The Confident Writer

The Confident Writer

FIFTH EDITION

Carol C. Kanar

Valencia Community College

Houghton Mifflin Harcourt Publishing Company

Boston   New York

Sponsoring Editor: Joann Kozyrev

Marketing Manager: Tom Ziolkowski

Discipline Product Manager: Giuseppina Daniel

Development Editor: Amy Gibbons

Project Editor: Aimee Chevrette

Senior Media Producer: Philip Lanza

Senior Content Manager: Janet Edmonds

Art and Design Manager: Jill Haber

Cover Design Manager: Anne S. Katzeff

Senior Photo Editor: Jennifer Meyer Dare

Senior Composition Buyer: Chuck Dutton

New Title Project Manager: James Lonergan

Editorial Associate: Daisuke Yasutake

Marketing Associate: Bettina Chiu

Editorial Assistant: Laura Collins

Printed in the U.S.A.

Library of Congress Control Number: 2008926002

Instructor's Annotated Edition
　　ISBN-10: 0-618-96289-1
　　ISBN-13: 978-0-618-96289-1
For orders, use student text ISBNs
　　ISBN-10: 0-618-95846-0
　　ISBN-13: 978-0-618-95846-7

123456789–DOW–12　11　10　09　08

Contents

UNIT 2
Patterns as Options   195

[8]   Narrating and Describing   195

[9]   Explaining a Process   224

[10]   Choosing Classification
          or Division   243

Thematic Contents

[Media]

[Language and Learning]

[Nature]

[On the Lighter Side]

Preface

Thank you for choosing *The Confident Writer,* Fifth Edition. Through four editions, this text has been a friend to both students and their instructors because of its optimistic tone, its clear presentation of skills, and its underlying theme that there is a confident writer in each of us. Its goal is to empower every student to become that writer and, in so doing, develop his or her own unique voice. With that aim in mind, *The Confident Writer*

- Begins with the assumption that *every* student is a writer
- Presents the writing process as a series of choices that writers make
- Makes a clear connection between reading and writing as complementary communication processes that share features and skills
- Utilizes both a process- and a skills-based approach that not only shows students how to manage the writing process, but also teaches them the skills that will allow them to confidently meet the writing demands of college, life, and work
- Provides abundant opportunities for writing through extensive, thought-provoking exercises and topic suggestions in each chapter
- Integrates grammar with the writing process and treats grammar as a series of choices available to writers for clear and effective communication

NEW TO THE FIFTH EDITION

The following new features have made *The Confident Writer* even more student- and instructor-friendly:

Greater emphasis on the theme of confidence, beginning with a chart on the inside front cover that lists the traits of confident writers. Each chapter opener features an inspirational quote addressing one of these traits. Chapter 1 opens the text with an increased focus on encouraging students to think like writers and empowering them to find their own voices.

A completely new design guides students through the most important parts of each chapter and makes the text a more effective teaching tool. New student-friendly chapter openers, for example, feature a series of statements designed to help students discover what they already know about the chapter topics, followed by a list of clearly stated objectives that are color-coded to the major chapter headings. The Fourth Edition's strong visual emphasis is enhanced in the Fifth Edition with many new photographs, charts, and bulleted lists.

Intelligent organizational changes have made *The Confident Writer* an even more streamlined and accessible text. Revising and editing are now covered in a single chapter (Chapter 6), eliminating unnecessary repetition and helping to clarify the differences between these two processes. Narrating and describing have also been combined into one chapter (Chapter 8)—a natural fit, as effective narration depends on vivid and descriptive details. This combined treatment also demonstrates that confident writers may choose to use multiple organizational patterns within a single essay.

A revamped research chapter (Chapter 7) contains new sections on researching and evaluating online sources; expanded coverage of plagiarism and documentation, with a clear comparison of MLA and APA styles; and an annotated MLA-format student research paper.

An expanded handbook (Unit 4) features new exercises throughout and an entirely new section, "ESL Concerns and Choices," that covers word order and the correct use of negatives, *there* and *it* as sentence openers, articles, prepositions, and idioms. This section was added in response to instructor requests for material addressing the particular concerns of non-native speakers of English.

New professional essays (eleven in all) open Chapters 1, 3, 11, 12, and 14 and appear in Unit 3, "More Choices: A Collection of Readings." These selections were carefully chosen to actively engage students and to represent the viewpoints of a diverse group of writers.

A new student essay feature, *Student Voices,* has been added to Chapters 8–14 to complement the professional essay in each of these chapters and to Chapter 8 to provide a model research paper.

Improved apparatus for the chapter-opening essays includes pre-reading features appearing under new names: *First Thoughts* helps students build background for the reading, while *Word Alert* calls their attention to words or terms in the reading that may be new or unfamiliar. *The Critical Thinker*, the set of post-reading questions for reflection, discussion, and writing, has been moved from the end of the chapter to directly follow *The Critical Reader*, the post-reading question set that focuses on the essay's structure and meaning.

Two or more new *Concept Check* **marginal notes in every chapter guide** students' reading of the text via cross-references, thought-provoking questions, or examples. These notes encourage students to think critically and creatively about the chapter topic or concept under discussion.

Expanded end-of-chapter features include *Topics for Writing* that have been divided into "React to the Reading," "Use Your Experience," "Make a Real-World Connection," and "Go to the Web" categories, making these writing suggestions even more varied and useful. In addition, updated *Checklists for Revision* provide students with thorough yet focused guidance on what they should look for as they revise and edit their essays.

Two new pattern-specific features have been added to Chapters 8–14, the chapters that introduce the organizational patterns. *Questions to Consider* boxes toward the ends of these chapters highlight ten thought-provoking questions designed to help students think critically about their topic, audience, purpose, and pattern as a prewriting strategy. These are followed by new charts that give students an overview of what to include in the introduction, body, and conclusion of their essays when they write in the pattern featured in the chapter.

More themed exercises, identified with marginal icons, throughout the Fifth Edition include *collaborative exercises* that build community and promote active learning, *Internet exercises* that send students online to complete a variety of writing-related tasks, and *learning styles exercises* that encourage students to use all of their senses and to develop the writing strategies that work best for them.

ORGANIZATION AND CONTENT

The Confident Writer has a flexible organization that can accommodate a variety of teaching and learning styles. Designed to take students logically through the writing process, the chapters can also be effectively presented in different sequences.

Unit 1, "The Writing Process," begins with an empowering first chapter that introduces students to the process of writing and explains the connection between reading and writing. Most importantly, Chapter 1 encourages students to think like writers and explains how they can find their own unique voices. Chapter 1 also retains the overview of the essay from the Fourth Edition. Other Unit 1 chapters focus on prewriting strategies, paragraph skills, stating and supporting thesis statements, and practical suggestions for revising and editing. A thoroughly revised research chapter, Chapter 7, familiarizes students with all the key steps in the research process. This chapter's important updates include new sections on researching and evaluating online sources; an expanded section on documentation, with a side-by-side comparison of MLA and APA documentation styles; and an annotated student research paper in MLA format.

Unit 2, "Patterns as Options," introduces the rhetorical patterns (narration and description, process, division and classification, comparison and contrast, cause and effect, definition, and argument), treating them as organizational choices that enable a writer to select the framework that best suits his or her purpose, audience, and thesis. The emphasis throughout is that a writer's choice of pattern proceeds logically from his or her goals. This unit also makes a connection between the patterns as writing options and their use in academic thought and writing.

Unit 3, "More Choices: A Collection of Readings," contains ten timely, high-interest, and culturally diverse essays that promote critical reading and thinking and also serve as models for writing. Six of these essays are new to the Fifth Edition. Instructors can use this collection in various ways—for example, as supplementary material or as starting points for discussion and writing assignments. Pre-reading and post-reading questions frame each essay.

Unit 4, "The Selective Writer: A Brief Handbook," focuses on grammar as yet another set of choices for the confident writer. Although the organization of Unit 4 remains the same as in the Fourth Edition, the content has been enhanced by the addition of many new exercises and a brand-new section that addresses ESL concerns.

ANCILLARIES

Annotated Instructor's Edition   Offered for the first time with the Fifth Edition, *The Confident Writer* Annotated Instructor's Edition contains on-page answers to the exercises in the text, as well as marginal notes that provide general teaching suggestions and tips for meeting the needs of ESL students.

The Confident Writer Instructor Website (college.hmco.com/pic/kanarTCW5e)

The Confident Writer instructor website features an Instructor's Resource Manual and a wealth of grammar exercises that supplement the text's handbook. The Instructor's Resource Manual includes an overview of the text, teaching suggestions for each chapter, sample syllabi, and correlations of the text content to the CLAST and THEA competencies.

The Confident Writer Student Website (college.hmco.com/pic/kanarTCW5e)

The Confident Writer student website supplements the text with chapter summaries, exercises, and quizzes; *Your Discovery Journal* activities for each chapter; a variety of downloadable forms; an extensive list of suggested writing topics; access to the exercises and resources of *Total Practice Zone*; and links to other helpful resources. New features include self-tests and a *Your Reflections* section with critical reading and thinking questions that address the new student essays in Chapters 8-14. The student website also provides access to HM WriteSPACE™, Houghton Mifflin's comprehensive location for interactive online products and services to accompany composition texts.

Houghton Mifflin Guide to Grammar

The *Houghton Mifflin Guide to Grammar* provides instruction and practice in essential grammar areas, including verb tenses, modals, noun clauses, subject-verb agreement, word forms, and parallel structure. Abundant exercises help students learn to recognize and avoid common grammatical mistakes. A valuable resource for anyone seeking to improve his or her writing skills, the *Guide* is particularly helpful for multilingual students. It is available as either a stand-alone (ISBN-13: 978-0-618-83289-7) or package item (ISBN-13: 978-0-618-91122-6).

ACKNOWLEDGMENTS

Writing a textbook is a monumental task that the writer does not accomplish alone. I am deeply grateful to the Houghton Mifflin family of editors and others who contributed to *The Confident Writer, Fifth Edition*. Special thanks go to Pat Coryell for approving this edition and to Joann Kozyrev for spearheading its execution and redesign. Amy Gibbons, I thank you for your devotion to this book and for always being accessible to answer questions and guide my thinking. To Aimee Chevrette for the expertise that brought this book through production and to Vici Casana for a superb job of copyediting, I offer many thanks. I also acknowledge and appreciate the marketing efforts of Tom Ziolkowski and the editorial assistance of Daisuke Yasutake. To the many others without whom this book would have never made it to production, you have my deepest appreciation. I thank my family and colleagues for their enthusiasm and support, and my husband, Stephen P. Kanar, for being the wonderful, indispensable person that he is. Finally, I thank my students for the delight and inspiration that they have given me over the years. This book is for them.

To the reviewers, whose excellent suggestions were a great help, I offer my thanks:

Jacqueline Blackwell, Thomas Nelson Community College
Candace Boeck, Cuyamaca College
Margaret Chandler, Williamsburg Technical College
Margo Eden-Camann, Georgia Perimeter College
Gwyn Enright, San Diego City College
Susan Ford, Thomas University
Anita Garner, University of North Alabama
Nikka Harris, Rochester Community and Technical College
Christine Heilman, College of Mount St. Joseph
Billie Jones, Shippensburg University
Lisa Kahookele, Des Moines Area Community College—Boone
Jennifer Kaufman, Ulster County Community College
Betty LaFace, Bainbridge College
Kevin Menton, California State Polytechnic University—Pomona
Theresa Mohamed, Onondaga Community College
Randall R. Mueller, Gateway Technical College
Amy C. Murphy, San Antonio College
Sharon Occhipinti, Florida Metropolitan University—Tampa
James Sodon, St. Louis Community College—Florissant Valley
Helen (Lyn) Ward Page, Oakton Community College
Guangping Zeng, Pensacola Junior College

Carol C. Kanar

CHAPTER 1

(((*Confident writers are self-motivated. Their motivation*

to write may be for self-expression,

academic success, or career advancement.)))

Becoming a Confident Writer

What you already know about *writing*

○ Considering the number of authors interviewed on cable news shows in a single week, you can tell that writing plays an important role in American life.

○ You probably have seen many examples of different types of writing—in books, magazines, letters, email messages, and other sources.

○ If you have done any writing in the past—either for a course, for work, or for personal reasons—then you already know something about the writing process and what it involves.

Your *goals* for this chapter

[1] Know how to develop the qualities, attitudes, and writing skills that will ensure your success in college and career.

[2] Know how to make good decisions about audience, purpose, thesis or central idea, supporting details, and ways to organize your ideas.

[3] Be familiar with the three stages of the writing process so that you can manage the process and make it work to your advantage.

[4] Use critical and creative thinking to discover and express your unique voice as a writer.

Unit 1 The Writing Process

Writing is one of the fundamental ways you express yourself, share ideas, and reveal your knowledge and experience. Like singing, dancing, speaking, or many other human capacities, writing is a skill that you can develop. Writing is an art that inspires, provokes discussion, or issues a call to action. Perhaps you have experienced the power of writing, either by producing your own work or by being moved by the work of others. On the other hand, you may be new to writing. You may be wondering, "Can I do this?"

Yes, you *can* become a confident writer. With a positive attitude, self-motivation, and the willingness to put into practice the skills taught in this book, you will be off to a good start. Persistence also helps; do not give up at the first sign of difficulty. Writing is both a journey within and a reaching out. As you gain knowledge and skills, you will find your voice as a writer. Your words will speak for you, and others will listen.

Being able to write well is one mark of an educated person. Your professors insist on good writing, your employers will expect it, and you can learn to write well. Are you willing to take the risk?

[First Thoughts]

To build background for reading, explore your thoughts about images of smoking in movies. Then answer the following questions, either on your own or in a group discussion.

1. How much influence do you think celebrities have on people's choices and behavior?

2. What effect do you think watching people smoke in movies has on young people?

3. Read the title, headnote, and first one or two paragraphs of the following essay. Based on this preview, what do you think will follow?

[Word Alert]

Before reading, preview the following words and definitions. During reading, use context clues and your dictionary to define any additional unfamiliar words.

raunchy (2)	obscene, vulgar
depicting (2)	representing in a picture
mitigating (3)	becoming less in force or intensity

cater (4)	to be attentive
dubious (11)	uncertain, undecided, filled with doubt
beckons (12)	invites, summons

Free Expression Gets Smoked

Stephen Chapman

In this essay, Stephen Chapman comments on a decision of the Motion Picture Association of America (MPAA) regarding the depiction of smoking in films. Chapman is a syndicated columnist.

1   The First Amendment, which guarantees freedom of speech and freedom of the press, takes the view that the people should dictate to the government, not the other way around. But no one told a group of 32 state attorneys general, who have taken it upon themselves to instruct the film industry on the appropriate content of movies.

2   This time, the cause is not raunchy sex, foul language or blood-spattering violence. It's cigarettes. Many experts think that when actors puff away, they cause teenagers to do likewise. One study went so far as to say that 38 percent of all the kids who acquire the habit do so because of the influence of films. So all these state government officials want filmmakers to stop depicting tobacco use.

3   They evidently have had an effect. Not long after the attorneys general sent a letter requesting action, the Motion Picture Association of America (MPAA) agreed to use smoking in determining each film's rating. "Depictions that glamorize smoking or movies that feature pervasive smoking outside of a historic or other mitigating context" would run afoul of the ratings board. Apparently it would be OK to show an unwashed lowlife taking a drag just before he drops dead of a heart attack.

4   The MPAA didn't go as far as demanded by some anti-tobacco groups that want to slap an R rating on just about every film in which actors light up. But it accepted the basic principle that public-health lobbyists and politicians should have a big role in deciding what people will see, instead of letting the industry merely cater to its audience.

5   It's hard to fully credit the notion that kids start smoking just because they see Scarlett Johansson doing it. Steven Milloy, publisher of the Web site JunkScience.com, points out that adolescent smoking has declined even as on-screen smoking has increased. If movies exert such a mammoth influence on impressionable youngsters, shouldn't teen tobacco use be on the rise?

6   The studies themselves are not as damning as they purport to be. They indicate that kids who watch more movies with smoking are more likely to smoke.

But a correlation does not necessarily show a cause: Just because there is lots of beer drinking at baseball games doesn't mean beer drinking causes baseball.

7   It may be that kids see a star light up and rush out to imitate him. Or it may be that teens who are inclined to smoke anyway are also inclined to see the sort of movies that feature smoking.

8   Michael Siegel, a physician and professor at the Boston University School of Public Health, believes the studies greatly exaggerate the impact of tobacco in films. "It is simply one of a large number of ways in which youths are exposed to positive images of smoking (which includes advertisements, television movies, television shows, DVDs, Internet, music videos, and a variety of other sources)," he told me in an e-mail interview. "To single out smoking in movies as THE cause of youth smoking initiation for a large percentage of kids is ridiculous."

9   Putting an R rating on smoky movies probably wouldn't do much to reduce teenagers' exposure. Some 75 percent of new releases that feature smoking are already rated R—and a lot of them are accessible even to preteens. In one survey of kids in grades 5 through 8, only 16 percent said their parents never let them see R-rated films.

10   Siegel points out that applying R ratings to films just because they feature full-frontal shots of cigarettes may backfire. Parents anxious about sex and violence may stop paying attention to the rating system once it factors in smoking. So you could actually end up with more kids seeing films with smoking.

11   If the MPAA were responding to the clear preferences of parents, this change might be merely dubious. In this case, though, it acted only after getting overt pressure from state governments—which have no more business determining what appears on movie screens than they do in deciding what goes into Judy Blume's next novel. In the minds of safety zealots, censorship in the name of public health is no vice.

12   The MPAA's response validates the politicians in their intrusions, and beckons them to find new ways to regulate art and other matters that are supposed to be exempt from their control. A shame it didn't give the attorneys general a simpler, better response: Snuff this.

Source: Chapman, Stephen. "Free Expression Gets Smoked." *Orlando Sentinel* 21 May 2007: A11.

⟪ The Critical Reader ⟫

[CENTRAL IDEA]

1. The author's central idea is that politicians should not tell the film industry how to make movies. Find a sentence in the essay that comes closest to stating this thesis.

2. In which paragraph does the author use a direct quotation to explain why the MPAA included smoking in its ratings decisions?

3. Who is credited with saying that smoking among adolescents had decreased even though onscreen smoking has increased?

4. Which sentence in paragraph 6 do the details in paragraph 7 support? (Hint: Find the main idea of paragraph 6.)

[**IMPLICATIONS**]

5. What is your opinion about smoking in movies? Do you think it adds to or detracts from the story? Does the amount of smoking in movies concern you or not? As a parent, are you more concerned about the amount of smoking, sex, or violence that is depicted in the movies your children see?

[**WORD CHOICE**]

6. In paragraph 11, to whom does the term *safety zealots* refer, and what does the choice of this term tell you about the author's attitude toward them? To help you decide, look up the meaning of *zealot*.

⟪ The Critical Thinker ⟫

To examine Stephen Chapman's essay in more depth, follow these suggestions for reflection, discussion, or writing.

1. In paragraphs 1 through 3, the author makes clear that he sees the MPAA's decision to use smoking in determining a film's rating as a free speech issue. Explain whether you agree or disagree and tell why.

2. In paragraph 2, Chapman says many experts think that teenagers smoke because they see actors smoking in movies. Where in the essay does Chapman disprove this claim, and has he provided enough evidence to convince you?

3. Explain the meaning of the essay's title in relation to the essay as a whole. What are all the possible meanings you can think of for the word *smoked*?

4. Some people believe that there is too much government interference with private businesses. Chapman probably supports this view. Others believe that some government regulation of some businesses, such as the film industry, is necessary. What do you think?

How to Be a Confident Writer

Goal 1 Know how to develop the qualities, attitudes, and writing skills that will ensure your success in college and career.

From this point on, think of yourself as a writer. Sports psychologists tell athletes to think of themselves as winners, to visualize making a perfect golf swing or sinking a basket, and then to practice. Their reasoning goes like this: If you see yourself as a winner, you will begin to do what it takes to win, and soon you will *be* a winner. If the sports psychologists are right, then perhaps the same principle can be applied to writing. To become a confident writer, first believe that you *are* a writer. Then do what writers do: Polish your skills and practice, practice, practice. As a starting point, take these five steps to confident writing:

1. **Adjust your frame of mind.** Have a positive attitude and be willing to take academic risks. For example, ask questions, try new strategies, think for yourself, and be creative.

2. **Schedule time for writing.** A project will go undone if you never get started. Are you a procrastinator? Take control of your time by knowing when assignments are due and by scheduling time to complete them. Get a calendar or daily planner, not only for scheduling writing assignments but also for keeping track of the work in all your courses. By managing your time effectively, you will always have time for writing.

3. **Motivate yourself.** If you have the opportunity to select your own topic for writing, choose a subject in which you have a genuine interest. Do not depend on the instructor to make writing enjoyable. Find your own sources of enjoyment.

4. **Develop your powers of observation.** Become more aware of your surroundings. Observe what people are doing and how they are acting. Listen to their tones of voice. Pay attention to current events. Get involved in campus life. Notice the sights, sounds, and smells around you. A good writer has highly developed senses. Develop yours.

Whether in a sport or in writing, success begins with the belief that you will succeed, followed by practice.

5. **Read.** Reading is a springboard for writing. Reading is a source of knowledge and wisdom. Writers get many of their ideas from reading. If English is your second language, reading newspapers and magazines will give you a feel for the rhythms and syntax of English. Reading and writing are intimately connected—more about that later.

6. **Get wired.** If you already know how to do word processing and to search the Internet, good. If not, a visit to your college library, media center, or computer center will help you get started. Most professors require that papers be typed on a computer, and using the Internet is a great shortcut to finding information for research papers and other assignments. Writing and researching in college will prepare you for the workplace, where computing skill is essential for most careers.

In addition to these six steps, a few words about reading and the types of writing assignments you can expect in college will also help you to think like a writer.

The Reading and Writing Connection

Reading and writing are connected in several ways. Both require analytical (logical) and creative thinking. Both operate on two levels, the literal level and the critical level. The literal level is about words and what they actually say, their dictionary meanings. The critical level is about reading between the lines to discover what words imply or suggest.

Each chapter of *The Confident Writer* begins with an essay for you to read and use as both a model and a springboard for writing your own essays. An **essay** is a relatively short piece of writing that may serve one or more purposes: to inform, persuade, entertain, explain, or merely express an idea, feeling, or impression. The essay is a powerful form of communication that you will find in the pages of newspapers, magazines, and books. Essays are a staple of college courses either as assignments or as tests. Mastering the essay will give you good experience in focusing your ideas on a single topic and supporting your opinions with facts. You will feel a sense of accomplishment when your essay empowers your readers with new knowledge and inspires them to improve their circumstances or take other positive actions. This experience and others can be applied in the workplace, where you may be called on to write reports, memos, letters, manuals, or other documents. The essay is the perfect proving ground for you to gain practice in writing clearly, authoritatively, and concisely on topics that are meaningful to you and your readers.

To read an essay with understanding, follow three steps. These steps are also useful for reading anything, including a textbook chapter.

☑ **CONCEPT CHECK**
Are you an active or
passive reader? Go to
The Confident Writer
website and take a survey
to find out.

1. **Build background before reading.** Determine what you already know about the topic. What are your opinions and assumptions? What experience related to the topic have you had?

2. **Read actively.** Take it one paragraph or section at a time. Stop and ask yourself what you have just read. If you have questions, look for the answers as you continue to read. Read with a dictionary. Define unfamiliar terms as you go. Pay attention to any guideposts the author has built in, such as headings, numbered lists, or graphics. Also pay attention to the author's choice of words, which may set a mood, create an image or feeling, or reveal a bias. Read with a pen or pencil in hand, underline key words or phrases, and take notes in the margin.

3. **Review after reading.** Read again the title, first paragraph, last paragraph, and your underlining. Try to reconstruct the author's central idea, one or two major supporting ideas, and the conclusion. Then determine why or how the information may be useful.

Why is reading important in a writing class? For one thing, reading is a great way to explore ideas from which you can develop topics for your own writing. Second, the more you read examples of good writing, the more you will begin to notice the different ways authors organize and support their ideas, the words they choose, and the types of details they select, all of which you can apply in your writing. Figure 1.1 compares reading an essay with writing an essay. This comparison illustrates the point that the things you look for in reading are the same things that you should include in your writing.

Several features in every chapter of *The Confident Writer* are designed to help you develop critical reading and thinking processes that you can also apply in writing. These features are *Thinking First, The Critical Reader, The Critical Thinker, Topics for Writing,* and *Your Discovery Journal.*

Writing an Essay: The Basics

The central idea of an essay is often called the *thesis.* A writer *develops,* or supports, a thesis with specific evidence, or information. The way the evidence is organized, or arranged, is the essay's *direction of development.* For example, the most usual direction of development is to start with an introduction that leads up to a thesis; continue by providing evidence to support, explain, or prove the thesis; and end with a concluding paragraph that summarizes major points or leaves readers with implications about the topic's significance in their lives.

Of course, there are many ways to develop an essay. Some essays have little or no introduction; others have a lengthy introduction. Some writers put the thesis at the end. As a beginning writer, you will probably want to follow the more usual direction of development: from introduction and thesis,

Figure 1.1   Reading an Essay and Writing an Essay

QUESTIONS TO ASK	WHAT TO LOOK FOR WHEN READING AN ESSAY	WHAT TO THINK ABOUT BEFORE WRITING AN ESSAY
What is the topic?	Read the title and first paragraph to determine what the essay is about.	Start with a general topic or subject; then narrow the topic to find a focus for your essay.
What is the purpose?	Determine what you, the reader, are expected to know, learn, or be able to do.	Decide what you, the writer, want your audience to know, learn, or be able to do.
Who is the audience?	Look for details that tell you whether the audience is general (the public) or specific (students, voters, job applicants, and so on).	Determine who your audience is and what you can assume about their beliefs or opinions.
What is the thesis, or central idea?	Determine what the author thinks. Look for a sentence that expresses an opinion about the topic or takes a position on an issue.	Decide what point you want to make or what is your opinion about the topic or your position on an issue.
What evidence supports the thesis?	What specific facts, reasons, or examples does the author provide to support the central idea?	Select details that clearly explain why you think or feel the way you do.
How are the ideas organized?	Try to spot certain organizational patterns, such as a comparison, a definition, or the stages of a process.	Choose the most appropriate patterns for organizing your ideas.
What do the ideas mean?	Make inferences: You know what the words say, but try to apply the author's ideas to your own life.	Determine why your ideas are significant and what they may mean to your readers.

through support, to conclusion. This direction of development helps you achieve an organization that is easy for both you and your readers to follow. The introduction, thesis, support, and conclusion are all important parts of an essay that have specific purposes, as explained in Figure 1.2.

For example, in Stephen Chapman's essay at the beginning of this chapter, the first two paragraphs introduce the topic by pointing out the free speech issue and by building background for the thesis, which does not come until near the end of the essay. Paragraphs 2 through 11 are the body of the essay, and they contain the major supporting evidence, which consists of facts

Figure 1.2   An Essay's Direction of Development

Introduction	Build readers' interest in your topic by making clear why you are writing about it (your purpose) and how you became involved with it or why readers should care or know about it (background).
Thesis statement	Write a sentence that states your opinion about the topic—the central idea of your essay.
Support	Select evidence in the form of main ideas and specific details to support your thesis and explain it to your readers.
Conclusion	End the essay by provoking a response from readers, either in the form of understanding or in the form of taking action.

gathered from several sources plus the author's opinions. Paragraph 12 concludes the essay with the implication that the MPAA's response could pave the way for more intrusive government action.

An essay's direction of development is reflected in its three parts: the *introduction*, which usually includes the thesis; the *body*, which contains the supporting evidence; and the *conclusion*, which ends the essay.

[Exercise 1.1] Write one or two pages on the topic *A movie or TV program that has had a positive (or negative) effect on viewers.* This will be a *discovery draft* that has two purposes. First, you will discover what you already know about the topic. Second, you may be able to identify the writing skills that you already possess and those that need improving. Follow these directions to complete your draft:

1. The following questions will help you brainstorm the topic for ideas. What is one movie or TV program that caused a strong positive or negative reaction in you or others? What did you like or dislike about the show or the way it was presented, and why? Why do you think this show is good or bad for viewers? What kind of ideas, actions, or behaviors do you think it could provoke?

2. Write everything you can think of on the topic. For now, do not be concerned with grammar; instead, concentrate on what you want to tell your readers.

3. Read your draft. Can you trace a direction of development? Can you identify parts of the draft that could become the introduction, body, and conclusion of a new draft?

4. Determine whether one of your sentences states a central idea, what the whole draft is about.

5. Finally, comment on what you did well in this discovery draft and on what needs improvement. Then save the draft for a future assignment and as a sample of your writing against which you can assess your progress later on.

Make Good Choices for Writing

Goal 2

Know how to make good decisions about audience, purpose, thesis or central idea, supporting details, and ways to organize your ideas.

From start to finish, writing is a process of making choices. Each choice leads to an outcome. If you do not like the outcome, you can make another choice. For example, suppose you are writing an essay. You start writing about the topic you have chosen, and you very quickly decide that you either do not like your topic or cannot think of anything to write. Now you have another choice: Will you keep writing and hope the ideas will follow, or will you choose a new topic and start over?

Some experts recommend discovery drafts, such as the one you wrote for Exercise 1.1, as a way of exploring a topic until an idea for a thesis emerges. Others suggest using a *prewriting* strategy, such as outlining or brainstorming, to plan before you write. Whatever strategy you use for thinking about and planning for writing, you will eventually have to make five choices:

✓ CONCEPT CHECK
Prewriting strategies are explained in Chapter 2.

1. Who will be your audience?

2. What will be your purpose?

3. What will be your thesis?

4. What evidence will support your thesis?

5. How will you organize your evidence?

Remember, too, that one of your privileges as a writer is that *all your choices are open to change.*

Who Will Be Your Audience?

Writing is a communication process between the writer and an *audience* of readers. When you write a letter to a good friend, you expect a reply. Your letter is probably filled with information that interests both you and your friend. You are aware of your friend's preferences, values, beliefs, and attitudes, and they influence what you write. If you know, for example, that your friend is interested in professional basketball, you might write a letter that contains a description of the exciting game you watched last week. When you sit down to write a letter and you begin to think about all the things you have done lately and what your friend would most like to know, you are involved in an essential part of the writing process: *You are considering your audience's needs and interests.*

Considering your audience's needs and interests is an essential part of the writing process.

CONCEPT CHECK
Whether you are writing an essay, giving a speech, or making a presentation, the same audience characteristics apply. For any writing or speaking task in college or career, addressing the ages, roles, knowledge base, assumptions, interests, and values of your audience will help you get your message across.

Similarly, when you write an essay for your composition class, or for any class, consider your audience. The audience for most college writing is professors and other students. If you write a term paper for your American government class, you know that your professor will be reading it to find out how much you know about the topic and which concepts from the material presented in class you have been able to apply to your analysis of that topic. The audience for most of your college writing will be either your professor and classmates or an imagined audience that you choose or your professor assigns. If you are attending a technical college or a business or professional school, the audience may be a work- or career-related group of people. To write effectively for any group of people, these are the **audience characteristics** you need to consider:

- **Age.** How old are your readers? What can you determine about their generational differences in background and experience that might affect how they respond to your topic?

- **Roles.** Who are your readers? Are they students, instructors, employees, consumers, parents, or business owners, or do they fill other roles? What are the concerns of people who fill those roles? To which role or concern do you intend to address your writing?

- **Knowledge base.** How familiar with your topic are your readers? What experiences have they had that may apply? Are they beginners or experts in your field or area of interest?

- **Assumptions.** What are your readers' opinions or preconceived ideas about your topic? Are they likely to respond positively or negatively to what you write? How can you get them to put aside their assumptions and carefully consider your ideas?

- **Interest.** Is your topic one that most readers would be interested in, or will you have to arouse their interest?

- **Values.** What personal preferences, beliefs, or attitudes can you assume your readers may have? How will their values affect the way they respond to your writing? How can you appeal to their values?
- **Culture/ethnicity.** How diverse is your audience? To what cultures, ethnic groups, or nationalities do they belong? What can you assume they have in common? In what ways might their interests differ?

What Will Be Your Purpose?

Having a *purpose* for writing is also important. Why are you attending college? Are you here to pursue a degree that is the first step toward a career? Do you want to upgrade your skills so that you can qualify for a promotion at work or a better job? Or are you taking classes for self-fulfillment, to enrich your life? Whatever your reasons, you probably had many decisions to make about which college to attend and what courses to take. Writing also involves many decisions: what topic to write about, what central idea to develop, what details and examples to choose, and which words will best express your ideas. Your *purpose,* or reason, for writing is what unifies all these decisions and gives you a goal to work toward.

To determine a purpose for writing, ask yourself these two questions:

- Why do I want to write about this topic?
- What do I expect readers to be able to understand or do after they read my essay?

Throughout the writing process, your *audience* and *purpose* should motivate every choice you make. Chapter 2 contains a more detailed explanation of these two essentials of good writing.

[**Exercise 1.2**] This exercise will help you practice determining the purpose and analyzing the audience for a specific writing task. Read the following scenario, then answer the questions.

You own a home in an urban neighborhood. Your home is similar to others in the area, and it is close to schools and shopping. Recently, the city planning board has notified you that a new highway extension is being routed through your part of the city and that a number of homes, including yours, will have to be demolished. Of course, you will be compensated financially for your loss. However, you are opposed to the project because it will break up the community and force you and many other residents to move further out from the city, a location that is not as convenient to shops and schools. You decide to write a letter to the editor of your local newspaper to make your views known. Answer the following questions to clarify your purpose and to determine the views of the audience—those who will read your letter.

[PURPOSE:]

1. What do you hope to accomplish by writing the letter?
2. What do you want readers to know or do in response to your letter?

[AUDIENCE:]

3. Who will be most likely to read your letter?
4. What assumptions can you make about readers' ages, backgrounds, and attitudes?
5. Why should they be interested in whether the road goes in or not?
6. How will the project affect them?
7. How can you convince them to support your efforts to stop the road?

[**Exercise 1.3**] Review Stephen Chapman's essay on pages 3–4. Why do you think he wrote the essay, and for whom? Try to determine his purpose and audience.

What Will Be Your Thesis?

Writing an essay involves more than choosing a good topic. What idea do you want to express about the topic? What is interesting, important, humorous, outrageous, or upsetting about the topic that you want to share with your readers, and why? Answering these questions will help you determine your central idea, or thesis. Your essay's thesis states your opinion about the topic and suggests the knowledge you bring to it. For example, a thesis could be a fact, idea, belief, or experience that you think is worth explaining. Stephen Chapman's thesis is that politicians should not tell the film industry how to make movies. Chapman believes that this is a First Amendment issue, and he wants to convince readers that freedom of expression is more important than whether movie stars smoke cigarettes on screen.

One way to make your central idea clear to readers is to write a *thesis statement,* a sentence that clearly shows what your topic is and what you plan to say about it in the body of your essay. Following are three topics and a sample thesis statement for each. As you can see, the topics are very general. The thesis statements are more specific and tell you exactly what the writers plan to say about their topics.

Topics	Thesis Statements
1. A movie many people will enjoy	*Pirates of the Caribbean* is a movie many people will enjoy for its interesting costumes and sets and for the way it combines fantasy with drama and suspense.
2. A relaxing place to visit	Tourists looking for a relaxing place to visit will enjoy a trip to coastal Maine.
3. A habit that is not worth the risk	Financial, social, and health concerns make smoking a habit that is not worth the risk.

✔ CONCEPT CHECK

Chapter 4 explains in detail how to write a thesis statement.

A good thesis limits the topic and controls your selection of evidence. For example, in the first thesis statement, the topic of movies is limited to one movie: *Pirates of the Caribbean.* The type of evidence you select to support this thesis would include one or more examples each of what makes the *costumes* and *sets* interesting and an explanation of how the film combines *fantasy* with *drama* and *suspense.* In the second thesis statement, the topic of relaxing places to visit is limited to *coastal Maine.* The evidence you select to support the thesis might include examples of activities, events, and attractions in coastal Maine that provide relaxation. In the third thesis statement, the topic of habits is limited to *smoking,* and the evidence you select to support this topic would explain the *financial, social,* and *health* risks of smoking.

Having a thesis that you care about and that clearly states what your essay covers may provide the sense of direction you need to write with confidence.

[Exercise 1.4]

Being able to find the central idea in another person's work is a good first step toward learning to write your own thesis statements. This exercise will help you practice identifying the thesis, or central idea, in a piece of writing. Bring to class an essay or article to share, or examine several pieces of writing that your instructor provides. After reading each article, answer these questions:

1. What is the article about? (topic)

2. What does the author say or think about the topic? (opinion)

3. In your own words, what seems to be the central idea? (author's topic plus opinion)

4. Can you find a sentence that states the central idea? (thesis statement)

5. Which of the three examples at the top of this page does the thesis statement most resemble?

[Exercise 1.5]

The Internet contains a wealth of sites that you can access for help with writing. Each chapter of *The Confident Writer* contains at least one exercise that makes use of online sources. For this online activity, go to *The Confident Writer* website and explore what is available there. Then complete the "Writer's Profile," print a copy of your results, and bring it to class to share in discussion. The profile is a survey questionnaire that addresses the process, skills, and attitudes that are essential to success in writing. The questions address topics covered in *The Confident Writer.* Take the survey now to find out where you are at the beginning of your writing course. Then take the survey again at midterm and at the end of the course to check your progress.

What Evidence Will Support Your Thesis?

You have probably learned from experience that people who ask you questions want reasons and explanations, and when they do not understand your answers, they want some examples that will enable them to relate your ideas to what they already know. In other words, you need to support your thesis, or central idea, with evidence. *Evidence* includes the facts, reasons, examples, opinions, and any other details that help support your thesis. As the thesis statement examples on page 15 illustrate, the thesis can control your selection of evidence by specifying what your essay covers. In the following short essay, the thesis statement and concluding sentence are underlined. Marginal notes point to the evidence.

☑ **CONCEPT CHECK**
For more on how to select evidence, see Chapters 3 and 5.

THE FUTURE OF LANGUAGE

1   English has long been the language of international commerce; therefore, you might expect English to be the world's most widely spoken tongue, right? Wrong. Mandarin Chinese is first, and it is the language of some 874 million people. Well, then English must be second, no? Actually, only about 341 million people speak English, which is the fourth most spoken language worldwide. Hindustani is second, Spanish is the third most spoken language, and these two languages account for roughly 426 million and 358 million speakers, respectively. These figures are from Dorling Kindersley's *The Top 10 of Everything,* and they reflect a changing role for English in the world community.

Ranking of languages

2   For one thing, although English as a first language may be in decline, its value as a basic skill, on a par with computer skills, is widely acknowledged and will only increase. The future of English may be as a second language for training bilingual and multilingual

Changing role of English

workers. As we look to the future of language in general, we may expect some other surprising developments.

Thesis

3   With Mandarin Chinese being the most widely spoken tongue, it is likely that the demand for college courses in this language will increase, especially among those in Asian Studies programs and those who intend to major in international business. One development that supports this prediction is the IBM company's work on an automatic speech translator. The new technology will instantly translate one spoken language into another, much as a human interpreter might. The software developed so far works for English and—you guessed it—Mandarin Chinese. If IBM's product is successful, then software for translating other languages will follow.

Demand for Mandarin Chinese

Automatic speech translator

4   Another development we can foresee is an increase in the number of people who are bilingual or even multilingual. As more American jobs go global, the need for both Americans and internationals to speak each other's languages will increase. Immigration, if only because of the sheer numbers of immigrants, may make having a second language not only a convenience but also a necessity.

More bi- and multilingual speakers

5   But as some languages are increasing in usage and others are declining, still others are disappearing altogether. This disturbing development does not bode well for the future of language in general. Linguists warn that as we move toward the end of the twenty-first century, many of today's languages will no longer be spoken. For example, the Siberian tongues of Middle Chulym and Tofa and many of the North American Indian languages are already in rapid decline. The loss of a language means the loss of a people and their culture, a tragedy by any account.

Loss of some languages

6   As with all things, the future of language is change. One of our challenges will be to preserve for tomorrow's generations those languages and cultures that are in danger of extinction.

Conclusion

[**Exercise 1.6**] Being able to identify the supporting details in another person's work is a good first step toward learning to select evidence to support a thesis in your own writing. Answer the following questions to identify the important details in "The Future of Language."

1. What is the author's topic?

2. What is the author's opinion?

3. In what four ways is the role of English changing?

4. Why might the demand for courses in Mandarin Chinese increase?

5. Why might we see an increase in the number of people who are bi- or multilingual?

6. What are three examples of languages that are in danger of disappearing?

How Will You Organize Your Evidence?

A filmmaker creates a film scene by scene. The scenes added together result in a movie in which the story and the characters' lives usually unfold in an orderly way. Have you ever arrived late to a movie, so that it took you several minutes to figure out what was going on? Your confusion may have occurred because you missed the opening scenes that introduced the characters and established the setting and situation. An orderly presentation of ideas is important in writing, too. How well your evidence is organized determines how understandable it will be to your readers.

Organization in writing involves two habits of critical thinking: *logic* and *analysis.* Ideas that are arranged logically follow one from the other. Beginning your sentences with words such as *first, next,* and *finally* helps your readers to keep up with the flow of your argument or explanation. Logic is also maintained when you stay on the topic and do not ramble or introduce confusing ideas. *Analysis* means presenting all sides of an argument or breaking down a complex issue into parts so that your readers can better understand it. To analyze your topic, you can select one or more of the common *organizational patterns,* many of which will be familiar to you because they are also thought patterns that you use all the time. The following are a few examples.

- **Finding a movie to rent:** At Blockbuster or other stores, movies are usually arranged by type, such as drama, comedy, TV series, and so on. We call this system *classification.*

☑ **CONCEPT CHECK**
Looking for thought patterns in your reading will improve your comprehension. For example, does the author explain a process, make comparisons, or define terms?

- **Reading and following a recipe:** The recipe explains step by step how to make a dish. This thought pattern is called *process.*

- **Explaining why an assignment is late:** You explain the causes such as "I forgot," or "I didn't understand," or "I was sick." Your excuses result in a lower grade. This situation illustrates the pattern of *cause and effect.*

- **Defining a word or term:** A friend who is learning to use the Internet asks you to explain what *search engine* means. You define the term and give a few examples. This thought pattern is called *definition.*

- **Explaining what life is like in a certain country:** A student who is from South Korea explains some similarities and differences between that country and the United States. This thought pattern is known as *comparison and contrast.*

Figure 1.3   Organizational Patterns for Thinking and Writing

PATTERN	PURPOSE	ESSAY TOPICS
Narration	To relate an event or series of events leading to an outcome	An award or special recognition you received
		The paintings of Picasso's blue period (humanities)
Description	To describe or create a vivid mental picture of a person, place, etc.	A person you will never forget
		The view from the pulpit of Chartres Cathedral (humanities)
Process	To explain how to do something or how something can be done	A difficult job or activity and how you learned to do it
		How a bill gets enacted into law (American government)
Classification and division	To break down a topic into categories	Types of restaurants in your community
	To divide a topic into parts	The division of labor within a kibbutz (sociology)
Comparison and contrast	To explain similarities and differences between two things	The car you own now versus the car you would like to own
		How Freud's and Jung's theories of personality differ (psychology)
Cause and effect	To explain the reasons for something, the results of something, or both	The positive or negative effects of an important choice you had to make
		The causes and prevention of AIDS (biology)
Definition	To define a term or even a situation, perhaps because you may think many people misunderstand it or because it has a unique meaning to you	Your definition of a *good friend*
		What are *fractals?* (math)

The same thought patterns we use in daily life are the organizational patterns you will use to analyze a topic and arrange your ideas in writing. Figure 1.3 lists the patterns that are covered in greater detail in Chapters 8 through 14. The figure shows each pattern's purpose and provides two possible essay topics for which the pattern would be an appropriate choice.

Effective writing has many characteristics that you will learn about in the chapters following, but these five—*audience, purpose, thesis, evidence,* and *organization*—are a good starting point.

Take Control of the Writing Process

Goal 3

Be familiar with the three stages of the writing process so that you can manage the process and make it work to your advantage.

Writing an essay is a process that begins with an idea and ends with a well-organized development of that idea. This process will probably involve three stages, each of which requires you to make choices. As you proceed through the chapters of this book, the writing process will gradually unfold, and you will have ample opportunity to explore and practice. What follows is a quick preview of the process and how it works.

Stage 1: Prewriting

☑ CONCEPT CHECK

See Chapter 2 for additional prewriting strategies.

Think of this stage as a *readiness* stage: You are getting ready to write. Your choices include selecting a topic, thinking about the topic, making some notes about it, and perhaps even coming up with a tentative thesis and outline. At this stage, you are generating ideas—what you know and do not know about your topic. Sometimes you need a reliable strategy to get the thinking process started. Writing a discovery draft is one strategy. *Clustering* is another prewriting strategy that can help you gather and organize evidence to support a topic. Figure 1.4 illustrates an idea cluster for the topic "A Behavior I Wish People Would Change."

The cluster in Figure 1.4 illustrates how one writer thought through her topic. First, she decided that chronic lateness was the behavior she wanted to write about, so she wrote that topic in the middle of her paper and circled it. As she thought some more about the topic, she asked herself: "What are some of the problems chronic lateness causes?" Branching out from the first circle, she wrote "creates a bad impression" inside a new circle. She then thought of three more problems, which she wrote inside more circles. Now she had four major divisions of an essay. To explain the problems of chronic lateness, she had to come up with some evidence. As she continued to think about her topic, she added new circles to her cluster. For example, one way that chronic lateness hurts the latecomer is that it "may earn you a bad recommendation." When the cluster was complete, the writer had a preliminary pattern of organization to follow. She would discuss chronic lateness in terms of four problems it causes and how these problems affect latecomers and those around them. Clustering not only helps you to organize your evidence but also provides a visual representation of your ideas so that you can *see* the organization clearly.

Stage 2: Drafting and Organizing

Think of this stage as an *exploratory* stage: You are experimenting with the ideas you gained during the prewriting stage to come up with a *first draft* of

Figure 1.4   Idea Cluster for "A Behavior I Wish People Would Change"

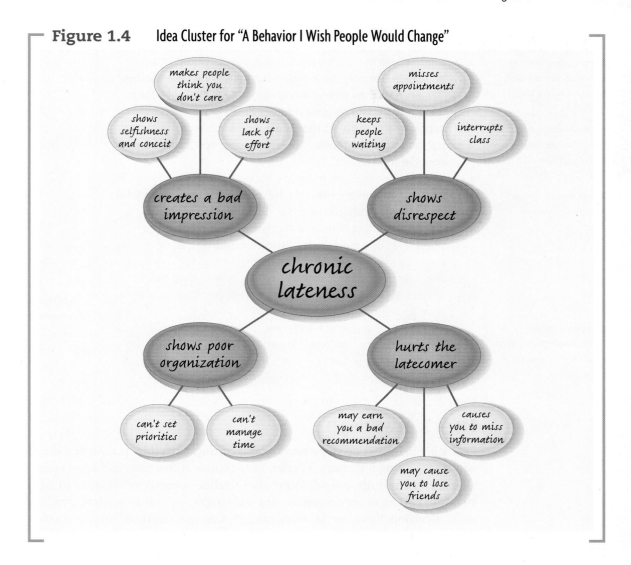

your essay. Later you will refine this draft to a *final draft* through successive revisions. A *draft* is a rough piece of writing. Your first draft will probably contain a tentative thesis, some support, and the beginning of an organizational plan. As you write, your choices include whether to stick with the thesis you have chosen, how much and what kind of support you need, and how to organize your ideas logically. These choices are explained in greater detail in Chapters 3 through 5. Following is a first draft developed from the idea cluster in Figure 1.4. As you can see, this draft is sketchy, and the instructor's comments suggest ways to develop the ideas in future drafts.

FIRST DRAFT OF "A BEHAVIOR I WISH PEOPLE WOULD CHANGE"

Introduction needs to establish purpose and background for thesis

1 Chronic lateness is a behavior I wish people would change because it not only hurts others but it also hurts themselves.

2 Jim has never arrived anywhere on time in his life. He is late for work, late for class, late for dates, late for appointments. Jim's <u>attitude</u> is a good example of how a person's chronic lateness shows disrespect and a lack of consideration.

Provide evidence to show "what" his attitude is and "how" it shows disrespect

3 Without realizing it, Jim is creating a <u>bad impression</u> on his boss and coworkers. However, he may need a recommendation someday, so he should take the job more seriously.

Again, explain "what" the impression is

4 Jim's lateness hurts him in other ways too. To be late to class sends a message to the instructor that <u>a student lacks organization</u>. Also, Jim does not date a woman for very long. She is just not going to keep seeing a guy who does not respect her enough to arrive on time. His friends do not even want to <u>invite him places where time is a factor</u>.

Add an example

Add an example

Can you expand conclusion? What might result from a change in behavior?

5 Most people who are chronically late are like Jim. They do not realize either the effect their behavior has on others or the ways lateness can hurt them. If they did, maybe they would make more of an effort to arrive on time.

Stage 3: Rewriting

Rewriting involves two steps: *revising* and *editing*. Each time you *revise* a draft, you are rewriting it to make it better. Your choices at this stage include whether to add content, improve organization, or refine your style. Whether to add, take out, or rearrange sentences and paragraphs are other choices you can make. Revision, therefore, is an ongoing process that starts the minute you begin to make changes in your first draft.

☑ **CONCEPT CHECK**
For more detailed information on the rewriting stage of the writing process, see Chapter 6 for *revising* and *editing*.

Editing is also part of the rewriting process. When you edit, you read your draft carefully to find and correct errors in grammar, spelling, and punctuation before writing your final draft. You also make an effort to tighten and trim your essay by eliminating unnecessary words and phrases. *Proofreading* is one last editing check before handing in your essay. Proofreading is a close reading to find any previously missed errors and to make sure that your essay is neat and legible. Following is a revised and edited draft of "A Behavior I Wish People Would Change."

REVISED DRAFT OF A BEHAVIOR I WISH PEOPLE WOULD CHANGE

1   Being late once in a while is excusable, but the chronically late are late for everything, all the time. They are rude and inconsiderate of others' feelings. What they do not seem to realize is that their lateness creates a bad impression, making them appear disrespectful and disorganized. Chronic lateness is a behavior I wish people would change because it not only hurts others but it also hurts the latecomers.

2   Jim has never arrived anywhere on time in his life. He is late for work, late for class, late for dates, late for appointments. As far as he is concerned, no one at work has complained, so why should he knock himself out to get there on time? As for his professors and the students in his classes, "They can start without me." He probably thinks his dates are so grateful to get to go out with him that they are willing to wait for hours for him to show up. As for appointments, well, everyone knows that dentists, doctors, and barbers overschedule. If he arrived on time, they would make *him* wait! Jim's attitude is a good example of how chronic lateness shows disrespect and a lack of consideration for others.

3   Without realizing it, Jim is creating a bad impression. His boss and coworkers can assume that Jim's job is not very important to him. For example, they may figure that the job is just something Jim has to do for the money while he is in school, so he does not put any more effort into it than necessary. But he may need a recommendation from these people someday, and he should take this job as seriously as any other.

4   Jim's lateness hurts him in other ways. Being chronically late to class sends a message to the instructor that Jim is disorganized and unable to manage time effectively. Students who do arrive on time are annoyed when he walks in late, interrupting a lecture by noisily getting into his seat and shuffling papers. Jim does not date a woman for very long. To hear him tell it, he is the one who ends the relationship, but I don't believe it. A woman is just not going to keep seeing someone who does not respect her enough to be on time. Even Jim's friends have begun to quit inviting him places where time is a factor. They do not want to miss the beginning of a concert or a movie because Jim is late.

5   Most people who are chronically late are like Jim. They do not realize either the effect their behavior has on others or the ways lateness can hurt them. If they did, maybe they would make more of an effort to arrive on time. Perhaps our lives would be improved as well. For example, we could get through a movie without latecomers tripping over us, spilling popcorn in our laps, and whispering loudly to their friends who had arrived on time, "What did I miss?"

The three stages of the writing process overlap. They are not entirely separate, nor do they necessarily follow in order. During the prewriting stage, you may do some organizing. During the drafting and organizing stage, you will do some revising and may even go back to prewriting. For example, you may discover that your evidence does not support your thesis. Then you might use a

Figure 1.5   Writing Is a Recursive Process

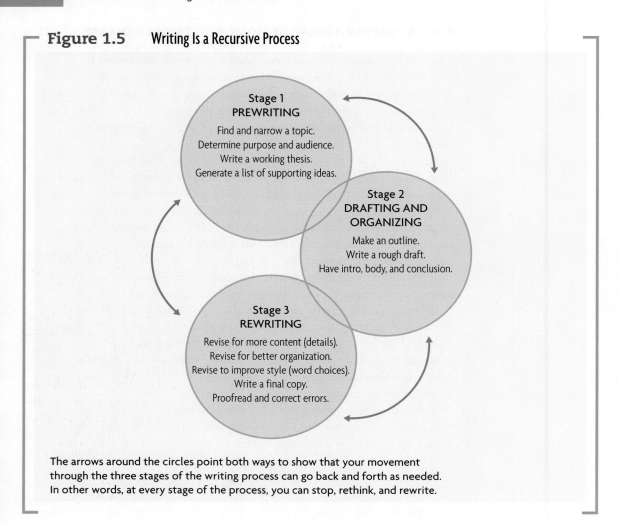

**Stage 1
PREWRITING**

Find and narrow a topic.
Determine purpose and audience.
Write a working thesis.
Generate a list of supporting ideas.

**Stage 2
DRAFTING AND
ORGANIZING**

Make an outline.
Write a rough draft.
Have intro, body, and conclusion.

**Stage 3
REWRITING**

Revise for more content (details).
Revise for better organization.
Revise to improve style (word choices).
Write a final copy.
Proofread and correct errors.

The arrows around the circles point both ways to show that your movement
through the three stages of the writing process can go back and forth as needed.
In other words, at every stage of the process, you can stop, rethink, and rewrite.

prewriting strategy to explore your subject some more and either rewrite your
thesis or collect new evidence. Even some editing may occur during the drafting and organizing stage. When you find an error, you may choose to correct
it then instead of waiting until you finish your draft. The overlap of the three
stages is called *recursiveness,* a term that means "falling back on itself." Writing
is a recursive process *because* the stages overlap and there is much moving
back and forth among them. Figure 1.5 illustrates the recursive nature of the
writing process.

There is no one best way to write an essay, but as you prewrite, draft and
organize, and rewrite essay after essay, you will develop a process that works
for you. What is important is that you state a thesis and support it, that you or-

ganize your ideas logically and state them clearly, and that you spend enough time revising and editing so that your essay represents your best achievement.

[**Exercise 1.7**]

Think about the most recent essay you have written. List the stages you went through in writing your essay. Compare your stages with the three stages of the writing process explained on pages 20–25. What conclusions can you draw? Which part of the process is easiest for you? Which part is most difficult? On which part of the process do you need to spend more time?

Find Your Voice

Goal 4 Use critical and creative thinking to discover and express your unique voice as a writer.

Your writing is unique, just as you are unique. The topics that interest you, the words you choose, and the way you put them together reflect who you are. Who are you, and how did you get to be that way? Where were you born, and where did you grow up? What is your cultural or ethnic heritage? Who have been the important people in your life, and what have they taught you? What values and beliefs do you find meaningful? Where have you traveled, what jobs have you held, and what experiences have you had that have left an impression on you? Do you have a favorite place, book, or activity?

Many students underestimate their knowledge and experience. If you have ever played a sport, learned a skill such as how to drive a car, served in the military, done volunteer work, played in a band, sung in a choir, or done other things, the experience you gained can serve as a prompt for writing. Also, your point of view on those experiences will be a little different from that of anyone else who has had the same experiences.

To find your voice, look to the past and remember the people, places, and events that have made you who you are. In the process, think critically and creatively. Above all, think for yourself.

Be a Critical Thinker

Critical thinking informs every part of the writing process, from prewriting, to drafting and organizing, to rewriting. Critical thinking is a necessary part of reading and researching. In an academic setting, critical thinking helps you go beyond learning facts to discover what the facts mean and how you can apply the information. In the workplace, critical thinking helps you make decisions and solve problems. Critical thinking is unhurried, deep thinking. If you want a more formal definition, critical thinking is *logical, analytical, conscious, purposeful, active,* and *self-reflective thinking.* To think critically about writing, you will do all of the following and more.

- Find a purpose for writing
- Define your audience's characteristics
- Write an outline for your paper
- Choose an organizational pattern to arrange your ideas
- Analyze your topic from all sides
- Reflect on what you have written and on ways to improve it

Finally, critical thinking is an *active* process. Critical thinkers do not think passively or answer questions "off the top of their heads." Critical thinking is work; it requires you to focus your attention on an issue or a problem and ask questions such as "Why?" and "How?" However, do not stop there; think creatively too.

Be a Creative Thinker

Where critical thinking is logical and analytical, creative thinking is nonlinear and inventive. To some people, creative thinking means "thinking outside the box." However, you first have to know what is in the box to think outside it. Critical thinking and creative thinking are complementary processes. In an academic setting, creative thinking might help you to produce an original work of art, a musical composition, or an inventive answer to a research question. In the workplace, creative thinkers are valued for their fresh ideas and unique solutions to persistent problems. As applied to writing, creative thinking includes all of the following and more.

- Choose a topic that challenges your thinking
- Question your assumptions and be open to change

Figure 1.6   Are You a Critical and Creative Thinker?

QUALITIES OF CRITICAL THINKERS	QUALITIES OF CREATIVE THINKERS
Logical	Imaginative
Analytical	Inventive
Purposeful	Open-minded
Active	Risk-taking
Conscious (aware of their thought processes)	Observant
Self-reflective	Inquisitive

Figure 1.7   **Roles and Responsibilities for Group Members**

Leader	The leader keeps time, interprets the exercise directions, keeps the discussion on target, and makes sure everyone participates.
Recorder	The recorder acts as secretary, taking notes and compiling the final group report, which consists of the group evaluation and any other writing called for in the exercise.
Researcher	The researcher consults the textbook, the instructor, or other resources as needed to settle matters of confusion or controversy.
Reciter	The reciter reports back to the class, using the recorder's report for reference.

- Write an introduction that engages readers
- Imagine yourself in the audience to better understand their needs
- Select words to create vivid images
- Take intellectual risks by asking questions and trying new strategies

Finally, creative thinkers look for ideas in unusual places. Like critical thinkers, creative thinkers ask "Why?" and "How?" but they also ask "What if?" Creative thinkers are not content with the status quo. They already know how things are. They would rather imagine how things could be. Figure 1.6 on page 26 compares some qualities of critical and creative thinkers.

[Exercise 1.8]

This exercise will help you practice thinking creatively. First, form a group of four. To ensure that everyone participates, each person should play a role within the group. On the inside back cover of *The Confident Writer,* you will find a list of group roles and responsibilities that you can use as a guide for your own group's work. See also Figure 1.7 at the top of this page.

Next, follow these directions to complete the exercise: Read and discuss each other's discovery drafts from Exercise 1.1 and answer the following questions: (1) What movies or TV programs did the members of your group select? (2) What positive or negative effects did they identify? (3) How did their explanations and conclusions compare? Take notes on your discussion, and be prepared to share your findings with the rest of the class. Evaluate your discussion as your instructor recommends, or go to *The Confident Writer* website to download the group evaluation form.

≪ Topics for Writing ≫

1. **React to the Reading.** Use one of the questions from *First Thoughts* on page 2, as your topic, or use this question as your topic: Should the movie industry let social or political pressure affect its decisions about what or what not to include in films?

2. **Use Your Experience.** Choose a topic from the following list, or go to *The Confident Writer* website for more suggestions. The topic you select should be the one that you know the most about or can relate to your own life and experience.

   - A political or social issue that should concern everyone
   - A charity or organization that deserves support
   - A person we should admire
   - A book that has made a lasting impression on you

3. **Make a Real-World Connection.** The First Amendment protects the freedom of speech, of religion, of the press, and of the people's right to assemble peacefully. Write about one of these issues in which you, your community, or your campus hae been involved.

4. **Go to the Web.** Read one or more reviews of a movie that you have seen recently. You can find reviews at http://www.moviefone.com or ask your instructor or librarian for another URL. Then write an essay in which you agree or disagree with the review based on your own viewing of the film.

≪ Checklist for Revision ≫

Did you miss anything? Check off the following items as you revise and edit your essay.

- ❑ Does your essay have an introductory paragraph?
- ❑ Can readers tell from your introduction what your topic and purpose are?
- ❑ Can you find one sentence that states your central idea (thesis)?
- ❑ Does your essay have body paragraphs?
- ❑ Do you have enough details in each paragraph to support the thesis?
- ❑ Are the details organized so that readers can follow them?
- ❑ Does your essay have a concluding paragraph?
- ❑ Is there a summary of your major points?
- ❑ Do you call for an action or change of thought from your readers?
- ❑ Have you proofread your essay and corrected the errors?

≪ Your Discovery Journal ≫

A journal is a place to record ideas, impressions, thoughts, and feelings—anything that may be useful to you as a writer. A journal also provides a place for reflection—a day-to-day review of what you are learning and how it is changing the way you think or act.

Your journal allows you to be creative. It can be a pocket notebook that you carry around with you, or it can be as large as you want to make it. You can jot notes in it, insert clippings, or personalize it by decorating the cover, for example. You and your instructor may decide that you will submit some journal entries by email and receive a response, or you may decide that the journal will be for private musings only. As an additional option, do journal activities online by going to *The Confident Writer* website.

Now turn to the inside front cover of this book and read the list of traits of confident writers. There are fourteen traits in all, one for every chapter. Chapter 1 opens with the first trait on the list, *self-motivation*. Which traits best describe you? Which traits would you like to develop? What else gives you confidence? For your first journal entry, complete the following reflective statement and explain your reasons:

One skill, quality, or trait that gives me confidence is _____.

≪ Website Resources ≫

This chapter's resources include

- Chapter 1 Exercises
- Chapter 1 Quiz
- Downloadable Charts: *Group Evaluation Form*
- Survey: *Active Reading*
- Survey: *Writer's Profile*
- Chapter 1 Summary

To access these learning and study tools, go to *The Confident Writer* website.

Confident writers are flexible. They are willing to try new strategies for planning, writing, and revising an essay.

Using Prewriting Strategies

What you already know about *prewriting*

- You may already know that *prewriting* is something you do before writing.

- Your experience tells you that planning ahead for writing, or any activity, will improve your chances for success.

- If you have ever written an outline, made a list, or discussed a topic before writing about it, then you have used a prewriting strategy.

Your *goals* for this chapter

[1] Know how to think like a writer, discover your values, and use your knowledge to connect with others.

[2] Know how to choose an appropriate topic and limit a topic so that it is neither too narrow nor too broad.

[3] Be able to use a prewriting strategy such as brainstorming, freewriting, or questioning to think through your topic.

[4] Use the START strategy to find your voice, choose a topic, and determine your audience, purpose, and tone.

[5] Know how to take essay exams without fear and write effectively in all timed situations.

You are sitting in your favorite study place, ready to write. Whether you are facing a blank sheet of paper or an empty computer screen, you have been staring at it for what seems like hours. If only you could get started. Perhaps you are taking an essay exam. Although you understand the topic and have studied sufficiently, you do not know where to begin. Suppose your supervisor at work has asked you to write a report. You know where to look for information and what format to follow. Now you have only one question in mind: "How do I get started?" Do any of these situations sound familiar? If so, you are not alone. Getting started can be a challenge for any writer, no matter what the writing task is.

All writing begins with an idea, and one idea leads to another. To get the first idea that starts the others flowing, many writers have a favorite prewriting strategy, a method for generating ideas and planning what to write. Writing a discovery draft, as explained in Chapter 1, is one of the many choices available. This chapter explains several other prewriting strategies that can help you get started. Try them all; then choose the one that works best for you and make it part of your writing process.

[First Thoughts]

To build background for reading, explore your thoughts about writing. Then answer the following questions, either on your own or in a group discussion:

1. Is getting started an easy or difficult part of the writing process for you? Why?

2. What helpful tips for getting started have you received from instructors or others?

3. Read the title, the headnote, and the first one or two paragraphs of the excerpt. Based on this preview, what do you think will follow?

[Word Alert]

Before reading, preview the following words and definitions. During reading, use context clues and your dictionary to define any additional unfamiliar words.

innovating (1)	introducing something new
extensively (1)	in great amount, or over a wide area
disparagement (2)	reduction in esteem

confirmed (4)	supported
drudge (4)	one who does boring, unpleasant work
insight (5)	the capacity to understand the true nature of a situation
trivial (13)	unimportant
mimicking (13)	copying

Start with One Brick

Robert M. Pirsig

The following excerpt is from Robert M. Pirsig's Zen and the Art of Motorcycle Maintenance. *The book is about a cross-country trip in which a man and his son search for life's meaning. This excerpt is about teaching, writing, and a common problem many student writers share: trying to think of something to say.*

1   He'd been innovating extensively. He'd been having trouble with students who had nothing to say. At first, he thought it was laziness but later it became apparent that it wasn't. They just couldn't think of anything to say.

2   One of them, a girl with strong-lensed glasses, wanted to write a five-hundred-word essay about the United States. He was used to the sinking feeling that comes from statements like this, and suggested with disparagement that she narrow it down to just Bozeman.

3   When the paper came due she didn't have it and was quite upset. She had tried and tried but she just couldn't think of anything to say.

4   He had already discussed her with her previous instructors and they'd confirmed his impressions of her. She was very serious, disciplined and hardworking, but extremely dull. Not a spark of creativity in her anywhere. Her eyes, behind the thick-lensed glasses, were the eyes of a drudge. She wasn't bluffing him, she really couldn't think of anything to say, and was upset by her inability to do as she was told.

5   It just stumped him. Now *he* couldn't think of anything to say. A silence occurred, and then a peculiar answer: "Narrow it down to the *main street* of Bozeman." It was a stroke of insight.

6   She nodded dutifully and went out. But just before her next class she came back in *real* distress, tears this time, distress that had obviously been there for a long time. She still couldn't think of anything to say, and couldn't understand why, if she couldn't think of anything about *all* of Bozeman, she should be able to think of something about just one street.

7   He was furious. "You're not *looking!*" he said. A memory came back of his own dismissal from the University for having *too much* to say. For every fact there is an *infinity* of hypotheses. The more you *look* the more you see. She really wasn't looking and yet somehow didn't understand this.

8   He told her angrily, "Narrow it down to the *front* of one building on the main street of Bozeman. The Opera House. Start with the upper left-hand brick."

9   Her eyes, behind the thick-lensed glasses, opened wide.

10   She came in the next class with a puzzled look and handed him a five-thousand-word essay on the front of the Opera House on the main street of Bozeman, Montana. "I sat in the hamburger stand across the street," she said, "and started writing about the first brick, and the second brick, and then by the third brick it all started to come and I couldn't stop. They thought I was crazy, and they kept kidding me, but here it all is. I don't understand it."

11   Neither did he, but on long walks through the streets of town he thought about it and concluded she was evidently stopped with the same kind of blockage that had paralyzed him on his first day of teaching. She was blocked because she was trying to repeat, in her writing, things she had already heard, just as on the first day he had tried to repeat things he had already decided to say. She couldn't think of anything to write about Bozeman because she couldn't recall anything she had heard worth repeating. She was strangely unaware that she could look and see freshly for herself, as she wrote, without primary regard for what had been said before. The narrowing down to one brick destroyed the blockage because it was so obvious she *had* to do some original and direct seeing.

12   He experimented further. In one class he had everyone write all hour about the back of his thumb. Everyone gave him funny looks at the beginning of the hour, but everyone did it, and there wasn't a single complaint about "nothing to say."

13   In another class he changed the subject from the thumb to a coin, and got a full hour's writing from every student. In other classes it was the same. Some asked, "Do you have to write about both sides?" Once they got into the idea of seeing directly for themselves they also saw there was no limit to the amount they could say. It was a confidence-building assignment too, because what they wrote, even though seemingly trivial, was nevertheless their own thing, not a mimicking of someone else's. . . .

≪ The Critical Reader ≫

[CENTRAL IDEA]

1. What is Pirsig's central idea about teachers and writing?

[EVIDENCE]

2. Pirsig states three examples of writing assignments that made students do original thinking. What are they?

3. How does the teacher in the excerpt compare himself to the girl who can't think of anything to say?

[IMPLICATIONS]

4. Does the teacher think that any student is capable of thinking originally and creatively? Use evidence from the excerpt to support your answer.

[**WORD CHOICE**]

5. Read the excerpt again, and underline all the adjectives the author uses to describe the girl who had nothing to say. How does the author's choice of words create an impression of what this girl is like? If you wanted to write about someone who was the opposite of the girl in Pirsig's essay, what adjectives would you use instead of the ones in the excerpt?

≪ The Critical Thinker ≫

To examine Pirsig's essay in more depth, follow these suggestions for reflection, discussion, and writing.

1. Review the section "Find Your Voice" on pages 25–27. Do the teacher's writing assignments in Pirsig's essay require students to think critically, creatively, or both? Explain your answer.

2. Explain what the author means by this statement from paragraph 7. "The more you *look* the more you see."

3. Based on what you have learned from this chapter and from Pirsig's essay, what would be your advice to a student writer who cannot think of anything to say? Make a list of suggestions to help the student get started.

4. In paragraphs 12 and 13, the author says that two writing assignments gave the students something to say. Discuss these assignments and explain why you think they worked. Then try one of the two assignments for yourself: either write about the back of your thumb or write about a coin.

Think Like a Writer

Goal 1 Know how to think like a writer, discover your values, and use your knowledge to connect with others.

To begin your voyage to self-discovery think about the roles you play. Whether you are someone's mother, father, son, daughter, sister, brother, friend, husband, wife, lover, boss, coworker, student, or classmate, you have a background of experiences associated with that role that affects how you see and relate to the world. For example, your positive and negative experiences as a student influence the way you interact with teachers and classmates, just as the way you were raised as a child has an effect on how you raise your children. You also have a private self, a part of you that has made decisions about what is right or wrong, and about what your political, social, and religious values are. Your *self* is the person you are in all of your outer roles and in all of your inner values. How much of this self you reveal as a writer depends upon what

seems most appropriate to your topic and your audience. To write about any issue, explore your experiences and values to determine where you stand and why. This process will help you arrive at the point of view from which you will write your essay.

The *self* you reveal in your writing also expresses your unique point of view. If you were writing on the issue of women in combat, would your point of view be that of a man or woman who has served in the military, a father or mother who has daughters to protect, a citizen who believes that equal opportunity should apply to women in the service, or a citizen who thinks that women have no place in the infantry? When the teacher in the excerpt on pages 32–33 asks the student to write about just one brick, he forces her to see for herself, instead of repeating what others have said—to use her experience to come up with a unique point of view. He asks her to relate topic to *self*. In other words, he wants her to think creatively, take a risk, and find her voice.

[**Exercise 2.1**]

✓ CONCEPT CHECK
For more on finding your voice, see Chapter 1.

To see yourself and your experiences in relation to the topics you write about, you first have to know who you are. Though some take the question "Who am I?" for granted, many great men and women have spent their lives trying to answer it. Listed below are some categories of experience. Write the categories on a sheet of paper, skipping several lines between them. Then make some notes about yourself under each category. The finished list should give you a picture of yourself and bring into focus what makes you unique. To explore your values in detail, go to *The Confident Writer* website and take the survey *My Values*.

- Origin, background, family heritage
- Special talents or accomplishments
- Places lived in or traveled
- Work experience
- Political views
- Social/moral values
- Personal likes and dislikes
- Life/career goals

Choose and Limit a Topic

Know how to choose an appropriate topic and limit a topic so that it is neither too narrow nor too broad.

The **topic** is the *subject* of your essay. In thinking about the topic, decide what you know about it, what experiences you have had with it, and what you would like to tell readers about it. Anything can become a topic for writing: people, places, objects, ideas, problems, and processes. The best topics are those that are familiar to you and that appeal to your interests.

Mai Chan is a college student who came to the United States from China several years ago. She works as a waitress in her family's restaurant. She hopes to finish college someday, but she has not decided what her major or her career will be. Like many students in her writing class, Mai often has difficulty getting started, but she is learning to use her experience as a source of ideas. A recent topic the professor assigned was "a favorite holiday and how you celebrate it." Many of the students wrote about Christmas, Hanukkah, or Thanksgiving. Mai chose to write about Chinese New Year and how it is celebrated in her native country. As she thought about her topic, she jotted down some notes about the traditions surrounding the holiday, the food and activities associated with it, and what the holiday means. The category of personal experience that Mai used to relate self to topic is *origin, background, family heritage.*

As you think about your topic, make sure it is not too broad. A broad topic is one that is general and covers a lot of territory. An important step in your prewriting process should be to *narrow,* or *limit,* your topic to something you can explain fully in a short essay. "Holidays," for example, is too broad. If you tried to write an essay about holidays in general or all the holidays you could think of, you might fill pages without saying much of significance about any one holiday. A good topic is one that has been limited sufficiently to focus on a single central idea that can be developed in an essay. Mai's topic, "a favorite holiday and how you celebrate it," limited her to one holiday and how she celebrates it. To get started, all Mai had to do was decide which holiday to write about, then gather her evidence on how the Chinese celebrate the new year.

Remember that in the excerpt on pages 32–33, the student at first wanted to write a five-hundred-word essay about the United States. The teacher narrowed the topic down to Bozeman, then to the main street of Bozeman, and finally to just the front of one building, starting with the upper left-hand brick. The student's first topic was too broad. Once she understood how to limit the topic, she was able to write a five-thousand-word essay.

[**Exercise 2.2**] Practice limiting topics by thinking about the following topics, then rewriting them so that they focus on a single idea. The first one is done as an example.

1. General topic: friends

    Limited topic: *the most important quality of a good friend* _____

2. General topic: family traditions

   Limited topic: _____

3. General topic: games or sports

   Limited topic: _____

4. General topic: ways to save energy

   Limited topic: _____

5. General topic: election campaigns

   Limited topic: _____

6. General topic: travel destinations

   Limited topic: _____

7. Write your own general topic: _____

   Write your own limited topic: _____

[**Exercise 2.3**]   Using your list from Exercise 2.1, decide which categories of personal experience would help you to think about and generate ideas from the topics you limited in Exercise 2.2. For example, if you wrote about the limited topic "the most important quality of a good friend," you would be drawing upon the categories of social/moral values and personal likes and dislikes.

Use a Prewriting Strategy

Goal 3 Be able to use a prewriting strategy such as brainstorming, freewriting, or questioning to think through your topic.

Many writers believe that it helps them to spend some time thinking about their topics and making notes before they begin to write. *Prewriting* is the planning stage of the writing process. During this stage, you think about your topic and make some decisions about what aspect of your topic you will cover, your central idea, your purpose, your point of view, and perhaps even how you will organize your essay. You also think about your audience and what you want readers to know about your topic. At this stage, your planning is tentative. You are giving yourself directions to follow so that you can get started. As you begin to draft your essay, your plans may change. Prewriting is also useful for rethinking your topic whenever you get stuck during the writing process. You might be in the middle of a rough draft, for example, and decide that what you have written so far isn't working out. Now you could use another prewriting strategy to generate some more ideas about your topic, or even to help you find a new topic.

Brainstorm Your Topic

Whether you are writing about a familiar topic or one that you need to research, *brainstorming* is a useful prewriting strategy for thinking about topics and generating ideas that may become the evidence to support a thesis or central idea of your essay. Start with a blank sheet of paper. Write your topic at the top. Think about the topic, and list everything that comes to your mind. Do not worry about whether the ideas are related, and do not try to write complete sentences. Jot down whatever words and phrases come to mind, and do not stop until you have at least twenty items on your list. Later you can decide which ideas to use, which ones to leave out, and how to organize those that are left. Following is a student's brainstorming list for the topic "grades and testing," which he limited to "final exams."

Final exams

cramming	test anxiety
staying up all night	worrying about grades
fast food	fear of failure
headaches	comfortable clothes
notes	good-luck charms
old exams	best place to sit
study groups	what to take to the exam
the need for breaks	how to relax
music or not?	what to study
ways to study	pressure
jitters	

After reading over his list, the student decided that his ideas fell into three categories. He then rearranged his ideas into three lists with new headings:

Problems students face during finals

cramming
staying up all night
fast food
headaches
test anxiety
jitters
pressure
worrying about grades

Preparing for exams

notes
old exams
study groups
music or not?
what to study
ways to study

Taking exams

comfortable clothes
good-luck charms
best place to sit
how to relax

Now the student had a clearer idea of what he wanted to write about. As a topic, "final exams" was still too broad. His lists reminded him of something he had learned from experience, though: that most of the problems students face when studying for and taking exams are the result of poor preparation. The student therefore limited his topic to "how to avoid exam-week jitters." He still needed to come up with a thesis statement, and he also realized that his lists needed more work. For example, he needed more ideas for "preparing for exams" and "taking exams." Even so, he knew that with the evidence he had collected so far, he was off to a good start.

[**Exercise 2.4**]   Choose a topic that interests you. What would you like to write about? Is there a problem you would like to see solved? Is there a piece of advice you would like to give readers that would make their lives easier or better? After choosing and limiting your topic, write a brainstorming list of twenty or more items. If you like the results, use the list as part of your planning for an essay.

Freewrite as a Data Dump

The term *freewriting* means exactly what it says: free, unrestrained writing. It is a process in which you write down whatever comes to mind without pausing to think about spelling or the rules of grammar. The purpose of this type of writing is merely to dump data or generate ideas and to get the writing process going. Some writers and educators disagree about the value of freewriting. Some say that most of what you get when you freewrite is unusable. But others find it a valuable tool to use when they have trouble getting started. For those writers, just the process of writing something—anything—helps them think about their topic.

Those who do find freewriting helpful say that it works best if you take the time to limit your topic first. Then your focus is narrowed to writing and thinking about a single idea. To begin, write your limited topic at the top of a blank sheet of paper. Using a timer if possible, write for ten minutes without stopping. Write everything you can think of about your topic. Do not worry about grammar or spelling. When you have finished, read what you have written. Much of it may not be useful, but some of it may contain a few details that you can use or an idea that you can develop into a thesis or central idea. If your freewriting did not generate a few useful ideas, then choose another topic and try again, or try another prewriting strategy.

Exercise 2.5

Writing on a computer engages your senses of touch, sound, and sight. If you have a learning style that responds favorably to visual and kinesthetic stimuli, then you may enjoy freewriting on a computer. Choose a topic, limit your topic, and freewrite for about five minutes to generate ideas. First, dim the computer screen so that you are not tempted to look at what you have written until you are finished. Next, begin typing. Write whatever comes to mind about your topic. The dark screen frees you from the need to stop, revise, or edit your ideas. When you are finished, brighten the screen and read what you have written. Delete anything that is not useful, and save anything that you might be able to use in a current or future writing assignment.

Ask Questions About Your Topic

When gathering facts for a story, journalists often ask six questions: *Who? What? Where? When? Why?* and *How?* For example, a journalist might ask: *Who* is involved? *What* happened to that person? *Where* did the event take place? *When* did it happen? *Why* did it happen? *How* did anyone find out about it? To help you remember the questions, think of them as *five W's and an H.* Answering these questions about your topic is another good way to generate ideas in the prewriting stage and come up with the evidence you need to support a thesis. Following are several examples that show you how to adapt the journalist's questions to different kinds of topics.

EXAMPLE 1: WRITING ABOUT A PERSON

Who am I writing about? Who is my reader? (audience)

What happened between me and the person? What is my opinion or viewpoint? (topic and central idea)

Where did we meet? Where did the event I describe occur? (evidence)

When did we meet? When did something significant happen in our relationship? When did we break up, and so forth? (evidence)

Why do I like (or dislike) this person? Why am I writing about him or her? (purpose)

How have my feelings changed or remained the same? How has this person affected my life, and so forth? (implications)

EXAMPLE 2: WRITING ABOUT A PLACE

Who was with me in this place? Who is my reader? (audience)

What place am I writing about? What is my opinion or viewpoint? (topic and central idea)

Where is the place? (evidence)

When did I go there? When did the event I describe occur? (evidence)

Why do I like (or dislike) the place? Why am I writing about it? (purpose)

How did I find out about the place? How did it affect me? (implications)

EXAMPLE 3: WRITING ABOUT AN ISSUE

Who influenced me or made me aware of the issue? Who is my reader? (audience)

What is the issue? What is my position, opinion, or viewpoint? (topic and central idea)

Where did I learn about the issue? Where did a certain event related to the issue occur? (evidence)

When did the issue become an issue? When did I become interested in it? (evidence)

Why do I think the way I do? Why am I writing about the issue? (purpose)

How has the issue or my involvement in it affected me? How does it affect others? (implications)

To think creatively about issues, add one more question to the journalist's list: *"What if?"* This question forces you to think about outcomes and consequences. For example, what if the residents in an inner-city neighborhood decided to take back control of their streets from gangs and drug dealers? How could they do it, and what if they were successful? Suppose that you have earned poor grades on the last two tests in one of your courses. What if you were to change your study habits? What if you were to do nothing? In either case, the outcome might be different. Thinking about outcomes and consequences is another way to generate ideas for writing and find solutions to problems.

Make an Idea Cluster

Clustering, as explained briefly in Chapter 1, pages 20–21, is a prewriting strategy that not only helps you generate ideas that you may later use as evidence but also helps you see relationships among your ideas. An idea cluster is an illustration or visual representation of how ideas relate. Figure 2.1 is an idea cluster for the limited topic "how to avoid exam-week jitters," which a student narrowed down from the topic "final exams."

Figure 2.1 Idea Cluster for "How to Avoid Exam-Week Jitters"

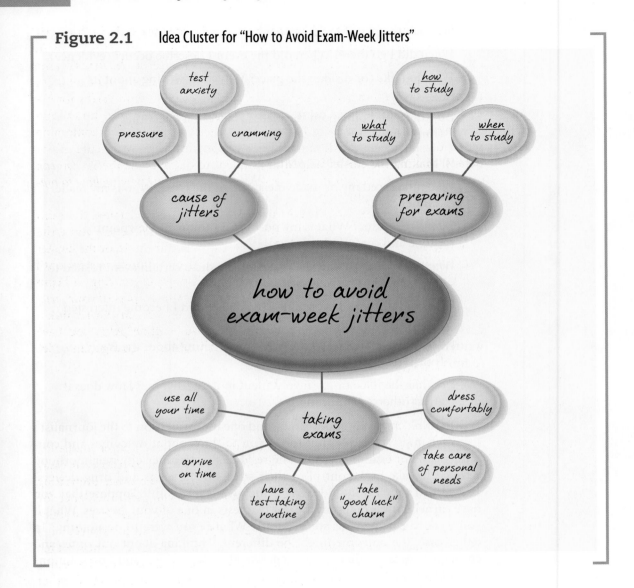

To make an idea cluster, first write your topic, or an abbreviated version of it, in a circle in the middle of a page of clean paper. As you think about your topic, decide how you would break it down into parts that you can discuss one at a time in your essay. These parts, or divisions, may become the main ideas of body paragraphs. As soon as you decide what one main idea will be, draw a line out from the center circle to another circle in which you write the idea. If you can break that idea down into more specific supporting details to use as evidence, draw lines out to additional circles and write the details in those circles. For example, in the cluster in Figure 2.1, one of the divisions, or main ideas, is "preparing for exams." As the student thought about the items on the brainstorming list he had made earlier, he decided he could improve on them by reorganizing them and by adding more items. From the "preparing for exams" circle, he drew three more circles: "what to study," "how to study," and "when to study." These were his major details. From the circles containing major details, he could add more circles to contain his more specific minor details. Making the cluster helped the student to discover his thesis: *You can avoid exam-week jitters by eliminating their causes and by knowing how to prepare for and take exams.*

How many circles you add to your idea cluster and how detailed you want to be in writing in them is up to you. The main ideas and details you write down may become the evidence you use to support your thesis, or the cluster may be only a starting point from which you will make more clusters until you have collected enough evidence and done enough organizing to begin drafting your essay. Moreover, you can use clustering in any part of your writing process, not just for prewriting. Sometimes it is necessary to rethink a draft you are working on. A cluster on which you "outline" what you have written so far may help you see what needs to be added or changed in order to finish your draft.

Plan Your Essay with START

Goal 4 Use the START strategy to find your voice, choose a topic, and determine your audience, purpose, and tone.

START is an acronym formed from the first letters of *self, topic, audience, reason,* and *tone*—five essentials to consider as you begin to plan your essay during the prewriting stage. Using START *and* one of the other prewriting strategies explained in this chapter not only will help you gather evidence for your essay but also will help you focus on your audience's needs. A student who was having difficulty choosing a major decided to visit her college's career center on the recommendation of a friend. She made an appointment for career counseling, took several tests and inventories, and based on the results decided on a major that would help her reach her goals. Because she felt that other students should know about the center and the services it provides, she decided to write an essay about it. Figure 2.2 illustrates how she used START to plan her essay.

The first two letters of *START* stand for *self* and *topic.* Always begin your prewriting process by thinking of yourself as a writer. Choose a topic that you can write about from your own experience or knowledge, and remember to limit your topic. Remember too that the self you bring to writing is also your *voice* as a writer. The following sections explain *audience, reason,* and *tone* as three more essentials to consider as part of your planning for writing.

Figure 2.2   Using *START* to Plan an Essay

QUESTIONS TO ASK		ANSWERS
Self	What roles do I want to reveal?	I am a student like many of those who might read my essay.
Topic	How will I limit my topic?	My topic is the career center and the services it offers to students.
Audience	Who is my audience, and what can I assume about my readers?	Other students are my audience, and I can assume that some of them are uncertain about their futures.
Reason	What is my purpose for writing about this topic?	I want to inform students about the center's services and the kind of help it provides.
Tone	What tone do I want? How do I achieve it?	I will choose words that make me sound serious and confident.

Determine the Audience

You can write for one of two possible audiences, a general one or a specific one. Most of the time in college, you will write for your peers—that is, your classmates and your instructor. What assumptions can you make about them? First of all, they are part of your college community, so they share your interests, concerns, and problems as a college student. Since they are also part of the larger community in which you live, they are members of a *general audience.* You can assume that they have shared many of your same experiences and that they may be aware of current events and of the social issues that affect everyone's lives. In addition, people of varying races, cultural backgrounds, nationalities, and ethnic groups are all part of a general audience in the United States today and are also part of your classroom audience. It is important to keep in mind that some of your readers will have had experiences that are very different from yours. Therefore, you cannot assume that readers will always know what you mean unless you explain it to them.

Sometimes you may write for a *specific audience.* Perhaps you have decided to write about a controversial topic—animal rights, for example—and you imagine that some of the people reading your essay will strongly disagree with you. To write effectively for this audience, determine what their views are so that you can choose your evidence and develop your thesis to answer these views.

☑ **CONCEPT CHECK**
See also "audience characteristics" in Chapter 1.

☑ **CONCEPT CHECK**
How to set up an argument and how to write an essay on a controversial topic are explained in Chapter 14, "Arguing Persuasively."

How you write about a topic will differ depending upon who the audience is and what your purpose is. In the following examples, the topic is the same, but the audiences are different. The topic is "competency testing for college students." Notice how the *purpose* and *audience* affect the writing.

The first example is a paragraph from a typical news article a journalist might write in response to a new state law requiring college students to take a competency test in math and English. The purpose of the article is to inform readers about the test. The general public is the audience.

EXAMPLE 1

Soon, all college students in our state will have to take a basic skills test. The test comes at a time when educators across the country are expressing concern about underprepared students and about employers' complaints that college graduates lack basic communication skills. The purpose of the test is to ensure that students who want to continue in college are able to demonstrate that they can read, write, and compute at a basic level. Students who fail one part of the test will have an opportunity to retake that part without having to repeat the whole test. Though the test is still in its experimental stages, eventually every student will have to take it in order to be eligible for an Associate of Arts degree and to continue his or her education. Students will have to pay a fee to take the test; however, the price has not yet been determined. . . .

The next two examples are possible letters to the editor of a local newspaper in a community where competency testing has been going on for some time. One writer defends the test, and the other condemns it. Parents of college students are the specific audience for both letters, and the writers' purpose is to persuade them to either support or reject the test.

EXAMPLE 2

Dear Editor:

When I was in school you either learned, or else. The "or else" came in the form of a rap on your knuckles with the teacher's ruler. No one passed to the next grade who had not learned the lessons. I remember one boy in the sixth grade who was 18 years old. Eventually, he graduated and went on to earn a living and support his family like the rest of us.

I don't advocate a return to those times. I know that all students are entitled to the opportunity to continue their education, not just those who can afford the tuition. However, I think it's a shame that so many kids graduate from college who can't even spell.

After all these years of social promotion and lack of accountability on the part of schools and teachers, I'm glad that my grandson will have to take the state competency test. Maybe because of this test, he'll work harder in school and his teachers will feel obligated to help him succeed. I hope all parents will get behind the state's efforts to upgrade education and support the testing program.

A Concerned Citizen

EXAMPLE 3

Dear Editor:

My daughter has always been a good student except in math. In high school she made mostly A's and B's. She has done well in her college courses too, but now her graduation is being delayed because she didn't pass the math part of the state competency test. She is spending another semester at the community college to brush up on her math skills so she can pass the test. I'm worried that she may never pass this exam because math is the one subject that has always given her trouble.

What a lot of parents do not realize is that students have to pay for this test, and in my case I am having to pay my daughter's tuition for another semester in college, which I had not planned on and I can ill afford.

Not only does the test cause students needless anxiety, but it is very discouraging to them when they fail. How can one test be a measure of a person's ability, and why should one test determine whether a student gets to continue her education? Furthermore, the test is timed. When students are under that kind of pressure, it is no wonder that they do not do well. I am sure I am not alone when I say that I think the test is unfair. I urge parents to write their legislators opposing the test.

A Concerned Parent

The writers of Examples 1, 2, and 3 know their audiences. Each knows the extent to which the audience is informed about the topic, what additional information about the topic the audience needs, why the audience should be interested in or concerned about the topic, and what new information would enlighten the audience.

The writer of Example 1 assumes that some readers may know about the new competency test but that most of them do not. He also assumes that most of them are aware that educators are concerned about college graduates' declining performance. He probably thinks that they do not know what the test covers or that all college students will have to take it. Because many of the members of this writer's audience are parents, they are probably interested in or concerned about competency testing because their children will have to take the test if they expect to graduate from college. As a result of reading the article, parents may be inclined to encourage their children to succeed in those subjects that the test covers. Though some readers of the article undoubtedly may have heard that their state had established competency testing, they may not have realized that failing the test could delay or even prevent graduation. That students would have to pay a fee to take the test may also have been new information for some readers. This writer states facts without making judgments, and the language is formal and unemotional.

The writers of Examples 2 and 3 are writing at a time when the competency test is an established fact. Therefore, they can assume that parents of college students and students who want to go to college are aware of the test, what it covers, and its cost and know that it is required. These writers can also assume that although some members of the audience are in favor of the test, some oppose it. Both writers make judgments about the test. They rely on personal examples and opinions more than on facts for their support, and their language is informal and emotional.

The writer of Example 2 believes that many readers remember the days when students did learn their lessons. She also believes that, like her, many of her readers take for granted that schools and colleges need reform. The test, she thinks, is an effort to improve education. She probably thinks that readers who do not support the test do not realize that it might have a positive effect on the state's education program. She is writing for an audience of readers who she believes would support the state's testing program were they to see it as both encouraging students to work harder and requiring teachers to provide more help.

The writer of Example 3, on the other hand, believes that those who favor the test do not realize its drawbacks. This writer cites the cost, the inconvenience, the discouragement of having to take all or parts of the test more than once to pass it, the time limit, and the added cost of delaying graduation—all hardships for students. For some members of the audience, this additional information may be of some interest and concern, particularly if they have college-age sons and daughters who have failed the test and encountered similar problems.

The writers of Examples 2 and 3 both hope their readers will take action in the form of either supporting the test or writing their legislators to complain about it. Both either know or have studied their audiences well enough to present facts and opinions that will appeal to their readers' interests.

In considering your audience's needs, ask yourself the questions listed on page 44 in addition to these three general questions:

- What do my readers already know?
- What do I think they need to know?
- What do I know that may surprise my readers and add to their knowledge?

[Exercise 2.6]

Apply what you have learned about purpose and audience by doing this exercise with group members. First, review the group roles and responsibilities listed on the inside back cover. Next, read and discuss the following scenario and complete the writing task. Then evaluate your work as your instructor recommends, or go to *The Confident Writer* website, where you can download the group evaluation form.

> In your state, all college students must take a competency test in English and mathematics to be eligible for graduation. As members of your college's student government association, you have decided to organize a prep session to help students get ready for the test. You have convinced an instructor to conduct the session and give a practice exam and exercises. You think all students who are planning to take the test should take advantage of the prep session. The session is free, but students do have to sign up in the student government office.

Write an article for your campus newspaper to advertise the prep session. Keep your article brief, 200 words or fewer, and give it a title. To help you generate ideas for your article, refer to the scenario and discuss the following questions.

1. Who is your audience for the article, and what are its members' needs?
2. What is your purpose?
3. Who is eligible to attend the prep session?
4. How much will it cost?
5. Who will conduct the session?
6. What will it cover?
7. Where will it be held?
8. When will it be offered?
9. Why should students attend?
10. Where do they sign up?

Have a Reason to Write

Now that you are in college, you write to answer test questions, to complete exercises and assignments, and perhaps even to fill out application forms for scholarships, financial aid, or part-time jobs. Before you graduate, you will probably write a résumé, or a summary of your work and other experience, which you will submit along with job applications. In the workplace, you may have to write reports or take the minutes of a meeting. In your personal life, you may write letters to friends and relatives, to the editor of your local newspaper, or even to your state representative or senator. In each of these situations, you have a clear *reason*, or *purpose*, for writing.

In each case, there is something you want—for example, a good grade, a good job, a promotion, or a favorable response. Your purpose should be just as clear before you begin writing an essay. One way to determine a reason for writing is to ask yourself, "Why am I writing this?" Most of the time your answer will reveal one of two reasons: *to inform* or *to persuade.* To inform means to explain, provide facts, and give out information for the purpose of clear understanding. To persuade means to influence another's thinking with the hope of perhaps changing a behavior. Persuading also relies upon explanations, facts, and information for the purpose of influencing rather than for simply increasing knowledge and understanding.

If your purpose is to inform readers, tell them something about your topic that will educate or enlighten them. Perhaps you work as a greeter in a popular restaurant. To some people it may look as if you have an easy job. You greet people when they come in, take their names if they do not have a reservation, show them where to wait, and then give their names to a server who seats them when their table is ready. However, there is more to this job than people think. You may decide to write an essay to inform your readers that being a restaurant greeter is not as easy as it looks.

If your purpose is to persuade readers, you will want to influence them so that they change their opinions or behavior. Perhaps you are a politically active college student who is concerned about the low turnout of young voters during the last election. You believe that the best way for young people to influence their country's future direction is by voting. You want to encourage students to register to vote and to become informed about candidates and issues. As a result, you decide to write an essay that will persuade your readers to take these actions.

Writers often have more than one reason for writing. In the process of *informing* readers that there is more to a job than might appear on the surface, you may find yourself *persuading* them not to consider taking this job unless they first find out what is involved. In order to *persuade* readers to become more politically active, you may first have to *inform* them that a problem exists.

Exercise 2.7   Read each of the following paragraphs and decide whether the purpose is primarily to *inform* or to *persuade.* Underline words or phrases in each paragraph that help you determine the writer's purpose.

1. From his broad, flat bill to his webbed feet, the furry duck-billed platypus is an odd animal. Awkward on land, he is a graceful swimmer. Shrimp are the platypus's favorite food, but you might wonder how he ever finds them since he swims with his eyes closed. Electric sensors on his bill can detect the tiny electric current given off by the movement of the shrimp's tail. Not only do the receptors in the platypus's bill help him find dinner, but they help him navigate, too. Flowing waters create electric fields through which the platypus glides with ease.

2. The last thing we need in our area is a baseball stadium. We already have two convention centers and one sports arena, which the taxpayers have financed—never mind the fact that whenever we were given the chance, we voted against such a waste of our tax dollars. For one thing, these stadiums are private businesses and should be paid for with private funding. Second, their owners, who care about nothing but making a profit, have gouged consumers to the point that many of us cannot afford to attend events taking place in facilities that we bought. For example, one ticket to a basketball game can cost as much as $150, parking costs $15, and a soft drink is $5. Third, in every case we were told that the center or arena would pay for itself, bring jobs to the community, and promote development from which everyone would profit. However, the only ones who have made any money at all are the owners. Now our city council and business leaders want to build a stadium to attract a major-league baseball team. I have one question for them: Are you willing to put up your own money to underwrite this venture? Neither are we.

3. "Canned hunts," that's what they're called, and what they are is an excuse for people who call themselves hunters to shoot exotic, often endangered, animals at as much as $3,500 a pop. Often the animals are drugged or chased out of cages into a fenced-in open area where they are trapped. Some sport that is. The real tragedy is that there is money in this grisly business, a lot of it. Exotic animal "preserves" are springing up in some states; these are the wildlife supermarkets where hunt organizers shop. Canned hunts are currently under investigation, but progress is slow because of weak and ambiguous laws. Legitimate hunters and sportsmen should deplore canned hunts and demand that their legislators become involved in this issue.

4. When it comes to mate selection, do you believe in true love or propinquity? Those who believe in true love believe that love happens only once and that there is just one "right" person for everyone. Those who believe in propinquity believe that anyone can fall in love with any number of people, and that the "right" person may be the one who is the most available at the time. Propinquity means closeness or nearness in a physical sense. Two people sitting next to each other in a movie theater have propinquity. One reason so many people marry the girl or boy next door is propinquity. So when you are looking for a mate, chances are you will select someone from your own neighborhood, someone you went to school with, or someone you met at work. Other factors that play a role in mate selection are physical appearance, race, nationality, age, educational level, socioeconomic status, religion, personality characteristics, and shared interests. In other words, you are probably going to marry someone very much like yourself; most people do.

Select the Right Tone

Your tone and choice of words can help readers determine your purpose and respond to the self that your tone reveals. As a writer, you have a voice. You can make the tone of your written voice sound different depending upon your attitude toward your topic and audience and the words you choose to express it. Consider how being in a restaurant where there is an unruly child at the next table may affect people in different ways. A person who is also a parent and has been through the process of teaching young children how to eat in restaurants might sympathize with the parents of the unruly child and therefore not become annoyed at the child's behavior. Someone else might be very annoyed. Perhaps this person came to the restaurant with a date for a quiet, pleasant evening and might think that the parents of the unruly child are inconsiderate. If these two restaurant goers were each to write an essay about the experience, their essays would be quite different. One might write with an amused, sympathetic tone. The other might choose an angry, annoyed tone.

Tone is the attitude you convey through your choice of words. Read paragraphs A and B below. They are written on the same topic, "office thieves," but each has a different tone. In the first paragraph, the writer is amused. In the second, the writer is angry. In each paragraph the words, phrases, or sentences that help convey the tone are underlined.

PARAGRAPH A

Humorous words and phrases that mean stealing

Creates a humorous visual image

Office thieves are like those people who are always trying to bum a cigarette: a little annoying, basically harmless, but not criminals. You would think that an office manager would have something more important to do than to waste time crying over a pilfered paper clip. So what if someone lifts a legal pad, rips off a ream of paper, bags a box of number 2 pencils? Surely the office orders a surplus to cover these losses. Some managers guard the supply cabinet with their lives. Just try to get a ballpoint pen out of them if you have already used your allotted quota for the year. If more managers would realize that one of an employee's perks is free supplies and look the other way, then maybe fewer office thieves would steal a colleague's stapler with one hand while bumming a cigarette with the other.

An act that usually causes laughter

Humorous exaggeration

PARAGRAPH B

Words and phrases that suggest anger

Office thieves make life difficult for the rest of us. While we try to cut costs by making supplies last, the thieves are taking more than their share and costing us more. They are selfish, wasteful, and inconsiderate. To them, taking a box of pencils

"Us" against "them"

home for their own use is not stealing. Their attitude is that there are plenty more where those came from. A box of pencils costs about $8.50. A box of manila folders or a ream of paper cost around $25.00. Who do these <u>thugs</u> think pays for the supplies? The cost comes out of the office management budget. If <u>we</u> could cut consumption by eliminating the stealing, <u>we</u> might have more money left to upgrade some of the equipment <u>we all have to use</u>. <u>We</u> ought to punish the <u>culprits</u> by adding up the cost of their <u>larceny</u> and deducting it from their paychecks.

An angry exaggeration

"We" and "they" pronouns emphasize angry conflict

Strong term for office stealing—angry exaggeration

"Us" against "them"

✔ CONCEPT CHECK
How many tones can you recognize? See Chapter 6 for a list of tone words and definitions.

Although you should consider tone during the prewriting stage, you may not know what tone you want until you write your first, or rough, draft. Read your draft to yourself, or have someone read it to you. Try to recall how you felt and what you were thinking as you wrote it. Were you sad, angry, or amused, or did you have a different feeling? Also, how do you want readers to respond as they read your essay? Your purpose, what you expect of the audience, and your attitude toward your topic should influence your choice of an appropriate tone.

[Exercise 2.8]

Examine five pieces of writing and determine the *tone* of each: the excerpt from *Zen and the Art of Motorcycle Maintenance* on pages 32–33, and the paragraphs in Exercise 2.7. Is the tone of each piece of writing appropriate for its purpose? Why, or why not? What could you add or change to make the tone more appropriate?

Write with Confidence Under Pressure

Goal 5   **Know how to take essay exams without fear and write effectively in all timed situations.**

The skills you will develop in your writing class can be applied to any writing you will do in your other courses. For example, your writing class may require you to write a final essay in a timed setting. Instructors in some of your other courses may give exams that call for written responses in the form of short essays. No matter what kind of writing task you may have, prewriting is an essential part of the process. Take a few minutes to think through your topic and do some preliminary planning. These efforts will give you the confidence you need to compose an effective answer that covers all the points your instructor expects.

You can minimize the discomfort of writing under pressure by following a few simple steps.

1. **Be prepared.** Find out how much time you will have, what topics are likely to be covered, and how much detail your instructor expects.

Figure 2.3   Instruction Words Commonly Used in Essay Questions/Assignments

INSTRUCTION WORDS	DEFINITIONS	EXAMPLES
COMPARE	Show similarities and differences.	Compare two forms of government.
CONTRAST	Show differences only.	Contrast the painting styles of two artists of the same period.
CRITICIZE or EVALUATE	Make a judgment about worth or merit: Examine strengths and weaknesses or positive and negative factors.	Write a critical review of a movie.
DEFINE	State a precise and accurate meaning of a word, term, or idea.	Define the terms *gas, solid,* and *liquid,* and give examples of each.
DESCRIBE	Create a mental impression, a detailed image or account.	Describe the architectural features of a building.
DISCUSS or EXPLAIN	Support a point with facts, reasons, or other details.	Discuss the impact of globalization on the U.S. economy.
ENUMERATE or LIST	State points or examples one by one.	List and explain the First Amendment freedoms.
ILLUSTRATE	Explain by using examples.	Provide examples of paintings to illustrate how "the horrors of war" has been a major theme for European artists.
INTERPRET	Explain meaning or significance; express an opinion.	Read "Those Winter Sundays" by Robert Hayden and give your interpretation of this poem.
JUSTIFY or PROVE	Construct an argument: Make an assertion and support it with evidence.	Argue for or against assisted suicide and justify your position.
OUTLINE	Provide a brief overview, the big picture.	Outline the major battles fought in the Civil War.
SUMMARIZE	Condense a complex issue into one or more main ideas and a few major supporting ideas.	Briefly summarize the elements of fiction and how they interact to develop a story's theme.
TRACE	Give a historical account, the stages of development, or a series of events leading to an outcome.	Trace the rise of television from its earliest beginnings to the present.

2. **Read the question carefully.** Determine what you are being asked to do. Pay attention to *instruction words* in the question that reveal the type of answer required. Figure 2.3 lists instruction words commonly used on essay exams, their definitions, and sample exam questions.

3. **Plan your essay.** Brainstorm the topic to access your prior knowledge and to generate a short list of related ideas. Then do a scratch outline that begins

with a working thesis, or central idea, followed by three to five supporting details that you will develop fully in the essay.

4. **Write a thesis statement.** Incorporate the question in your thesis statement. For example, suppose this is the question: *Based on your reading of Chapter 2, what is meant by* prewriting, *and what examples can you give?* The question calls for a definition followed by examples. This might be your thesis: *Prewriting is the first step in the writing process whose purpose is to generate ideas from a topic by using strategies such as brainstorming, freewriting, and clustering.* Now you have defined the term and suggested your direction of development—the three strategies that you will explain in detail.

5. **Leave personal opinions out of it.** Unless the instructor specifically asks for your opinion, support your thesis with well-chosen facts from your reading, lectures, or class discussion.

6. **Organize your ideas.** Remember the three-part development explained in Chapter 1: introduction, body, and conclusion. Introduce and state your thesis in the introductory paragraph. Develop one of your major supporting details in each body paragraph, and summarize your thesis and support in the concluding paragraph.

7. **Leave time to proofread and correct errors.** However, if you do not have time to finish, briefly list the other supporting ideas you would have developed if you had had the time. Some instructors will give extra consideration when calculating a grade if they can see where your discussion was headed.

In addition to following the previous seven steps, try these suggestions to relieve pressure and perform your best: Arrive on time, bring a dictionary if one is allowed, and maintain a positive attitude. Remember that your primary goal in writing an exam essay is to demonstrate your knowledge. With good preparation, you will meet this goal.

≪ Topics for Writing ≫

1. **React to the Reading.** When Pirsig's teacher asks his student to write about "just one brick," he is challenging her to focus on a single aspect of the building and to write about it in great detail. Look closely at the photograph on page 35. What interesting architectural features do you see? What do you think is the building's purpose? Who might go there, and why? Put yourself in the place of Pirsig's student and write about just one aspect of the building.

2. **Use Your Experience.** Look over all the writing you completed for the exercises in this chapter. Which prewriting strategy helped you generate the most and the best ideas from the topic you chose? Using these ideas, now write an essay.

3. **Make a Real-World Connection.** Use this chapter's strategies for prewriting and writing under pressure the next time that you have an essay exam in one of your courses. When your paper is returned, make notes on what you did well and where you had trouble. Then use these notes to share in class discussion or for writing in your journal, as your instructor directs.

4. **Go to the Web.** First, go to *The Confident Writer* website and choose a topic for writing. Then use one of the prewriting strategies explained in this chapter to plan and write an essay. Hand in your plans along with your essay.

≪ Checklist for Revision ≫

Did you miss anything? Check off the following items as you revise and edit your essay.

- ❏ Did you use a prewriting strategy to think through your topic?
- ❏ Is your topic sufficiently limited?
- ❏ Are your purpose and audience clear?
- ❏ Does your essay have an effective introduction?
- ❏ Does your essay have a clearly stated central idea?
- ❏ Do you have enough evidence to support your central idea?
- ❏ Does your essay have a good conclusion?
- ❏ Are your sentences error free?

≪ Your Discovery Journal ≫

An inference you can make from Robert M. Pirsig's essay is that good writers are close observers of the world around them. How observant are you? To answer this question, complete the following reflective statements and explain your reasons.

As an additional option, do journal activities online by going to *The Confident Writer* website.

Like many people, I am probably more observant of some things than of others; for example, the kinds of details I pay attention to are _____.

I will try to improve my powers of observation by _____.

‹‹ Website Resources ››

This chapter's resources include

- Chapter 2 Exercises
- Chapter 2 Quiz
- Self Tests: *My Values*
- Downloadable Charts: *Group Evaluation Form*
- More Topics for Writing
- Chapter 2 Summary

To access these learning and study tools, go to *The Confident Writer* website.

(((*Confident writers are positive. They believe that*

writing is a skill that anyone can develop or improve.)))

Improving Your Paragraph Skills

What you already know about *paragraphs*

o You are probably familiar with the terms *paragraph, topic sentence,* and *main idea.*

o You may have written paragraphs in the past.

o In discussion you may have heard people say, "Get to the point," or "Don't change the subject," and this can also be said about writing paragraphs.

Your *goals* for this chapter

[1] Know how to determine your main idea; then clearly state the main idea in a topic sentence.

[2] Choose specific details such as facts, reasons, and examples to support your main idea.

[3] Know how to write unified, coherent paragraphs, and choose among several patterns to organize the details in your paragraph.

[4] Apply all the paragraph skills explained in this chapter to write a summary that is objective and concise.

A *paragraph* is a part, or division, of an essay that develops a main idea that is relevant to the whole essay. At the same time, the paragraph is complete in itself. Though a paragraph may be as short as one sentence or as long as a page or more, the paragraphs you write will usually consist of several sentences that support one main idea. The *main idea* of a paragraph expresses its topic and focus. A *topic sentence,* when present, states the main idea. If there is no topic sentence, the main idea may be implied. To *imply* a main idea means to hint at it or to suggest it without stating it directly. If a paragraph has no topic sentence, you can figure out what the main idea is by asking yourself what single idea the details all seem to support or explain.

Essays and articles that you read in magazines, newspapers, and elsewhere will reveal a variety of writing styles and paragraph lengths and types. Professional writers may not always write paragraphs that have topic sentences. As a beginning writer, however, you should strive for a clearly stated main idea. The topic sentence will guide your selection of details and will keep you on topic. To help you improve your paragraph skills, this chapter explains three keys to writing good paragraphs: main idea, support, and organization.

[First Thoughts]

To build background for reading, explore your thoughts about what makes you happy. Then answer the following questions either on your own or in a group discussion.

1. Do you think people are entitled to happiness?

2. What can people do to improve their quality of life?

3. Read the title, the headnote, and the first one or two paragraphs of the following essay. Based on this preview, what do you think will follow?

[Word Alert]

Before reading, preview the following words and definitions. During your reading, use context clues and your dictionary to define any additional unfamiliar words.

cultivate (3)	nurture, foster, promote
jubilance (4)	extreme joy or happiness
revel (8)	delight in, take pleasure in

abounds (9)	being great in number or amount
avid (14)	eager, passionate, enthusiastic
bolstering (18)	supporting, reinforcing

15 Ways to Put More Joy in Your Life

Leigh Anne Jasheway-Bryant

Leigh Anne Jasheway-Bryant is a humorist, columnist, and motivational speaker. This essay is an inspirational piece that was published in *Family Circle*.

1   One of my favorite songs of all time is "Joy to the World" by Three Dog Night. It always makes me think about how much better the world would be if we all tried, every day, to bring a little joy into each other's lives. Now I know this isn't something you think about most of the time, even though feeling joyful is a basic human need. The truth is, many of us think joy is something we can experience only when things are going right in our lives—the birth of a child, getting a promotion, moving into that dream house. But you can invite joy into your life even when things aren't going as well as you'd like, and especially when you're feeling sad, frightened or confused. Now more than ever, you need to reach out and find happiness in the world—and teach your kids to do the same. Here's how:

2   **Give yourself permission to be joyful.** You know that little voice inside your head that pops up in certain situations and whispers, "It's wrong to be happy now"? Well, guess what. Humans are complicated creatures capable of feeling many emotions at the same time. To deprive yourself of joy under any circumstances is to deny yourself a complete life. So write yourself a permission slip: "Dear self: I hereby grant you permission to be joyful whenever you feel like it!"

3   **Find happiness in nature.** Don't get so caught up in the day's to-do list that you forget to make time to enjoy the world around you. Watch your dog the next time she's outside. Chances are she'll sniff everything in the yard, her tail wagging a mile a minute. To your dog, every inch of the world is worth exploring. Everything has the potential to bring joy. Cultivate that behavior (the curiosity and enthusiasm, not the sniffing!) in yourself and your kids.

4   **Search for jubilance.** Don't wait for it to come knocking at your door. Instead, seek out the things that give your life meaning and purpose. Imagine you're writing a personal ad listing everything that brings you pleasure. You might include things like feeling loved, raising happy and healthy children, maintaining strong friendships, mentoring a child, and being the kind of person others turn to in times of need. To find joy, do more of the things that give your life meaning.

5   **Heed the call of pleasure.** The world's happiest people are those who have found what they are meant to do in life and are doing it every day. If your job or career fills your heart and you know that—even in a small way—what you do helps to make the world a better place. Then joy is sure to seep into your daily life.

6   **Teach your children well.** Have you ever asked your kids, "What brought you joy today?" If not, then perhaps this should be the question of the day, every day. (Just ignore the funny looks your kids may give you at first!) By asking the question, you remind them (and yourself) that they should be grateful for the things that make them happy and focus on those things instead of on life's negatives.

7   You can also pass along the lesson of joy by helping your kids choose after-school activities that truly make them happy, not just those that look good on their transcript or may someday get them a scholarship.

8   **Create delight in everyday things.** Every moment has the potential to bring you joy if you let it. Shoveling snow can be an opportunity to revel in the crisp white beauty of the landscape and the wonder of seeing your own breath; your daily workout can provide a chance to admire the strength of your own body; even paying bills can be a happy experience if you think about it as reflecting your ability to provide for your family.

9   **Make a joyful noise (part one).** Most of the noises we humans make aren't very pleasant, are they? We whine, complain and dwell on past wrongs. For years now, I've lived by one simple rule: for every one thing I complain about, I must say something good (out loud) about three other things. This focus on what's positive in my life increases my awareness that even in tough times, joy abounds.

10   **Make a joyful noise (part two).** Sing an uplifting song. Giggle with delight. Whistle your approval. Do whatever you can to add your voice to those expressing appreciation for life.

11   I live down the block from an elementary school. Every day at recess, I can hear the squeals of delight from children on the playground. No matter how badly my day might be going, their laughter always reminds me that there is joy to be found somewhere.

12   **Spread the gladness.** We all know that happiness is multiplied many times when shared with others. Another little rule that I follow in my life is that in every interaction, I must try to make the other person laugh. This simply means that I am always conscious of what I can do to add some sparkle to someone else's life. Try it. You'll like how it makes you feel.

13   **Jump with delight.** You don't actually have to jump. (Although if you feel like it, why not?) Just demonstrate unbridled enthusiasm for those things you care passionately about, and you'll achieve the same result. After all, enthusiasm is joy in action. If you're enthusiastic, all those you come in contact with will want to share in whatever it is that has stimulated you so.

14   **If happiness isn't in the picture, refocus your lens.** If you can't find joy in the big things, look at the small things, or vice versa. I'm an avid gardener, which means that I often look at my yard in terms of what needs to be done: weeds to pull, trees to prune, soil to till. But I'm also an amateur photographer, and I find that grabbing my camera and really focusing in on a flower or a leaf changes my whole perspective. Through the lens, I see the beauty, not the chore.

15   Conversely, sometimes you need to look at the bigger picture to find the joy. By stepping away from your troubles and focusing on, say, a beautiful sunrise or the loving support of your family and friends, you'll be able to refocus on the joy in your life.

16   **Go for a ride.** Sometimes the path you're on seems hopeless, and no matter how slowly you walk or how hard you look, you just can't see anything on the horizon. This is a sure sign that it's time to take a new life path. You don't necessarily have to take a huge detour (like quitting your job). Take baby steps.

17   Ask for a new project at work that motivates you. Take a different route home from the supermarket and explore neighborhoods you've never driven through. Learn a new language. Make friends with someone who thinks differently than you do. There's no single road to joy. You have to be willing to follow whatever road will get you there.

18   **Wake up happy.** As soon as you wake up in the morning, think about at least one thing that brings you joy. Now smile. A simple smile can make you feel more hopeful about the day ahead. It can also improve your resistance to stress by bolstering your immune system. Now, before you actually begin your day, do something that delights you. Snuggle with your spouse, bury your face in your cat's soft fur or listen to the birds chirping.

19   **Plan for merriment.** If you have something to look forward to, the anticipation helps to fill the days with happiness until the actual event. The event doesn't have to be something big like a wedding. It can be as simple as a family picnic or lunch with a good friend. You should have at least one joyful event on your calendar every three weeks so you can experience the giddiness of anticipation.

20   **Bring joy to the world.** A truly happy person looks outside herself to see how she can make the world a better place. This is an important time to start thinking about your role in the world and what you can do to reduce suffering outside yourself and your community. Whether by sponsoring a hungry child, working to save an endangered species or volunteering with an international organization, you can be a beacon of hope in the lives of people you may never actually meet. It really *is* one planet, and the more you work to bring joy to everyone on it, the more your life will feel truly blessed and enriched.

‹‹ The Critical Reader ››

[CENTRAL IDEA]

1. What is Jasheway-Bryant's central idea?

2. Who is Jasheway-Bryant's audience, and how can you tell?

[EVIDENCE]

3. What type of evidence does the author use to develop her central idea?

4. What strategy does the author suggest for those who can't seem to find happiness.

[IMPLICATIONS]

5. The author says that "feeling joyful is a basic human need," but she also suggests that finding joy does not necessarily come naturally. Do you agree or disagree, and why?

[WORD CHOICE]

6. The author's focus is on joy. What are some of the terms that the author uses that suggest joy?

‹‹ The Critical Thinker ››

To examine Jasheway-Bryant's essay in more depth, follow these suggestions for reflection, discussion, and writing.

1. Do you think the author would agree or disagree with this statement: "Happiness is your responsibility"? Explain your answer.

2. Read the first and last paragraphs again. How do the author's introduction and conclusion support her central idea?

3. What would inspire an author to write about ways to put more joy in one's life? Do people need the kinds of suggestions she offers? Is happiness that hard to find? What do you think?

4. What is one thing that can raise your spirits when you are feeling down? Explain your answer in writing.

State Your Main Idea

Goal 1

Know how to determine your main idea; then clearly state the main idea in a topic sentence.

The main idea of a paragraph is what the whole paragraph is about. A paragraph has just one main idea. Often, the main idea is stated in a *topic sentence*. The topic sentence of a paragraph has two characteristics:

1. *Topic:* The topic sentence tells you who or what the paragraph is about.

2. *Focus:* The topic sentence tells you what the writer thinks about the topic or what aspect of the topic the writer plans to discuss.

In addition to having a topic and a focus, a good topic sentence is neither too narrow nor too broad. It is broad enough to tell your readers what the whole paragraph is about, but it is narrow enough to focus on a single idea that you can explain. Read the next three examples.

EXAMPLE 1: Everyone recognizes that crime is a problem.

This statement is too broad to be a topic sentence because it lacks a *focus*. Although the statement expresses an opinion, neither the crimes nor the problems they cause are specified.

EXAMPLE 2: My parents' home was burglarized two months ago.

This statement is too narrow to be a topic sentence because it simply states a fact that need not be further explained.

EXAMPLE 3: My subdivision's neighborhood watch program has shown us how to discourage robbers.

This statement is neither too broad nor too narrow. It would make a good topic sentence because the topic, "neighborhood watch program," has a focus: "how to discourage robbers."

Suppose you choose *drinking* as your topic. As you brainstorm the topic, you recall spending spring break at the beach along with hundreds of other college students who had flocked there in search of fun and relaxation. Looking back, you begin to think that a number of drinking establishments promoted activities and engaged in advertising tactics designed to appeal to young people. Drawn to these places by their party atmosphere and encouraged to drink more than they should, many students overindulged in alcoholic beverages. For some, spring break ended in tragedy. Although you see nothing wrong with students having a good time, you do see something wrong with adults who exploit them. Your thinking leads you to write this topic sentence:

Advertising tactics that make drinking seem safe, fun, and cheap take advantage of students on spring break.

✓ CONCEPT CHECK
When reading, keep this point in mind: A topic sentence may be anywhere in a paragraph—beginning, middle, or end. Also, some paragraphs have no topic sentence. However, when writing your own paragaphs, it is a good idea to begin with a topic sentence.

In this topic sentence, the topic is *advertising tactics that make drinking seem safe, fun, and cheap,* and the focus is that they *take advantage of students on spring break.* The sentence is neither too broad nor too narrow because it focuses on a single idea that you can explain, using specific examples to describe the advertising tactics. As you begin to make notes, you think of three examples to use.

1. Bars that welcome spring breakers and provide a party atmosphere seem like safe places to have a few drinks.

2. Bars that sponsor wet t-shirt and bikini contests attract students who will order drinks while enjoying these events.

3. Bars that advertise two-for-one specials and free drinks for women attract students seeking lots to drink for little cash.

The topic can be developed more fully by adding details to explain each example. To explain the first example, you could add that inexperienced students who may have avoided drinking in bars in the past might be enticed to join in the fun. To explain the second example, you could point out that students attracted to contests are likely to stay for the outcome and drink more as a result. To explain the third example, you could suggest that two-for-one specials and other "free" offers may have a hidden cost, especially if the bar has a two-drink-minimum policy. A good topic sentence will give your topic the focus it needs to help you think of examples or other types of evidence to support it.

[Exercise 3.1] Read each of the topic sentences below. Underline the topic and bracket the focus. Be prepared to explain your answer.

1. Fast-food junkies can break the habit by following three simple steps.

2. Those who are against the building of a new city hall can think of better ways to spend the money it will cost.

3. Both the supporters and the detractors of the war in Iraq can present facts to defend their positions.

4. Cereal commercials are aimed at two main groups: children and nutrition-conscious adults.

5. Binge drinking among college students is a serious problem that should be treated like other addictions.

[Exercise 3.2] Choose three topics from the following list. For each, limit the topic and write a topic sentence. Make sure your sentences have a topic and a focus. Make sure each sentence is neither too narrow nor too broad. The first one is done as an example.

1. Cellular phones
    a. limited topic: cellular phone etiquette
    b. topic sentence: When using your cell phone in public, several rules of good behavior apply.
2. Addictive behaviors
3. Roommates
4. Weight-loss programs
5. Voting
6. Reality TV
7. Types of music

Though some of the paragraphs you read have topic sentences, in others the main idea is *implied,* which means that there is no topic sentence. Instead, you have to infer, or guess, the main idea by reading the whole paragraph, paying attention to the details, and asking yourself such questions as "What is this whole paragraph about?" and "What one idea do all the details explain?" In the next paragraph, the main idea is implied.

> The turquoise water blends into the pale aqua sky at the horizon. From my seat at the table on the private porch outside my resort hotel room I can see that it is going to be a hot, humid day just like the last three. I am beginning to like the luxury of having my breakfast brought to me, coffee poured from a silver teapot, an array of fresh tropical fruit from which to choose. A large blackbird shares my breakfast, pecking at the muffin I have tossed on the floor for his culinary pleasure. What will I do today? Take a swim in the Caribbean sea? Visit a pineapple plantation? Check out the sidewalk market in Montego Bay for bargains? Whatever I do, I will not think of two days from now when I will be back at my desk day-dreaming about these quiet moments, wondering when they will come again.

Though the paragraph has no topic sentence, the last sentence suggests that the writer is on vacation, and the rest of the details describe what a morning at the hotel is like. A topic sentence for the paragraph might be: "Mornings are always the same on my Caribbean island vacation."

[**Exercise 3.3**]

Apply what you have learned about topic sentences and implied main ideas by doing this exercise with group members. First, review the list of group roles and responsibilities listed on the inside back cover. Next, read and discuss the following paragraph. Then discuss and answer the questions. When you are finished, evaluate your work as your instructor recommends, or go to *The Confident Writer* website, where you can download the group evaluation form.

> The first thing to go wrong was that all the parking spaces were taken, so I had to park on the grass and hope that I would not get a ticket. When I got to the admissions office, there was already a long line. By the time it was my turn to register, all of the sections for one of the courses I needed were filled, and I had to go back to my counselor and make out a whole new schedule. Although I did register for all my courses and pay my fees, I missed lunch. The next thing to go wrong was that the bookstore had sold out of one of the textbooks I needed. As I was leaving, I wondered what else could possibly happen. Then I saw a campus cop standing beside my car and writing out a ticket.

1. Who is the *I* in the paragraph, and how can you tell?
2. What is the person doing, and what details tell you so?
3. How does the person feel about what he or she is doing?
4. What is the whole paragraph about? What one situation do all the details explain?
5. Using the information you have gathered from answering questions 1–4, write a sentence that you think expresses the main idea of the paragraph and that has a topic and a focus.

As a beginning writer, you will find topic sentences very helpful. A good topic sentence will control your selection of details because every detail must explain or relate in some way to the topic sentence. As you gain experience, you may want to experiment with writing paragraphs that have implied main ideas. You can add variety to the paragraphs within an essay by stating some main ideas and implying others.

Support Your Main Idea

Goal 2

Choose specific details such as facts, reasons, and examples to support your main idea.

To support a main idea means to explain or prove it with evidence. The evidence you choose to support your opinion about your topic may include *facts, reasons,* or *examples.* These types of details make it possible for your readers to understand why you think the way you do.

State Facts to Be Convincing

A fact is anything that can be proven right or wrong through research, direct observation, or questioning. Facts include statistics and other numerical data; information gathered through the senses of sight, hearing, smell, taste, and touch; and information collected from books, other printed sources, or the testimony of experts. A fact is also anything we have observed so often that we commonly accept it as true, such as the laws of gravity or the process of photosynthesis. An opinion is more convincing if you support it with facts. Following are three topic sentences that state opinions and the facts that support them:

Topic Sentences	Facts
Public officials have done a poor job of solving our city's traffic problems.	The city's main highway is operating at four times its intended capacity. Rush "hour" lasts from 6:45 A.M. to 8:30 A.M. and from 4:45 P.M. to 6:30 P.M. Traffic accidents, according to the highway patrol, have more than doubled in the past five years.
Julia Roberts is a versatile actress.	In *Pretty Woman* she plays a likeable prostitute. In *Notting Hill* she plays a famous actress who falls in love with an ordinary man. In *Erin Brockovich,* a movie based on a true story, she plays an outspoken legal assistant who uncovers the illegal dumping of hazardous chemicals. In *Mona Lisa Smile,* she plays an unconventional professor at a traditional women's college in the 1950s.
This winter a destructive storm ravaged our area.	Heavy snow and ice caused numerous traffic accidents. Sixty-mile-an-hour winds damaged houses and property. Tides of twelve feet caused flooding in some areas. Several towns had to be evacuated.

In the first example, facts about the highway's operating capacity, rush-hour times, and accident rate support the main idea. In the second example, facts about the types of characters Roberts has played in four of her movies support the main idea. In the third example, facts about the storm's destructiveness support the main idea. The facts listed in these three examples provide readers with a basis for evaluating the accuracy of the opinions stated in the topic sentences.

[**Exercise 3.4**] Choose one of the topic sentences you wrote for Exercise 3.2 and list the facts you could use to support it.

Provide Reasons to Explain

Reasons help explain why something happens or why something is the way it is. Words and expressions such as *because, since, the causes are,* and *the purpose is* may help readers identify statements in your writing that contain reasons. Because there may be many different reasons to explain just about everything, you need to carefully consider your reasons for thinking the way you do about your topic. You also need to be aware of the reasons others may have for thinking differently. Following are three topic sentences with reasons that support them:

☑ **CONCEPT CHECK**
Most of us have strong opinions that go unchallenged. Do you have a strong opinion on an issue? What are your reasons?

Topic Sentences	Reasons
Though there are several colleges I could have attended, I chose Valencia Community College.	The campus is only three miles from my house. I can save money by living at home. The tuition is affordable. The atmosphere at Valencia is friendly and personal. The programs and services available are helping me plan my future.
To overcome math failure, you must first understand why so many students fail.	Math anxiety afflicts many students who have a "fear of failure." A fear of success can also affect students' performance in math. Equating math grades with self-esteem can lead to negative feelings that direct attention away from the task. Procrastination is the reason many math students get behind and never catch up.
So far, our community has remained safe even though we live near a high-crime area.	One reason is that the city has installed quartz halogen bulbs in the street lights to make it harder for criminals to hide. Police make regular neighborhood patrols. Also, we have a successful neighborhood watch program. Our school board approved a crime-prevention program for grades K–12 that has been in effect for several years.

In the first example, Valencia's affordability, atmosphere, programs, and services are the reasons that explain why the writer chose that college. In the second example, the writer cites math anxiety, fear of success, equating grades with self-esteem, and procrastination as the reasons for math failure. In the third example, the community's lighting, police patrols, neighborhood watch program, and crime-prevention program are the reasons that support the main idea. The reasons listed in these examples help readers understand the logic behind the opinions stated in the topic sentences.

[**Exercise 3.5**]   Make a list of your reasons for attending the college you have chosen. Then, write a topic sentence for a paragraph on your reasons for attending that college.

Give Examples to Clarify

An example is an illustration that clarifies a general statement, such as a topic sentence. Examples usually appeal to one or more of the five senses—sight, sound, taste, touch, and smell—and they help create clear and vivid pictures in your readers' minds. Examples are one more kind of evidence you can use to support your main idea and explain your opinions. You can use the phrases *such as, for example,* and *to illustrate* to signal your readers that an example follows. An effective use of examples can help you clarify your ideas for readers. Following are three topic sentences with examples that support them:

Topic Sentences	Examples
Some name their cars after people, but I call mine "Unreliable."	Sometimes it will not start. The gas gauge gives incorrect readings. The oil light comes on even though I have just added oil. The tires will not stay balanced. This morning the brakes failed. For the last year it has been in the shop at least once a month.
My grandmother's house is a collection of aromas, odors, and fragrances.	The aroma of chocolate chip cookies or a turkey baking in the oven fills the house. The fragrances of roses and gardenias come in through the windows when there is a breeze. The clean smells of wax, furniture polish, and freshly washed linens pervade the rooms.

My job as a volunteer firefighter is a rewarding experience.

On clear, cool days when the wind is in the right direction, the unpleasant odors from a paper mill and a charcoal plant mingle with the fragrances in the house.

I have earned the respect of my male coworkers by proving that I am willing to work as hard as they do.
I know I am making an important contribution to my community because of the commendations our department has received.
I have felt the gratitude of the people I have helped to safety during a fire.
I have developed new confidence in myself because I am doing a job that in the past women were not supposed to be able to do.

In the first example, the problems the writer is having with the car's gas gauge, oil light, tires, brakes, and trips to the shop are examples that support the main idea. In the second example, the writer supports the main idea with examples of the food aromas, flower fragrances, cleaning smells, and outside odors that fill his grandmother's house. In the third example, the writer provides examples of her job's rewards, such as the respect of coworkers and the gratitude of those she has helped. The lists of examples that support each of the topic sentences appeal to readers' senses and feelings and may help them to identify with the situations the writers describe.

[Exercise 3.6] This exercise will sharpen your senses and call on your powers of observation—both are indispensable tools of the writer.

Carefully examine the photograph on page 71, paying attention to every detail. Then write a paragraph in which you use examples to explain what you see in the photo: the situation pictured and the meaning that you derive from it.

Visual exercises, such as examining the details in a photograph, will sharpen your senses and your powers of observation.

Organize Your Ideas

Goal 3 Know how to write unified, coherent paragraphs, and choose among several patterns to organize the details in your paragraph.

Organization is a key principle in every aspect of life. Having places for everything you own makes it easy for you to find what you need, when you need it. Weekly schedules or daily lists help you organize and keep track of your activities and obligations. Many of life's mistakes and missed opportunities are the result of poor organization.

Organization is a key factor in writing, too. A paragraph in which the ideas flow smoothly, the details are arranged logically, and all the evidence supports one main idea is a joy to read. A fully developed, well-organized paragraph has three qualities:

- Three levels of development
- Unity
- Coherence

Use Three Levels of Development

Whether you support a topic sentence with facts, reasons, examples, or some of each, be specific. You can learn to do this by using a three-level development plan that moves from (1) the general statement (topic sentence) to (2) the primary evidence (major details) to (3) the secondary evidence (minor details). For example:

Topic sentence:	**Level 1** My health club has become more of a social gathering place than a fitness center.
First major detail that supports the general statement	**Level 2** For one thing, people come here to see and be seen.
Minor detail that supports the first major detail	**Level 3** The men and women wear skimpy outfits that show off their bodies.
Minor detail that supports the first major detail	**Level 3** The women wear makeup, and their hair is attractively styled as if they were going on dates.
Minor detail that supports the first major detail	**Level 3** The men seek to impress the women by trying to outdo each other lifting weights.
Second major detail that supports the general statement	**Level 2** Also, some people use the health club as a meeting place.
Minor detail that supports the second major detail	**Level 3** Men and women join because they have heard it is a safe place to meet people.
Minor detail that supports the second major detail	**Level 3** They can observe each other's behavior and get to know each other before going out.

The major details illustrate two ways in which the health club has become a social gathering place. People come there to see and be seen and to meet each other. The minor details provide specific examples of what people *do* in order to see and be seen, and *how* they use the club as a meeting place.

[**Exercise 3.7**] The paragraph below is followed by a partially filled-in outline that illustrates three levels of development: main idea, major details, and minor details. Read the paragraph. On a sheet of paper, complete the outline.

Getting a college education has not been easy for me. One thing that makes it difficult is that I am a working mother of two children who are still in school. I have to get up early to make their breakfast and see them off. Also, I try to arrange my schedule to be at home when they arrive. Helping them with their homework is important to me but leaves me less time to do my own studying. My job is another thing that makes it hard for me to get an education. I work as a receptionist in a doctor's office in the mornings from 8:00 A.M. until 11:30 A.M. If a class I need is scheduled at these times, then I have to postpone taking it until it is offered at a more convenient time. Because of my job, it will probably take me a long time to get my degree. Studying adds to these difficulties. It has been a while since I attended school, and my skills are a little rusty. Though getting a college education is difficult, the struggle is worth it not only for me but also for the good example I am setting for my children.

Level 1   I. **Topic sentence:** Getting a college education has not been easy for me.

Level 2   A. One thing . . .

Level 3   1.

      2.

      3.

      4.

   B.

      1. I work as a receptionist from 8:00 A.M. to 11:30 A.M.

      2. I have to postpone taking classes offered at these times.

      3. It will take me a long time to get my degree.

   C. Studying adds to these difficulties.

      1.

      2.

II. **Concluding Sentence:** Though getting a college education is difficult . . .

Write Unified Paragraphs

Unity means *oneness* or *wholeness*. Animal rights activists are *united* in their efforts to protect animals from being exploited. Environmental activists are *united* by their common goal to preserve resources. Members of professional, political, and social organizations are *united* by shared beliefs, values, and goals. The sentences of a paragraph are *united* when they all work together to support a main idea, and paragraphs within an essay are *united* when they all work together to support a thesis or central idea. Your paragraphs will have *unity* if you state your main idea clearly and stay on topic. When one or more sentences or details within a paragraph do not support the main idea, then unity is interrupted, and the paragraph strays from its topic. The next paragraph contains a sentence that keeps it from being unified. Find the off-topic sentence before reading the explanation that follows the paragraph.

   If you would like to get fit and are thinking about joining a health club or gym, you should also consider the advantages of a membership in a hospital wellness center. Unlike some health clubs or gyms, wellness centers hire only trained staff members who have degrees or other certification in such fields as nutrition and fitness. These people are qualified to assess your level of fitness and design a safe program for you that is based on the results of a blood test, a stress test, and your doctor's recommendation. In fact, you cannot even join a wellness center without your doctor's approval. Some health clubs serve as meeting places for young singles. Another advantage of wellness centers over health clubs and gyms is that they offer services other than fitness training, such as nutritional counseling, stress reduction seminars, and weight-loss classes. At a health club or gym you may be left on your own after your first visit, but at a wellness center, someone monitors your progress and continually updates your program as your fitness level increases. Surprisingly, a wellness center membership may cost you a lot less than a membership in a health club or gym, and that is another advantage.

In this paragraph, the unity is disrupted by the sentence "Some health clubs serve as meeting places for young singles." The paragraph compares wellness centers and health clubs or gyms on the basis of their fitness advantages, not on their social advantages.

Following this very simple rule will help you achieve unity in your paragraphs: *State your main idea clearly and stay on topic.*

[**Exercise 3.8**]

Read the following paragraphs and evaluate them for unity. If you find any sentences that are off-topic, underline them. Be able to explain your results. For an additional exercise on paragraph unity, go to *The Confident Writer* website.

1. Count Dracula is a character who continues to appeal to filmgoers. Many actors have played him, each one adding something different to the role. In *Nosferatu,* a silent film of the 1920s, Max Shreck plays Dracula as a supernatural being having a ratlike appearance. Frankenstein is another character who appeals to filmgoers. In 1931, Bela Lugosi portrayed Dracula as an attractive, cultured man whose genteel manner barely concealed his violence. Christopher Lee's performances in the 1950s emphasized Dracula's sex appeal. George Hamilton was the first to make us laugh at Dracula in *Love at First Bite,* a cult favorite. The 1970s gave us an updated version of *Nosferatu* in which Klaus Kinski combines aspects of the Shreck and Lugosi roles. In the 1980s, Frank Langella showed us a sensitive Dracula who falls in love with a "liberated" woman. Lon Chaney plays the Wolfman as an ordinary fellow fallen on bad times. *Interview with the Vampire* in the 1990s and *Shadow of the Vampire* in 2001 prove that every decade recreates the old and popular vampire legend.

2. American politics has always been a two-party system, but change seemed possible with the campaign of Ross Perot in the 1992 presidential

election. Perot is a Texas billionaire who ran for president as the nominee of the Independent party, a third party that has never aroused much interest or support. During the week of the Democratic National Convention, Perot announced that he would not run. Barbara Jordan and Jesse Jackson, both Clinton supporters, addressed the convention. But Perot rejoined the campaign, debated the other two candidates, then lost the election to Bill Clinton. The successful campaign of an Independent Party candidate proved, however, that the Republicans and Democrats were losing some of their influence over the American voter.

3. Though being a dental hygienist may not be everyone's idea of the perfect job, Kelly would not want to do anything else. For a brief time, she had thought she wanted to be a court reporter. One reason she likes her job is that she can schedule her hours so that she works four days a week and is off in the afternoons. This allows her to be at home when her children arrive from school. Since she does not work on Fridays, she has a three-day weekend. Another reason Kelly likes her job is that the work is challenging and pleasant. For example, cleaning children's teeth is a challenge because Kelly has to find ways to distract the children so that they will let her do what she needs to do without making a fuss. Kelly's work is pleasant because just about everyone likes the way his or her mouth feels after a cleaning, and they compliment Kelly on what a good job she does. But Kelly's best reason of all for liking her job is that she gets to be with her family while she is at work. After all, the dentist Kelly works for is her dad, and her sister is his receptionist.

Check Your Paragraphs for Coherence

Cohere means *to stick together.* A paragraph has **coherence** when it is so well organized that the evidence seems to flow smoothly and to "stick together." To give your paragraphs coherence, use a pattern, or organizing principle, that is appropriate for your topic.

Coherence patterns in paragraphs correspond to organizational patterns in essays in that they provide a logical framework for your ideas. For example, in the essay at the beginning of this chapter, Leigh Anne Jasheway-Bryant uses an organizational pattern called *enumeration* or *listing.* Her topic is stated in the title "15 Ways to Put More Joy in Your Life." To develop the topic, she lists and explains the fifteen ways. Listing is a pattern you will often encounter in the popular press and in your textbooks. Some instructors may encourage you to avoid listing in favor of using more sophisticated patterns. However, instructors in the sciences often encourage listing for its clarity and directness.

Although there are many other ways to organize the details within a paragraph, the three most common patterns are *time order, emphatic order,* and *spatial order.*

Time Order

Another name for time order is **chronological order,** and it is appropriate for any subject that can be explained with details that follow a time sequence. Suppose you are reading a textbook chapter on human reproduction that explains what happens during pregnancy. After making some notes, you decide to write a paragraph in which you summarize what you have read. Since pregnancy occurs over nine months, you arrange your details into three 3-month periods. Your informal outline might look like this:

1. The first three months

    a. Little increase in size.

    b. Embryo becomes a fetus.

2. The next three months

    a. Fetus becomes larger.

    b. Heartbeat and movement occur.

3. The last three months

    a. Fetus continues to grow.

    b. Fetal movements increase.

    c. Body prepares itself for birth.

When you are using time order, help your readers follow your ideas by beginning some of your sentences with signal words and phrases that serve as *time markers,* such as *first, next, third,* and *finally;* times of day, such as *at 10:30;* or phrases that indicate time of day, such as *this morning.* Time order signals help readers to understand when you have finished explaining one step or stage and have moved on to another. In the following excerpt from N. Scott Momaday's *The Names, A Memoir,* signal words and phrases that serve as time markers are underlined for you.

> ☑ **CONCEPT CHECK**
> For a practical example of time order, think about news reports of crimes or disasters. People interviewed about these events are often asked to reconstruct them in chronological order.

NAVAJO DOG

Dusk was falling <u>at five o'clock,</u> when the dancing came to an end, and <u>on the way home</u> alone I bought a Navajo dog. I bargained for a while with the thin, wary man whose dog it was, and we settled on a price of five dollars. It was a yellow, honest-to-goodness, great-hearted dog, and the man gave me a bit of rope with which to pull it home. The dog was not large, but neither was it small. It was one of those unremarkable creatures that one sees in every corner of the world. If there were only thirty-nine dogs in Creation, this one would be the fourth, or the thirteenth, or the twenty-first, the archetype, the common denominator of all its kind. It was full of resistance, and yet it was ready to return in full measure my deep, abiding love. I could see that. It needed only, I reasoned, to make a small adjustment in its style of life, to shift the focus of its vitality from one frame of reference to another, in order to be perfectly at home with me. Even as it was nearly strangled on the way, it wagged its bushy tail happily all the while. That night I tied the dog up in the garage, where there was a warm, clean pallet, wholesome food, and fresh water, and I bolted the door. And the next morning the dog was gone, as in my heart of hearts I knew it would be, I believe. I had read such a future in its eyes. It had gnawed the rope in two and squeezed through a vent in the door, an opening much too small for it, as I had thought. But, sure enough, where there is a will there is a way, and the Navajo dog was possessed of one indomitable will. I was crushed at the time, but strangely reconciled, too, as if I had perceived some truth beyond billboards. The dog had done what it had to do, had behaved exactly as it must, had been true to itself and to the sun and moon. It knew its place in the order of things, and its place was away out there in the tracks of a wagon, going home. In the mind's eye I could see it at that very moment, miles away, plodding in the familiar shadows, its tail drooping a little after the harrowing night, but wagging, in its dog's mind contemplating the wonderful ways of mankind.

The story of the Navajo dog develops in a time sequence from late afternoon, through that night, to the following day.

Emphatic Order

Sometimes it makes sense to arrange details in their order of importance, especially if one of your details is clearly more important than another, if you want to save the best of your suggestions for last, or if you want to emphasize the conclusion. Suppose you have learned from experience that cramming for a test does not work, and you write a paragraph that explains an effective way to study for an exam. You may think that the most important thing students can do to ensure success is to review periodically. You might save this suggestion for last and conclude with tips on how to make periodic review easier. Use *words of emphasis* to signal your readers when another important idea is coming or to show a progression of ideas from least important to most important. Words and phrases such as *equally important, the most important of all, major* and *minor,* and *of primary concern* are helpful signals for readers and may improve the coherence of your paragraphs. In the following paragraph, words of emphasis are underlined.

✓ CONCEPT CHECK
What are three qualities you look for in a friend? How would you rank these qualities in their order of importance?

The power of television news to capture the public's attention became apparent in the 1960s. In 1963, the nation was gripped by horror and grief at the assassination of President Kennedy; the event and its aftermath kept the nation riveted to television screens for days. Other major events, though reported in newspapers and magazines as well, were likewise widely and instantaneously experienced on television. Several incidents occurred in 1968 alone: the first expedition to set foot on the moon, the assassination of Senator Robert F. Kennedy, the riots at the Democratic National Convention, and North Vietnam's Tet offensive—television coverage of which brought into American homes bloody images from a war that previously had seemed quite remote.

Each of these events, seen over several days by a huge section of the American public, became part of a shared set of experiences, all seen through the eye of television. Since then, television has become the primary source of news information for a large section of the American public, with newspapers, magazines, and radio assuming supplemental roles. . . .

The excerpt explains how television became the primary, or most important, source of news information because of a progression of several televised major events that began with the assassination of President Kennedy in 1963.

Spatial Order

If you want to describe a place or recreate a scene in which the placement of objects is important, follow these steps to give readers a sense of being there. Imagine yourself in the place. Tell readers what they would see in front of them, behind them, on either side of them, directly overhead, and beneath their feet if they were to stand in the same spot as you. When you use spatial order, words or phrases such as *in front, behind, near, north,* or *south* can signal a reader where to "look" in his or her mind's eye. The following excerpt is from the first paragraph of "Home," a chapter in *Lake Wobegon Days* by Garrison Keillor. Spatial details provide a description of Lake Wobegon, a Minnesota town. The order of details creates a view of the town that you would see by looking or walking in the direction the writer suggests. Spatial details and the words that signal their order are underlined.

☑ CONCEPT CHECK
To practice using spatial order, visualize yourself standing in the middle of your dorm room or a room at home. What do you see above your head, below your feet, and on all sides?

The town of Lake Wobegon, Minnesota, lies on the shore against Adams Hill looking east across the blue-green water to the dark woods. From the south, the highway aims for the lake, bends left by the magnificent concrete Grecian grain silos, and eases over a leg of the hill past the SLOW CHILDREN sign, bringing the traveler in on Main Street toward the town's one traffic light, which is almost always green. A few surviving elms shade the street. Along the ragged dirt path between the asphalt and the grass, a child slowly walks to Ralph's Grocery, kicking an asphalt chunk ahead of him. It is a chunk that after four blocks he is now mesmerized by, to which he is completely dedicated. At Bunsen Motors, the sidewalk begins. A breeze off the lake brings a sweet air of mud and rotting wood, a slight fishy smell, and picks up the sweetness of old grease, a sharp whiff of gasoline, fresh tires, spring dust, and, from across the street, the faint essence of tuna hot-dish at the Chatterbox Cafe. . . .

The spatial details in this paragraph help you to visualize the imaginary town of Lake Wobegon. The order of details leads you on a visual trip through

Figure 3.1   Choosing Coherence Patterns for the Topic "My Typical Day at Work"

MAIN IDEA	TYPE OF SUPPORT	COHERENCE PATTERN
My typical work day consists of the things I do before lunch and after lunch.	Use details that explain what the duties are and *when* you do them.	Time order
A typical work day for me is filled with several important tasks.	Use details that explain what the tasks are and their order of *importance*.	Emphatic order
My typical work day is easy because of the way my office is arranged.	Use details that explain *where* everything is.	Spatial order

the town by following the highway south to Main Street, then along Main Street, where your eyes travel down the dirt path beside the street and to the sidewalk. You *see* the town through Ralph's grocery, Bunsen Motors, and the Chatterbox Cafe. Sensory details such as the breeze and smells of mud, rotting wood, fish, grease, gasoline, tires, and spring dust complete the picture. The order of spatial details gives them coherence. They draw you into Keillor's image of Lake Wobegon just as the arrangement of colors, shapes, and figures in a painting draws you into the picture.

Coherence comes with practice. You may have to revise a paragraph several times to make the ideas flow smoothly and to make one sentence lead logically to the next. In choosing patterns for your paragraphs, let your guide be the main idea and the type of support you have chosen to explain it. Figure 3.1 illustrates three choices for main idea, type of support, and coherence pattern for the topic "my typical day at work."

[Exercise 3.9] Read the following three paragraphs and decide whether the details are organized according to *time order, emphatic order,* or *spatial order.* Underline words or phrases that help you decide. Then write your answer beside each paragraph.

_____ 1. When interviewing for a job, it is important to look your best. Wear a conservative outfit; stick to neutral colors, and avoid fashion fads. Let the interviewer run the show. Answer questions clearly and completely; stick to the point and do not ramble. Not only should you dress carefully and follow the interviewer's lead, but you should also refrain from doing anything that may be out of place. Do not smoke even if the interviewer offers you a cigarette. Let your actions show that you know the difference between a social situation and a business situation. Most important, be yourself. You have heard this many times, and it is still good advice. The interviewer wants to know who you are, not who you *think* you are.

_____ 2. It is easy to get a part-time job at my college. Whether you would like to work as an office assistant or a tutor, follow these steps. First you have to qualify. Financial aid is not available to everyone. To find out whether you qualify, go to the financial aid office and fill out the appropriate form. Next, you will be given a list of job openings. Before accepting the first one on the list, determine what each job pays, whether it conflicts with your schedule, and what the duties are. Once you have selected the right job for you, then you are ready to go to work. The whole process, from application to first day on the job, may take several days. Following these steps in the right order may save you a lot of time.

_____ 3. The "new" theater at the Peabody Arts Center is not new. It is a reconstructed opera house brought over from Europe and assembled piece by piece. Once you get past the modern lobby and walk into the theater itself, it is like stepping into another world. If you are sitting about halfway down the aisle in the center of your row, you can look directly overhead and see an immense crystal chandelier suspended above you. In front of you are rows of red plush-covered seats, then the orchestra pit, then the stage flanked on either side by heavy red velvet curtains. When they are closed, you can see the initials PAC. The intertwined letters measure several feet from bottom to top, and they are embroidered in gold and silver thread. To the left and right and in back of you are more rows of seats. Follow the rows to the end in each direction; then let your gaze travel up the walls, which are decorated with ornate wallpaper. Carved columns support balcony areas on three levels. No matter where you look, the view is sumptuous, reflecting the elegance of another age.

As you have seen, signal words at the beginnings of some sentences and elsewhere in your paragraph can help your readers follow the coherence pattern you have chosen. Figure 3.2 summarizes the signal words that indicate time order, emphatic order, and spatial order.

To help you write fully developed, well-organized paragraphs, remember these three keys:

Figure 3.2   Signal Words That Identify a Coherence Pattern

COHERENCE PATTERN	SIGNAL WORDS TO USE
Time order	*first, second, third, before, after, next, then, finally,* times (10:30), dates (year, month, day of the week), *morning, afternoon, evening*
Emphatic order	*important, most important, significant, primary, major, minor, unimportant, insignificant, of major concern*
Spatial order	*in front, behind, near, far, above, below, left, right, north, south, east, west, low, high, up, down, over, under, sideways, close, distant*

- Main idea   State your main idea in a topic sentence.
- Support   Support your main idea with plenty of specific details.
- Organization   Organize your evidence so that the details are logically arranged, unified, and coherent.

Write an Effective Summary

A **summary** is a condensed version of a piece of writing or oral account that presents just the central idea and a few major supporting points. One familiar example is a textbook chapter summary that presents the key ideas for your review. Being able to summarize information is a useful skill. Your instructor might ask you to summarize the important points in an article. During the process of researching a topic, you might summarize information from various sources to compile in a research paper. A classmate who missed a lecture might ask you to summarize the information given. An employer might assign you the task of reading a report and summarizing the information to present in a meeting. An effective summary has the following characteristics:

- **Objectivity:** A summary includes only the essential information, stated in your own words, but without your comment or opinion.
- **Brevity:** A summary is shorter than the original text because it condenses the information into a few key ideas. However, some summaries may be longer than others, depending on the length and complexity of the original.
- **Conciseness:** A summary focuses on essential elements, the key ideas in an argument or the central idea, and a few examples.

Your summary of an article or other piece of writing should clearly state the author's central idea and the major supporting points, and it should conclude with any final observations the author may have made about the information's use or significance. To write an effective summary, follow these five steps:

☑ CONCEPT CHECK
See Chapter 7 for more information on summarizing and documenting information for a research paper and to learn the difference between a paraphrase and a summary.

1. Either annotate or take notes from the reading. Identify the author's thesis or central idea and the major supporting points.

2. Identify the source (author's name and title of the piece), and include that information in your summary.

3. In a well-developed paragraph, state the central idea and the major supporting points. Do not copy from the text; instead, use your own words but maintain the meaning of the original.

4. If you quote any material directly, surround it with quotation marks. You should keep quotations to a minimum.

5. Do not insert your own opinion or reveal your attitude toward the topic.

As an example, read the following summary of the chapter-opening essay. This example meets the three characteristics of an effective summary and also applies the five steps discussed above.

> In the essay "15 Ways to Put More Joy in Your Life," Leigh Anne Jasheway-Bryant provides a list of suggestions that anyone can follow to lead a happier life. The author believes that not only should we look outside ourselves to find happiness, but we should also teach our children how to be joyful. Four of Jasheway-Bryant's "Ways" that are representative of all her suggestions include looking for happiness in nature, finding joy in everyday life, waking up happy, and spreading joy to others. The author concludes by saying that by making ourselves joyful, we can also bring hope to others.

[**Exercise 3.10**] To apply what you have learned about summarizing information, choose one of the following activities.

a. Select an essay from Unit 3 of your textbook. Read the essay, take notes, and write a one-paragraph summary to share in class.

b. Listen to a lecture and take notes; then write a summary of the lecture. Hand in your notes and the summary.

≪ Topics for Writing ≫

1. **React to the Reading.** Review the chapter-opening essay. Which one of the author's suggestions for putting more joy in your life appeals to you most, and why? Write a paragraph to answer this question.

2. **Use Your Experience.** Choose a topic from the following list that will allow you to write from experience. Organize your details, using the coherence pattern in parentheses that follows each topic.

   a. A typical day for me (time order)

   b. An ideal weekend (time order)

   c. An event that changed history (time order)

   d. My reasons to vote for a certain candidate (emphatic order)

   e. A behavior that is harmful or beneficial (emphatic order)

   f. My best or worst job (emphatic)

   g. A good study place (spatial order)

   h. A city park (spatial order)

   i. A favorite place (spatial order)

3. **Make a Real-World Connection.** Use facts, reasons, or examples to write a paragraph about something interesting you have learned in one of your courses. End your paragraph by explaining what makes the information important or how you plan to use it.

4. **Go to the Web.** Most people who are in the public eye have websites. Think of someone whom you admire or would like to know more about, for example, a politician, an author, or an athlete. Using a search engine such as Google and the person's name as your search phrase, find out what you can about him or her. Then write a paragraph in which you summarize the person's key biographical data such as place of birth, education, employment history, and major accomplishments.

⟨⟨ Checklist for Revision ⟩⟩

Did you miss anything? Check off the following items as you revise and edit your paragraphs.

❏ Does your paragraph have a topic sentence?

❏ Are your topic and focus clear?

❏ Do your supporting details include specific facts, reasons, or examples?

❏ Do all of your sentences support the main idea?

❏ Is your paragraph well organized?

❏ Have you used either time order, emphatic order, or spatial order as a coherence pattern?

❏ Does your paragraph have an effective concluding sentence?

❏ Are your sentences error free?

❑   Have you identified the source of the information summarized?

❑   Have you stated the central idea of the article or other piece of writing?

❑   Does your summary include the major supporting ideas?

❑   Have you used your own words but avoided giving your opinion?

❑   Is your summary objective, brief, and concise?

≪ Your Discovery Journal ≫

Assess what you have learned about paragraph skills by completing a quiz on Chapter 3. Go to *The Confident Writer* website and select the test to take on-line. Then complete the following reflective statement and explain your reasons, which you can also do online if you choose.

Based on what I have learned about paragraph skills from Chapter 3, my strengths and weaknesses in this area are _____ .

≪ Website Resources ≫

This chapter's resources include

- Chapter 3 Exercises
- Chapter 3 Quiz
- Downloadable Charts: *Group Evaluation Form*
- Chapter 3 Summary

To access these learning and study tools, go to *The Confident Writer* website.

(((*Confident writers are focused. They have a point to make that controls all of their other choices for writing.*)))

Stating Your Thesis

What you already know about a *thesis* or central idea

- When you ask someone to state his or her position, belief, or opinion, you are asking for a thesis statement.
- When you read a newspaper article and wonder what the point is, you are looking for the writer's thesis.
- Your experience with writing topic sentences (Chapter 3) is good background for learning how to write thesis statements.

Your *goals* for this chapter

[1] Know how to tell the difference between a thesis statement and a simple statement.

[2] Be able to write a thesis statement that has a limited topic and expresses your viewpoint toward that topic.

[3] Recognize the four parts of a thesis statement and be able to supply any missing parts in your own thesis statements.

[4] Know five ways to write an introduction, and be able to choose the best introduction for your topic and purpose.

Broadly defined, a *thesis* is a subject for discussion or analysis supported by reasoning. For example, suppose this is your thesis: *American companies that send jobs overseas are helping, not hurting, our economy.* By itself, this statement is merely an opinion with which many will disagree. However, if you can support your thesis with convincing evidence, readers may decide that your position is worth considering.

Just as a paragraph has a main idea, an essay has a *thesis* or central idea. A paragraph provides a brief but detailed development of a main idea. An essay provides a more lengthy development of a thesis. The main idea of a paragraph is stated in a topic sentence. The central idea of an essay is put forth in a thesis statement. Your essay's thesis controls everything else you will write.

The *thesis statement* is usually one sentence in the introductory part of your essay that states your central idea. A good thesis statement clearly identifies your topic and sets limits that keep your details focused on your central idea. Everything you write, especially the main idea or topic sentence of every paragraph, should relate to your thesis. This chapter explains how to write a thesis statement and also suggests strategies for beginning your essay with an effective introduction.

[First Thoughts]

To build background for reading, explore your thoughts about the questions readers ask authors. Then answer the following questions, either on your own or in a group discussion:

1. Have you ever met an author or attended a book signing? Describe the experience.

2. What questions do you think most people would be likely to ask a famous author?

3. Read the title, headnote, and first two paragraphs of the following essay. Based on this preview, what do you think will follow?

[Word Alert]

Before reading, preview the following words and definitions. During your reading, use context clues and your dictionary to define any additional unfamiliar words.

penal (3)	of or relating to punishment
morbid (4)	a preoccupation with unwholesome things

laconic (7)	terse, using few words
enumerate (10)	list or name one by one
grovel (13)	cringe, behave in a submissive manner
toady (13)	flatter, compliment excessively or insincerely
query (22)	to question
impotent (22)	powerless, helpless
cunningly (22)	cleverly, shrewdly
flagellate (24)	to whip or flog
self-abnegation (24)	self-denial
sidles (27)	moves sideways
obligatory (28)	morally or legally binding
modicum (30)	small or token amount

Ever Et Raw Meat?

Stephen King

Stephen King is one of the best-selling authors of all time. His books have sold millions of copies worldwide. He is a favorite among readers who enjoy novels and stories whose themes involve the mysterious, the supernatural, or the horrifying. In this essay, which was published in the *New York Times Book Review* in 1987, King discusses his responses to the questions readers ask.

1   It seems to me that, in the minds of readers, writers actually exist to serve two purposes, and the more important may not be the writing of books and stories. The primary function of writers, it seems, is to answer readers' questions. These fall into three categories. The third is the one that fascinates me most, but I'll identify the other two first.

The One-of-a-Kind Questions

2   Each day's mail brings a few of these. Often they reflect the writer's field of interest—history, horror, romance, the American West, outer space, big business. The only thing they have in common is their uniqueness. Novelists are frequently asked where they get their ideas (see category No. 2), but writers must wonder where this relentless curiosity, these really strange questions come from.

3   There was, for instance, the young woman who wrote to me from a penal institution in Minnesota. She informed me she was a kleptomaniac. She further informed me that I was her favorite writer, and she had stolen every one of my books she could got her hands on. "But after I stole *Different Seasons* from the library and read it, I felt moved to send it back," she wrote. "Do you think this means you wrote this one best?" After due consideration, I decided that reform on the part of the reader has nothing to do with artistic merit. I came close to

4   writing back to find out if she had stolen *Misery* yet but decided I ought to just keep my mouth shut.

From Bill V. in North Carolina: "I see you have a beard. Are you morbid of razors?"

5   From Carol K. in Hawaii: "Will you soon write of pimples or some other facial blemish?"

6   From Don G., no address (and a blurry postmark): "Why do you keep up this disgusting mother worship when anyone with any sense knows a MAN has no use to his mother once he is weaned?"

7   From Raymond R. in Mississippi: "Ever et raw meat?" (It's the laconic ones like this that really get me.)

8   I have been asked if I beat my children and/or my wife. I have been asked to parties in places I have never been and hope never to go. I was once asked to give away the bride at a wedding, and one young woman sent me an ounce of pot, with the attached question. "This is where I get my inspiration—where do you get yours?" Actually, mine usually comes in envelopes—the kind through which you can view your name and address printed by a computer—that arrive at the end of every month.

9   My favorite question of this type, from Anchorage, asked simply: "How could you write such a why?" Unsigned. If e.e. cummings were still alive, I'd try to find out if he'd moved to the Big North.

The Old Standards

10   These are the questions writers dream of answering when they are collecting rejection slips, and the ones they tire of quickest once they start to publish. In other words, they are the questions that come up without fail in every dull interview the writer has ever given or will ever give. I'll enumerate a few of them:

11   Where do you get your ideas? (I get mine in Utica.)

12   How do you get an agent? (Sell your soul to the Devil.)

13   Do you have to know somebody to get published? (Yes; in fact, it helps to grovel, toady, and be willing to perform twisted acts of sexual depravity at a moment's notice, and in public if necessary.)

14   How do you start a novel? (I usually start by writing the number 1 in the upper right-hand corner of a clean sheet of paper.)

15   How do you write best sellers? (Same way you get an agent.)

16   How do you sell your book to the movies? (Tell them they don't want it.)

17   What time of day do you write? (It doesn't matter; if I don't keep busy enough, the time inevitably comes.)

18   Do you ever run out of ideas? (Does a bear defecate in the woods?)

19   Who is your favorite writer? (Anyone who writes stories I would have written had I thought of them first.)

20   There are others, but they're pretty boring, so let us march on.

The Real Weirdies

21 Here I am, bopping down the street, on my morning walk, when some guy pulls over in his pickup truck or just happens to walk by and says, "Hi, Steve! Writing any good books lately?" I have an answer for this; I've developed it over the years out of pure necessity. I say, "I'm taking some time off." I say that even if I'm working like mad, thundering down homestretch on a book. The reason *why* I say this is because no other answer seems to fit. Believe me, I know. In the course of the trial and error that has finally resulted in "I'm taking some time off," I have discarded about 500 other answers.

22 Having an answer for "You writing any good books lately?" is a good thing, but I'd be lying if I said it solves the problem of *what the question means*. It is this inability on my part to make sense of this odd query, which reminds me of that Zen riddle—"Why is a mouse when it runs?"—that leaves me feeling mentally shaken and impotent. You see, it isn't just *one* question; it is a *bundle* of questions, cunningly wrapped up in one package. It's like that old favorite, "Are you still beating your wife?"

23 If I answer in the affirmative, it means I may have written—how many books? two? four?—(all of them good) in the last—how long? Well, how long is "lately"? It could mean I wrote maybe three good books just last week or maybe two *on this very walk up to Bangor International Airport and back!* On the other hand, if I say no, what does *that* mean? I wrote three or four *bad* books in the last "lately" (surely "lately" can be no longer than a month, six weeks at the outside)?

24 Or here I am, signing books at the Bett's Bookstore or B. Dalton's in the local consumer factory (nicknamed "the mall"). This is something I do twice a year, and it serves much the same purpose as those little bundles of twigs religious people in the Middle Ages used to braid into whips and flagellate themselves with. During the course of this exercise in madness and self-abnegation, at least a dozen people will approach the little coffee table where I sit behind a barrier of books and ask brightly "Don't you wish you had a rubber stamp?"

25 I have an answer to this one, too, an answer that has been developed over the years in a trial-and-error method similar to "I'm taking some time off." The answer to the rubber-stamp question is "No, I don't mind."

26 Never mind if I really do or don't (this time it's my own motivations I want to skip over. You'll notice); the question is, why does such an illogical query occur to so many people? My signature is actually stamped on the covers of several of my books, but people seem just as eager to get those signed as those that aren't so stamped. Would these questioners stand in line for the privilege of watching me slam a rubber stamp down on the title page of *The Shining* or *Pet Sematary?* I don't think they would.

27 If you still don't sense something peculiar in these questions, this one might help convince you. I'm sitting in the café around the corner from my house, grabbing a little lunch by myself and reading a book (reading at the table is one of the few bad habits acquired in my youth that I have nobly refused

giving up) until a customer or maybe even a waitress sidles up and asks, "How come you're not reading one of your own books?"

28   This hasn't happened just once, or even occasionally; it happens *a lot.* The computer-generated answer to this question usually gains a chuckle, although it is nothing but the pure, logical and apparent truth. "I know how they all come out," I say. End of exchange. Back to lunch, with only a pause to wonder why people assume you want to read what you wrote, rewrote, read again following the obligatory editorial conference and yet again during the process of correcting the mistakes that a good copy editor always prods, screaming from their hiding places (I once heard a crime writer suggest God could have used a copy editor, and while I find the notion slightly blasphemous, I tend to agree).

Stephen King

29   And then people sometimes ask in that chatty, let's-strike-up-a-conversation way people have, "How long does it take you to write a book?" Perfectly reasonable question—at least until you try to answer it and discover there *is* no answer. This time the computer-generated answer is a total falsehood, but it at least serves the purpose of advancing the conversation to some more discussable topic. "Usually about nine months," I say, "the same length of time it takes to make a baby." This satisfies everyone but me. I know that nine months is just an average, and probably a completely fictional one at that. It ignores *The Running Man* (published under the name Richard Bachman), which was written in four days during a snowy February vacation when I was teaching high school. It also ignores *It* and my latest *The Tommyknockers. It* is over 1,000 pages long and took four years to write. *The Tommyknockers* is 400 pages shorter but took five years to write.

30   Do I mind these questions? Yes . . . and no. Anyone minds questions that have no real answers and thus expose the fellow being questioned to be not a real doctor but a sort of witch doctor. But no one—at least no one with a modicum of simple human kindness—resents questions from people who honestly want answers. And now and then someone will ask a really interesting question, like, Do you write in the nude? The answer—not generated by computer—is: I don't think I ever have, but if it works, I'm willing to try it.

≪ The Critical Reader ≫

[CENTRAL IDEA]

1. What is Stephen King's central idea in this essay, and where is it stated?

[EVIDENCE]

2. King's major details are the three types of questions he gets from readers. What are the three types and their characteristics?

3. What are some of King's examples that help explain each type of question?

[IMPLICATIONS]

4. What purpose does King's first paragraph serve?

5. According to King, where does he get his inspiration for writing? Read again paragraph 8 and explain what the last sentence means.

[WORD CHOICE]

6. King's subject is the questions readers ask. What do King's word choices and examples tell you about his attitude toward his subject? For example, does he take readers' questions seriously, or does he make fun of them? Is the essay designed merely to make you laugh, or does it also have a serious message? Explain your answer using specific words and phrases from the essay.

≪ The Critical Thinker ≫

To examine Stephen King's essay in more depth, follow these suggestions for reflection, discussion, and writing.

1. Which paragraphs make up the introduction, body, and conclusion of King's essay? What purpose do the headings serve? How does King's choice of a structure for his essay help readers follow his ideas?

2. Are the questions that readers ask King similar to or different from the kinds of questions fans might ask of any celebrity? Give some examples of questions fans might ask of celebrities in the fields of sports, music, or film.

3. To Stephen King, some readers' questions are interesting, some are annoying, some are amusing, and some are boring. Examine the essay for examples of questions that provoke these emotional responses.

4. Look at the photograph of Stephen King on page 90 and think about his categories of the questions fans ask. If you had the opportunity to meet King, what would you ask him and why?

[**Exercise 4.1**]

Most authors have an Internet website. To find an author on the Web, you can try the following: Type the author's full name, with no spaces between first and last name, into the location box on your web browser, followed by *.com*. If there is a listing for your author, his or her home page will appear on screen. Or you can use a search engine like Google, Excite, Yahoo!, AltaVista, or HotBot, to name a few. Remember to use quotation marks when you type in your keyword in the dialog box.

As a follow-up to reading Stephen King's essay, search the Web to find out more about him. You may be able to find an interview, a review of his most current book, or a list of books he has published. Then share your results in a class discussion or written report.

What Is a Thesis Statement?

Goal 1

Know how to tell the difference between a thesis statement and a simple statement.

The *thesis* of an essay is its *central idea*. The thesis is a writer's opinion, viewpoint, or special insight about a topic. Suppose you choose *cartooning* as the topic of an essay. You choose this topic because cartooning is one of your interests. You like drawing cartoons, and you enjoy reading graphic novels and comic strips. In your opinion, cartooning is an art form that, like other art forms, requires technical expertise and that expresses political ideas or social values. Based on this background, you write the following thesis statement:

> Contrary to what many people believe, cartooning is an art form that depends on technical skill, political and social awareness, and a consistently expressed viewpoint.

If this were your thesis statement, the body of your essay should clearly and convincingly support your central idea with evidence that explains what you mean by "technical skill," to what extent "political and social awareness" is involved in cartooning, and why a "consistently expressed viewpoint" is important. In addition, your body paragraphs should be packed with facts and other details that support each part of your thesis. *A thesis statement is usually one sentence that combines a writer's topic (subject) and comment (opinion, viewpoint, or insight).*

Not just any sentence will do as a thesis statement. In fact, there is a big difference between a thesis statement and a simple statement of fact. A simple statement stands on its own, requiring no further explanation. The following statements are all simple statements:

- The dollar is a unit of currency in Australia, Taiwan, and more than twenty other countries as well.
- English is a second language for many students in American colleges and universities.
- Best-selling author Stephen King lives in Bangor, Maine.
- Martin Luther King Jr.'s birthday is celebrated in January.

As you can see, these statements are merely factual statements that do not call for additional support, explanation, or clarification. However, a thesis statement issues a challenge to readers in the sense that it may give rise to questions, comments, or personal feelings. A thesis statement expresses a writer's topic and comment. For example, in the thesis statement about cartooning, explained earlier in this section, the topic is *cartooning* and the comment is that *it is an art form.* The last part of the sentence tells you that cartooning depends on three things: *technical skill, political and social awareness,* and a *consistent viewpoint.* These terms suggest that the essay will have three major divisions. Following are two more examples. The first one is a simple statement, and the second is a thesis statement.

- Algebra is a required course at my college.
- Students can improve their performance in algebra by applying ten strategies for success in math courses.

The first statement contains a topic only. All you can do is agree or disagree with the statement. The second statement contains both a topic and a comment. The topic is *performance in algebra,* and the writer's comment is that *students can improve their performance by applying ten strategies.* You can do a lot more with this statement than agree or disagree with it. You can ask yourself what the ten strategies are, how to apply them, and whether they will help you improve your performance in algebra.

In the following examples of thesis statements, the topic is underlined and the comment is bracketed for you.

Example 1	Television commercials on Saturday morning cartoon shows [encourage the development of bad habits in children].
Example 2	[Parents should find a more beneficial activity to occupy their children on Saturday mornings than] watching cartoons on TV.
Example 3	So-called Reality TV [reflects neither real people nor real-life situations].

[Exercise 4.2] Read and discuss each sentence below; then circle an answer to indicate whether it is a thesis statement (TS) or a simple statement (SS). In the thesis statements you identify, draw a line under the writer's *topic* and bracket the writer's *comment,* as in the examples on page 93. Be prepared to explain your choices.

1. I have been working as a teller at First Union Bank on Center Street for the last fifteen years.   TS   SS

2. As a bank teller, I have learned several effective ways to deal with difficult customers.   TS   SS

3. Some women work as volunteer firefighters.   TS   SS

4. I like my job as a firefighter because it is both personally rewarding and socially responsible.   TS   SS

5. Armadillos should not be sold as pets because most people cannot provide the food, climate, and habitat that these animals need.   TS   SS

[Exercise 4.3]

Apply what you have learned about thesis statements by doing this exercise with group members. First, review the group roles and responsibilities listed on the inside back cover. Next, read and discuss the following simple statements. Decide how you could rewrite them to make them into thesis statements. What would you have to add or change? Then write the new statements to share with the rest of the class. As a final step, evaluate your work as your instructor recommends, or go to *The Confident Writer* website, where you can download the group evaluation form.

1. American politics is dominated by a two-party system.

2. Some students study at home while others prefer the library.

3. As many viewers do, I watch reality shows on television.

4. Most people have a favorite author.

5. Anyone in the United States who meets the qualifications can get a driver's license.

How to Write a Thesis Statement

Goal 2
Be able to write a thesis statement that has a limited topic and expresses your viewpoint toward that topic.

Though the thesis statement has two basic parts, *topic* and *comment,* the comment can be broken down further into *opinion, purpose,* and *parts.* Suppose you believe that participating in a sport is beneficial in several ways. You have arrived at this opinion because you play tennis, and it has become an important part of your life. You choose tennis as your topic because it has given you

Figure 4.1   Writing a Thesis Statement: Five Questions

QUESTION	ANSWER
1. What is the *general topic?*	Sports.
2. What is my *limited topic?*	The benefits of tennis.
3. What is my *opinion* about the limited topic?	Playing tennis is a sport I enjoy because of its benefits.
4. What is my *purpose* in writing about this topic?	I will tell readers why I enjoy tennis so that they will have a better understanding of the benefits of playing this game.
5. How will I break down my topic into parts I can explain in two or more body paragraphs?	I will tell readers what the benefits of playing tennis are for me: social interaction, improved fitness, and challenge of the game.

To write a thesis statement that contains *topic, opinion, purpose,* and *parts,* combine your answers to the five questions, and write a complete sentence like the ones below:

    Opinion   **Topic**   **Purpose**

1. I enjoy playing tennis because it gives me the benefits of [social interaction, improved fitness, and a challenging game].

                      Parts
                    Topic   **Purpose**

2. Attending a major league baseball game is better than watching one on TV [because the crowd's excitement is contagious, the view of the field is unlimited, and it provides good entertainment for a date].

                Purpose and parts are combined.

☑ **CONCEPT CHECK**
Your thesis statement is the point you want to make about your topic. To find your thesis, ask yourself why you want to write about your topic, what it means to you, and why readers should care.

a great deal of pleasure, but you are having difficulty deciding what comment to make about it. Figure 4.1 lists five questions to ask that will help you think through your topic and come up with a comment to write an effective thesis statement. Answering the questions will help you limit your topic and identify the opinion, purpose, and parts of your comment.

[**Exercise 4.4**] Choose any two topics from the list on page 96, or make up your own topics based on what interests you. Answer the five questions in Figure 4.1 to limit each topic and break down your comment into opinion, purpose, and parts. Next, write a thesis statement for each of your two topics. The first one is done as an example.

1. U.S. government
    a. General topic: U.S. government
    b. Limited topic: the three branches of the U.S. government
    c. Opinion: Each branch has a different function and purpose.
    d. Purpose: I want to inform readers about the way our government works.
    e. Parts: I will explain the purpose and function of each branch of government.
    f. Thesis: The executive, legislative, and judicial branches of the U.S. government have different purposes and functions, which are designed to keep any one branch from assuming too much power over the others.

2. College courses

3. Current fashions

4. Recreational activities

5. Places to visit

6. Restaurants

7. Careers

Although writers may place the thesis statement anywhere in an essay, you will usually find it near the beginning of a short essay or near the end of an introduction to a longer one, as in Stephen King's essay on pages 87–90. It is important for you as a beginning writer to state your thesis at the beginning of your essay for two reasons. First, your thesis lets your readers know what to expect. Second, just as the topic sentence of a paragraph limits and controls what you write in the rest of the paragraph, the thesis statement limits and controls what you write in the rest of your essay and helps you stay organized and on topic. In fact, topic sentences and thesis statements have several characteristics in common, as illustrated in Figure 4.2 on page 97.

Is Your Thesis Statement Complete?

Goal 3 Recognize the four parts of a thesis statement and be able to supply any missing parts in your own thesis statements.

If your thesis statement is missing a topic, opinion, purpose, or parts, you may run into one of several common problems. Read the next example:

1a. We need to do something to solve the problem of crime in our cities.

This statement might work as an interest grabber in an introductory paragraph, but it is not a suitable thesis statement. Although it expresses a topic (crime in our cities) and an opinion (we need to do something) it lacks the *purpose* and *parts* that would limit the thesis and clarify the writer's central

Figure 4.2   Comparison of Topic Sentence and Thesis Statement

TOPIC SENTENCE OF PARAGRAPH	THESIS STATEMENT OF ESSAY
Limits the topic covered in the paragraph	Limits the topic covered in the essay
States the main idea of the paragraph	States the central idea of the essay
Controls the selection of evidence to support the essay's thesis	Controls the selection of evidence to support the essay's thesis
Suggests how the writer has organized the paragraph	Suggests how the writer has organized the essay
Helps the writer maintain unity in the paragraph	Helps the writer maintain unity in the essay

idea. It is not clear *why* the writer chose the topic or *what* the writer wants to tell us about it. Also, "crime in our cities" covers a lot of ground. The writer should limit the topic to something more specific, such as "burglaries in our neighborhood." Below is a revision of example 1a that includes purpose and parts:

Purpose and opinion are combined—we started the program because we want to prevent burglaries.

                                                                          Topic
1b. To prevent burglaries in our neighborhood, we have
      started a neighborhood watch program that includes
      a five-point plan for home protection.
                        Parts

The sentence in example 2a below is a simple statement of fact, telling you only what the latest polls show. It is not suitable as a thesis statement because it does not indicate what the writer thinks about the decline in alcohol abuse or what it may mean to readers. Statement 2a lacks an opinion, purpose, and parts. Example 2b is a revision that includes the missing parts.

2a. The latest polls show that alcohol abuse among college
      students is decreasing. (unsuitable)

Purpose and opinion are combined—why the polls are misleading and who is affected by alcohol abuse.

                                                                  Topic
2b. Although the latest polls show that alcohol abuse among
      college students is decreasing, many students do abuse
      alcohol and cause problems for themselves and for their   *Opinion*
      communities. (better)

The topic in example 3a is study skills. The opinion is that study skills are important, and the writer has broken the topic down into three parts: time management, goal setting, and note taking. But what is the writer's *purpose?*

As a thesis statement, this sentence is unsuitable because readers cannot tell what the writer wants them to know or do about study skills. Example 3b provides the missing information.

3a. Time management, goal setting, and note taking are three important study skills. (unsuitable)

Parts

3b. Time management, goal setting, and note taking are

Topic   three important study skills college students can   *Purpose*
develop that may help them improve their grades.
(better)   *Opinion*

The writer of the sentence in example 4a has expressed two different opinions about two different topics in her thesis, so the statement is confusing. As a result, the purpose is also unclear. A thesis statement should cover only *one* topic. Examples 4b and 4c illustrate two ways to revise the statement.

4a. I disagree with people who want to abolish college sports, and I also think college athletes should have to maintain good grades. (unsuitable)

Purpose and parts are combined: why the disagreement, how the topic breaks down.

Opinion   *Topic*

4b. I disagree with those who want to abolish college sports because sports are a source of revenue for the college, an extracurricular activity that appeals to most students, and an opportunity for athletic scholarships. (better)

Purpose and parts are combined: why athletes should keep good grades; which parts (requirements and careers) will be explained.

Topic   *Opinion*

4c. College athletes should have to maintain good grades because they should have to meet the same requirements as all students and because they should prepare themselves for careers outside the field of professional sports. (better)

[**Exercise 4.5**] Check the thesis statements below for completeness; then rewrite them to add any missing parts.

1. Teenage alcohol abuse is on the rise.

2. People who run for office may have their private lives exposed in the press.

3. Many students are opting for careers in health care.

4. Even if I had the opportunity, I would not want to be sixteen years old again.

5. To gain the approval of voters, a new president of the United States must keep campaign promises, choose qualified people to serve in the cabinet, and act decisively in times of crisis.

6. Right-to-work laws are in effect in several states.

☑ CONCEPT CHECK
For an additional exercise on writing thesis statements, go to the student website.

In addition to stating the writer's topic and comment, a well-written thesis statement is grammatically correct. For example, a thesis statement should be a *complete* sentence, not a sentence fragment or a run-on sentence. If you tend to write fragments or run-ons, if your memory of these terms is rusty, or if you need help writing grammatically correct sentences, see Unit 4.

Write an Effective Introduction

Goal 4
Know five ways to write an introduction, and be able to choose the best introduction for your topic and purpose.

Writing a good introduction to your essay is a way of building readers' interest and placing your thesis within a meaningful context. Your essay's introduction, therefore, is also the introduction to your thesis statement. Though you can choose among many strategies for writing effective introductions, the five listed below may be especially helpful to you. Each strategy helps create a context for your thesis.

- Supply *background information.*
- Relate an *anecdote.*
- Begin with a *quotation and explanation.*
- Use interesting *facts and figures.*
- Ask a revealing *question.*

Build Background for Your Thesis

Supplying background information creates a context for your thesis much like setting the scene for a play. To build background, lead up to your thesis by identifying the situation, events, or issues that are relevant to it. Suppose that a certain intersection in your community is known to be dangerous. Residents take other, less convenient routes through residential areas to avoid this intersection, Your thesis is that by lowering the speed limit approaching the intersection, lives will be saved and traffic will not be diverted into neighborhoods where school children are present. To build background for your thesis, you tell readers that the intersection is at the bottom of a hill. The posted speed limit leading up to the intersection is fifty-five miles per hour, and most vehicles are traveling much faster when they reach the intersection. Truckers especially have difficulty stopping. Some people who could not stop their vehicles in time have caused accidents that resulted in serious injuries and death. By supplying this background information, you place your thesis in the context of a problem that requires a solution.

The following excerpt from "I Married an Accountant" by Joe Queenan introduces a thesis by supplying background information. The thesis is underlined.

> At the mature age of 39, a somewhat immature 220-pound friend of mine took up ice hockey. Though he had never before strapped on ice skates and is far from fit, he has spent virtually every Sunday evening for the past two summers barreling up and down the ice in a special hockey league for aging neophytes. He may be strange, but he is not boring.
>
> Another person I know moved to Teheran in the late 1970s, met an Iranian woman, converted to Islam so he could marry her, and had to undergo a circumcision—all of this took place against the backdrop of massive civil unrest in Iran. He too may be strange, but he is not boring.
>
> This is equally true of my wife, who for three years wrote video scripts for a man who had previously directed the Gothic soap opera "Dark Shadows." Though the subject of her continuing-education scripts had few ghoulish elements, she can nevertheless claim to have worked closely with a colleague of Jonathan Frid's, the famous TV vampire. It is an honor she will take to her grave. She, like the aging hockey player and the intrepid voyager to Iran, has led a rich, interesting life and has done exciting, unpredictable things. Like them, she is also an accountant.
>
> Accountants have long been the targets of satirists and have been mercilessly lambasted by everyone from Monty Python to the rock group The Kinks. Personally, I hold no brief for accountants as a unit and would be loath to argue that they are, collectively or individually, electrifying fireballs. Yet nothing in my experience would lead me to the conclusion that accountants are quantifiably less interesting than people in other occupations.
>
> <u>Thus I have often wondered why these attacks on accountants continue at a time when numerous other professions would make</u> equally suitable targets. . . .

Queenan's article takes a humorous look at the prevailing stereotype of accounting as boring. Queenan believes that many other professions would make suitable targets as "most boring job." To introduce his thesis, he provides background information in the form of three examples of accountants he knows who have led interesting lives. The rest of the article contains examples of the professionals Queenan thinks are boring—for example: systems engineers, investment bankers, public relations consultants, and writers. Queenan's opinion is that accountants are no less interesting than anyone else. His implied purpose is to persuade readers through the use of humor that other professions are as boring, or even more so, than accounting. The phrase "numerous other professions" implies the parts of Queenan's thesis to be developed in the essay: examples of boring professions.

Relate an Anecdote

An *anecdote* is a brief story or narration of an event. Used as an introductory strategy, the anecdote can vividly establish a context for your thesis.

In the following example, a personal anecdote introduces an essay on the topic of "how to succeed in college."

✔ CONCEPT CHECK
To write an anecdote, think about your topic and try to recall a related event from your experience. What story can you tell in a few sentences that will introduce readers to your topic?

> One of my most memorable experiences as a first-year student at a large state university was an orientation address that we were required to attend. I was from out of state, nervous, and hadn't made any friends yet. I sat in that big auditorium among strangers, hoping for some encouragement from the professor who stood at the podium. The first words out of his mouth were "Look to your left; look to your right. Only one of you will still be here at midterm." I've never forgotten that moment because I took those words as a personal challenge. I vowed that not only would I still be in college at midterm, but I would graduate four years later.
>
> Now I am a senior, and I have made good on my vow. I will graduate at the end of this semester. College has not always been easy for me. Some of my courses were harder than others, but persistence and a positive attitude have paid off. To all those students who may be feeling discouraged, I have these words of advice. If you want to succeed in college, attend class regularly, take advantage of the support services that are available, and try these strategies for getting the most out of your courses. . . .

The essay goes on to explain several strategies for improving study skills and classroom performance. The anecdote builds a context for the thesis by establishing the writer's authority as someone who has succeeded despite some earlier misgivings.

Begin with a Quotation and Explanation

Quotations from books, poems, articles, experts in a certain field, or interviews you have had with people who are involved in some way with your topic can add authority to your opinions. Using quotations shows readers that others have thought about your topic and formed opinions about it. If you begin with one or more quotations, be sure to explain what they mean and how they relate to your thesis. The quotation may illustrate your thesis or back it up with an expert's opinion. The following excerpt is from "The Straight Path of Islam," an essay by Huston Smith. The thesis statement is underlined.

> If a Muslim were asked to summarize the way Islam counsels people to live, the answer might be: It teaches them to walk the straight path. The phrase comes from the opening *surah* of the Koran, which is repeated many times in the Muslim's five daily prayers.
>
> In the Name of Allah the Merciful, the Compassionate:
> Praise be to Allah, Creator of the worlds,

> The Merciful, the Compassionate,
> Ruler of the day of Judgment.
> Thee do we worship, and Thee do we ask for aid.
> Guide us in the straight path,
> The path of those on whom Thou hast poured forth Thy grace.
> Not the path of those who have incurred Thy wrath and gone astray.

> This *surah* has been called the heartbeat of the Muslim's response to God. At the moment, though, the question is why "the straight path"? One meaning is obvious; a straight path is one that is not crooked or corrupt. The phrase contains another meaning, however, which addresses something that in Islam is distinctive. The straight path is one that is straightforward; it is direct and explicit. Compared with other religions, Islam spells out the way of life it proposes; it pinpoints it, nailing it down through clear injunctions. Every major type of action is classified on a sliding scale from the "forbidden," through the "indifferent," to the "obligatory." This gives the religion a flavor of definiteness that is quite its own. Muslims know where they stand. . . .

The rest of Smith's essay explains the human duties that make up the content of Islam's straight path: the Five Pillars of Islam and the Koran's social teachings. His purpose is to explain the teachings of Islam to practitioners of other faiths. The quotation from the Koran establishes the context for Smith's explanation.

Use Interesting Facts and Figures

Facts and figures such as dates, times, names of people, places, and statistics add interest and realism to your writing, and statistics can act as evidence to support your thesis. Suppose you are disturbed by the commercials on children's television programs that promote sugared cereals. To gather evidence, you count the number of times *sugar* or other words that refer to sweetness are mentioned in several commercials. You find that the number is surprisingly large, and you decide to use it in your introduction to establish a basis for your opinion that there is too much of this kind of advertising aimed at children.

Dates establish a historical context for your thesis. For example, when you are writing about a past event such as an election you thought was significant or a social movement that changed history, dates are factual details that give your argument credibility. Names of people and places can interest readers in your topic, as illustrated in the following example, in which the thesis statement is underlined.

> To the list of professional basketball players such as Magic Johnson, Michael Jordan, and Larry Bird who have become household words, we have added

another name: Shaquille O'Neal, or "Shaq" for short. It seems like only a few short years ago when Shaq was yet another high school basketball player who had dreams of becoming an NBA player. But unlike the great majority of high school hopefuls, Shaq had the unbeatable talent of which sports fame and fortune are made. Shaq began his career with the Orlando Magic. He now plays for the Phoenix Suns. <u>How Shaquille O'Neal was discovered and how he became a nationally known player make an interesting story.</u> . . .

People who follow sports will recognize the names of famous athletes that help provide a context for the thesis. Orlando, Florida, is a place many readers may recognize whether they follow sports or not. Shaquille O'Neal is the topic; the writer's opinion is that Shaq's rise to fame is an interesting story, and the writer plans to discuss how Shaq was discovered and how he became a nationally known player. The writer's purpose is to inform readers about Shaq, another household name in the world of professional basketball.

The following excerpt from "The Trouble with Television," an essay by Robert MacNeil, makes use of statistics to introduce the thesis, which is underlined.

It is difficult to escape the influence of television. If you fit the statistical averages, by the age of 20 you will have been exposed to at least 20,000 hours of television. You can add 10,000 hours for each decade you have lived after the age of 20. The only things Americans do more than watch television are work and sleep.

Calculate for a moment what could be done with even a part of those hours. Five thousand hours, I am told, are what a typical college undergraduate spends working on a bachelor's degree. In 10,000 hours you could have learned enough to become an astronomer or engineer. You could have learned several languages fluently. If it appealed to you, you could be reading Homer in the original Greek or Dostoyevsky in Russian. If it didn't, you could have walked around the world and written a book about it.

<u>The trouble with television is that it discourages concentration.</u> Almost anything interesting and rewarding in life requires some constructive, consistently applied effort. The dullest, the least gifted of us can achieve things that seem miraculous to those who never concentrate on anything. But television encourages us to apply no effort. It sells us instant gratification. It diverts us only to divert, to make the time pass without pain. . . .

Using facts and figures as an introductory strategy builds a context for Mac-Neil's thesis statement by establishing the pervasive influence of television. MacNeil's topic is television; his comment is that there is *trouble* with television; he specifies the kind or *part* of this trouble he will discuss as *discourages concentration*. Although MacNeil's purpose is not directly stated in his thesis, you can assume that he means to inform readers of the ways television discourages concentration. The rest of the essay explains how television's appeal to the short attention span has affected our language, the way we think, and our tolerance for effort.

Ask a Revealing Question

Beginning an essay with a question works best if the question you ask is new, surprising, or something readers may not have thought to ask. The question must also be a *revealing* one that clarifies what the essay is about. The following excerpt is from a section of the first chapter of *The Practical Entomologist* by Rick Imes. The thesis statement is underlined.

☑ **CONCEPT CHECK**
When introducing a thesis with a question, make sure that you frame the question with a sentence or two of explanation that creates a context for it.

Just what are insects, anyway? Often, any small creature with more than four legs is indiscriminately labeled a "bug," but true bugs represent only one of many different groups of insects. What's more, many of these creepy, crawling critters are not insects at all, but may belong to one of several related but very different groups.

Insects, as it turns out, are characterized by several easily recognized traits that set them apart from any other group of organisms. Like other members of the Phylum Arthropoda (which, literally translated, means "jointed foot"), and unlike mammals, for example, insects possess an external skeleton, or *exoskeleton*, which encases their internal organs, supporting them as our skeleton supports us and protecting them as would a suit of armor on a medieval knight. Unlike other arthropods, their body is divided into three distinct regions—the *head, thorax,* and *abdomen.* Insects are the only animals that have three pairs of jointed legs, no more or less, and these six legs are attached to the thorax, the middle region of the body. . . .

The first chapter of Imes's book is titled "The Basics of Entomology," and in the excerpt above, his thesis, or central idea, is that several traits determine which organisms can be classified as insects. The rest of the excerpt following the thesis describes more of the traits. The question that introduces the thesis is a surprising one because most readers think they know what an insect is. Furthermore, the question is central to the development of Imes's chapter, which sets forth the basics of the study of insects and their behavior.

[**Exercise 4.6**] Identify which of the following introductory strategies the writers of the next four passages use. In addition, underline the thesis statement in each passage. Explain the reasons for your choices.

- Supply *background information.*
- Relate an *anecdote.*
- Begin with a *quotation and explanation.*
- Use interesting *facts and figures.*
- Ask a revealing *question.*

1. If you heard in a television commercial that half the dentists surveyed recommended SMILE toothpaste, you might want to try it. But if you were a wise consumer, you would realize that the other half didn't recommend the toothpaste, so maybe "half" isn't such a good number after all. You would also realize that although half of 2,000 is 1,000 and that is a lot of dentists, half of two is just one dentist. In either case, however, 50 percent is still 50 percent, which means that half the dentists surveyed did not recommend SMILE toothpaste. Untrained consumers have a way of hearing only the positive side of the messages in television commercials. You can become a wise consumer by learning to spot the seven common tricks that advertisers use to make you want to buy their products. . . .

2. Is high school football a luxury we cannot afford? A school district in our area is considering abolishing athletic events as a way to cut costs. Uniforms cost money. So do coaches' salaries, equipment, concessions at football games, electricity for running the scoreboard and field lights, transportation to away games, and other related expenditures. The money saved from these could be used to buy science lab equipment, new books for the library, and computers, to name a few of our needs that the school board has been exploring. High school football is something most community members take for granted, and surely the students will be the losers if they do not have the experience of cheering their teams to victory. Perhaps if we can find other ways to cut costs, then football may be the luxury that we *can* afford. . . .

3. When the late president John F. Kennedy said, "Ask not what your country can do for you but what you can do for your country," he exhorted a nation of young people to get involved in the political process and to take an active role in the fashioning of their government. For the first time in the history of the United States, a president appealed to young people as adults, not as children, and they rose in force to meet his challenge, joining the Peace Corps and the ranks of others in service to humankind. Kennedy was their man, and since his death there has been no one like him. If future presidents of the United States want to capture the youth vote, they will have to do several things to gain young people's respect and support. . . .

4. The story of the search for radium is a romantic and stirring one. Behind it is a woman who was passionately curious, daring in her convictions, and determined to work in an age hardly encouraging to professional aspirations among those of her sex. From a dilapidated shed, described by one German chemist at the time as a "cross between a stable and a potato-cellar," came a discovery that would throw light on the structure of the atom, open new doors in medicine, and save lives in future generations.

Marie Sklodowska came to Paris and the Sorbonne in 1891 as a reticent Polish woman of twenty-four. Taking a solitary room in the Latin Quarter, she began her studies in mathematics and physics. By 1897 she had two university degrees and a fellowship, as well as a husband and a newborn daughter. In the physicist Pierre Curie, Marie had found both an adviser and a lover, someone as serious as she, who shared her interests and became drawn into her quest. . . . (Excerpted from "How Did They Discover Radium?" in *How Did They Do That?* by Caroline Sutton)

The way you begin your essay can arouse your reader's interest and create a context for your thesis. Choose an introductory strategy that best suits your purpose and audience. For example, suppose you had written the following thesis statement for an essay on weight management. What introductory strategy would you choose?

To lose weight sensibly and without health risks, limit calorie intake, eat balanced meals, and exercise regularly.

For a general audience, either of the following introductory strategies and example sentences would introduce your thesis effectively:

QUOTATION AND EXPLANATION

The headline "Dieters Gain Back Lost Weight on Starvation Diet" says it all. A new study reveals that people who lost weight quickly while on a popular diet regained the lost pounds and more once they returned to normal eating habits. Nutritionists counsel that *to lose weight sensibly . . .*

FACTS AND FIGURES

Only about 10 percent of those who lose pounds on some highly advertised weight-loss programs actually keep them off. The other 90 percent gain back the lost weight and then some in about three to six months. "Diets" do not work; a change in eating habits does. *To lose weight sensibly . . .*

For the specific audience of college students, the following introductory strategy would be a good choice.

ANECDOTE

A year of studying, partying, fast-food eating, and no exercising had left Terry several pounds heavier. A quick-loss plan advertised in the local paper seemed just the ticket. A few weeks later, Terry was lighter in body and spirit until the pounds came creeping back. Like many dieters, Terry learned a lesson: *To lose weight sensibly . . .*

As explained in this chapter, the strategies for writing and introducing a thesis statement are among the many choices available to you as a writer. A well-thought-out introduction and clearly stated thesis will give direction to your essay.

[Exercise 4.7]

Of the five methods for introducing a thesis statement, which one appeals to you most, and why? How do your topic, audience, and purpose influence your choice of an introductory method?

≪ Topics for Writing ≫

1. **React to the Reading.** Is there an author or other famous person such as an athlete, entertainer, or politician of whom you would like to ask some questions? Write an essay in which you explain who the person is, what questions you would like to ask, and why.

2. **Use Your Experience.** Choose a topic from the list below and write an essay. Follow the suggestions offered in this chapter for writing, introducing, and correcting your thesis statement.

   a. Write about the qualities you admire in a U.S. president.

   b. Write about a sport that has either harmful or beneficial effects on those who participate in it.

   c. Write about a time when you accomplished something that you wanted to do. Explain how achieving success affected you.

   d. Go to *The Confident Writer* website and choose your own topic.

3. **Make a Real-World Connection.** Think about an issue that is currently being discussed in the news. What are some of the different positions people are taking on this issue? What is your opinion? Write about the issue, and make your point in a clearly written thesis statement. Remember to introduce your thesis with one of the five methods explained in this chapter.

4. **Go to the Web.** Find an official website for Stephen King. Look for a biography and list of his work. Using the information you find, write an essay about King.

≪ Checklist for Revision ≫

Did you miss anything? Check off the following items as you revise and edit your essay.

- ❑ Does your essay have a thesis statement?
- ❑ Is the thesis statement complete? Can you identify a topic, opinion, purpose, and parts?
- ❑ Does your introductory paragraph create a context for the thesis?
- ❑ Have you used one of this chapter's five strategies for introducing a thesis?
- ❑ Do your body paragraphs have topic sentences?
- ❑ Do you have enough supporting facts, reasons, or examples in each body paragraph?
- ❑ Does your essay have a conclusion?
- ❑ Are your sentences error-free?

≪ Your Discovery Journal ≫

It may sound strange, but reading can help you improve your writing. Reading builds awareness of the many ways in which writers use words and structure their ideas. By choosing reading materials that appeal to your interests, you will enhance your enjoyment of the process.

For your next journal entry, briefly summarize some material you have read recently that you enjoyed or that aroused your interest. Begin your summary by completing the reflective statements below. Then explain your reasons.

As an additional option, do this activity online by going to *The Confident Writer* website.

Recently, I read _____, which was about _____.

I (would, would not) recommend _____ to others for the following reasons.

≪ Website Resources ≫

This chapter's resources include

- Chapter 4 Exercises
- Chapter 4 Quiz
- Downloadable Charts: *Group Evaluation Form*
- More Topics for Writing
- Chapter 4 Summary

To access these learning and study tools, go to *The Confident Writer* website.

(((*Confident writers are organized. They plan their essays, taking the time to choose the best details to support their thesis.*)))

Supporting Your Thesis

What you already know about *supporting* a thesis

- In everyday conversation, you expect people to explain what they mean, and this is also true in writing.

- Think of an important decision you have made. What were your reasons behind the decision?

- Because you know that your thesis statement tells readers *what you think,* you can probably guess that your support for the thesis explains *why you think that way.*

Your *goals* for this chapter

[1] Be able to support your thesis with facts, reasons, and examples that are relevant to your topic and purpose.

[2] Know how to use levels of development to organize your details logically.

[3] Understand how using transitions and finding a controlling idea can help you make connections between the paragraphs of your essay.

[4] Know how to write a concluding paragraph that effectively ends your essay and makes readers think critically.

Two college students are sitting outside the student center when an attractive member of the opposite sex walks by. The students exchange looks that clearly indicate what they are thinking, yet no word passes between them. Seeing the grade on a composition the professor has just returned, one student says, "Yes!" Though no conversation follows, the other students in the class know this writer did well and are hoping for similar results on their papers. In both cases, either a word or a look effectively communicates an idea that would probably take several sentences to write about in an essay.

Writing is not like having a conversation. When people read your essay, you may not be available either to explain an unclear thesis or to provide additional evidence to support your opinions. In writing, everything needs explaining; words have to do the work of gestures, facial expressions, and tone of voice. As explained in Chapter 4, an essay needs a thesis or central idea. Equally important is how you support your thesis—how clearly and completely you explain what you mean so that your readers can identify with you and follow your ideas. This chapter explains how to support your thesis with specific evidence and how to reinforce your thesis in the conclusion of your essay.

[First Thoughts]

To build background for reading, explore your thoughts about stress and life expectations. Then answer the following questions, either on your own or in a group discussion:

1. What is your outlook for the future; for example, do you expect your life to be better or worse than that of previous generations, and why?

2. To what extent does stress affect your performance in your courses or at work?

3. Read the title, the headnote, and the first two paragraphs of the following essay. Based on this preview, what do you think will follow?

[Word Alert]

Before reading, preview the following words and definitions. During your reading, use context clues and your dictionary to define any additional unfamiliar words.

paradox (3), (4)   a seemingly contradictory statement that may be true

materialism (3)   excessive regard for material things or worldly concerns

prosperity (3)	success
phenomenon (5)	an occurrence or fact that is perceived through the senses
inevitable (6)	predictable, unavoidable
engenders (6)	causes, gives rise to
fosters (11)	promotes, nurtures, advances
tumultuous (15)	prone to sudden change, upsetting

Stress Is the Dirty Secret of Success

Gregg Easterbrook

Gregg Easterbrook is the author of books and articles on American life and culture. His latest book is *The Progress Paradox: How Life Gets Better While People Feel Worse.* The following article originally appeared in the *Los Angeles Times.*

1   By practically every objective measure, American life has been getting better for decades.

2   Standards of living keep rising, with the typical house now more than twice as large as a generation ago; middle-class income keeps rising, although more slowly than income at the very top; more Americans graduate from college every year; longevity keeps rising; almost all forms of disease, including most cancers, are in decline; crime has dropped spectacularly; pollution, except for greenhouse gases, is in long-term decline; discrimination is down substantially. Yet despite all these positive indicators, the percentage of Americans who describe themselves as "happy" has not increased since the early 1950s, while incidence of depression keeps rising—and was doing so long before the morning of Sept. 11, 2001.

3   This is the progress paradox: Life gets better while people feel worse. Many explanations suggest themselves. One is the depressing effect of excess materialism, which I call "the revenge of the credit card." Another is fear that Western society will break down, which might be called "collapse anxiety." A third is the uneasy feeling that accompanies actually getting what you dreamed of. Today, tens of millions of Americans have things their parents or grandparents could only dream of—nice houses, college educations. Although that is obviously good, Americans are finding that merely possessing the good life does not ensure happiness. This may tell us there is a "revolution of satisfied expectations"—that general prosperity brings with it an empty feeling.

4   Here is another possible explanation of the progress paradox: that along with getting better at manufacturing cell phones, DVD players and SUVs, society gets ever better at manufacturing stress.

5   Stress is hardly a new phenomenon. To have been a pioneer prairie farmer in the 1800s, cracking hard soil with a hand plow; to have been a seamstress working 14-hour days for starvation wages in a sweatshop in the 1800s; these and many other past life circumstances were surely stressful. But the contemporary

increase in stress is not in your mind; researchers believe Americans suffer from ever-higher levels of nervous tension. Higher stress, in turn, may be offsetting our appreciation of a better life.

6   Consider, first, that nature designed us to experience stress. "Stress is inevitable and not necessarily bad," says Bruce McEwen, a researcher at Rockefeller University in New York and a leading authority on the biology of stress. In reaction to noise, sudden movements or perceived dangers, an area of the brain called the amygdala secretes a hormone called cortisol that engenders stress. Stress hormones heighten the awareness of surroundings, while slightly improving vision and hearing.

7   Researchers believe the stress response evolved in mammals because stress decreases the odds of being caught and eaten by something. Today, the stress response is no less important as an evolutionary "adaptation" than it was in the era of saber-toothed tigers. Drive at 75 mph with other vehicles only a car-length away, and you'd better have heightened awareness of sudden small movements.

8   Stress is also a coping mechanism for the demands of life. At the workplace or at school, the stress response helps people be on guard regarding problems, and helps them work harder. Studies show that successful or high-income individuals tend to have more cortisol pumping through their systems. (Whether the pressures of their positions cause the stress or the stress-response helps them attain their positions is not known.)

9   However, research also shows that those who enjoy career success and exhibit stress symptoms are twice as likely as the population at large to describe themselves as "very unhappy." That the stressed-out are likely to be unhappy is a warning sign, because stress, measured either by emotional state or by cortisol levels, is rising in American society. One reason is that the media get ever better at presenting us with information to worry about.

10   The 1800s prairie farmer would have fretted a great deal about the weather and the arrival of the Wells Fargo wagon, but he would have known hardly anything about crimes in distant cities or angry chanting mobs in other nations. Today, everyone gets minute-by-minute readouts of killings, natural disasters and social unrest the world over. Even as most things get better for most people, there are ever more entries on the list of worries, activating more stress.

11   The contemporary lifestyle also fosters stress. Americans now spend an average of almost an hour per day in the car, and being stuck in traffic is stressful compared with walking, which can be relaxing and pleasant. A century ago the typical American walked three miles a day; today it's well less than a quarter of a mile. Ever-decreasing physical exertion coupled with ever more calories means that, today, the typical American is overweight. Stress and weight are related, as overweight people have a higher proportion of cortisol in their bodies than the lean.

12   The national decline in sleep is another factor in rising stress. Cortisol production stops during sleep; one of the fundamental reasons mammals sleep

may be to give their bodies a break from stress hormones. Researchers believe 10 hours of sleep nightly was the norm for most of human history. By a generation ago, the U.S. average had fallen to eight hours per night; the average is now seven hours and still falling.

13   We don't sleep well, either, owing to bad habits such as eating or watching TV just before bed. Those who watch TV until lights-out often experience interrupted sleep, researchers say, whereas our ancestors, who read or knitted before bed, slept more soundly.

14   What can we do to reduce stress? First are short-term lifestyle changes. Cut calories; engage in 30 minutes of physical activity daily; turn off the television at least an hour before bedtime.

15   Long-term goals should be more ambitious. Society needs to find ways to make society less of a rat race; to render the economy less tumultuous and ease job anxiety; to slow the hectic pace of existence so that we can step back and appreciate our own lives. If living standards and stress continue rising in sync, we'll endlessly be better off but not happier.

‹‹ The Critical Reader ››

[CENTRAL IDEA]

1. What is Gregg Easterbrook's thesis?

2. What strategy does he use to introduce the thesis?

[EVIDENCE]

3. What evidence does the author provide to explain his statement in paragraph 3 that "Life gets better while people feel worse"?

4. What facts explain that stress is not a new phenomenon?

5. What examples does the author provide to explain that stress is a coping mechanism?

[IMPLICATIONS]

6. According to the author, higher stress may be offsetting our appreciation of a better life. What do you think he means?

7. The author says that for most people, there are "ever more entries on the list of worries, activating more stress." Do you agree with this statement? What worries do you have today that you did not have when you were younger?

[WORD CHOICE]

8. Do you think the author's use of the term *progress paradox* (paragraphs 3–4) is effective? Explain your answer.

◁◁ The Critical Thinker ▷▷

To examine Gregg Easterbrook's essay in more depth, follow these suggestions for reflection, discussion, and writing.

1. Preview the concluding devices explained in this chapter. Which one does Gregg Easterbrook use? Is it an effective choice, and why?

2. Throughout the essay, the author compares American life today to that of a prairie farmer in the 1800s. What purpose does this comparison serve?

3. What is the significance of the title in relation to the essay as a whole? For example, what *is* "the dirty secret of success"?

4. How does the author suggest that we "slow" the pace of life and increase our appreciation of our circumstances? What suggestions do you have? Write an essay in which you answer these questions.

Find Evidence to Support Your Thesis

Goal 1

Be able to support your thesis with facts, reasons, and examples that are relevant to your topic and purpose.

When you have chosen a topic and written your thesis, the next step is to select the evidence to support your thesis. How you arrange the evidence determines what the major divisions of your essay will be. One way to begin is to make an informal outline by writing your thesis statement and breaking it into several subpoints or main ideas, each of which can be explained in a body paragraph. Read the following two examples of a thesis statement and informal outline.

EXAMPLE 1

A good weight-training program should concentrate on how to build and tone the muscles in four major parts of the body.

1. The muscles of the chest

2. The muscles of the back

3. The muscles of the arms

4. The muscles of the legs

In this outline, the writer shows that the essay will have four major divisions. Each of these divisions will become a main idea or subpoint that supports the thesis statement. The four main ideas will specify which muscles receive weight training.

EXAMPLE 2

Many people who have stage fright believe that there is nothing they can do about it, but they are wrong.

1. Stage fright is a type of stress.

2. To eliminate or control stage fright, determine its cause.

3. Use relaxation techniques to reduce stage fright.

4. Be well prepared for a speech or performance.

This outline specifies that the writer's essay will have four major divisions to support the thesis. The first division of the essay will define *stage fright* and explain how it is a type of stress. The second major division will explain what causes stage fright. The third and fourth major divisions of the essay will explain two strategies for reducing stage fright. Each major division of the essay can be dealt with in a body paragraph, and the writer can use facts, reasons, or examples to support each paragraph's main idea. Together, the body paragraphs will support the overall point, or thesis, that people can indeed do something about stage fright.

[**Exercise 5.1**] Following are three informal outlines. Each begins with a thesis statement followed by two or more subpoints that could become the main ideas of body paragraphs. Read the outlines; then add one more subpoint to each.

1. Malls not only provide a place to shop but are popular entertainment centers as well.

   a. They provide teenagers with a place to hang out.

   b. They provide endless subjects for people watchers.

   c. They provide . . .

2. The behavior of some moviegoers is enough to drive me from the theater to the nearest video store.

   a. Some moviegoers do not make their children behave.

   b. Some moviegoers disturb others by leaving their seats frequently.

   c. Some moviegoers litter the theater.

   d. Some moviegoers . . .

3. Going to the movies is better in some ways than it was when I was a child, but in other ways it is worse.

   a. Better

      1. There are more theaters to choose from.

    2. There is a wider variety of snacks available.

    3.

  b. Worse

    1. Moviegoers are not as considerate as they used to be.

    2. There are not as many good shows for children.

    3.

[Exercise 5.2] Following are two thesis statements. For each of them, list two to four main ideas that could be developed into the body paragraphs of an essay.

1. Acquaintances come and go in our lives, but true friends show their continuing support for us in several ways.

2. Everyone knows you cannot cure the common cold, but while you are waiting for one to go away, try my method to make yourself comfortable.

Arrange Your Supporting Evidence

Goal 2

Know how to use levels of development to organize your details logically.

Choose specific details and arrange them logically to help give your essay unity and coherence. The thesis is your central idea. *It is also your controlling idea* in that it determines your essay's development and your selection of details. To support your central idea and prove your thesis, break it down into subpoints, which are the main ideas of your body paragraphs. Then support each subpoint or main idea with specific details. If you follow this logical plan from *thesis* to *topic sentence* to *major* and *minor supporting details,* your essay will be unified and coherent.

✔ **CONCEPT CHECK**
See also the section on levels of development in Chapter 3.

Example 1 on page 114 shows a thesis statement and an informal outline of the main ideas that support it. The formal outline shown here adds major and minor details and gives you a clearer picture of how the writer will develop the thesis.

THESIS: A good weight-training program should concentrate on how to build and tone the muscles in four major parts of the body.

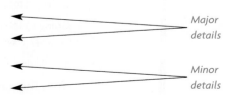

Main idea   → I. The muscles of the chest: pectorals

       A. How we use these muscles   ← *Major details*

       B. Type of training required

         1. Horizontal bench press   ← *Minor details*

         2. Incline bench press

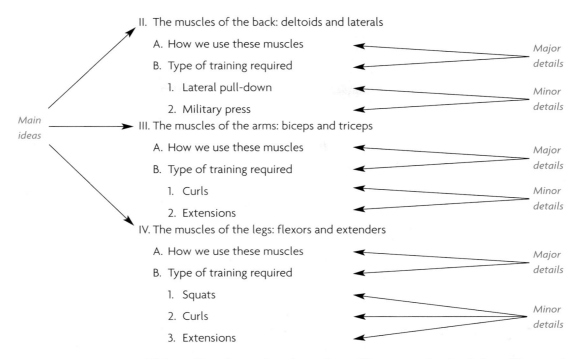

This outline shows that the writer will support the thesis by telling readers which muscles to train, what these muscles help them do, which exercises to do, and how to build and tone each muscle. The details are now more specific, and the outline has helped the writer to arrange them logically so that readers will be able to follow the writer's organizational pattern. Someone else writing on the same topic might choose to arrange the details differently or choose different details. How you support a thesis is up to you, as long as your details are specific and are arranged logically.

Achieve Coherence Between Paragraphs

Goal 3

Understand how using transitions and finding a controlling idea can help you make connections between the paragraphs of your essay.

Coherence means how well ideas hold together. Just as the sentences of a paragraph must flow smoothly and be logically related, so must the paragraphs of an essay. What ties the introductory, body, and concluding paragraphs together are your thesis, your controlling idea, and the transitional words and phrases within and between paragraphs. The following excerpt from the beginning of "Vocabulary Building," a chapter from Jess Stein's *The Word-a-Day Vocabulary Builder,* illustrates how the author uses a thesis and transitional words and phrases to achieve coherence between paragraphs.

> In borrowing so freely, the English language did just what we do as individuals to increase our personal vocabularies.

[When we see something strange or experience something new, either we take the name for it that someone else—whether a foreigner or not—is using or, on the basis of some real or fancied resemblance, we take an old word and apply it in a new situation.**]** This gives it a new meaning and us a new word.

Thesis

Kangaroo is an example. Captain Cook first saw a kangaroo during his exploration of the South Pacific (1768–1771). No European language had a name for this animal, much less an idea of it. It was a very strange and exciting thing. Therefore, it *had* to be talked about at once and that meant it had to have a name. There is a story that when Cook asked a native what the animal was, the native, in his own tongue, said, "I don't understand you." Since that statement sounded something like kangaroo," Cook mistook it for the creature's name and forthwith called it that.

Relates back to "We take the name . . . that someone else is using"

Repetition of a key word or term

Though Cook does not tell the story himself, it is a very old story and may very well be true. Nobody has ever found any word in any known Australian native language that describes the beast and sounds like kangaroo. But then, according to the story, that wasn't what the native really said anyway. And the story certainly illustrates a common event in conversation. A asks B a question which B doesn't understand. B gives A an answer which A doesn't understand, but thinks he or she does. Both go along under the impression that they have communicated with each other.

Repetition of a key word or term

At any rate, *kangaroo* is now the animal's name in English. A word which had never appeared in any European tongue before the latter part of the seventeenth century, and has never been traced to any Australian dialect, is now as fixed in the language as if it could be traced back to Latin. It's accepted as much as *wolf* or *rabbit* or any other name for an animal. . . .

These paragraphs are tied together by one controlling idea: how English borrows from other languages, either by accepting a word that someone else is using or by applying an old word to a new situation. Stein develops the thesis by the extended example of how *kangaroo* became part of the English language: Captain Cook adopted the word he thought he heard an Australian call the animal now known as a kangaroo. Three types of transitions help achieve coherence in Stein's paragraphs:

- Signal words that establish a relationship between paragraphs
- Repeating a word, phrase, or idea in one paragraph that is mentioned in the previous paragraph
- Repeating a key word or term throughout the passage

☑ CONCEPT CHECK
To achieve unity and coherence *within* paragraphs, use the strategies explained in Chapter 3.

The word *example* in the first sentence of Stein's second paragraph signals that an idea mentioned in the previous paragraph will now be illustrated. In the first sentence of the third paragraph, the phrase "the story" echoes the phrase "there is a story" from the previous paragraph. This transition indicates that the third paragraph will tell readers more about "the story." Throughout the four paragraphs, Stein's repetition of the word *kangaroo* lets readers know that the example continues and keeps their attention focused on the author's thesis.

Suppose you had written the first thesis statement in Exercise 5.1:

> Malls not only provide a place to shop but are popular entertainment centers as well.

Imagine also that you had begun writing an informal outline using the two subpoints given in the exercise.

1. They provide teenagers with a place to hang out.

2. They provide endless subjects for people watchers.

With a little rewriting, you could use these sentences as the topic sentences of the first and second body paragraphs following your introduction. To achieve smooth transitions between paragraphs, you could add a signal word or phrase to your topic sentences, as shown here.

If you visit a shopping mall on any weekend, you will probably see more people milling, or should I say "malling," around than buying. The mall is a place to hang out. For some, it is a place to exercise. For many, the mall is a cheap way to spend an evening. <u>Malls not only provide a place to shop but are popular entertainment centers as well.</u>

Thesis

"For example" signals that an example follows to illustrate one way the mall functions as an entertainment center

<u>For example</u>, the mall is a popular (hang-out) for teenagers. Teenagers looking for an afternoon or evening's (entertainment) will find it at their <u>local</u> mall. Even if they don't have any money, they can (hang out) in a video arcade and watch their friends play "World Heroes," or they can roam the aisles of Waldenbooks and see what's new in fiction. If the mall has a food court, they can get an inexpensive meal at a Nature's Table, Chik-fil-a, or Sbarro. They might even take in a movie, check out the new clothes in their favorite stores, or indulge a popular pastime, (people watching.)

Circles indicate repetition of key ideas.

"Another source" indicates that another example of the mall as entertainment center follows

Endless subjects for the (people watcher) stroll the mall, providing <u>another source of entertainment</u>. Mall walkers keep up a steady pace in their Nikes and warm-up suits. This group includes men, women, the old, the young—anybody who wants a good aerobic workout in a safe, stimulating, temperature-controlled environment. . . .

To complete the essay, you could add more examples of "subjects" for the people watcher, then one or more paragraphs that explain other ways in which the mall is an entertainment center. Finally, you could conclude your essay using one of the strategies explained later in this chapter.

Each time you revise your essay, look for ways to improve the coherence between paragraphs. For example, in the mall essay you might use "entertainment" or a related concept such as "pastime" or "recreation" as a controlling idea to repeat throughout the essay. You as a writer are free to organize your essay any way you like and to select whatever examples, facts, or reasons you think will support your thesis. Of course, not everyone lives near a large shopping mall. Where do city dwellers shop, and where do urban teenagers hang out with their friends? In your neighborhood or community, where do people go for entertainment, and what do they do? Let knowledge and experience shape what you write.

Whatever you write, remember to keep your audience in mind. Smooth transitions between paragraphs will give your essay coherence and help your readers keep up with you.

| Exercise 5.3 | Examine Gregg Easterbrook's chapter-opening essay for the three types of transitions listed below. Find and mark them in the text; then share your results with the rest of the class. |

- Signal words that establish a relationship between paragraphs
- Repeating a word, phrase, or idea in one paragraph that is mentioned in the previous paragraph
- Repeating a key word or term throughout the essay

Write an Effective Conclusion

Goal 4
Know how to write a concluding paragraph that effectively ends your essay and makes readers think critically.

A good conclusion brings your essay to a close that satisfies readers and does not leave them hanging. Have you ever turned the page of a book, story, or article, only to find you were at the end when you had expected to read more? This might happen to your readers if you do not end your essay on a note of finality that makes it clear that you have said all you intend to say about your topic. Of course, you do not want to say to readers, "Now I have concluded my essay." Instead, you need to be less obvious and more creative with your endings. Four of the introductory strategies explained in Chapter 4 also work well as concluding devices:

1. End with an anecdote that reinforces your thesis
2. End with a quotation and an explanation that relate to your thesis

3. Use additional facts and figures to reinforce your central idea

4. Ask one last revealing question that makes readers think about what you have said

The following examples illustrate possible thesis statements and concluding paragraphs of essays using each of these devices:

EXAMPLE 1: END WITH AN ANECDOTE

Thesis: *Superstitions are of three major types: those that come from religious beliefs and practices, those that have a historical basis, and those that have cultural or national origins.*

Concluding paragraph with anecdote underlined:

. . . A friend of mine accompanied me on a shopping trip recently. As we were walking down the street, talking and looking at the window displays, we suddenly had the choice of continuing on our path, which led directly under a ladder, or walking out of our way to avoid it. Without so much as a pause in the conversation, we walked around the ladder. In doing so, we did not stop to think that we were observing an age-old practice to ward off evil. If you should catch yourself falling into an old superstitious habit, just remember that it probably has some religious, historical, or cultural significance.

EXAMPLE 2: END WITH A QUOTATION AND AN EXPLANATION

Thesis: *To successfully prepare for an exam, be sure you first understand the material you want to remember; then use one of several common memory aids to help you study.*

Concluding paragraph with quotation and explanation underlined:

. . . Someone once said, "You cannot remember what you do not understand." Preparation alone is not enough, especially when your preparation consists of memorizing without understanding. To make the best use of the tips we have explained, first determine what will be on your test. Next, review your lecture and textbook notes and any other materials until you are sure you understand them. Then apply the memory aids that work best for you.

EXAMPLE 3: USE ADDITIONAL FACTS AND FIGURES

Thesis: *The evidence is conclusive that smoking is a health hazard and that those who smoke should make every effort to kick the habit.*

Concluding paragraph with a fact and a figure underlined:

. . . If you, like some smokers, still believe that the claims of tobacco use causing lung cancer, emphysema, and other diseases are largely exaggerated, talk to your doctor. Better yet, visit a hospital ward for emphysema patients. Although you may not realize it, deaths from tobacco-related illnesses outnumber deaths from drug abuse two to one. In fact, more people die every year from smoking than from automobile accidents.

EXAMPLE 4: ASK ONE LAST REVEALING QUESTION

Thesis: *Selecting a home computer is difficult unless you know exactly what you want your computer to do.*

Concluding paragraph with question underlined:

. . . Selecting a computer for home use is no easy task because technology is changing so rapidly that your computer will be outdated almost as soon as you get your programs running. If you do not require "state-of-the-art" equipment, pick a model that will do what you want it to do and will last for several years. Consider all the jobs you normally use a computer for, and buy one that does those tasks. Two years from now, will you still be happy with your computer, or will you be kicking yourself for the extra money you spent on fancy features you have never used?

You may also want to try these additional concluding strategies:

- Summarize thesis and support.
- Predict the future.
- Challenge your readers.

Summarize Thesis and Support

To summarize your thesis and support in a concluding paragraph, restate your thesis in different words, and briefly summarize the main ideas of your body paragraphs. Suppose you had written an essay using the expanded outline on pages 116–117. You could write the following concluding paragraph:

. . . Though there are many weight-training programs to choose from, one that focuses on building and toning the chest, back, arms, and legs will give you the best results. If you join a health club or gym, make sure you get the right type of training for each of these muscle groups.

This short paragraph restates the thesis and summarizes main ideas I–IV on the outline.

Predict the Future

Another way to conclude an essay is to point to some future outcome that readers can expect as a result of what you tell them in your essay. For example, you might conclude the essay on a good weight-training program by telling readers what they can expect and how long it will take.

The following paragraph concludes an essay about the presidential election of November 2000 and its outcome. The author believes that the problems associated with this election have lead to election reforms.

> . . . In conclusion, the presidential race of 2000 finally ended in a photo-finish, with both candidates carrying 49 percent of the popular vote and with George W. Bush winning by a nose in Florida—enough to give him that state's electoral votes. However, this election dragged on until voters tore up their racing forms, so to speak, and no one was placing any bets on its outcome. Two unprecedented events had voters steaming: Several major networks called the Florida vote for Al Gore before all the ballots were in, and hassles involving confused voters and confusing ballots, recount discrepancies, and lawsuits on both sides prolonged the outcome. As a result, many state legislatures have examined their election laws, and reforms have followed.

The paragraph begins with a summary of the election's outcome and the problems leading up to it and ends with a prediction about the future of presidential elections in the United States.

Challenge Your Readers

If you are writing persuasively about a topic, one of your purposes might be to get readers to change their behavior or to consider a better way of doing something.

The following conclusion from "Rock Lyrics and Violence Against Women," an essay by Caryl Rivers, is an example. Rivers's thesis is that rock music that depicts violence against women sends a subtle message to its listeners that the violence is OK.

> . . . I think something needs to be done. I'd like to see people in the industry respond to the problem. I'd love to see some women rock stars speak out against violence against women. I would like to see disc jockeys refuse air play to records and videos that contain such violence. At the very least, I want to see the end of the silence. I want journalists and parents and critics and performing artists to keep this issue alive in the public forum. I don't want people who are concerned about this issue labeled as bluenoses and bookburners and ignored.

> And I wish it wasn't always just women who were speaking out. Men have as large a stake in the quality of our civilization as women do in the long run. Violence is a contagion that infects at random. Let's hear something, please, from the men. . . .

Rivers's conclusion challenges readers to do something about the violence against women that is expressed in some rock music lyrics. Rivers also challenges men in particular to speak out.

[Exercise 5.4]

☑ **CONCEPT CHECK**
As a review of this chapter, go to *The Confident Writer* website and take the quiz for Chapter 5.

Apply what you have learned about concluding devices by doing this exercise with group members. First, review the group roles and responsibilities listed on the inside back cover. Next, complete the four-step activity that follows. Then evaluate your group's performance as your instructor recommends, or you can download the form from *The Confident Writer* website.

1. Read and discuss the concluding paragraphs of two essays of your choice from Unit 3.

2. Identify the concluding device each author uses.

3. Be able to explain whether or not the conclusion ends the essay on a note of finality and how it helps reinforce the essay's thesis.

4. Explain your group's results in writing to share with the rest of the class.

[Exercise 5.5]

Go to the home page of a newspaper or news service on the Internet. The *New York Times*, CNN, and Fox News are three sources to try. If you need help finding URLs and accessing these sources or others, ask your instructor or a librarian.

Next, read the lead article, or an article of your choice, and answer the following questions. Then share your results in a class discussion.

1. What is the title of the article? Who is the author?

2. What is the author's thesis?

3. What are at least two major pieces of evidence that support the thesis?

4. Read the opening and closing paragraphs. What introductory and concluding devices does the author use?

[Exercise 5.6] Look closely at the photo above. What are the people doing? What might they be thinking? How does the scene depicted in the photo relate to Gregg Easterbrook's chapter-opening essay? Find a sentence in the essay that would serve as a caption for the photograph.

‹‹ Topics for Writing ››

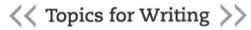

1. **React to the Reading.** In the chapter-opening essay, Gregg Easterbrook writes about stress and the toll it takes on our lives and expectations. What makes you stressed out? Write an essay in which you explain how to reduce stress.

2. **Use Your Experience.** Choose a topic from the list below and write an essay. Follow the suggestions offered in this chapter for supporting your thesis and concluding your essay.

   - How students can avoid exam-week stress
   - Ways voters can show support for a candidate
   - A leisure-time activity that has workplace advantages
   - A change you have lived through that has had a positive effect on your life

3. **Make a Real-World Connection.** Dressing for success is a theme of corporate business. Do clothes affect others' perceptions of us? Can the way that we dress determine the opportunities that are available to us? Write an essay in which you answer these questions.

4. **Go to the Web.** Search a job or career website for an article that provides tips for reducing stress at work. Write a short essay in which you summarize this information. Remember to include the source: title, author, URL, and your date of access.

‹‹ Checklist for Revision ››

Did you miss anything? Check off the following items as you revise and edit your essay.

- ❑ Do your body paragraphs represent major divisions of your essay?
- ❑ Do your paragraphs have topic sentences that relate to your thesis?
- ❑ Are your details in each paragraph specific and on topic?
- ❑ Have you arranged your ideas logically?
- ❑ Do you have smooth transitions between paragraphs?
- ❑ Have you concluded your essay on a note of finality?
- ❑ Have you used one of the concluding devices explained in this chapter?
- ❑ Are your sentences error free?

‹‹ Your Discovery Journal ››

Remember that a well-written essay has three parts: introduction, body, and conclusion. The introduction and conclusion, as explained in Chapters 4 and 5, help provide an organizational framework for your essay.

To reflect on what you have learned about introductory and concluding strategies, complete the following statements and explain your responses.

As an additional option, do this activity online by going to *The Confident Writer* website.

An introductory (or concluding) strategy that I have used successfully is _____.

A strategy that I have not yet used but would like to try is _____.

‹‹ Website Resources ››

This chapter's resources include

- ▬ Chapter 5 Exercises
- ▬ Chapter 5 Quiz
- ▬ Downloadable Charts: *Group Evaluation Form*
- ▬ More Topics for Writing
- ▬ Chapter 5 Summary

To access these learning and study tools, go to *The Confident Writer* website.

(((*Confident writers are persistent. They seek the*

positive results that come with revising

and editing, however long those processes take.)))

Revising and Editing Your Essays

What you already know about *revising* and editing

○ You may have had the experience of redoing an assignment or project that did not work out right the first time.

○ You know that people value persistence because of familiar sayings such as "Never give up" and "Don't be a quitter."

○ You have probably had to "take back," revise, or change what you have said at some time because you were misunderstood. The same holds true in writing.

Your *goals* for this chapter

[1] Know how to revise an essay by finding ways to improve its content, organization, and style.

[2] Be able to identify and eliminate the common errors in grammar, punctuation, and spelling that can cause confusion.

[3] Understand how to edit your essays for three common mistakes that cause needless clutter: wordiness, passive voice, and tired expressions.

[4] Know how to proofread, and remember to do a final editing check before handing in your paper.

Your writing represents you. Therefore, an essay you hand in to your instructor, an essay you write as part of a job application, or any other important piece of writing should be your best work. Your first draft is not your best work; it is a starting point. Through the rewriting process, you can improve the quality of your work and take pride in the message your writing sends.

Rewriting consists of two tasks: revising and editing. *Revising* an essay means making structural changes in content, organization, and style. *Editing* an essay means finding and correcting errors in grammar, spelling, and punctuation. Editing also involves trimming and tightening your essay to eliminate wordiness, passive voice, and tired expressions. Both revising and editing may take you through several drafts. Even when you think you have written your final draft, *proofreading* is a final editing check for any additional errors you may have overlooked.

Revising and editing take time. Give yourself enough time to complete your writing assignments. Many experienced writers let their ideas *incubate*. They write a first draft, let it sit for a day or two, and then come back to it with a whole new perspective. With each draft, your writing has the potential for more improvement. Use the strategies explained in this chapter to revise and edit with confidence.

[First Thoughts]

To build background for reading, explore your thoughts about revising and editing. Then answer the questions either on your own or in a group discussion:

1. What kinds of mistakes do you find when you edit your essays? Which ones do you usually overlook?

2. What does the word *clutter* mean to you? What sorts of things could create clutter in an essay?

3. Read the title, headnote, and first two paragraphs of the following excerpt. Based on this preview, what do you think will follow?

[Word Alert]

Before reading, preview the following words and definitions. During reading, use context clues and your dictionary to define any additional unfamiliar words.

laborious (4)	difficult
pompous (5)	boastful, self-important

ponderous (6)	burdensome
euphemism (6)	flattering term that replaces an unflattering one
tenure (9)	term of office or length of service
arsenal (10)	collection, storehouse
tedious (10)	boring, dull, tiresome
insidious (11)	not obvious
stupefied (11)	bored, made dull
component (12)	part
appended (12)	added on
festooned (13)	draped, adorned, covered with
prune (14)	cut, trim

Clutter

William Zinsser

William Zinsser has written many books, both fiction and nonfiction. He has also worked as a journalist and a college professor. The following excerpt comes from *On Writing Well.*

1   Fighting clutter is like fighting weeds—the writer is always slightly behind. New varieties sprout overnight, and by noon they are part of American speech. Consider what President Nixon's aide John Dean accomplished in just one day of testimony on television during the Watergate hearings. The next day everyone in America was saying "at this point in time" instead of "now."

2   Consider all the prepositions that are draped onto verbs that don't need any help. We no longer head committees. We head them up. We don't face problems anymore. We face up to them when we can free up a few minutes. A small detail, you may say—not worth bothering about. It *is* worth bothering about. Writing improves in direct ratio to the number of things we keep out of it that shouldn't be there. "Up" in "free up" shouldn't be there. Examine every word you put on paper. You'll find a surprising number that don't serve any purpose.

3   Take the adjective "personal," as in "a personal friend of mine," "his personal feeling" or "her personal physician." It's typical of hundreds of words that can be eliminated. The personal friend has come into the language to distinguish him or her from the business friend, thereby debasing both language and friendship. Someone's feeling *is* that person's personal feeling—that's what "his" means. As for the personal physician, that's the man or woman summoned to the dressing room of a stricken actress so she won't have to be treated by the impersonal physician assigned to the theater. Someday I'd like to see that person identified as "her doctor." Physicians are physicians, friends are friends. The rest is clutter.

4   Clutter is the laborious phrase that has pushed out the short word that means the same thing. Even before John Dean, people and businesses had stopped saying "now." They were saying "currently" ("all our operators are currently assisting other customers"), or "at the present time," or "presently" (which means "soon"). Yet the idea can always be expressed by "now" to mean the immediate moment ("Now I can see him"), or by "today" to mean the historical present ("Today prices are high"), or simply by the verb "to be" ("It is raining"). There's no need to say, "At the present time we are experiencing precipitation."

5   "Experiencing" is one of the worst clutterers. Even your dentist will ask if you are experiencing any pain. If he had his own kid in the chair he would say, "Does it hurt?" He would, in short, be himself. By using a more pompous phrase in his professional role he not only sounds more important; he blunts the painful edge of truth. It's the language of the flight attendant demonstrating the oxygen mask that will drop down if the plane should run out of air. "In the unlikely possibility that the aircraft should experience such an eventuality," she begins—a phrase so oxygen-depriving in itself that we are prepared for any disaster.

6   Clutter is the ponderous euphemism that turns a slum into a depressed socioeconomic area, garbage collectors into waste-disposal personnel and the town dump into the volume reduction unit. I think of Bill Mauldin's cartoon of two hoboes riding a freight car. One of them says, "I started as a simple bum, but now I'm hard-core unemployed." Clutter is political correctness gone amok. I saw an ad for a boys' camp designed to provide "individual attention for the minimally exceptional."

7   Clutter is the official language used by corporations to hide their mistakes. When the Digital Equipment Corporation eliminated 3,000 jobs its statement didn't mention layoffs; those were "involuntary methodologies." When an Air Force missile crashed, it "impacted with the ground prematurely." When General Motors had a plant shutdown, that was a "volume-related production-schedule adjustment." Companies that go belly-up have "a negative cash-flow position."

8   Clutter is the language of the Pentagon calling an invasion a "reinforced protective reaction strike" and justifying its vast budgets on the need for "counterforce deterrence." As George Orwell pointed out in "Politics and the English Language," an essay written in 1946 but often cited during the wars in Cambodia, Vietnam and Iraq, "political speech and writing are largely the defense of the indefensible. . . . Thus political language has to consist largely of euphemism, question-begging and sheer cloudy vagueness." Orwell's warning that clutter is not just a nuisance but a deadly tool has come true in the recent decades of American military adventurism. It was during George W. Bush's presidency that "civilian casualties" in Iraq became "collateral damage."

9   Verbal camouflage reached new heights during General Alexander Haig's tenure as President Reagan's secretary of state. Before Haig nobody had thought of saying "at this juncture of maturization" to mean "now." He told the American

people that terrorism could be fought with "meaningful sanctionary teeth" and that intermediate nuclear missiles were "at the vortex of cruciality." As for any worries that the public might harbor, his message was "leave it to Al," though what he actually said was: "We must push this to a lower decibel of public fixation. I don't think there's much of a learning curve to be achieved in this area of content."

10   I could go on quoting examples from various fields—every profession has its growing arsenal of jargon to throw dust in the eyes of the populace. But the list would be tedious. The point of raising it now is to serve notice that clutter is the enemy. Beware, then, of the long word that's no better than the short word: "assistance" (help), "numerous" (many), "facilitate" (ease), "individual" (man or woman), "remainder" (rest), "initial" (first), "implement" (do), "sufficient" (enough), "attempt" (try), "referred to as" (called) and hundreds more. Beware of all the slippery new fad words: paradigm and parameter, prioritize and potentialize. They are all weeds that will smother what you write. Don't dialogue with someone you can talk to. Don't interface with anybody.

11   Just as insidious are all the word clusters with which we explain how we propose to go about our explaining: "I might add," "It should be pointed out," "It is interesting to note." If you might add, add it. If it should be pointed out, point it out. If it is interesting to note, *make* it interesting; are we not all stupefied by what follows when someone says, "This will interest you"? Don't inflate what needs no inflating: "with the possible exception of" (except), "due to the fact that" (because), "he totally lacked the ability to" (he couldn't), "until such time as" (until), "for the purpose of" (for).

12   Is there any way to recognize clutter at a glance? Here's a device my students at Yale found helpful. I would put brackets around every component in a piece of writing that wasn't doing useful work. Often just one word got bracketed: the unnecessary preposition appended to a verb ("order up"), or the adverb that carries the same meaning as the verb ("smile happily"), or the adjective that states a known fact ("tall skyscraper"). Often my brackets surrounded the little qualifiers that weaken any sentence they inhabit ("a bit," "sort of"), or phrases like "in a sense," which don't mean anything. Sometimes my brackets surrounded an entire sentence—the one that essentially repeats what the previous sentence said, or that says something readers don't need to know or can figure out for themselves. Most first drafts can be cut by 50 percent without losing any information or losing the author's voice.

13   My reason for bracketing the students' superfluous words, instead of crossing them out, was to avoid violating their sacred prose. I wanted to leave the sentence intact for them to analyze. I was saying, "I may be wrong, but I think this can be deleted and the meaning won't be affected. But *you* decide. Read the sentence without the bracketed material and see if it works." In the early weeks of the term I handed back papers that were festooned with brackets. Entire paragraphs were bracketed. But soon the students learned to put mental

14   brackets around their own clutter, and by the end of the term their papers were almost clean. Today many of those students are professional writers, and they tell me, "I still see your brackets—they're following me through life."

You can develop the same eye. Look for the clutter in your writing and prune it ruthlessly. Be grateful for everything you can throw away. Reexamine each sentence you put on paper. Is every word doing new work? Can any thought be expressed with more economy? Is anything pompous or pretentious or faddish? Are you hanging on to something useless just because you think it's beautiful?

15   Simplify, simplify.

≪ The Critical Reader ≫

[CENTRAL IDEA]

1. "Clutter" is a broad topic. How does Zinsser limit his topic? What does he mean by "clutter"?

2. In your own words, what is Zinsser's thesis?

3. What is Zinsser's purpose—what does he want writers to be able to do?

[EVIDENCE]

4. Does Zinsser support his thesis with mainly facts, reasons, or examples?

5. Is Zinsser's essay coherent? What transitional words and phrases do you find?

[IMPLICATIONS]

6. Zinsser's first paragraph contains a *metaphor,* a figurative comparison that makes a point: "Fighting clutter is like fighting weeds." Zinsser continues the metaphor later in that same paragraph when he says that new varieties "sprout" overnight. Can you find other metaphors in the essay?

7. Are there occasions when it may be appropriate to use a tired expression in writing? For example, could you use one appropriately in dialogue, in direct quotations, or in certain kinds of business correspondence? Or should you always substitute a fresh expression for a tired one?

[WORD CHOICE]

8. Jargon is occupational slang. It may be acceptable on the job, but it clutters writing because people outside the occupation do not know what it means. Zinsser's examples of political jargon include "at this point in time" for *now* and "reinforced protective reaction strike" for *invasion.* Business jargon includes terms such as "finalize" for *end* and "empower" for *strengthen.* What other examples of jargon can you think of, and where have you heard them?

‹‹ The Critical Thinker ››

To examine William Zinsser's essay in more depth, follow these suggestions for reflection, discussion, and writing.

1. Who is Zinsser's audience, and how can you tell?

2. In his essay, Zinsser explains seven types of clutter. Explain each type, using at least one of Zinsser's examples.

3. Read an article from your local newspaper, an article from your college newspaper, an article from a popular magazine, and a scholarly article from a journal. Your college librarian can help you locate sources. As you read each article, list any examples of clutter that you find. What conclusion can you draw from the type and frequency of clutter you found in these articles?

4. Review Zinsser's examples of clutter and the tired expressions listed in Figure 6.5 on page 149. What additional examples of clutter can you recall from either your reading, your writing, or conversation?

How to Revise Your Essay

Goal 1

Know how to revise an essay by finding ways to improve its content, organization, and style.

It is hard to try to think of everything at once. Most of us do better when we concentrate on one thing at a time. Rather than trying to make your first draft perfect and, therefore, your only draft, think of the first draft as a *discovery draft*, as explained on page 10. In this draft you will *begin* to explore your subject, come up with a preliminary thesis and support, and perhaps discover an organizational pattern that seems right for your topic and purpose. You may need to rewrite your first draft several times to improve its content, organization, and style.

Improve the Content

☑ CONCEPT CHECK
Changing only one or two words, or merely correcting errors, is not revising. Revising means rethinking, reworking, and rewriting the entire essay to make it better.

If you were to ask other students what they find difficult about writing, many of them would answer, "Thinking of something to say." Because you too may find it difficult to think of what to say, your writing may be filled with *generalities,* statements that are too broad to provide readers with a clear vision of what you mean. Specific details not only make your writing clear; they also make it interesting, alive. The following example shows a general statement that has been rewritten to make it more specific.

General   A large wave came out of nowhere, causing damage at Daytona Beach.

Specific   At Daytona Beach on July 3, 1992, a towering twelve-foot wall of water crashed to shore, overturning cars and causing injury to beachgoers who were unable to scramble to safety. Scientists could not account for "the mystery wave," though some thought it may have resulted from an earthquake. One survivor, who was driving along the beach at the time the wave hit, later said, "You haven't surfed 'til you've done it in a Jeep."

The general statement becomes more specific because *content* was added in the form of specific details: a date, a description of the wave, examples of the type of damage that occurred, a possible explanation of the wave's cause, and a quotation from someone who was there. The addition of content not only creates a picture of the wave in readers' minds but also gives them a sense of being there.

To rewrite an essay for *content,* read it one paragraph at a time, and underline general words, phrases, or statements that you can make more specific. Make notes in the margin to remind yourself where you need to add content. To gather information, explore your memory, use firsthand observation, interview people, or do some research. For example, if you want to write about Daytona's mystery wave or some other natural disaster, such as a hurricane or flood, you can get all the information you need by going to the library or the Internet and researching newspaper articles that reported the story.

The following essay is annotated to show where the writer needs to add content.

EARTHQUAKE!

What had you heard that made you want to live there?

Last summer, I visited my cousins in California. I had really looked forward to this trip because I had heard so much about California. In fact, I used to think I wanted to live there someday. Now I am not so sure. On my visit, we had an earthquake. No one was hurt, but the damage it caused and the cleaning up we had to do afterward made me realize how disastrous an earthquake can be.

What month? What city? What are your cousins' names?

How did it feel? Compare it to something. Replace "things" with specific words. Add details to explain what each person did. Describe the damage more. Add examples—dishes? lamps?

We were all sitting around the living room watching television when we felt this little tremor. Then there was another one that lasted longer and got worse. The house began to shake, and things were falling off the shelves. My uncle told us all to either find a doorway and brace ourselves against it or get under a table. When it was all over, the whole house was a mess.

How long? How much worse? Can you describe it? Add one or two examples.

The damage was just unbelievable. Part of the roof had caved in. Just about anything that could break was broken. My aunt lost some of her prized possessions. We were without water and electricity.

What did you do?

It took us about a week to clean up the mess, fix the roof, and make the house look halfway decent again. When my visit was over, there were still some things left to be done. Even with all this trouble, I still had a good time. In a way, disaster brought us closer.

How long?

Add examples.

Give an example.

[Exercise 6.1] Rewrite the general statements below to add *content* in the form of specific details. To find information, use resources such as your college catalog for Question 1, your experience for Questions 2 and 3, and firsthand observation for Questions 4 and 5. Questions in parentheses indicate which parts of the statements need specific details added.

1. My college provides support services (What kind?) that can be helpful (How?) to students (Which ones?).

2. Recently (When?), I had a bad car accident (What was the damage? How did it happen? Who was involved?).

3. I plan to support (How?) my candidate (Who?) in the next (Date?) election (For what office?).

4. A certain television program (Which one?) is harmful for children (How?) because of the bad values it expresses (What values? How does it express them? What makes them bad?).

5. I would recommend (To whom?) a certain movie (Which one?) for several reasons (What are the reasons?).

[Exercise 6.2] Read your draft of an essay in progress and identify sentences or paragraphs that need rewriting for content. Determine what kind of information you should add. Then rewrite the essay.

Achieve Better Organization

Chapter 1 explains that the direction of development in an essay moves from the *introduction* and *thesis statement,* to the *support* of the thesis with *evidence,* to the essay's *conclusion.* The direction of development is expressed in the essay's three basic parts: *introduction, body,* and *conclusion.* Each part has a specific function.

The introduction builds a context for your thesis by either supplying background information, relating an anecdote, explaining a quotation relevant to the thesis, supplying interesting facts and figures, or asking a revealing question. These introductory devices set the stage for the thesis, which is the central idea of your essay. The introduction also clarifies your purpose for your readers and tells why you have chosen the topic and what you want to tell readers about it. To achieve better organization in the introduction, revise to achieve one of the following goals: make better use of an introductory device; have a more specific or clearly stated thesis that meets the criteria of *topic* and *comment* broken down into *opinion, purpose,* and *parts.*

The body of your essay should contain enough specific details, such as facts, reasons, and examples, to fully develop your thesis. In addition, the details should be unified and coherent. To achieve better organization in the body of your essay, revise each paragraph so that it has the following:

- A topic sentence that clearly relates to your essay's thesis
- Details that do not stray from the topic so that each paragraph has unity
- Transitional words and phrases between paragraphs to achieve coherence
- Signal words within paragraphs to achieve coherence

The conclusion ends the essay on a note of finality by summarizing your thesis and support, predicting a future outcome for readers, or challenging readers to change an opinion or to take action. Other concluding devices are an anecdote, a quotation and explanation, a question that reinforces the thesis, or an additional fact or figure that brings home your central idea. To achieve better organization in the conclusion, revise it to make better use of a concluding device or to more clearly reinforce the thesis.

Before you begin the revision process, determine whether your draft has the three essential parts and whether they fulfill the needed functions. Either make an outline of your essay to find out what is already there and what needs revising, or ask yourself the questions listed in Figure 6.1.

☑ **CONCEPT CHECK**
If you have problems with organization, try outlining your draft. You will quickly see which parts of your essay are logically organized and which ones are not.

[Exercise 6.3]

Using the questions listed in Figure 6.1, evaluate one of your own essays for organization. Or go to *The Confident Writer* website, and click on "Charts for Downloading." Print out the chart *Organization Checklist* and use it to evaluate your essay for organization.

Figure 6.1   Questions to Ask About Organization

PARTS OF AN ESSAY	QUESTIONS TO ASK YOURSELF
Introduction	Have I used an appropriate *introductory strategy*?
	Is my *purpose* clearly stated or implied?
	Do I have a sufficiently *limited topic*?
	Do I have an effective *thesis statement*?
	Is my writing directed to a specific *audience*?
Body	Does each paragraph have a *topic sentence* or clearly implied main idea?
	Do *topic sentences* relate to the thesis?
	Does my essay have *coherence*; that is, are my ideas arranged in a logical sequence, and do they flow smoothly?
	Do I have appropriate *transitions* between paragraphs and between ideas within paragraphs?
	Does my essay have *unity*; that is, do I stay on the topic?
Conclusion	Have I used an appropriate *concluding device*?
	Does my conclusion end my essay on a *note of finality,* or does it leave readers hanging?

Sharpen Your Style

The way you express yourself in writing is your writing *style*. Though many factors influence a writer's style, keep these three basic factors in mind as you revise your essays: *diction, tone,* and *sentence variety.*

Diction means *word choice.* Good diction is a matter of selecting words that are appropriate for your audience and purpose and that clearly convey your meaning. In the following passage, the writer's purpose is to convince readers that bats are interesting mammals that we should appreciate for the important ecological role they play. The writer assumes that the audience may include readers who fear bats or who react to them with disgust.

BATS

1   Every evening about sundown bat-lovers, skeptics, and the just plain curious gather at the Congress Street bridge in Austin, Texas, where one of nature's most dramatic events unfolds. The bridge is the home of more than half a million Mexican bats, one of the largest colonies in the United States. As the sun fades and as the lights in high-rise buildings across the river slowly blink on, the bats begin their exodus from under the bridge. For several minutes thousands of the small, furry mammals form what looks like two columns of black smoke

originating at opposite ends of the bridge. The bats spiral upward until the two columns merge into one over the middle of the river. Still the bats come, their long black trail spiraling upward over the river until it is too dark to see them.

2   Despite their bad reputation as disease carriers and their association in the public imagination with horrific images of vampirism, bats, like most wild animals, are harmless to humans if left alone. Though there are about a thousand species of bats, they have certain similarities in appearance. Most of them have furry bodies and dog-like faces with bright eyes and sharp teeth. Their wings consist of membranes stretched over bone that look like the halves of an umbrella. Bats are not blind, although most of them use high frequency sounds to communicate, navigate, and find prey. Much to the delight of humans, most bats eat insects. A large colony of bats can consume billions of insects in one season. Scientists say that without bats to control their numbers, insect populations would increase at a rate that would endanger crops and other forms of plant life.

3   So we owe a debt of gratitude to our friend the bat. In fact, many people encourage the formation of small bat colonies in their own backyards by building bat houses: wooden boxes that are partitioned inside and open at the bottom. Bats hang onto the partitions to sleep, hibernate, and nurse their young. At sundown people who have installed bat houses can sit on their porches and watch a mini-version of Austin's nightly drama with the added benefit of a reduction in their backyard mosquito population.

The choice of words in this passage characterizes the bat as a friendly creature in the sense that it performs an essential service for humans: keeping the insect population under control. For example, the word *home* describes the bat's habitat under the bridge. *Home* has pleasant associations for most readers, so it is a better choice than the more scientific *habitat*. The writer could have said that the bat has a rat-like face but instead chose *dog-like*, a descriptive phrase that will seem friendlier to most readers. The repetition of *drama* to describe the colony's flight at sundown characterizes this event as an awe-inspiring natural occurrence and underscores the idea that we should not fear bats.

Tone, as explained in Chapter 2, means *voice*—how you would want your voice to sound if you were reading your essay aloud. "Tone" also means *mood:* the overall feeling readers get when they read your essay. Diction is a part of tone. Diction is the choice of words, and tone is the overall effect or "sound" of those words. A textbook chapter has a teaching tone that fits its informational purpose. A political speech may have a tone that varies from folksy to outraged to match whatever persuasive purpose the speaker has in mind. Tone, therefore, is linked to purpose. The tone you choose depends upon your purpose in writing and what you expect readers to feel as they read your essay.

A tone can be amusing, angry, objective, serious, or pleading, to mention a few of the many choices available to you as a writer. The tone in "Bats" is in-

formal and conversational. The writer has avoided using scientific or technical terms and has chosen words for their visual effect to appeal to a general
audience. For example, *smoke* describes what the mass of bats in flight looks
like. The bats' wings are compared in appearance to the *halves of an umbrella.*
Though perhaps not a scientifically accurate comparison, it creates a familiar
image for readers. In the essay, the sun *fades;* the buildings *across the river* are
high-rise ones; and the lights *slowly blink on.* These words and phrases create
an image of an urban setting in which the natural drama takes place, and they
create a *peaceful* mood. Following are a few brief passages and their tones.
Words and phrases that establish each tone are underlined.

Passages	Tones
1. In discontinuing its mosquito control program, the county commission has once again displayed poor judgment. With a reported encephalitis outbreak threatening our continued health, we voters should send a message to the so-called guardians of public health who advised the commission to make this unwise budget cut.	Angry (The choice of words encourages readers' mistrust of the commission and its decision.)
2. Still water is a breeding ground for mosquitoes. They lay their eggs in moist environments where water collects in pools. Swamps, for example, are a typical breeding place, as are pools of water that stagnate in drainage ditches and canals.	Objective (Examples and definitions are hallmarks of this tone, as are word choices that are free of emotion and judgment.)
3. Parents, please do not send your children outdoors to play without protection from insect bites and stings. Mosquitoes and flies carry diseases. Yellow jacket stings can be deadly, and many children have allergic reactions to insect bites. I urge you to shop for a safe insect repellent and to use it. I implore you to keep your children's arms, legs, and feet covered during times of the year when biting and stinging insects are most prevalent.	Pleading (The three underlined words indicate a pleading tone, one that begs readers to feel or act in a certain way. A plea is stronger than a simple request.)

4. I doubt that you could live on a steady diet of mosquitoes, though you may enjoy them as an appetizer or delicacy. Covered with chocolate, they are a sweet source of protein. Of course, you may have to eat a glob of them the size of a raisin to taste them, and you may enjoy the experience more if you close your eyes.

Amusing (The tone results from the contrast between seriousness in the underlined food terms, and humor in the slang term *glob*.)

[**Exercise 6.4**] Compare the tones of any two essays from *The Confident Writer* that you have read. How are their tones different? How does each writer's tone fit the purpose? What specific words or phrases help you identify the tone in each essay?

Sentence variety can keep your writing from becoming monotonous. If all your sentences are short, simple sentences, your writing may sound choppy and unsophisticated. If you *vary* your sentence length and type so that you have a mix of short and long sentences that begin in different ways, your writing will be more interesting, and you will begin to develop a more mature style. Using coordination (Unit 4, B.4) and subordination (Unit 4, B.5) to combine sentences is one way you can begin to add variety to your sentences.

To revise an essay for style, first read through the whole essay and ask yourself whether the tone is what you want and one that suits your purpose. If it is, read through your essay again, one paragraph at a time, underlining all your descriptive words and phrases. Examine each one of these to see if your word choices, or diction, effectively convey your tone. If they do not, then substitute better choices. A dictionary and thesaurus are helpful guides. If your tone is unclear, think about your whole essay in terms of your purpose and decide which tone you want, then proceed as above, underlining descriptive words and choosing more appropriate ones. Second, one paragraph at a time, analyze your sentences for length and type. If you are using mostly sentences of one length or type, rewrite some of your sentences to achieve variety. See Unit 4, B.7 for four ways to add variety to your sentences. See also Figure 6.2 for a list of tone words and their meanings.

Figure 6.2   Tone Words and Definitions

amused	comical, provoking laughter
angry	showing rage
apathetic	indifferent, unconcerned
arrogant	displaying undeserved importance or pride
bitter	harsh and resentful
cheerful	happy, expressing goodwill
condescending	displaying a superior attitude
compassionate	showing pity and sorrow for others' suffering
critical	judgmental, evaluating on the basis of worth
cynical	scornful and bitterly mocking
detached	unemotional, uninvolved, impersonal
distressed	upset, worried
earnest	deeply sincere
evasive	vague, intending to be unclear
formal	proper, conventional
indignant	angry with feelings of injustice
intense	profound, showing depth of feeling
ironic	saying one thing but meaning another
mocking	making fun of
objective	considering all sides without judging
outraged	shocked, morally offended
optimistic	positive, looking on the good side
playful	humorous and full of fun
pleading	begging, showing urgency
pompous	displaying an inflated sense of self-worth, egotistical
reverent	respectful
sentimental	overly sensitive or emotional
serious	concerned, responsible
solemn	serious and dignified

A writer's tone *conveys a mood, feeling, or attitude toward the topic.*

[**Exercise 6.5**]

As previously explained, *tone* in writing refers to the mood or feeling that an author's words convey. One way of understanding tone is to think of it as *attitude expressed in words.* A visual exercise may help.

Look at the panel of photographs above. Examine each facial expression. Then choose one photograph and write a paragraph about it. First, find the tone word in Figure 6.2 that best describes the person's expression. Then explain what the person seems to be feeling or thinking and why. Finally, choose a partner and read each other's paragraphs. Then select one paragraph to share in a class discussion.

Eliminate Surface Errors

Goal 2 · Be able to identify and eliminate the common errors in grammar, punctuation, and spelling that can cause confusion.

Surface errors are the mistakes in grammar, punctuation, and spelling that distract from the content of your essay. Because surface errors stand out, they call attention to themselves, and readers may notice them before they have a chance to consider your thesis and support. If your writing contains surface errors, you need to understand why you make them and what you can do to eliminate them. Surface errors usually result from one or both of the following conditions:

1. Inconsistent application of the rules of Standard English

2. Careless mistakes, like typographical errors, that occur when you are paying more attention to content than to mechanics

To apply the rules of Standard English consistently, brush up on them by reviewing the explanations and exercises throughout Unit 4. To find your careless mistakes, proofread.

Edit for Grammar, Punctuation, and Spelling

Become aware of the kinds of errors you most frequently make by carefully examining essays that have been graded and returned to you. Suppose, for example, that your essays often contain pronoun agreement errors. When you proofread, check every pronoun to make sure it agrees in number with the person or thing it refers to. Proofreading essays before you hand them in should help you find typographical errors and other mistakes.

Figure 6.3 on the following page lists examples of some common grammatical errors and how to correct them. Read the figure, and find the type of mistake you most often make.

[Exercise 6.6] Practice your editing skills on the following paragraph by reading it carefully to find and correct grammatical errors. Share your findings with the rest of the class.

> Recently my husband and me took our children to visit my father who lives on a farm in Pennsylvania. He raises cattle and pigs he grows all his own vegetables. He sell most of them, but he saves enough to have all he wants to eat. He has an apple orchard and he has a pretty good deal going with an Amish settlement near where he lives. He gives them apples for making cider in exchange for all the cider you can drink. We thought it would be good for our children to see what it is like living in the country, and it will not hurt them to participate in the chores. The trip was one of the best we have ever had. Much to our surprise, the children loved helping their grandfather milk the cows, feed the pigs, and tend the garden. Our sixteen-year-old sold vegetables from my father's produce stand at the entrance to his property and was thrilled that they let her keep some of the proceeds. Driving home, the visit was one we decided to repeat in the future.

When you are editing, check for correctly punctuated sentences. When you are drafting, and even when you are writing your final copy, it is easy to leave out commas and end punctuation marks. A quick review of what to look for may help you find and correct punctuation errors. See Unit 4, Sections C.1–C.8 for an explanation of how to use commas and for more punctuation rules.

Spelling errors can interfere with the good ideas you are trying to communicate. If you know you have a spelling problem, use the dictionary when you write. Spelling errors may result from two major problems: not knowing the common rules of spelling, and confusing the spelling of words that

Figure 6.3   Correcting Common Grammatical Errors

ERROR	EXAMPLE	CORRECTION
Fragment	When the lights went out.	Connect the fragment to an independent clause: "When the lights went out, we were plunged into darkness."
Comma splice	John felt his way around the room, he was looking for candles and matches.	Replace comma with period or semicolon: "John felt his way around the room; he was looking for candles and matches."
Run-on sentence	We waited for the lights to come back on after an hour we decided to call the power company.	Find the two independent clauses. Separate them with a period or semicolon: "We waited for the lights to come back on. After an hour we decided to call the power company."
Dangling modifier	Sitting in the dark, light came into the room from the full moon outside.	Who was sitting in the dark? After the comma following the modifier, insert *who* or *what* the modifier describes: "Sitting in the dark, we saw the light that came into the room from the full moon outside."
Pronoun-antecedent agreement	Someone remembered that they had a battery-operated radio.	*Someone* is singular, and it is the antecedent of *they*. Change *they* to either *he* or *she* to agree with *Someone:* "Someone remembered that she had a battery-operated radio."
Pronoun case	John and her went to look for the radio	*Her* is one of the subjects of the sentence. *Her* is an objective-case pronoun. Change *her* to *she*, which is a subjective-case pronoun: "John and she went to look for the radio."
Subject-verb agreement	We heard on the news that people's lights was out all over the county.	Make the verb agree with the subject: "We heard on the news that people's lights were out all over the county."
Inconsistent tense	It was a power blackout, so we listen to the radio and waited for the lights to come back on.	Since the blackout took place in the past, all the verbs should be in the past tense. Make *listen* a past-tense verb: "It was a power blackout, so we listened to the radio and waited for the lights to come back on."
Inconsistent point of view	When the lights came back on, we had gotten so used to being in the dark that you had to adjust your eyes.	*You* is inconsistent because the point of view is first-person plural. Change *you* to *we* and *your* to *our* for consistency: "When the lights came back on, we had gotten so used to being in the dark that we had to adjust our eyes."

look or sound alike. See Unit 4, E.3 for an explanation of common spelling rules. See also Unit 4, E.2 for an explanation of the most commonly confused words.

Learn from Your Mistakes

How much editing you have to do depends upon how many errors you usually make. If your only problem is a misspelled word now and then, one reading may be enough for you to find and correct your spelling errors. If you usually make several errors in grammar, punctuation, and spelling, you may have to do several readings: one for grammar, one for punctuation, one for spelling, and a final reading to see whether you missed anything. Figure 6.4 below contains an editing checklist that will help you analyze your essays for errors. To download copies of the checklist, go to *The Confident Writer* website.

Your analysis of several essays may reveal that your errors are either random or of certain types. Once you know your most common type of error, you can concentrate on looking for it while you are editing.

Figure 6.4   Your Editing Checklist

	NUMBER OF ERRORS PER ESSAY					
TYPE OF ERROR	**ESSAY #1**	**ESSAY #2**	**ESSAY #3**	**ESSAY #4**	**ESSAY #5**	**ESSAY #6**
Fragment						
Comma splice						
Run-on sentence						
Dangling modifier						
Pronoun-antecedent agreement						
Pronoun case						
Subject-verb agreement						
Inconsistent tense						
Inconsistent point of view						
Punctuation						
Spelling						
Other error						
Other error						

What kinds of surface errors do you make? What is your most frequent type of error? Search the Internet for a website that provides free exercises or tests for grammar review, practice, and skill building. Many colleges have such material available on their websites. Find an exercise that addresses your most frequent type of error. Complete the exercise and download it if possible or summarize your results to share in class. Your instructor or librarian can help you with URLs.

Trim and Tighten Your Writing

Understand how to edit your essays for three common mistakes that cause needless clutter: wordiness, passive voice, and tired expressions.

William Zinsser's essay on pages 129–132 explains how our writing can become cluttered with empty words and phrases that interfere with effective communication. *Trimming and tightening* an essay means editing it to eliminate three kinds of clutter:

- wordiness
- passive voice
- tired expressions

As you trim clutter from your essay, tighten it by eliminating wordiness, changing passive voice to active voice, and substituting original ideas for tired phrases.

Eliminate Wordiness

Wordiness is what results when you use two or more words to say what you could say in one carefully chosen word. *Due to* and *due to the fact that* are wordy phrases that mean *because*. Another good replacement for these phrases is *since*. As Zinsser says, *now* is a better word choice than *at this point in time* or *at present*. If you find *until such time as* in your essay, cross it out, and write *until*. You will say the same thing and do it in fewer words. Wordiness is also called *filler* because it pads your writing with needless words and phrases.

Trim and tighten the following paragraph to eliminate wordiness. Share your results with the rest of the class.

> Due to the fact that many students work and have families to care for, attending college in today's society can become a juggling act. A student's responsibilities are like a juggler's clubs. There is one club for attending classes, one for doing homework, and another for studying. All three clubs have to be kept in the air. If students drop just one club, for example, if they miss too many classes, they

may find themselves withdrawn from a course. There are other clubs in the juggling act of students who have jobs and families. They have to add housework clubs and work-responsibility clubs to their school-responsibility clubs. There is only one way to keep all those clubs in the air, and that is to manage time effectively. Students can do this by making schedules for completion of work, working with employers to arrange convenient hours, and delegating chores to family members. Until such time as they are willing to take these steps, students may find that their juggling acts have flopped.

Change Passive Voice to Active Voice

Verbs are either *active* or *passive*. If the subject of the sentence performs an action, the verb is in *active voice.*

> The student wrote the essay.

The student writes, so the verb is in active voice. If the subject of the sentence receives the action, the verb is in *passive voice.*

> The essay was written by the student.

In this sentence, the subject receives the action, so the verb is in passive voice.

Active voice is usually more effective than passive voice because sentences written in active voice are less wordy and more direct. Passive voice can also be confusing when the performer of the action is not specified. For example:

> The essay was left in the instructor's mailbox.

In this sentence, it is not clear who left the essay. To change this sentence into active voice, add a subject:

> Toby left the essay in the instructor's mailbox.

Some form of the verb *to be*, such as *is* or *was*, precedes the main verb in a passive-voice sentence. When you edit a sentence by changing the passive voice to active, you get rid of the extra *to be* verbs that precede the main verb and any other words that do not fit the new sentence.

> Ryan's hair was cut by Nina.   (passive)
> Nina cut Ryan's hair.   (active)

The active-voice sentence leaves out the extra words *was* and *by.*

☑ CONCEPT CHECK
Do you use the passive voice? Check one of your essays. Underline any examples of passive voice you can find. Then rewrite them in active voice.

[Exercise 6.9] Trim and tighten the following paragraph by finding and changing passive voice to active. Share your results with the rest of the class.

Ben is angry with Cloudy Vale Utilities Company because he feels that he is not getting satisfactory service. His bills keep going up and up, yet the service gets worse and worse. Every day the power goes off for a few seconds. It can happen at any time; for example, one day the power may go off at 3:30 P.M., and the next day it may go off at 6:00 A.M. Although the electricity stays off for only a short time, a lot of trouble is caused by it. Ben's daughter's homework is done on a computer. When the power goes off, everything on the screen is lost, and it has to be rewritten from memory. On weekends, Ben likes to record the football games on his DVD player. If the power goes off during the recording process, it wipes out his programming, and he gets some other show instead of the game. Another problem is that whenever the electricity goes off, all the clocks in the house have to be reset. Ben's family has seven digital clocks: one on the microwave oven, one in each bedroom, one in the utility room, and one each in the family and living rooms. Several letters of complaint have been written, and phone calls have been made to top executives at Cloudy Vale Utilities. Though they listen politely, nothing has been done about Ben's problem. That is why he has concluded that the service is unsatisfactory.

Replace Tired Expressions

A *tired expression,* also called a "cliché," is any word or phrase, old saying, or slang expression that has lost its freshness and originality because of overuse. Since normal everyday conversation is filled with tired expressions, you may have to work at keeping them out of your writing. When you edit, eliminate tired expressions and replace them with more interesting and appropriate choices. Figure 6.5 on the next page lists some tired expressions to avoid.

[Exercise 6.10]

Apply what you have learned about tired expressions by doing this exercise with group members. First, review the group roles and responsibilities listed on the inside back cover of *The Confident Writer*. Next, complete the following three-step activity, and share your results with the rest of the class. Evaluate your discussion as your instructor recommends, or go to *The Confident Writer* website, where you can download the group evaluation form.

1. Read and discuss each other's essays in progress.

2. Make a list of any tired expressions you find in the essays.

3. Work together to write a fresh and interesting replacement for each tired expression on your list.

Figure 6.5   Tired Expressions to Avoid

in today's society	at a loss for words	You're history.
in this world in which we live	a blessing in disguise	been there, done that
in this fast-paced society	through thick and thin	in your dreams
Mother Nature	day in and day out	whatever
after all is said and done	hustle and bustle	a no-brainer
last but not least	the whole nine yards	clueless
short but sweet	over and done with	pretty as a picture
live and let live	now and then	sigh of relief
easier said than done	I'm outta here.	sick and tired
it goes without saying	your worst nightmare	nine times out of ten
time and time again	no pain, no gain	

Use Proofreading Strategies

Goal 4 — **Know how to proofread, and remember to do a final editing check before handing in your paper.**

Save proofreading as a last step before handing in your essay. This is your final editing check to make sure you have not overlooked any surface errors. Your final copy should be as neat and error-free as possible.

Most instructors require typewritten essays, so if you have never typed an essay using a word processor, now is a good time to learn. Your college may provide computer access and training for students. If it does, take advantage of this service. In addition, try the following suggestions to make proofreading a productive task.

- **Let your ideas incubate.** Write your essay well enough ahead of the due date so that you can put it aside for a day or two. When you go back to it, the ideas will seem fresh. You will have a different perspective and may be able to see new ways to improve your work. Proofreading may help you spot errors that you might have missed earlier.

- **Pace yourself.** Proofread one line at a time. Take a wide ruler or folded sheet of paper and move it slowly down the page, revealing only one line at a time. When you find an error, circle, underline, or highlight it, or annotate in the margin to indicate what type of error it is. Use correction symbols such as *sp* for spelling. When you have finished marking your draft, go back and correct your errors. Develop and use a marking system that works for you.

- **Read backwards.** It may sound silly, but reading backwards works. It is easy to overlook errors when you are paying attention to the content.

Reading backwards interrupts the logical flow of ideas and makes any errors stand out. Go to the end of your essay. Starting with the last word of the last sentence, read back to the beginning. This strategy works especially well for spotting spelling errors.

- **Read aloud.** Many errors that you might overlook when reading silently will stand out when you read your essay aloud. Errors in subject-verb agreement and pronoun-antecedent agreement can produce awkward-sounding sentences. To make the process of proofreading even more productive, exchange essays with a partner and take turns reading them aloud. An error that you missed may stand out when you hear someone else reading your essay.

- **Use a writer's tools.** Proofread with a dictionary at hand. Look up words when you are in doubt. Do not rely on computer spelling and grammar checking features because they can be wrong. Not all misspelled words register as errors, and some sentence structures that are correct may register as mistakes. When in doubt, using a good dictionary and handbook is your best bet.

- **Proofread with a purpose.** If you frequently make a certain type of error, proofread the first time with that error in mind. Then proofread once again to find any other errors you may have made.

[**Exercise 6.11**]

Examine any of your essays that have been graded and returned thus far. What did you do well? What needs improvement? Choose one of the essays and write a revision and editing plan that you will follow to rewrite the essay. Choose from among the strategies explained in this chapter to find the ones that you think will work best for you.

‹‹ Topics for Writing ››

1. **React to the Reading.** Read paragraphs 12 and 13 of the chapter-opening essay, and then put Zinsser's idea into practice. Proofread one of your essays for clutter. Bracket any words, phrases, expressions, or even whole sentences that you think do not add anything new to your essay. Then write a new draft, eliminating or revising the bracketed items.

2. **Use Your Experience.** Choose a topic from the following list. Then write an essay and revise it to improve its content, organization, and style.

   - a public official from your state, city, or county who should or should not be re-elected

   - a product that is not worth the cost

- a lesson learned the hard way
- a college course that does or does not have practical value

3. **Make a Real-World Connection.** Choose any one of the revising or editing strategies explained in this chapter. Write an essay explaining how you have used this strategy, or plan to use it, either in another course or for writing at work.

4. **Go to the Web.** Select an essay topic from the list on *The Confident Writer* website. Decide what tone you want your essay to have, and then choose words that reflect that tone. In the revision process, examine your word choices carefully, making any changes that are needed.

⟪ Checklist for Revision ⟫

Did you miss anything? Check off the following items as you revise and edit your essay.

Revise your essay for improved content, organization, and style.

- ❑ Do you have a limited topic?
- ❑ Are your purpose and audience clear?
- ❑ Is your thesis statement complete?
- ❑ Do you introduce your thesis effectively?
- ❑ Does each body paragraph have a main idea?
- ❑ Are all your paragraphs fully developed with specific details?
- ❑ Have you used appropriate transitions within and between paragraphs?
- ❑ Are your paragraphs unified and coherent?
- ❑ Do you conclude your essay effectively?
- ❑ Have you made good word choices throughout your essay?
- ❑ Is your tone clear and effective?

Edit your essay to trim, tighten, and eliminate errors.

- ❑ Does your essay have any grammar, punctuation, or spelling errors?
- ❑ Have you eliminated wordiness?
- ❑ Have you used active voice rather than passive voice?
- ❑ Do you need to replace any tired expressions?
- ❑ Have you done a final proofreading check?

≪ Your Discovery Journal ≫

This chapter explains four kinds of clutter to identify and eliminate from your essays: surface errors, wordiness, passive voice, and tired expressions. Reflect on the type of clutter you find in your essays most often. Then complete the following statement and explain your answer.

As an additional option, you can do this activity online by going to *The Confident Writer* website.

The kind of clutter that gives me the most trouble is _____.

≪ Website Resources ≫

This chapter's resources include

- Chapter 6 Exercises
- Chapter 6 Quiz
- Downloadable Charts: *Organization Checklist*
- Downloadable Charts: *Editing Checklist*
- Downloadable Charts: *Group Evaluation Form*
- More Topics for Writing
- Chapter 6 Summary

To access these learning and study tools, go to *The Confident Writer* website.

(((*Confident writers are inquisitive. They have questioning minds and the will to keep searching for answers.*)))

Researching for Writing

What you already know about *researching*

- You search through periodicals to learn about products or current events.
- You probably know how to search the Internet to find information.
- You may have used online resources and databases available in your library.

Your *goals* for this chapter

[1] Manage your time through effective planning, and apply what you have learned about writing essays to writing a research paper.

[2] Know how to use online catalogs and databases, search and evaluate Internet sources, and interview experts.

[3] Avoid plagiarism by quoting, paraphrasing, and summarizing information accurately and by keeping a record of your sources.

[4] Follow proven steps to write your paper and document your sources, using in-text citations and a list of works cited.

ollege assignments and workplace writing tasks often require you to back up your own ideas with other people's opinions, knowledge, or experience. Researching a topic is a starting point for making an effective speech, writing a persuasive essay, or doing a fact-finding report for your employer. Knowing how to conduct research is an essential academic and career skill.

To *research* a topic means to gather information on it from several sources such as books, periodicals, online materials, and interviews. As a writer, your most important choices include selecting information from different sources and deciding how to incorporate that information in your paper. To help you make appropriate choices, this chapter introduces you to the processes of researching, evaluating, and documenting sources for writing a research paper.

[First Thoughts]

To build background for reading, explore your thoughts about plagiarism. Then answer the following questions, either on your own or in a group discussion:

1. What does *plagiarism* mean to you?

2. Should there be a penalty for handing in a paper taken from the Internet or for quoting from an article without crediting its source? Explain your answer.

3. Read the title, headnote, and the first one or two paragraphs of the following excerpt. Based on this preview, what do you think will follow?

[Word Alert]

Before reading, preview the following words and definitions. During your reading, use context clues and your dictionary to define any additional unfamiliar words.

sleuth (1)	a detective
locution (1)	a particular word or style of speaking
purloining (2)	stealing
salacious (2)	appealing to sexual desire, lewd
gaffes (5)	glaring errors

vulnerable (7)	unprotected
empathy (8)	the quality of being able to identify with another's situation or feelings

It's a Bird, It's a Plane, It's Plagiarism Buster!

Gillian Silverman

In this *Newsweek* essay, the author explains how she rescues words from literary bandits. Gillian Silverman is an assistant professor of English at a public university.

1   At around this time each year, I transform from mild-mannered English professor to take-no-prisoners literary sleuth. The beginnings are fairly undramatic. They usually involve myself, a Starbucks and a large stack of mediocre college-student papers. My mind numbs in response to the parade of hackneyed phrases ("And in conclusion, these books are both very similar and very different . . .") when suddenly something catches my eye—a turn of phrase or an extraliterary locution. "Paradoxically . . . ," writes one, "In lieu of an example . . . ," writes another. My breathing quickens, my heart skips, I reach for the red pen. And behold Plagiarism Buster, armed with a righteous sense of justice that would rival that of any superhero.

2   Plagiarism is the purloining of ideas or language from another source. It is literary theft, deriving from the Latin *plagiarius,* meaning kidnapper. Perhaps the dramatic derivation of the word is what attracts the academic set. We spend our days in libraries, classrooms and archives. Given the scant opportunities for stimulation, a kidnapping, literary or otherwise, offers perhaps the only taste of salacious activity we may experience all year.

3   Maybe this is why the disappointment I feel upon discovering a suspected case of plagiarism is always mixed with a bit of excitement. A plagiarized paper presents itself as an act of aggression, a taunt behind a title page. To ignore the challenge would be worse than irresponsible; it would be cowardly. And so, I begin the chase.

4   The Web is always a productive place to start. With thousands of sites dedicated to armchair literary criticism, nothing has done more to accommodate paper pilfering. The thing my students don't seem to realize, however, is that as easily as they can steal language from the Web, I can bust them for it. All it takes is an advanced search on Google.com. Plug in any piece of questionable student writing and up pops the very paper from which the phrase originates. I've discovered papers plagiarized from collaborative high-school projects and from essay services like screwschool.com. My personal favorite involved a paper cribbed from an Amazon.com reader's report for the CliffsNotes of Herman

Melville's "Bartleby the Scrivener." Really, why take the trouble to cheat directly off the Cliffs Notes when you can simply crib from the reviews?

5   It's not that my students are bad performers. Many of them do outstanding and original work. But on the whole, they are terrible cheaters. They will mooch just as readily from an adolescent chat room as they will from an online academic journal. And they can be sloppy in their deceptions: referencing page numbers to editions other than those we used in class or printing out essays without deleting underlined links. With gaffes like these, the job of Plagiarism Buster is often less than taxing.

6   This past semester, I discovered eight cases of plagiarism from the Internet, a new record. The confrontations that followed often verged on the comical. One student swore up and down that she had not cheated, and when I pointed to the proof on the computer screen, she looked genuinely perplexed and asked how her essay got there. "That's what I want to know," I told her. "Yeah," she said as if empathizing with my plight, "me too." Another student spent 10 minutes insisting that her brother wrote her paper for her and therefore it was *he* who was guilty of plagiarism.

7   Despite their efforts at defense, however, these students generally end up miserable. I fare little better. While I anticipate these confrontations will leave me victorious, they usually just make me depressed. The answer that I most frequently receive to my repeated inquiries of "why?" makes me think that plagiarism comes out of a misplaced effort to please. "You didn't like my last paper," one student told me. "I thought you'd be happier with this one." As if this weren't enough, I know that in the public university where I teach, it is largely my students' overtaxed lives that leave them so vulnerable to the temptations of cheating. They're not off rowing crew instead of writing their literature paper. They're working 12-hour night shifts and caring for elderly parents. In the end, I'm forced to realize that my students are not bad guys; they're just guys trying to get by.

8   And yet, while empathy for my students is important, in cases of plagiarism it has little educational value. And so I fail them. With compassion, sure, but I fail them nonetheless. And then, feeling more villain than superhero, I head to the movies for some moral clarity.

Source: From *Newsweek*, July 15, 2002, ©2002 Newsweek, Inc. All rights reserved. Reprinted by permission.

≪ **The Critical Reader** ≫

[CENTRAL IDEA]

1. Find and underline the author's thesis statement.
2. Who is Gillian Silverman's audience, and how can you tell?

[EVIDENCE]

3. How does Silverman define *plagiarism,* and where is the definition stated?

4. What does the author say is her favorite example of questionable student writing?

5. What example does the author give of a "comical" confrontation with a student over plagiarism?

[IMPLICATIONS]

6. To whom or what do the essay's title and the phrases "Plagiarism Buster" and "mild-mannered English professor" refer? Is this an effective image? Why or why not?

7. Is the author's attitude toward her students generally favorable or unfavorable? Find details in the essay to support your answer.

[WORD CHOICE]

8. How many terms does the author use that mean "stealing"? What are these terms, and what purpose do they serve?

9. Is Silverman's tone mainly serious, playful, outraged, or pompous? What words or details in the essay reveal the author's tone?

⟪ The Critical Thinker ⟫

To examine Gillian Silverman's essay in more depth, follow these suggestions for reflection, discussion, and writing.

1. Some of the author's examples of plagiarism include buying a paper from an essay service, copying from a review, and stealing from online journals. What other examples of plagiarism have you seen or heard of on your campus?

2. In paragraph 5, the author says that her students on the whole are "terrible cheaters." In your opinion, how widespread is student cheating of any kind, and what are some of the reasons for it? What are you own views about cheating?

3. In paragraph 7, the author says, "The answer that I most frequently receive to my question of 'why?' makes me think that plagiarism comes out of a misplaced effort to please." What does the author mean, and do you agree or disagree with her? Explain your reasons.

4. Explain the author's meaning in this sentence from paragraph 8: "And then, feeling more villain than superhero, I head to the movies for some moral clarity."

This cartoon takes a humorous look at plagiarism—a serious problem on college campuses.

Plan Your Research Paper

Manage your time through effective planning, and apply what you have learned about writing essays to writing a research paper.

Research begins with a subject that might be an issue (global warming), a question (What is global warming?), or a problem to solve (how to reduce global warming). A **research paper** is, basically, a long essay in which you state a thesis and support it with evidence collected from several sources.

Writing a research paper takes time and planning. Schedule plenty of time to do an information search, choose relevant sources, and take notes. To plan your paper, consider your thesis, purpose, audience, evidence, organization, and implications, just as you would for any essay. Figure 7.1 on the following page lists the steps to follow.

Manage Your Time Effectively

As soon as you know when your paper will be due, make a plan for completing it and start early. By starting early, you may avoid such problems as not being able to find enough information on your topic or discovering that a book you need is not available. Also, you may need to change your topic or revise your thesis. By planning ahead, you will have time to make these adjustments.

✔ **CONCEPT CHECK**
For help in planning a research paper, go to *The Confident Writer* website and view or download the form *My Research Schedule.*

Using a calendar or planner, set deadlines for completing each stage of the writing process. For example, if your paper is due in six weeks, plan to decide on your topic, audience, and purpose within the first few days. By the end of the first week, you should be able to write a working thesis statement. Set aside days and times to do your research, and follow your schedule. Planning effectively will enable you to write, revise, and complete your paper during the last week to ten days before it is due.

Choose and Narrow a Topic

Some of your courses may require you to write a research paper. In some cases, you will be free to select your own topic or choose from a list. In other cases, your instructor may assign a topic and may specify the number and kinds of sources from which you are required to gather information. If you have a choice, keep these guidelines in mind:

- **Be realistic.** Select a topic for which library and Internet resources are readily available.

- **Choose a significant topic.** Choose a topic of general interest and concern. Avoid trivial or overly technical topics. Avoid overworked topics such as abortion, capital punishment, and gun control unless you can approach them in innovative ways.

Figure 7.1   Overview of the Research and Writing Process

1. Choose a topic.
2. Narrow the topic to an issue (problem or question to be researched).
3. Determine your audience and purpose (who will read your paper and why).
4. Write a preliminary thesis statement (the central idea of your research paper).
5. Gather and evaluate information.
6. Compile a working bibliography (list of possible sources).
7. Write your final thesis statement.
8. Synthesize (put together) information from all your sources, using an outline, chart, or other organizer.
9. Draft your paper.
10. Revise your paper and write your final copy.
11. Compile a final bibliography (list of sources actually used).

■ **Choose a topic of personal interest.** Avoid boredom and burnout by selecting a topic that arouses your curiosity or that you think is important.

■ **Ask your instructor for ideas.** Your instructor may have some helpful hints for narrowing topics. He or she will also be able to tell you the names of major works or authors in your field of interest and steer you in the right direction as you begin your research.

Suppose the human memory has always interested you. "Why do we forget?" and "How can we improve memory?" are questions for which you would like answers. Suppose you do some research into ways to improve memory and stumble upon the idea that listening to music may enhance learning and improve retention. Since you have heard that listening to music interferes with learning and remembering, you begin to wonder what kind of music could enhance learning, and under what conditions it could act as a memory cue. Does listening to music work as a memory aid for only certain kinds of information, or can it improve retention of any material? Now you have a topic to research, a question to answer, and a way to narrow your topic: *Does listening to music help or hinder your memory?* The topic of memory itself is too broad for a research paper. Your narrowed topic deals with only one of the many possible aids to memory.

The prewriting strategies explained in Chapter 2 are useful for narrowing a topic for a research paper. To help you generate ideas, you can brainstorm, freewrite, make a cluster, or ask the journalist's questions. Any one of these strategies may help you to zero in on a narrowed topic suitable for your paper.

[**Exercise 7.1**] Following is a list of ten possible research topics. Choose any two and narrow them down to topics you could write about if they were assigned.

1. an environmental issue
2. the works of an artist
3. taxes
4. health care reform
5. same-sex marriage
6. reality TV shows
7. immigration policies
8. identity theft
9. obesity issues
10. the Olympics

Example topic: U.S. presidents

Example limited topic: President Reagan's library

1.

Topic: _____

Limited topic: _____

2.

Topic: _____

Limited topic: _____

Determine Audience and Purpose

The *audience* for your paper will be either the general public, which includes students and instructors, or a specific group of readers. For example, suppose you are in favor of offshore drilling because you believe that we need to become less dependent on foreign oil. Many people oppose offshore drilling. In fact, there are valid arguments both for and against this issue. Whatever position you take, you will be more convincing if you know what the objections on the other side are and can answer them with facts. To improve your *audience awareness,* answer these questions:

✔ CONCEPT CHECK
For more information on audience and purpose, see Chapters 1 and 2.

- Why is my topic important?
- What can I assume readers already know about my topic?
- What more do I think readers should know about my topic?
- How will their lives or thinking be affected by what I have learned through my research?

The *purpose* for your paper will be either to inform or to persuade readers. To determine your purpose, turn your topic, or issue, into a question. If the question can be answered by facts and an explanation, your purpose is to inform. If the question can be answered by your opinion based on a consideration of the evidence you've gathered, then your purpose is to persuade. Consider the following questions:

What kinds of music enhance learning and retention of information?

Should students listen to music while studying?

The first question can be answered by facts gathered from research; the purpose, therefore, is to inform. The second question can be answered by stating your opinion based on your understanding of the evidence; the purpose, therefore, is to persuade.

Another way to arrive at a purpose for writing is to consider what effect you want your research to have on your audience. If you expect your readers to be enlightened (to know more about your topic than they did before reading your paper), then your purpose is to inform. If you expect your readers to change their minds or decide to take action after reading your paper, then your purpose is to persuade.

| **Exercise 7.2** | For the topics you narrowed in Exercise 7.1, who would be your audience? Would your purpose be to inform or to persuade? Why? |

1. Topic _____

   Audience _____

   Purpose _____

   Explanation _____

2. Topic _____

   Audience _____

   Purpose _____

   Explanation _____

Write Your Thesis Statement

The thesis statement of any essay or research paper is its central idea. To arrive at a thesis statement, ask and answer these questions:

What is my narrowed topic (issue)?	*Sex education in middle school*
What question do I have about my topic/issue?	*Why should sex education begin in middle school?*
What is my answer (thesis statement)?	*For sex education to have an impact on teenagers, it must begin in middle school as children near puberty.*

It is common to write a *preliminary,* or working, thesis statement before you begin your research so that you have a clear direction to follow. Knowing

✔ **CONCEPT CHECK**
For more information on
thesis statements, see
Chapter 4.

the central idea of your paper may guide your research because your primary purpose in writing a research paper is to support the thesis statement. As you learn about your topic, you may revise your thesis statement many times until you arrive at a final thesis statement. On the other hand, you may prefer to wait until you have done some research before you write your first thesis statement.

Suppose that after writing the previous example thesis statement about sex education and researching several sources, you decide that focusing on the age when sex education should begin is too narrow. What you really want to write about is what makes an effective sex education program. Therefore, you compose the following revised thesis statement:

> An effective sex education program should include an ethics and values component as well as instruction in birth control methods and safe sex.

A good thesis will control your research paper's development and help you separate relevant from irrelevant information.

[Exercise 7.3]

Using the topics, audiences, and purposes from Exercise 7.2, now write a thesis statement for each one. Follow the steps outlined here.

Topic #1

1. What is my narrowed topic (issue)?

   _____

2. What question do I have about my topic/issue?

   _____

3. What is my answer to the question (thesis statement)?

   _____

   _____

Topic #2

1. What is my narrowed topic (issue)?

   _____

2. What question do I have about my topic/issue?

   _____

3. What is my answer to the question (thesis statement)?

   _____

   _____

Research Your Topic

Goal 2 **Know how to use online catalogs and databases, search and evaluate Internet sources, and interview experts.**

Now you are ready to begin your search for information. Many resources are available to you, and which ones you choose are up to you. Your college library contains a wealth of information in its online catalogs and databases and in its collection of books and periodicals. Through interlibrary loan, you have access to a wide range of materials from other libraries as well. In addition to using these resources, you can do your own Internet searches, interview experts and others who are familiar with your topic, and conduct your own direct observations of places and processes that have an impact on your topic. If you are new to doing research, then your college library may be the best place to begin.

Ask a Librarian

Your librarian is an important resource person who can help you with topic selection and finding material. Librarians work closely with instructors to make the research process both rewarding and efficient. Most college libraries provide orientation tours, flow charts, or manuals that serve as guides to their resources and services. Library personnel welcome the opportunity to teach you how to use online catalogs and databases and to help you refine your searches.

Find out what your library's resources are, where they are housed, and how to use them. By familiarizing yourself with these resources now, you will gain valuable experience that you can apply throughout college and whenever you need to conduct research in the future. Figure 7.2 is a general guide to the resources that you will find in most libraries.

Use Online Catalogs

Online catalogs have all but replaced the traditional card catalog at most libraries. Online catalogs allow you to access sources by author, title, subject, and keywords. Online systems vary. For example, the display screen for your library's catalog may look different from others you have seen, but you can expect to see some or all of the following standard source information displayed.

- Title and author
- Date and place of publication
- Description (number of pages, illustrations, features)
- Location and call number (where to find the source in the library)
- Status (whether the source is available for checkout)

Figure 7.2   A Library's Resources

RESEARCH AREA	USUAL LOCATION	RESOURCES/SERVICES AVAILABLE
Circulation	Near main entrance	Book checkout and return
Reference	Main floor	Dictionaries, encyclopedias, almanacs, indexes, yearbooks, guides, and other reference books—both print-based and electronic
Catalog	Main floor, near circulation or reference area	Computer terminals for accessing print, audiovisual, and electronic information sources
Stacks	Bookcases that may be housed on several floors	Books and other bound volumes, arranged according to Library of Congress or Dewey Decimal system
Current periodicals	Display racks or shelves	Magazines, newspapers, and journals
Government documents	May be separated from general collection	Statistical and other information on a wide variety of subjects—both print and online
Microfilm	A section housing film cases and readers (projectors)	Collections of special materials such as back issues of periodicals and newspapers—many stored electronically
Media center	An area identified as "Multimedia," "Audiovisual," etc.	Films, records, videotapes, CDs, DVDs, CD-ROMS, etc.
Preshelving	An area on each floor	Recently returned books stored temporarily before being reshelved
Special collections/ libraries	In main library or another building on campus	Rare and oversized books, Braille editions, specific collections such as medical or law books, etc.
Interlibrary loan	Near circulation desk	Checkout and return of materials borrowed from other libraries
Reserve desk	Near circulation desk	Books, periodicals, etc., reserved by instructors or groups for a limited time
Computer area	Terminals may be on each floor	Internet access for students; email, word processing, or other services

- Edition (second edition, revised, etc.)
- Notes on special features such as bibliography or index
- Table of contents
- Subject classification (type of material)

Since online catalogs allow you to access sources by author, title, subject, and keywords, try all these options to determine which one yields the best results for you.

In addition, learn to find and make sense of search screens for online systems. For example, the *library home page* displays all the features available at your library. The *title and author search screens* may be separate or combined, and most provide a free-text field in which you can type either author or title. The *keyword search screen* is where you begin your search by typing keywords to access information on your subject.

Begin your search by typing keywords to access information on your subject. For example, suppose you are interested in the way that nutrition affects memory. You select the keywords "nutrition and memory" to get a list of sources in which your keywords appear. If the list is quite long, or if none of the sources listed seems to provide the kind of information you want, then you may have to change your keywords or change the way you type them. For example, you might modify your phrase to be "effects of nutrition on memory." If you have trouble, look for a Help menu or ask a librarian for suggestions. See Figure 7.3 on page 167 for an example of a search screen.

Check Your Library's Website

Your library may have a website that can help you both to navigate your library and to find useful information. Like your college website, the library website is an empowering tool that helps integrate you into the college community and orient you to its resources. Following is a representative listing of the kind of information you might find on a library website. Check your library's website to see what is available.

- A site map, showing the library's layout
- Library hours
- A list of resources and services
- Links to electronic resources that are free to library users
- Special events, displays, and programs
- Research and study tips

Figure 7.3   A Library Search Screen

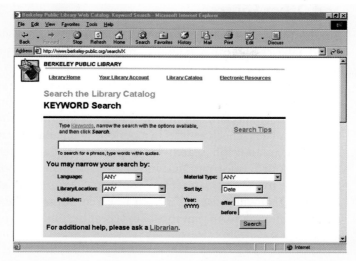

*Use search screens, such as this one, to help you browse your library's
online systems. (Courtesy of the Berkeley Public Library)*

Exercise 7.4

Take a tour of your college library. Your purpose is to find out what resources
and services are available for students. As you walk through the library, make a
list of the resources and services and note their locations. Then be prepared
to share your list in a class discussion. You can do this exercise by yourself or
with a partner. Either explore on your own, or ask a librarian to give you a
guided tour.

Exercise 7.5

Use your library's online card catalog to make a list of possible sources for a
research topic that interests you. Find the following:

1. A recent book that provides an overview of your topic

2. An article from a magazine on your topic

3. An article from a newspaper on your topic

4. An article from a journal on your topic

5. A passage on your topic from an online reference such as *Encarta*

Ask a librarian for any help you may need in locating these sources or in
choosing appropriate search words. Then share your results in class discussion.

Use Reference Tools: Indexes, Databases, and Other Sources

Besides the online catalog, your college library also provides access to various databases and other reference materials, which will give you access to a tremendous amount of information.

A good way to begin your research is by consulting a general reference work, such as an encyclopedia, to get an overview of your topic. From here, move to more specialized references in an academic discipline that relates to your topic. Next, check articles in a periodical database such as Lexus-Nexis or ProQuest. In addition, search more specific databases such as ERIC (Educational Resource Information Center) or ScienceDirect. Finally, consult books for a more in-depth treatment of your topic. Figure 7.4 lists several common resources that will assist you in your research. Some of these materials may be available in book form, but most are accessible online or on CD-ROM.

[**Exercise 7.6**]

Apply what you have learned about specialized references by doing this exercise with group members. First, review the group roles and responsibilities listed on the inside back cover of *The Confident Writer*. Complete the activity that follows and share your results with the rest of the class. Then

Figure 7.4   Where to Look for Information

REFERENCES	INFORMATION THEY CONTAIN	EXAMPLES
Periodical indexes and databases	Articles from magazines, journals, and periodicals	*InfoTrac, Lexus-Nexis, NewsBank, New York Times Index, Readers' Guide to Periodical Literature*
Specialized indexes	Articles and other resources in disciplines such as history, literature, science, and education	*Who's Who in American Literature, Biological Abstracts,* ERIC
Encyclopedias	General resources that provide an introduction to or brief overview of many subjects	*Encyclopedia Britannica, Encarta*
Statistical sources	Facts, figures, and other data such as climate, population, and crime statistics; birth and death rates (to name a few examples)	almanacs; websites for government agencies such as the Census Bureau, CDC (Centers for Disease Control), and U.S. Department of Labor

evaluate your group's performance as your instructor recommends, or go to *The Confident Writer* website to download the group discussion form.

1. Select an academic discipline from the following list.

business and economics	philosophy and religion
education	political science
fine arts	science and technology
history	social sciences
literature	performing arts (film,
mathematics	television, theater)

2. Go to the library and make a list of up to five print and online references available in your discipline.

3. Briefly summarize what kind of information each reference contains.

4. If you have trouble finding the references, ask a librarian for help.

Search the Internet

By the time they reach college, many students are already familiar with the Internet, having used email, downloaded music, participated in chat rooms, or visited blogs. Some have already researched a topic for a high school or work assignment. However, if you are not an experienced Internet user, do not feel alone. Help is available in your library, computer center, or tutorial center. The Web is easy to navigate, and there is plenty of information available there on any topic. The difficulty comes in deciding which sources are useful and credible. Anyone can post anything on the Internet. This section offers basic guidelines for finding and evaluating online information.

Let's begin with a few terms. Every website has an address, called a *URL* (uniform resource locator). Two URLs you may recognize are www.amazon .com, an online bookstore, and www.moviefone.com, a site where you can purchase movie tickets and see movie previews. Notice that both of these addresses have the extension *.com,* which identifies them as commercial sites. Listed below are four other common extensions and their meanings:

- *.edu:* educational institution such as a college

- *.gov:* government agency

- *.net:* commercial, business, or personal site

- *.org:* nonprofit organization

Generally speaking, government and educational sites tend to be reliable. Nonprofit organizations tend to promote their own views and agendas and are, therefore, less reliable. The reliability of commercial, business, or personal sites varies. Consider the reputation of the business or author of the information presented on the site, and check the home page to learn more about the site or its provider.

Suppose you are looking for information on your topic, but you do not know what sites to look for or the URLs of any sites that might contain what you want. In this case, use a *search engine,* a site that gathers and stores huge amounts of information that you can access by typing keywords or phrases related to your topic. Every search engine has a Help feature that explains how to use the engine and offers tips for choosing keywords. Google is the best-known and most widely used search engine; others include Alta Vista, Lycos, Excite, and Yahoo! Your instructor or librarian may suggest others.

When you type a keyword or phrase into Google or another search engine, you will get a listing of sites that may address your topic. Some will be useful; some will not. The more specific your keywords are, the more likely you will be to find relevant sites. If your search does not turn up any useful information, try again, using different keywords. If you have carefully selected your keywords, you should get a manageable list of clearly related sites to explore. If your list is too long, then you may need to narrow your topic further or use more specific keywords. Figure 7.5 shows a screen from Google that was accessed using a phrase (*global warming*) plus an additional term in quotation marks ("hurricanes"). Notice that both the list of sources and the sponsored links provide many options for researching this topic. You should also be aware that Google lists sites by their popularity, or number of "hits." However, a popular site may not necessarily provide the information you want.

[Exercise 7.7]

Using one of your narrowed topics from Exercise 7.1, select a keyword or phrase and do a Google search. Read through the list of sites that your search generates, and answer the following questions about them.

1. What is your topic?

2. What keywords or phrase did you use?

3. How many sites did your search generate?

4. Of the sites generated, how many seem related to your topic?

5. Is one of the sites an official site of an organization, company, or individual related to your topic?

6. What questions do you have about the search process or the sites on your list?

Figure 7.5 A Typical Google Search

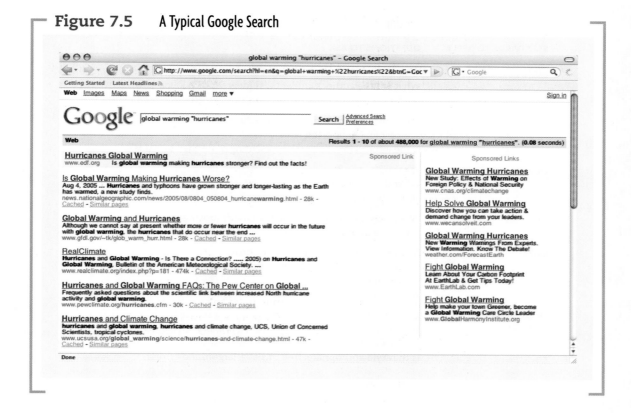

Evaluate Online Sources

☑ CONCEPT CHECK
For more information on what makes an argument invalid, or unreliable, see Chapter 14.

Once you have used a search engine to find sites related to your topic, it is time to select the most relevant ones, examine the information presented, and evaluate those sources for their *reliability, objectivity,* and *usefulness.* A source is *reliable* if the information is accurate, current, and written by persons whose credentials clearly reveal them to be knowledgeable about the subject. Primary sources are more reliable than secondary sources. A *primary source* is an author's own work, firsthand report, observations, or research. *Secondary sources* interpret data from primary sources. A reporter's analysis of a candidate's speech is a secondary source, but a recording of the speech is a primary source. Which would be more reliable—the transcript of an interview with your state's governor or a state representative's summary of the points that the governor made in that interview? Secondary sources are only as reliable as the quality of their authors' research or the degree of their expertise on their subjects.

A source is *objective* if its author relies on facts rather than unsubstantiated opinions to support claims, presents more than one side of an issue, and

Figure 7.6   Tips for Evaluating Online Sources

STANDARDS TO APPLY	QUESTIONS TO ASK
Authority	Who is the author of the information provided?
	What are the author's credentials? (degrees or publications)
	Is a bias revealed? (an affiliation with known groups or companies)
Coverage	Is the information thorough and detailed?
	Are opinions supported with facts?
	Is the information balanced, presenting more than one side?
Domain	What is the URL?
	What does the extension (*.com, .gov, .edu, .net, .org*) suggest about the site's reliability?
Currency	When was the information last updated? (posting date)
	Is the site updated regularly?
Links	Is the site linked to other related sites?
	Can the site be accessed from a variety of other sites (an indication of usefulness)?
	Are the site and its links of the same quality?
Documentation and Style	Is the information on a site attributed to a source?
	How much information comes from a *primary* source, such as an author's own words, writing, or original research?
	Is the style appropriate: free of slang, jargon, and errors?

Adapted from Kanar, *The Confident Student,* 6th ed. (Boston: Houghton Mifflin, 2008).

avoids using defamatory language such as name calling. For example, how objective are the views expressed in publications of the National Rifle Association or the National Organization for Women?

A source is *useful* if it is relevant to your topic and contains information that furthers your knowledge or fulfills some other intended purpose. Listed below are five tips for evaluating either print or online sources. Figure 7.6 lists more tips for evaluating online sources, more standards to apply, and questions that you should ask.

1. **Is the author an authority?** Check a reference such as a discipline-specific Who's Who for the author's credentials and accomplishments.

2. **Does the author have name recognition?** Recognized experts will be cited in textbooks, reference works, bibliographies, and journal articles and will be well known among other experts in the field.

3. **Can you trust the source?** Respected periodicals such as *Newsweek, U.S. News and World Report,* major newspapers, and *Scientific American* are

generally considered reliable. Also trustworthy are books published by well-known publishers and university presses.

4. **Is the source current?** The copyright date or date of publication will tell you how up-to-date the research is, information that is especially important in medicine and technology.

5. **Are ideas presented fairly?** Unsupported opinions, one-sided arguments, and emotional language are not characteristic of authoritative or scholarly research.

[Exercise 7.8] Select one of the websites you found for Exercise 7.7 and evaluate it by answering the questions listed in Figure 7.6. To answer the questions effectively, you will first have to read some or all of the information posted on the site.

Interview an Expert

An expert can offer an opinion on your topic or provide information that will either affirm or deny what you have already learned. An expert may even suggest ways to approach your topic that you have not considered. Experts include college faculty, business and professional people who know something about your topic, and public officials and employees who act as spokespersons for their various agencies or corporations. To conduct effective interviews, try these tips.

- **Schedule far ahead.** Most people have busy schedules. Make an appointment for the interview far enough ahead to allow for flexibility in case one of you must reschedule.

- **Prepare a list of questions.** Go to the interview with a clear idea of what you want to find out. Make a list of questions that call for an explanation rather than a yes or no answer.

- **Seek permission to quote the expert.** Also, ask permission to tape the interview if you want to review it later. If your expert does not want to be taped, be prepared to take notes.

- **Evaluate information.** An expert may have a personal bias or special interest that colors his or her views on your topic. It may be useful to interview several people or to weigh the information gained from the interview against that gathered from other sources.

- **Express your thanks.** Show your appreciation by thanking the expert and sending a thank-you note.

Take Notes to Avoid Plagiarism

As Gillian Silverman says in the essay at the beginning of this chapter, "Plagiarism is the purloining of ideas or language from another source." Plagiarism is, literally, stealing. When you use an author's ideas without attributing their source, you are guilty of plagiarism. If you download a research paper from the Internet and turn it in to your instructor with your name on it, you are guilty of plagiarism. Did your roommate write your paper? Did you copy a sentence or a paragraph from a magazine article into your paper and try to pass it off as your own? Both are examples of literary theft!

Sometimes plagiarism is unintentional, the result of bad note taking or failing to write down the source of an idea or a quotation. After time passes, you may forget where you found the information or confuse it with your own ideas. To prevent plagiarism, take good notes and prepare a working bibliography that you update regularly. Also, learn how to quote, paraphrase, and summarize ideas that are not your own.

Quote Sources

If you need to *quote,* or state directly, what an author has said, do so, but use quotations sparingly and use them only to support your ideas. Do not use a quotation as your thesis statement or topic sentence. Quotations should be integrated within the text of your paper and *framed* by introductory and concluding remarks that explain the quotation's significance, as in the following example from a paper on Edith Wharton's *The Age of Innocence.*

> As the novel opens, the Archers and Wellands are attending the opera. They are only peripherally interested in the music and story; their primary interest is to see who is there and to be seen. The opera is more a social obligation than an entertainment as the narrator suggests in Chapter 1 when commenting on the hasty departure of the spectators after the opera: "It was one of the great livery-stableman's most masterly intuitions to have discovered that Americans want to get away from amusement even more quickly than they want to get to it." This observation hints at one of the novel's minor themes: that European art and culture were merely affectations of old New York's upper class, things they knew they should appreciate but did not enjoy, or if they enjoyed them then they did so for the wrong reasons.

Remember to set off direct quotations in quotation marks and to document them according to the style you are using. When your quotation is five lines or longer, single space, indent, and omit quotation marks. See Unit 4, Section C.8 for an explanation of how to use quotation marks.

Paraphrase Ideas

Like quotations, paraphrases should be used to support your thinking and should not form the bulk of your evidence. A *paraphrase* is a restatement in your own words of someone else's words or ideas. A paraphrase restates the entire passage, whether it be a sentence, paragraph, or longer piece of writing, so your paraphrase should be about as long as the original. Paraphrasing from authorities adds weight to your conclusions. To paraphrase accurately, use your own words and sentence structure to restate what the author says. Maintain the intent and emphasis of the original passage, and make sure you copy into your notes all the information you need to correctly document the source. The following examples show an original passage and two paraphrases for comparison.

ORIGINAL PASSAGE

These two forces—a powerful surge among American blacks toward freedom, mostly inspired by the *Brown* decision, and a quantum leap in the power of the media—fed each other; each made the other more vital, and the combination created what became known as the Movement. Together, the Movement and the media educated America about civil rights.

From David Halberstam, The Fifties. *New York: Villard Books, 1993, p. 429.*

PARAPHRASE 1 (UNACCEPTABLE)

Two forces—a surge among blacks toward freedom and a quantum leap in the power of the media—fed each other and made each other more powerful. Together, the Civil Rights Movement and the media taught Americans about civil rights.

PARAPHRASE 2 (ACCEPTABLE)

The Civil Rights Movement, fueled by the decision for Brown in *Brown* v. *Board of Education,* was the effect of two forces: a growing desire for freedom among African Americans and a powerful media that brought their struggle into America's living rooms (Halberstam 429).

Paraphrase 1 is unacceptable because it copies many of the author's words and does not credit the ideas. Paraphrase 2 is acceptable because it maintains the author's intent, but the wording is different and the source is properly documented.

Summarize Information

A *summary* condenses the central idea and major details of a passage into a few sentences. Therefore, your summary of a passage will be much shorter than the original and should contain only the main idea and a few significant details. The following examples show an original passage and two summaries for comparison. The passage is about Maria Mitchell (1818–1886), the first woman astronomer in the United States.

ORIGINAL PASSAGE

Mitchell was a self-taught astronomer, reading mathematics and science while a librarian at the Nantucket (Mass.) Atheneum (1836–56). In 1847, while helping her father, William Mitchell, survey the sky for the U.S. Coast Survey, she discovered a comet, for which she received worldwide attention. In 1848 she became the first woman elected to the American Academy of Arts and Sciences.

In 1865 Mitchell was appointed professor of astronomy at Vassar College. There she gained distinction as a teacher of some of America's leading women scientists, including Christine Ladd-Franklin and Ellen Swallow-Richards. In 1873 her concern with the status of professional women led her to help found the Association for the Advancement of Women.

Mitchell pioneered in the daily photography of sun spots; she was the first to find that they were whirling vertical cavities, rather than clouds, as had been earlier believed. She also studied comets, nebulae, double stars, solar eclipses, and the satellites of Saturn and Jupiter.

From New Encyclopedia Britannica, *Vol. 8, 1992, p. 164.*

SUMMARY 1 (UNACCEPTABLE)

Maria Mitchell taught herself astronomy by reading math and science. She was a librarian at the Nantucket Atheneum from 1836 to 1856. She received worldwide attention when she discovered a comet while helping her father, astronomer William Mitchell. She had a distinguished career that included being appointed professor of astronomy at Vassar College in 1865, teaching leading women scientists such as Christine Ladd-Franklin and Ellen Swallow-Richards, helping to found the Association for the Advancement of Women, and pioneering in the daily photography of sunspots. She studied such phenomena as comets, nebulae, and the satellites of Saturn and Jupiter.

SUMMARY 2 (ACCEPTABLE)

According to an entry in the *New Encyclopedia Britannica,* Maria Mitchell was a self-taught astronomer who discovered a comet and gained wide recognition. The first woman to be elected to the Academy of Arts and Sciences, the first to discover the true nature of sun spots, a professor of astronomy at Vassar College, and a founder of the Association for the Advancement of Women, Maria Mitchell had a distinguished career.

Summary 1 is unacceptable because it borrows phrases from the original without crediting the source and because it includes too much information.

A summary should focus on the key ideas. Summary 2 is acceptable because it does credit the source, and it condenses the original passage into a few significant details that support a main idea.

Whether you quote, paraphrase, or summarize information, remember to credit your sources. To keep track of the sources you use and to help you avoid plagiarism, compile a working bibliography.

☑ CONCEPT CHECK
For a detailed explanation of how to document sources using MLA or APA style, see pages 179–186.

Prepare a Working Bibliography

A *working bibliography* is a running list of all the sources you have consulted while doing your research. As you take notes from a book, article, or other source, add to your bibliography the title of the source, author, publisher, date and place of publication, and numbers of pages where you found the information. You can record this information on note cards or in a computer file. The bibliography is for your information and will help you avoid plagiarism. Later, you will use your working bibliography to compile a *Works Cited list,* which is an alphabetized listing of the sources that you actually used in writing your paper. If your instructor requires that you hand in the working bibliography as well, then it too should be an alphabetized list. Following is the type of information you should record in your bibliography for books, articles, and websites. To see an example of a Works Cited list, turn to page 191.

- **Book:** Author, complete title, date published, name and location of publisher, pages that contain a quotation or other information you might use

- **Article:** Author, title of article, title of periodical, publication date (day, month, year), page number(s)

- **Website:** Author, page or site title, publication date or date of latest posting, sponsoring organization, date you obtained the source, online address in single brackets <URL>

When you take notes from a source, indicate whether you are quoting, paraphrasing, or summarizing the author's ideas. Label your notes with the symbols *Q* for quote, *P* for paraphrase, and *S* for summary. Doing this will help you to distinguish an author's ideas from your own comments, which you may later decide to add to your notes.

Assemble Your Research Paper

Your research paper should demonstrate that you have thought about your topic, considered the evidence from other sources, and arrived at your own viewpoint. Rather than being merely a report of what others have said about your topic, your paper should lay out the facts from your research that prove your thesis. As mentioned before, writing a research paper is like writing any other paper. You will introduce and support a thesis, develop that thesis with sufficient relevant evidence, and then draw a conclusion. What makes the research paper different is its length, the way that you integrate other writers' ideas with your own, and the fact that you must document information taken from other sources. Following are a few suggestions for writing your paper and documenting your sources.

Outline, Write, Revise

In the planning stage, you selected a topic, came up with a working thesis, and then took notes. Now you are ready to refine your working thesis into a thesis statement that will be the central idea of your paper. If you have trouble writing your thesis, try one of these three models:

- **A question to be answered:** Global warming is a hot topic that arouses controversy among supporters and skeptics, but what is global warming, and why should we be concerned about it?

- **A problem to be solved:** Global warming is a growing problem for future generations that we as individuals can begin to solve by making small changes in our daily lives.

- **A position on an issue:** Though marginalized by their opponents, who greatly outnumber them, global warming skeptics also have evidence to support their claims.

Next look over your notes and decide what information to use to support your thesis. Break down your thesis into several points, or main ideas, that you can support with facts from your notes. Organize the information into an outline, beginning with your thesis statement and followed by several sections that list your main ideas and the details that support them. The last section of your outline should be a concluding statement that you can develop into a concluding paragraph for your paper.

Working from your outline, write a draft of your paper. Your *first draft* is an attempt to put your notes and ideas together in a coherent way. As you write *additional drafts,* you will refine your content and organization until you are ready for the *final draft,* which you will proofread for errors and correct before submitting it to your instructor.

Figure 7.7   Organizing Your Research Paper

THE PARTS	WHAT EACH PART CONTAINS
Introduction	• Your thesis statement
	• Background or context for the thesis that arouses readers' interest and explains why they should be concerned or what they will learn
	• A brief preview of the evidence you will use to support your thesis
Body	• Several paragraphs, each of which develops one main idea related to your thesis
	• Supporting details to develop each main idea
	• Evidence from your notes integrated into each paragraph by using quotation, paraphrase, and summary
Conclusion	• Restatement of thesis in different words
	• A brief summary of major points that support the thesis
	• Your comment, observation, or challenge for readers, based on the information presented

As with any other paper, your research paper will have three basic parts: an introduction, a body, and a conclusion. Because your research paper will be longer than a typical college essay, you may have one or two introductory paragraphs, several body paragraphs, and one or two concluding paragraphs, depending on the amount of evidence you have to support the thesis. Figure 7.7 shows what to include in each part of your paper.

Document Your Sources

Quoting, paraphrasing, summarizing, or any other use of an author's original words or ideas must be acknowledged. The way you acknowledge a source is by *documenting,* or citing, it with a brief description that follows one of several specific formats or styles. The style you choose will depend on the discipline for which you are writing your paper, or your instructor may have a preference.

The following two styles are the most widely used:

- **MLA (Modern Language Association):** Writing in the humanities uses this style.

- **APA (American Psychological Association):** Writing in the social sciences uses this style.

Both the MLA and APA styles require you to follow specific guidelines for documenting print-based and online materials and other types of sources. In general, you will use two types of citations in your research paper: *in-text citations* throughout the paper and a *works cited list* at the end of the paper. In-text citations refer readers to an author and page number listed in your works-cited list. Although this section of the text provides some examples of how to cite sources, you can find more examples in any handbook for writers and on the official websites for the MLA and APA, which illustrate the documentation styles explained in this chapter. Ask your instructor or a librarian for the URL for the MLA or APA.

Figure 7.8 lists the types of sources that require MLA or APA documentation.

☑ CONCEPT CHECK
Because the MLA and APA style guidelines are updated from time to time, you should supplement this chapter with a visit to an official website for these styles. A librarian can provide the latest URLs.

In-Text Citations

Instructors in the humanities usually require documentation in the MLA style, but instructors in the social sciences may prefer that you use the APA style. In-text citations using either the MLA or APA style may call for the author's last name, the page number, or both in parentheses following the source material. However, APA style also requires the publication date. Following are several examples that show several different types of in-text citations.

1. To paraphrase or summarize material from a book by one author, insert last name and page (MLA) or last name and publication date (APA) in parentheses.

MLA

It took a court decision, a continued struggle on the part of blacks, and the influence of a powerful media to create the Civil Rights Movement (Halberstam 429).

APA

It took a court decision, a continued struggle on the part of blacks, and the influence of a powerful media to create the Civil Rights Movement (Halberstam, 1993).

Notice that both styles place the parentheses before the end punctuation. The MLA style uses no punctuation between the name and page number, but the APA style places a comma between the name and date.

2. To introduce a quotation with a statement containing the author's name and source:

MLA

In Howard Gardner's *Intelligence Reframed,* the author defines *intelligence* as "a biopsychological potential to process information that can be activated in

Figure 7.8   Sources That Require Documentation

SOURCE	TYPICAL EXAMPLES
Books	Single and multivolume works, edited collections, works within a collection, articles from encyclopedias or other reference works
Documents and Pamphlets	Government documents, annual reports, conference proceedings, dissertations
Periodicals	Articles in monthly or weekly magazines, journal articles, newspaper articles, editorials, letters to the editor, reviews
Orally Delivered Information	Speeches, presentations, interviews, performances
Graphics	Maps, graphs, tables, charts, cartoons, diagrams
Media	Films, television or radio broadcasts, recordings, transcripts
Museum Holdings	Artworks, exhibits
Internet and Other Electronic Sources	Online projects or databases; professional or corporate websites; online books, encyclopedias, or other reference works; online documents, reports, magazines; online transcripts of lectures and interviews; exhibits, recordings, and graphics; CD-ROM sources; and email interviews

a cultural setting to solve problems or create products that are of value in a culture" (34).

APA

In Howard Gardner's *Intelligence Reframed,* the author defines *intelligence* as "a biopsychological potential to process information that can be activated in a cultural setting to solve problems or create products that are of value in a culture" (1999, p. 34).

3. For quoted material for which you do not provide a statement containing the author's name and source title:

MLA

"Together the Movement and the media educated America about Civil Rights" (Halberstam 429).

APA

"Together the Movement and the media educated America about Civil Rights" (Halberstam, 1993, p. 429).

Figure 7.9 lists more guidelines for in-text citations using the MLA or APA style.

Works Cited List

The *Works Cited* page goes at the end of your research paper, and it lists all the sources you have quoted, paraphrased, or summarized. Follow these general guidelines for compiling your list. If you are using MLA style, type and center the words *Works Cited* at the top of the page. If you are using APA style, your title will be *References*. Both MLA and APA styles require you to alphabetize your list by the authors' last names. If an entry is not attributed to an author, then list it by the first main word in the title of the source. Do not number your entries. If an entry requires more than one line, indent the next and any following lines. MLA style requires you to list an author's full name, last name first. If there is more than one author, then only the first author's name is listed in reverse order. However, APA style requires you to list only an author's last name, followed by initials. The first letters of all major words in a title are capitalized in MLA style. However, APA style requires that only the first word in a title or subtitle be capitalized. In MLA style, titles of books, periodicals,

Figure 7.9   More MLA and APA Guidelines for In-Text Citations

TYPE OF CITATION	MLA	APA
More than one work by the same author	Author's last name, short title, and page number	Last name followed by publication date
A work by two authors	Last names separated by *and,* then followed by page number	Last names separated by &, then followed by publication date
A work by more than three authors	Last name of the first author plus *et al.* and page number	Last name of first author plus *et al.* and publication date
A work that has no named author	Title (or a few words from the title) followed by page number	Title (or a few words from the title) followed by publication date
A multivolume work	Last name, volume number followed by a colon, space, and page number	Last name and publication date (2001) or range if more than one volume (2001–2004)
Web documents	Treat these the same way that you would print sources. If no page numbers are given, use author's name only. If author is not given, use title.	Author or title, year, or most recent update

journals, databases, and websites are underlined. In APA style, only titles of books, periodicals, and journals are italicized. There are other differences between the two styles, as the following examples show.

1. A book by one author

MLA

> Covey, Stephen R. <u>The Eighth Habit: From Effectiveness to Greatness</u>. New York: Free Press, 2004.

APA

> Covey, S. R. (2004). *The eighth habit: From effectiveness to greatness.* New York: Free Press.

2. A book with two or more authors

MLA

> Lakoff, George, and Mark Johnson. <u>Metaphors We Live By</u>. Chicago: U of Chicago P, 1980.

APA

> Lakoff, G., & Johnson, M. (1980). *Metaphors we live by.* Chicago: University of Chicago Press.

3. A work from an edited collection or anthology

MLA

> Ferris, Timothy. "Stumbling into Space." <u>The Best American Science and Nature Writing</u>. Ed. J. Weiner and T. Folger. Boston: Houghton Mifflin, 2005. 66–76.

APA

> Ferris, T. (2005). Stumbling into space. In Jonathan Weiner & Tim Folger (Eds.), *The Best American Science and Nature Writing* (pp. 64–76). Boston: Houghton Mifflin.

4. An entry from an encyclopedia

MLA

> "Antarctica." <u>The Columbia Encyclopedia</u>. 6th ed. 2000.

APA

> Antarctica. (2000). In *The Columbia encyclopedia* (6th ed., pp. 116–115).

5. A magazine article

MLA

> Whitelaw, Kevin. "Rwanda Reborn." <u>U.S. News and World Report</u> 23 Apr. 2007: 43–47.

APA

> Whitelaw, K. (2007, April 23). Rwanda reborn. *U.S. News and World Report,* 43–47.

6. A newspaper article

MLA

> Engeler, Elaine, and Alexander G. Higgins. "Seven Wonders Race Puts Great Wall, Taj Mahal, in Running for New Honor." <u>Daily Commercial</u> 17 Apr. 2007: B1.

APA

> Engeler, E., & Higgins, A. G. (2007, April 17). Seven wonders race puts Great Wall, Taj Mahal, in running for new honor. *Daily Commercial,* p. B1.

7. A magazine or newspaper editorial lacking a named author

MLA

> "Stick With Winner." Editorial. <u>Orlando Sentinel</u> 17 Apr. 2007: A18.

APA

> Stick with winner [Editorial]. (2007, April 17). *The Orlando Sentinel,* p. A18.

If the editorial is attributed to an author, begin with the author's name as you would for any other newspaper article, using MLA or APA style.

8. A letter to the editor

MLA

> Scott, Kathryn. Letter. <u>Newsweek</u> 21 May 2007: 16.

APA

> Scott, K. (2007, May 21). [Letter to the editor]. *Newsweek,* 16.

9. Electronic sources: You will probably do much of your research online, using library, U.S. government, or other databases. Because information on websites and in databases is subject to change, always note the date when you accessed your information. Next is a list of general information that you need to know to cite sources from a database, followed by examples 10 through 15 that show how to document various online sources. For more extensive information on documenting different types of online sources, visit the official MLA or APA website, or consult a style manual.

- URL (web address)
- Name of the database or website
- Name of the provider, such as Lexis-Nexis or InfoTrac, or the sponsor, such as Cable News Network
- Name of the library system, if you are using one, such as Purdue University
- Your date of access: day, month, and year as shown on your printout
- Title and author of the article you found
- Print information for the article, such as the publication or source from which it came, the date, and the page numbers, if applicable

10. An entire website, journal, or database

MLA

Healthfinder. 29 June 2007. U.S. Department of Health and Human Services. 27 July 2007 ‹http://www.healthfinder.gov›.

APA

Healthfinder. (2007, June 29). U.S. Department of Health and Human Services. Retrieved July 27, 2007, from http://www.healthfinder.gov

11. A document on a website

MLA

Gandossy, Taylor. "Chatting with America's Gas Price Survey Maven." CNN.com 11 July 2007. Cable News Network. 31 July 2007 ‹http://www.com.cnn.com/ 2007/10/fa.lundberg.qa/index/html›.

APA

Gandossy, T. (2007, July 11). Chatting with America's gas price survey maven. *Cable News Network.* Retrieved July 31, 2007, from http://www.com.cnn .com/2007/10/fa.lundberg.qa/index/html

12. An article from an online periodical such as a newspaper or magazine

MLA

Pitts, Leonard Jr. "Firing of Imus Removes Leader of Sorry Band." MiamiHerald.com 13 Apr. 2007. McClatchy Company. 21 June 2007 ‹http://www.miamiherald .com/285/story/72285.html›

APA

Pitts, L. (2007, April 13) Firing of Imus removes leader of sorry band. *The Miami Herald.* Retrieved from http://www.miamiherald.com/285/story/72285.html

13. A posting to a discussion board or blog

MLA

Tahmincioglu, Eve. "For Many Small Business Owners, Health Care System is 'Sicko.'" Online posting. 23 July 2007. Your Biz Blog. 31 July 2007 ‹http://www.yourbiz.msnbc.msn.com/archive/2007/07/23/204892.aspx›.

APA

Tahmincioglu, E. (2007, 23 July). For many small business owners, health care system is "sicko." Message posted to *Your Biz Blog*. Retrieved July 31, 2007, from http://www.yourbiz.msnbc.msn.com/archive/2007/07/23/204892.aspx

14. Online Dictionary

MLA

"Ethnocentric". Merriam-Webster's Online Dictionary, 4 Mar. 2008 ‹http://www.merriam-webster.com/dictionary/›.

APA

Ethnocentric. (n.d.). In *Merriam-Webster's* online dictionary, retrieved March 4, 2008, from http://www.merriam-webster.com/dictionary

15. An email

MLA

Ripley, Terry. "Re: Online Resume." Email to James Shroeder. 12 Nov. 2006.

APA

Cite email in the body of your paper as "personal communication." Do not include email in your list of references.

16. An interview (by telephone, or in person)

MLA

Collins, Sarah. Personal interview. 7 Dec. 2006.

APA

Cite interviews in the body of your paper as "personal communication." Do not include interviews in your list of references.

Student Voices: A Research Paper

Paragraphs are numbered for easy reference in class discussion only. Do not number paragraphs in your own essays. Annotations point out features such as in-text citations, parts of the paper, and formatting. Your instructor may have additional guidelines as well. For critical reading and thinking questions related to this essay, go to Chapter 7, Your Reflections, on *The Confident Writer* website.

Top of each page: last name and page number → Bjork 1

1"

↔ Cassandra Bjork
Professor Brandt
English 101
December 5, 2007

Double-space paper throughout

Americans: Bigger by the Day ← *Center title*

Introduction asks two questions and states a problem

1   Why are Americans getting bigger by the day? And what's so bad about that anyway? Studies have shown that there are many negative effects associated with obesity. Obesity has been accused of contributing to many long-term conditions, such as heart disease, stroke, high blood pressure, osteoarthritis, diabetes, and cancer (Pennybacker 15). Along with the fact that obesity is the most common from of malnutrition in the Western world, it also affects sixty-four percent of Americans (Pennybacker 15; Brownell 1). Obesity is one of today's most visible yet most neglected conditions, affecting more Americans each day.

Obesity is defined

In-text citations

2   Obesity is defined as "a condition characterized by excessive bodily fat" (Merriam-Webster). Moreover, the Centers for Disease Control and Prevention have labeled the obesity problem an "epidemic" (Brownell 1). Basically, obesity is the long-term result of a diet that delivers more calories than are consumed through daily activity. Nevertheless, obesity is a serious medical condition that affects a high percentage of Americans and should be treated with concern.

Thesis statement

Topic sentence

3   There are many possible factors for the rise in the number of overweight and obese Americans. Brownell outlines these factors very well in <u>Food Fight</u> and writes, "The reasons for this growing problem

are simple and complex at the same time. People eat too much and exercise too little" (Brownell 2). Furthermore, by taking a look at the modern lifestyle of our world today, one could say it does not discourage obesity in the least way. One obstacle Americans need to overcome is to find the time in their busy schedules to exercise. It is much too easy to travel in cars, as opposed to walking or biking. Many people sit all day in an office, and do not get much physical activity at all. The conveniences and technology of today contribute to a very sedentary lifestyle for much of the population. According to <u>Food Fight</u>, one study found that twenty-three percent of all deaths from major chronic disease could be attributed to sedentary lifestyles (Brownell 70). The lack of exercise is one of the main causes of obesity in the United States.

4   Another possible contribution to obesity, which is still in the process of being further researched, is genetics. According to the Centers for Disease Control and Prevention, studies indicate that inherited genetic variation is an important risk factor for obesity. It was also pointed out that genetic factors are starting to be questioned as to the degree of effectiveness of diet and physical activity interventions for weight reduction ("Obesity and Genetics"). Learning how genetic variations affect obesity will make it much easier to prevent and treat the condition of obesity.

5   In addition to the many other causes of obesity fast food receives much of the blame. With the continual growth of the fast-food industry in the United States, obesity is becoming a bigger problem every day. The connection between fast food and obesity is one of the primary criticisms in the book <u>Fast Food Nation</u> by Eric Schlosser. Due to the high-calorie, high-fat food choices offered at many restaurants, both consumers and experts are quick to point their fingers at fast-food restaurants. In the book, Schlosser states, "If you look at the rise of the obesity rate in the United States, it's grown pretty much in step with the rise of fast-food consumption . . . and now it's the second leading cause of death in the United States, after smoking" (1). When McDonald's was asked to respond to Schlosser's charges, they stated

Causes of obesity are listed

Topic sentence

Fast food cited as another cause of obesity

Author's name introduces the quote, so only page is given in citation

Bjork 3

that forty-five million customers make the choice to dine at McDonald's every single day ("Fast Food"). The point McDonald's was trying to get across is that the fast-food restaurant customers are responsible for the persistent growth of the fast-food industry. Customers are the ones choosing to put this type of food into their digestive systems. Fast-food restaurants would not be so profitable if it were not for the high demand for their food products by consumers. Another source provided a statement from Dr. Cathy Kapica, former Global Director of Nutrition for McDonald's, regarding the responsibility of the customer: "It is not where you eat, but the food choices you make, and especially how much you eat." She then addressed the fact that McDonald's offers a wide variety of different foods and portion styles that can be a significant part of a healthy diet ("Meet McDonald's").

An opposing viewpoint is offered

6   An opposing opinion on the correlation between fast food and obesity came from HeartInfo.org. According to Amanda Gardner, a study was conducted on individuals' dietary habits. There were 3,301 adults surveyed between ages eighteen and thirty. The results showed that individuals who ate fast food more than twice a week gained an extra ten pounds in just six months and had a twofold greater increase in insulin resistance than people who ate fast food less than once a week (Gardner). The outcome of the study indicates that eating a high-fat diet can lead to weight gain and, eventually, obesity.

Causes of obesity are summarized

7   Although fast food is often blamed because of its high caloric content, it is simply a contributing factor. Obesity is caused by overeating, poor food choices, genetics, and lack of exercise as well. Whether it is from fast food or not, extra weight is put on by not burning as many calories as the number taken in. Dining in restaurants can encourage this unhealthy habit by providing enough food for two or more people on a single plate. Frequent visits to restaurants can then compound the effect of too much food too often. According to Kelly Brownell, more than forty percent of adults eat at a restaurant on a typical day. The frequency of eating out if associated with higher calorie and fat intake and increased body weight, while eating meals at

Bjork 4

home is associated with better calorie intake (Brownell 36). When it comes to healthy eating, it can be easier for one to make better healthful choices in his or her own kitchen.

8   In our world today, obesity affects people of all ages. A common misconception is that obesity is only an adult problem. In the United States, more children suffer from obesity than ever before. The Centers for Disease Control estimate that twenty-three percent of American children are overweight, in comparison to only four percent in the 1960s. Obesity causes the young to be at risk for problems that used to be common only in adults, such as cardiovascular disease, high cholesterol and blood pressure, and type 2 diabetes (Pennybacker 15).

9   There are many different suggestions for the prevention of and fight against obesity. The first and most obvious recommendation is to lose weight. Because obesity is a condition requiring continuous attention, any behavioral changes required to maintain weight loss must be lifelong. In order to lose weight, it is necessary to decrease caloric intake, increase caloric expenditure, or do both ("Fast Food"). According to Greg Critser in Fatlands, the response is simple but not always easy: We need to burn at least as many calories as we take in (Schlosser 2). It has been proven that physical activity is a vital component of a healthy lifestyle, whether a person is overweight or not. It is recommended [for a person] to participate in moderate levels of physical activity for thirty to forty minutes, three to five times each week (Mathur). It can be difficult to meet this recommendation, but it eventually causes a positive long-term result.

10   Obesity is one of today's most visible yet most neglected conditions, affecting more Americans each day. The possible causes of obesity include fast food, genetics, and lack of physical activity. Although it is a growing problem, today we have the resources and knowledge available to overcome obesity. It is up to Americans to

Bjork 5

assist in the prevention of this condition that affects such a high percentage of our people.

↕ *1"*

Works Cited

Brownell, Kelly D. <u>Food Fight</u>. Boston: McGraw, 2004.

"Fast Food, Fat Children." <u>CBSNews.com</u>. 21 Apr. 2001. CBS News. 15 Sept. 2007 ‹http//www.cbsnews.com›.

Gardner, Amanda. "Fast Food Linked to Obesity." <u>HeartInfo.org</u>. 30 Dec. 2005. 15 Sept. 2007 ‹http://www.heartinfo.org/ms/news/ 523168/main.html›.

Mathur, Ruchi. "Obesity (Weight Loss)." Ed. Dennis Lee. <u>MedicineNet.com</u>. 22 July 2003. 15 Sept. 2007 ‹http://www.medicinenet.com/ obesity_weight_loss/article.htm›.

"Meet McDonald's Nutrition Expert, Dr. Cathy Kapica." <u>McDonald's.com</u>. 2005. McDonald's Corporation 15 Sept. 2007 ‹http://www.rhmc .com/usa!_eat/nutritionist.html›.

"Obesity." <u>Merriam-Webster's Collegiate Dictionary</u>. 11th ed.

Pennybaker, Mindy. "Reducing 'Globesity' Begins at Home." <u>World Watch</u> Sept./Oct. 2005: 15.

Schlosser, Eric. <u>Fast Food Nation: The Dark Side of the All-American Meal</u>. Boston: Houghton, 2001.

United States. Centers for Disease Control and Prevention. "Obesity and Genetics." June 2006. 15 Sept. 2007 ‹http://www.cdc.gov/ genomics/training/perspectives/files/obesedit.htm›.

In your paper, the Works Cited would begin on a new page.

List sources alphabetically and indent all lines after the first one.

✓ CONCEPT CHECK
Check and update URLs before you submit your paper because sites change and documents can move to new sites.

≪ Topics for Writing ≫

1. **React to the Reading.** Using *plagiarism* as your topic, write a research paper about ways to avoid it or explain why it is a problem for students and instructors. How does your college treat plagiarism? What have other colleges done to prevent or deal with this problem?

2. **Use Your Experience.** Write a research paper on a topic that interests you. To find a good topic, answer one or more of the following questions: What would you like to know more about? What is your career goal? What favorite activity, pastime, or personal interest would you like to research?

3. **Make a Real-World Connection.** Choose a topic from one of your college courses that would be appropriate for a research paper. Or research and write about a work-related issue.

4. **Go to the Web.** Choose a topic from the following list and follow this chapter's suggestions for planning and writing a research paper. Ask your instructor or a librarian to suggest some websites where you can begin to search for information on your topic.

   - A good place for a vacation
   - A problem and its solution
   - A controversial issue
   - A person worthy of admiration
   - A social or political concern

≪ Checklist for Revision ≫

Did you miss anything? Check off the following items as you revise and edit your paper.

- ❑ Does your title capture your readers' interest?
- ❑ Are your audience and purpose clear?
- ❑ Do you introduce and state your thesis effectively?
- ❑ Do your paragraphs have topic sentences?
- ❑ Do you have sufficient support for your thesis?
- ❑ Are your paragraphs unified and coherent?
- ❑ Have you paraphrased, quoted, or summarized information and cited your sources?
- ❑ Do you conclude with a summary of your research or a challenge for readers?
- ❑ Have you proofread your paper and corrected any errors in spelling, grammar, or documentation?

‹‹ Your Discovery Journal ››

To make research as enjoyable and challenging as possible, choose topics that are of vital interest to you whenever you have a choice. Reflect on your interests and some possible research topics that might arise from them. Then complete the following statements and explain your answers.

As an additional option, you can do this activity online by going to *The Confident Writer* website.

A social problem that is of great concern to me is _____.

One thing I have always wanted to know is _____.

‹‹ Website Resources ››

This chapter's resources include

- Chapter 7 Exercises
- Chapter 7 Quiz
- Downloadable Charts: *My Research Schedule*
- Survey: *What Do You Know About Research?*
- Chapter 7 Your Reflections
- More Topics for Writing
- Chapter 7 Summary

To access these learning and study tools, go to *The Confident Writer* website.

(((*Confident writers are observant. They choose details that appeal to the five senses and create images in readers' minds.*)))

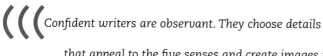

Narrating and Describing

What you already know about *narrating* and describing

- When you tell the story of how you got your driver's license or how you survived a car accident, you are narrating.

- When you begin a sentence with "It smells like . . . ," or "It tastes like . . . ," or "It feels like . . . ," you are describing.

- You use both narration and description in everyday conversation to talk about people, places, and events.

Your *goals* for this chapter

[1] Know how to use the sequence and significance of events, a clear point of view, and dialogue to tell a compelling story.

[2] Select details that are appropriate for your audience and purpose, that appeal to your readers' senses, and that create an overall effect or impression.

[3] Ask the questions that will help you determine what you know about your topic and whether narration or description is an appropriate choice of pattern.

[4] Use the tools of narration or description to help you plan, organize, and write your essay.

Unit 2

Patterns as Options

As explained in Chapter 1, organizational patterns for writing are the same thought patterns that are characteristic of logical thinking and everyday conversation. For example, it is normal to make comparisons, define terms, explain methods and processes, tell stories, and describe what you see or feel. The patterns explained in the next seven chapters are merely a writer's options for achieving unity and coherence. An organizational pattern serves as a framework for your ideas, and your choice of a pattern will depend on your topic, audience, and purpose.

Narration is the storytelling pattern. *Description* is the soul of writing because it brings subjects to life and allows your readers to see people, places, and events through your eyes. Both patterns work best when you have a clear purpose for using one or the other. To determine your purpose, ask yourself, "Why is the story important?" or "Why does my description matter?"

Because it is difficult to tell a story without also describing the people and places involved, Chapter 8 explains the tools and processes of both narration and description. Careful observation and attention to detail are the primary tools of both patterns, but each pattern has its own tools and processes as well.

[First Thoughts]

To build background for reading the following essay, explore your thoughts about conversion experiences, those events in our lives that act as turning points and change us in profound ways. Then answer the questions, either on your own or in a group discussion:

1. In a religious sense, what does it mean to be "saved" or to be "born again"? How is salvation a conversion experience?

2. In a secular (nonreligious) sense, what other conversion experiences can you describe? What are some of the events that change people's lives?

3. Read the title, the headnote, and the first two paragraphs of the following essay. Based on this preview, what do you think will follow?

[Word Alert]

Before reading, preview the following words and definitions. During your reading, use context clues and your dictionary to define any additional unfamiliar words.

revival (1)	a meeting for the purpose of awakening religious faith
dire (3)	dreadful, terrible

rounder (6)	an immoral person
wail (7)	a long, loud, high-pitched cry
serenely (7)	calmly
knickerbockered (11)	wearing knee pants
ecstatic (14)	joyful
deceived (15)	misled

Salvation

Langston Hughes

Langston Hughes, one of America's foremost African American authors, has written novels, poetry, short stories, and autobiographical essays. The following essay from Hughes's autobiography, *The Big Sea*, tells what happened to him the night he answered a preacher's call to be saved from sin. Hughes died in 1967.

1   I was saved from sin when I was going on thirteen. But not really saved. It happened like this. There was a big revival at my Auntie Reed's church. Every night for weeks there had been much preaching, singing, praying, and shouting, and some very hardened sinners had been brought to Christ, and the membership of the church had grown by leaps and bounds. Then just before the revival ended, they held a special meeting for children, "to bring the young lambs to the fold." My aunt spoke of it for days ahead. That night I was escorted to the front row and placed on the mourners' bench with all the other young sinners, who had not yet been brought to Jesus.

2   My aunt told me that when you were saved you saw a light, and something happened to you inside! And Jesus came into your life! And God was with you from then on! She said you could see and hear and feel Jesus in your soul. I believed her. I had heard a great many old people say the same thing and it seemed to me they ought to know. So I sat there calmly in the hot, crowded church, waiting for Jesus to come to me.

3   The preacher preached a wonderful rhythmical sermon, all moans and shouts and lonely cries and dire pictures of hell, and then he sang a song about the ninety and nine safe in the fold, but one little lamb was left out in the cold. Then he said: "Won't you come to Jesus? Young lambs, won't you come?" And he held out his arms to all of us young sinners there on the mourner's bench. And the little girls cried. And some of them jumped up and went to Jesus right away. But most of us just sat there.

4   A great many old people came and knelt around us and prayed, old women with jet-black faces and braided hair, old men with work-gnarled hands. And the church sang a song about the lower lights are burning, some poor sinners to be saved. And the whole building rocked with prayer and song.

5   Still I kept waiting to *see* Jesus.

6   Finally all the young people had gone to the altar and were saved, but one boy and me. He was a rounder's son named Westley. Westley and I were

surrounded by sisters and deacons praying. It was very hot in the church, and getting late now. Finally Westley said to me in a whisper: "God damn! I'm tired o' sitting here. Let's get up and be saved." So he got up and was saved.

"... the whole building rocked with prayer and song." —Langston Hughes

7   Then I was left all alone on the mourner's bench. My aunt came and knelt at my knees and cried, while prayers and songs swirled all around me in the little church. The whole congregation prayed for me alone, in a mighty wail of moans and voices. And I kept waiting serenely for Jesus, waiting, waiting—but he didn't come. I wanted to see him, but nothing happened to me. Nothing! I wanted something to happen to me, but nothing happened.

8   I heard the songs and the minister saying: "Why don't you come? My dear child, why don't you come to Jesus? Jesus is waiting for you. He wants you. Why don't you come? Sister Reed, what is this child's name?"

9   "Langston," my aunt sobbed.

10   "Langston, why don't you come? Why don't you come and be saved? Oh Lamb of God! Why don't you come?"

11   Now it really was getting late. I began to be ashamed of myself, holding everything up so long. I began to wonder what God thought about Westley, who certainly hadn't seen Jesus either, but who was now sitting proudly on the platform, swinging his knickerbockered legs and grinning down at me, surrounded by deacons and old women on their knees praying. God had not struck Westley dead for taking his name in vain or for lying in the temple. So I decided that maybe to save further trouble, I'd better lie, too, and say that Jesus had come, and get up and be saved.

12   So I got up.

13   Suddenly, the whole room broke into a sea of shouting, as they saw me rise. Waves of rejoicing swept the place. Women leaped in the air. My aunt threw her arms around me. The minister took me by the hand and led me to the platform.

14   When things quieted down, in a hushed silence, punctuated by a few ecstatic "Amens," all the new young lambs were blessed in the name of God. Then joyous singing filled the room.

15   That night, for the last time in my life but one—for I was a big boy twelve years old—I cried. I cried, in bed alone, and couldn't stop. I buried my head under the quilts, but my aunt heard me. She woke up and told my uncle I was crying because the Holy Ghost had come into my life, and because I had seen Jesus. But I was really crying because I couldn't bear to tell her that I had lied, that I had deceived everybody in the church, that I hadn't seen Jesus, and that now I didn't believe there was a Jesus any more, since he didn't come to help me.

≪ The Critical Reader ≫

[CENTRAL IDEA]

1. What is the writer's thesis? Can you find one or more sentences that state the central idea? If not, state the thesis, or central idea, in your own words.

[EVIDENCE]

2. Hughes uses time order to organize the details that explain what happened. Find and mark the transitional words that help you follow the story.

3. Identify the specific details that describe the church, the service, and the congregation. In which paragraphs do you find these details?

[IMPLICATIONS]

4. At the end of the essay, Hughes says he does not believe in Jesus because he did not *see* him. His aunt had said that he would see Jesus, or did she? What possible differences do you find in the meaning of the word *see* as the boy and his aunt interpret it?

[WORD CHOICE]

5. What does the dialogue add to the narrative? Would the story have been more effective if the dialogue had been left out? Why, or why not?

≪ The Critical Thinker ≫

To examine Langston Hughes's essay in more depth, follow these suggestions for reflection, discussion, and writing. Then choose one of them as a topic for writing.

1. Hughes's essay begins with two contradictory sentences. What is the author's meaning in these sentences? Use evidence from the essay to explain your answer.

2. Using examples from the essay, contrast Westley's and Hughes's attitudes toward being saved. What conclusion can you draw about the character of the two boys?

3. Disillusionment, a common theme in fiction and in autobiographical writing, is the process by which we become aware that something we believed in or thought to be true is incorrect. For example, children learn that there is no Santa Claus. A person's first love may be disillusioning. Someone we thought was a friend may betray us. Such experiences change us—for better or worse. How is "Salvation" a story of disillusionment?

4. Langston Hughes is also well known for his poetry. Read "Theme for English B." Check your library's holdings for a book that contains this poem or go to a poetry website. Your instructor can suggest a URL. Read the poem, then answer these questions about it in writing: What situation does the poem describe? Who are the people involved, and what do the author's details tell you about them? What specific details or ideas expressed in the poem are especially meaningful to you, and why?

Use Narration to Tell a Story

You would choose narration as your organizational pattern if you can see an advantage to developing your topic as a story. For example, if you think readers would be more interested in your topic and more likely to relate to your ideas if you tell them a story, then narration is your pattern. Topics such as "my first date" or "the day I got my driver's license" or "my registration nightmare" might work very well as narrative essays. Any of these topics can be related as a series of events that take place over a period of time. To bring organization to those events, you can explain what you did to prepare for the date, the driving test, or registration; what actually happened; and how you felt about the experience afterward.

The story will be even more compelling to readers if you explain what you learned from the experience and why they, too, should care about the lesson. This is called the story's *meaning* or *significance*. However, your story does not have to be about you. Instead, you might want to write about a person you admire or a day in the life of someone you know who has an interesting job. You might decide to write about the opening day at a new theme park, a concert you attended, or a historical event. If the event is important to you, you can make your readers care about it, too, by using effective writing strategies.

Although we usually associate narration with novels and short fiction, it is also an effective pattern for nonfiction writing. You can find many good examples of narration in professional essays, in magazine articles, in news stories, and even in your textbooks. It is not unusual for a textbook author to introduce a complicated topic with an *anecdote,* a brief story that puts the topic in perspective for students. In other words, a writer may decide to use narration whenever the topic or purpose requires it. If you choose narration as your organizational pattern for an essay, then use these tools and processes to tell your story:

1. Determine the story's significance.

2. Follow the sequence of events.

3. Choose a point of view.

4. Add dialogue for accuracy and variety.

Determine the Story's Significance

Suppose you are writing about an event such as witnessing the birth of a child, winning an award, achieving a victory in a sport, or surviving a catastrophe. First decide why this event is important to you or what you learned from the experience. In other words, try to understand the *meaning* of the event, not only for yourself but also for your readers. By analogy, whatever you learned from an experience, your readers should also be able to understand, either by having had similar experiences or by relating to yours. You can help them by having a purpose for writing and by communicating that purpose clearly. In his classic essay "Salvation," Langston Hughes describes the time he got saved. The significance of the event for him is that at the age of twelve he lost his faith because getting saved was not what he had expected. The significance of the event for readers may be that they, too, have questioned their faith or lack of it, or that they had a nonreligious conversion experience that changed their lives. These turning points mark the stages of personal growth that build character.

[**Exercise 8.1**] On a sheet of notebook paper, list three to five important events in your life, leaving several blank lines between them. Think about these events, and decide what is meaningful or significant about each one. To determine the significance, ask yourself, "What did I learn from the experience?" Following each event on your list, briefly explain its significance. When you have finished, decide which of the events you would like to write about. Then save your notes for a future assignment.

Follow a Sequence of Events

Events take place within a time frame. Every big event is marked by a series of little events from start to finish. Something happens first, then something happens next, then something else may occur, and finally the event is over. If you have a car accident, the highway patrol officer will ask you to explain the series of events that led up to the impact. If you decide to write about your car accident, begin by jotting down, in order, everything you remember about what happened to you. Next, go over your list and decide whether you need to tell *everything* that happened. If some of the events you have listed are not necessary to complete your narration, leave them out. Finally, decide how to organize the events.

While explaining what happened on a date might follow a before-during-after sequence, you might need to use another sequence to describe a different event. Suppose you are writing about the last five minutes of an exciting

Figure 8.1   Twenty-Two Transitions for Maintaining a Time Sequence

after	later
at the same time	meanwhile
before	never
beginning	next
during	now
earlier	once
ending	previously
finally	soon
first, second, third, ...	suddenly
following	when
last	whenever

football game. You might begin with a summary of what had led up to those last five minutes and then explain in detail what happened during each remaining minute. Transitional words and phrases are a big help in connecting ideas so that you maintain the sequence without losing coherence and so that your readers can follow your narration. Notice that many of Hughes's sentences in the chapter-opening essay begin with a time marker, such as *every night, that night,* or *suddenly.* Figure 8.1 lists some of the transitions you can use to show the passage of time.

In "How Did They Start the Breakfast Cereal Industry?" from Caroline Sutton's *How Did They Do That?* the author describes how the breakfast cereal industry developed. Dates help to mark the passage of time.

1   The Reverend Sylvester W. Graham preached that, rather than being born again, one's life could be salvaged by vegetarianism and bran. Living in New England in the early 19th century, the former Presbyterian preacher was an early champion of the low-fat, low-salt diet, brown bread as opposed to the socially sanctioned white, and fruits and vegetables as against beef or pork. If the Reverend Graham could only see how his flocks have multiplied a century and a half later. As it was, espousing coarse, unsifted flour; slightly stale bread; and lots of bran, he left his name to a flour and a cracker.

2   Graham had some notable followers in the 19th century—Thomas Edison, Amelia Bloomer, and Horace Greeley among them. Most critically, though, his influence led Mother Ellen Harmon White of the Adventist Church to found the Western Health Reform Institute at Battle Creek, Michigan, in 1866, where people

with stomachaches, too much fat or too little, high blood pressure, and assorted other ailments might find physical and spiritual health. Dr. John Harvey Kellogg, acting as manager, changed the name to Battle Creek Sanitarium and, along with his brother, developed a cereal called Granose, an immediate success. Among the patients at Battle Creek was Charles W. Post. While the absence of meat and lack of stimulants did not cure his ulcer, Post did invent Postum and Grape Nuts, the latter called Elijah's Manna until marketing problems provoked a change of name. The sanitarium must have been a creative place because there, too, Dr. Kellogg invented the corn flake for a suffering patient who broke her false teeth on a chunk of hard egg bread.

[**Exercise 8.2**] Identify and underline as many transitional words, phrases, and other time markers as you can find in the breakfast cereal passage. Then be able to share with the rest of the class how these transitions help readers follow the sequence of events.

Choose a Point of View

Writers narrate events from a *point of view*. If you describe events in your own life using the pronoun *I*, you are writing from the *first-person point of view*. If your narrative is about what happened to someone else and you use the pronoun *he, she,* or *they,* you are writing from the *third-person point of view*. Sometimes writers speak directly to the reader using the pronoun *you*, which is the *second-person point of view*. The following excerpt from Maxine Hong Kingston's *The Woman Warrior: Memoirs of a Girlhood Among Ghosts* illustrates the first-person point of view:

1 When I went to kindergarten and had to speak English for the first time, I became silent. A dumbness—a shame—still cracks my voice in two, even when I want to say "hello" casually, or ask an easy question in front of the check-out counter, or ask directions of a bus driver. I stand frozen, or I hold up the line with the complete, grammatical sentence that comes squeaking out at impossible length. "What did you say?" says the cab driver, or "Speak up," so I have to perform again, only weaker the second time. A telephone call makes my throat bleed and takes up that day's courage. It spoils my day with self-disgust when I hear my broken voice come skittering out into the open. It makes people wince to hear it. I'm getting better, though. Recently I asked the postman for special-issue stamps; I've waited since childhood for postmen to give me some of their own accord. I am making progress, a little every day.

2   My silence was thickest—total—during the three years that I covered my school paintings with black paint. I painted layers of black over houses and flowers and suns, and when I drew on the blackboard, I put a layer of chalk on

top. I was making a stage curtain, and it was the moment before the curtain parted or rose. The teachers called my parents to school, and I saw they had been saving my pictures, curling and cracking, all alike and black. The teachers pointed to the pictures and looked serious, talked seriously too, but my parents did not understand English. ("The parents and teachers of criminals were executed," said my father.) My parents took the pictures home. I spread them out (so black and full of possibilities) and pretended the curtains were swinging open, flying up, one after another, sunlight underneath, mighty operas.

3   During the first silent year I spoke to no one at school, did not ask before going to the lavatory, and flunked kindergarten. My sister also said nothing for three years, silent in the playground and silent at lunch. There were other quiet Chinese girls not of our family, but most of them got over it sooner than we did. I enjoyed the silence. At first it did not occur to me I was supposed to talk to pass kindergarten. I talked at home and to one or two of the Chinese kids in class. I made motions and even made some jokes. I drank out of a toy saucer when the water spilled out of the cup, and everybody laughed, pointing at me, so I did it some more. I didn't know that Americans don't drink out of saucers....

In this excerpt, Kingston explains her difficulty in learning English and how she coped with the language barrier by remaining silent. Perhaps becoming a writer was one way for her to overcome the silence of those early years. Through her use of the first-person point of view, Kingston controls the way you, as the reader, see her early school years.

The first-person point of view allows you to describe events and people's actions, thoughts, and feelings as *you* see them. A disadvantage for readers, however, is that they have to depend upon your interpretation of events. Suppose you write a first-person account of a car accident. You may describe the events differently from the way someone else would describe them, so readers do not have access to another point of view. When writing from the first-person point of view, use these pronouns: *I, me, my, mine, we,* and *ours.*

For an example of the third-person point of view, compare the following excerpt from Carin C. Quinn's "The Jeaning of America—and the World":

> ☑ **CONCEPT CHECK**
> A point of view is the perspective from which you tell a story. Narratives are often written in the first person, but they don't have to be. Experiment with writing from different points of view.

1 This is the story of a sturdy American symbol which has now spread throughout most of the world. The symbol is not the dollar. It is not even Coca-Cola. It is a simple pair of pants called blue jeans, and what the pants symbolize is what Alexis de Tocqueville called "a manly and legitimate passion for equality...." Blue jeans are favored equally by bureaucrats and cowboys; bankers and deadbeats; fashion designers and beer drinkers. They draw no distinctions and recognize no classes; they are merely American. Yet they are sought after almost everywhere in the world—including Russia, where authorities recently broke up a teenaged gang that was selling them on the black market for two hundred dollars a pair. They have been around for a long time, and it seems likely that they will outlive even the necktie.

2   This ubiquitous American symbol was the invention of a Bavarian-born Jew. His name was Levi Strauss.

3   He was born in Bad Ocheim, Germany, in 1829, and during the European political turmoil of 1848 decided to take his chances in New York, to which his two brothers already had emigrated. Upon arrival, Levi soon found that his two brothers had exaggerated their tales of an easy life in the land of the main chance. They were landowners, they had told him; instead, he found them pushing needles, thread, pots, pans, ribbons, yarn, scissors, and buttons to housewives. For two years he was a lowly peddler, hauling some 180 pounds of sundries door-to-door to eke out a marginal living. When a married sister in San Francisco offered to pay his way West in 1850, he jumped at the opportunity, taking with him bolts of canvas he hoped to sell for tenting.

4   It was the wrong kind of canvas for that purpose, but while talking with a miner down from the mother lode, he learned that pants—sturdy pants that would stand up to the rigors of the diggings—were almost impossible to find. Opportunity beckoned. On the spot, Strauss measured the man's girth and inseam with a piece of string and, for six dollars in gold dust, had [the canvas] tailored into a pair of stiff but rugged pants. The miner was delighted with the result, word got around about "those pants of Levi's," and Strauss was in business. The company has been in business ever since. . . .

In this excerpt, Quinn does not describe her own experience; instead, she reports on a series of events that happened to another person, Levi Strauss. She explains what Strauss and others thought and did, not what she thinks or has done. Notice that Quinn uses third-person pronouns—*he, his, him, them,* and *their.* Which point of view you choose for your essay will depend upon whether you are describing your own experience or someone else's.

One advantage for both you and your readers of writing from the third-person point of view is that you may look beyond the events themselves to the different ways people perceive them. The third-person point of view is characteristic of academic and other types of informational writing. This point of view relies more on information you gain by observing, thinking, and reading, and less on direct experience. Pronouns to use when writing in the third person are: *he, she, they, his, her, their, theirs, him, her,* and *them.*

The following excerpt from Tom Bodett's "Mood Piece" illustrates the second-person point of view.

1   . . . The bad mood scenario goes typically like this.

2   You wake up late, bound out of bed, and jam your foot under the closet door. This dislodges the big toenail from its setting, which hurts worse than if you'd taken the whole leg off at the knee. Recovering through rapid breathing, you throw on some clothes and fire up the coffeepot. While urging the brew cycle to its conclusion you sift through a stack of yesterday's mail and find a piece you'd overlooked, an official envelope from the City. It's one of those "Hold firmly here,

grasp and snap" deals that never work. You put your fingers at the indicated points and give it a stiff pull, nearly tearing the entire packet in two. It turns out to have been your personal property tax statement, and the rip went precisely through the amount due, rendering it unreadable.

3 Your temples start to throb, so you pour a fresh cup of coffee and turn on the radio to try and settle down. A little music usually soothes, but instead of music you're met with a barrage of incomprehensible jazz being forced through a saxophone at a pressure of ninety pounds per square inch. It's about as soothing as listening to an aircraft engine seize up in a small room, so you snap off the radio with a finality that sends the volume knob rolling under the stove. You figure it's time to stop screwing around and go to work. . . .

CONCEPT CHECK
For an explanation of pronoun types, errors, and how to correct them, see Unit 4, A.2 and D.1.

In this excerpt, Bodett describes how a typical morning begins for a person who is about to develop a bad mood that will last several days. In the essay from which the excerpt is taken, Bodett concludes that bad moods are predictable, they happen to everyone, and the only way to get through them is to maintain a sense of humor.

By using the pronouns *you* and *your*, Bodett is able to address his readers directly, encouraging them to identify with him. As you read the excerpt, you probably thought of your own bad moods, and you may have recalled experiences similar to those Bodett mentions.

An advantage of the second-person point of view is that it puts you and your readers on the same level: They are participants in the discussion rather than outside observers.

Whether you are writing from the first-person, second-person, or third-person point of view, be consistent. Readers will be confused if the point of view shifts unnecessarily or if your essay contains pronoun reference and agreement errors.

Exercise 8.3

Determine the point of view in "Salvation" on pages 197–198, and in the breakfast cereal excerpt on pages 202–203. Are the points of view similar or different? What do you think motivated each writer's choice of point of view? How would each piece of writing be different if the point of view were different, and why?

Add Dialogue for Accuracy and Variety

Dialogue adds variety to your writing. When you are describing actual events, you can give your readers a sense of "being there" by directly quoting what people said. Dialogue makes people come alive. Instead of describing them, you show them in action when you let them speak for themselves. The next time you read a newspaper account of a current event, look for dialogue. No-

☑ **CONCEPT CHECK**
Knowing where and when to use quotation marks is essential to writing good dialogue. Quotation marks are explained in Unit 4, C.8.

tice that people involved in the story are quoted so that you get the story not just from the reporter's point of view, but from the point of view of those who were there. To sharpen the accuracy of your memory when you are writing about an event, try to remember what the people involved said. Add to your essay only those bits of dialogue that you think will improve readers' understanding of the people, places and events you describe.

[**Exercise 8.4**] In Hughes's essay "Salvation" on pages 197–198, put a check beside each paragraph that contains dialogue. Then reread the paragraphs. Choose the paragraph that you think does the best job of using dialogue to create a picture in your mind of the person who is speaking or that helps you draw a conclusion about what the person is like. Then share your results with the rest of the class.

Your narrative essay should do more than list a sequence of events. Like any other essay, your narrative essay should have an overall point or central idea, which you will make clear to readers in your thesis statement. Use appropriate examples and descriptive details to tie your events together and make your point as Langston Hughes does in "Salvation." For another example of how narration and description work together, read the following passage from Zora Neale Hurston's autobiography, *Dust Tracks on a Road.* In this passage, Hurston recalls a story her family told about how she learned to walk.

1 . . . They tell me that an old sow-hog taught me how to walk. That is, she didn't instruct me in detail, but she convinced me that I really ought to try.

2 It was like this. My mother was going to have collard greens for dinner, so she took the dishpan and went down to the spring to wash the greens. She left me sitting on the floor, and gave me a hunk of cornbread to keep me quiet. Everything was going along all right, until the sow with her litter of pigs in convoy came abreast of the door. She must have smelled the cornbread I was messing with and scattering crumbs about the floor. So, she came right on in, and began to nuzzle around.

3 My mother heard my screams and came running. Her heart must have stood still when she saw the sow in there, because hogs have been known to eat human flesh.

4 But I was not taking this thing sitting down. I had been placed by a chair, and when my mother got inside the door, I had pulled myself up by that chair and was getting around it right smart.

5 As for the sow, poor misunderstood lady, she had no interest in me except my bread. I lost that in scrambling to my feet and she was eating it. She had much less intention of eating Mama's baby, than Mama had of eating hers.

6 With no more suggestions from the sow or anybody else, it seems that I just took to walking and kept the thing a-going. . . .

Can you see the scene clearly: the little child eating cornbread, the sow and her piglets nosing around in the crumbs, and the child scrambling to her feet and hugging the chair for support? Hurston creates a picture in words with details that appeal to your five senses. You can *see* the cornbread crumbs falling to the floor, recall what cornbread *tastes* and *smells* like, *hear* the child's screams, and experience *tactile* sensations in suggestive words and phrases such as *nuzzle* and *eat human flesh*. Other descriptive details give you a sense of place. These are country people who probably do not have running water, because Hurston's mother takes the greens down to the spring to wash them. The setting is the rural South, where *collard greens* are a regional dish and "right smart" is a familiar expression that in this context probably means "fast."

The next section explains the tools and processes of description, a pattern that will give life to your narrative essay.

Use Description to Enliven Your Writing

Goal 2 — Select details that are appropriate for your audience and purpose, that appeal to your reader's senses, and that create an overall effect or impression.

Like narrating, describing comes naturally to people. Description is a familiar means of self-expression that you use whenever you want to tell a friend about a movie you have seen, a book you have read, a person you care about, or a place you have been. When you visit the doctor, he or she asks you to describe your symptoms. A prospective employer will ask you to describe your previous work experience. In all these exchanges, the people you are talking with can ask questions to clarify anything they may not understand. The readers of your essays, however, have only your words to go on. Therefore, your descriptions should be clear enough to prevent any misunderstanding. You can improve your ability to choose descriptive details by doing the following:

- Find a controlling idea.
- Choose sensory details.
- Consider your audience and purpose.

Find a Controlling Idea

A *controlling idea* is the overall impression that a person, place, or object conveys. The controlling idea is part of your thesis, and it *controls* the details you select to support it. In the following short passage, a witness describes a suspect. The controlling idea of the description is the dullness, or ordinariness, of the suspect, and the descriptive details support this idea. The controlling idea is circled, and the supporting details are underlined.

You ask me to describe the man I saw fleeing from the building. Very well, then, he was a (dull) man. From his <u>medium-length mousy</u> <u>brown</u> hair to his <u>brown</u> shoes, he was an <u>ordinary-looking</u> fellow, a <u>middle-aged</u> man. He wore trousers <u>neither grey nor brown but some shade in between</u>. His shirt may have been white, or beige, or possibly a light yellow. It could have been a polo shirt with one of those little knit collars; then again it might have been a short-sleeved polyester sport shirt or a long-sleeved oxford cloth number. Was there a belt? There may have been a belt. Did he have any distinguishing marks or characteristics? None that I saw. He was clean-shaven, and he was of <u>medium height</u>; I do remember that. No, wait a minute; I think he had a beard. And now I seem to recall that the shirt was definitely the white polo, but I could be wrong.

There was a crowd of people at the end of the block waiting for the light to change. I think the suspect merged with the crowd, and, after that, I lost track of him. Would it help if you showed me some pictures? I do not think so. <u>He could be anyone, or no one.</u>

☑ **CONCEPT CHECK**
For more information on brainstorming and other prewriting strategies, see Chapter 2.

To find a controlling idea, begin by observing the person, place, or object you have chosen as your topic. Then make a brainstorming list. As you read over your list, try to think of one word or phrase that summarizes the overall impression the items on your list convey. For example, suppose you live in a dorm, and you have decided to write a short essay about your roommate, Ray. Your list might look like this:

saves money
takes shortcuts
buys used textbooks
saves time
makes instant coffee with tap water
reverses sheets to "clean" side
lets hair grow
skates to class
sprays deodorant on shirts
finds cheap or free entertainment
cools sodas on window sill in cold weather
trades paperbacks and tapes
blacks out light from windows
blocks out light from under door with black towel
stuffs cotton in ears
uses electric fan to muffle noise

brings food from home
brings toothpaste and other necessities from home

Reading over your list, you choose *resourceful* as a controlling idea, and you write the following preliminary thesis statement: *My roommate Ray is the most resourceful person I know.* Using this as your working thesis, you look at your brainstorming list again and decide that most of the items can be grouped under two major categories of resourcefulness, as listed here:

Saves Time

takes shortcuts
makes instant coffee with tap water
skates to class
reverses sheets to "clean" side
sprays deodorant on shirts

Saves Money

buys used textbooks
lets hair grow
finds cheap or free entertainment
trades paperbacks and CDs
brings food from home
brings toothpaste and other necessities from home

However, you have five items left over from your original list that do not seem to fit into either of your two categories. Asking questions about these items may help you find a third category for them. For example, why does Ray cool sodas on the window sill? Dorm rooms do not have refrigerators. Why does he black out light from windows and under the door? Perhaps he wants the room to look dark to discourage friends from interrupting his studying. Stuffing cotton in his ears and using a fan to muffle noise may be necessary to achieve quiet. What the items all seem to have in common is that they reflect some of the stresses of dorm life. Now you have a third category, *relieves dorm frustrations,* and an idea for revising your thesis statement: *My roommate, Ray, is a resourceful person who knows how to save time and money and how to relieve the frustrations of dorm life.*

Using your thesis, categories, and lists of items, you can now write an outline for your descriptive essay. After adding details and improving the organization, your final outline might look like this one:

I. Ray is resourceful in saving time.

    A. He knows all the campus shortcuts.

    B. He makes instant coffee with tap water.

    C. He skates to class.

D. He hates to waste time doing laundry.

    1. He reverses sheets to the "clean" side.

    2. He sprays deodorant on his shirts to keep from having to wash them.

II. Ray is resourceful in saving money.

A. He buys used textbooks.

B. He trades paperbacks and CDs instead of buying them.

C. He lets his hair grow to save money on haircuts.

D. He brings food from home.

    1. He raids the refrigerator and pantry.

    2. His mom makes cookies for him.

E. He brings toothpaste and other necessities from home.

F. He finds cheap or free entertainment.

III. Ray is resourceful in relieving dorm frustrations.

A. Having no refrigerator is a frustration.

    1. He keeps an ice chest in our room.

    2. He cools sodas on the window sill in winter.

B. Friends and noise can also be frustrating.

    1. To discourage unwanted visitors, Ray blocks the light from our windows with black paper.

    2. He uses a black towel to block the light that shines out from under our door, creating the impression that we are not at home.

    3. He uses an electric fan to muffle noise from the hall, and he stuffs cotton in his ears when studying.

Description is useful in any essay, no matter what other patterns you may choose to combine it with. A controlling idea will help you select appropriate descriptive details. To find a controlling idea, use the strategies of observation and brainstorming. To organize your details effectively during the planning stages of your writing process, try the strategies of listing and grouping related ideas and outlining. Choose descriptive words that appeal to your readers' five senses and that reinforce your controlling idea.

[**Exercise 8.5**] This visual exercise will help you gain a better sense of what a *controlling idea* is. Look at the photograph on page 198, and think about the scene it shows. In one word, describe how the scene makes you feel or what kind of thoughts it stimulates in your mind. The word you think of is the photograph's controlling idea. Using this idea as a starting point, write a paragraph in which you explain what the photograph means to you. Include in your paragraph details from the photograph that appeal to your senses.

Choose Sensory Details

Sensory details appeal to your five senses. Everything you *see, hear, smell, taste,* and *touch* makes an impression on you. To describe your impressions so that they come alive for readers, observe carefully. Then choose details that will appeal to your readers' five senses. For example, suppose you are writing about what it is like to ride on a subway. Go there. Take a ride, and make notes. What do you see, hear, and smell? Record your impressions as accurately as you can. When you write about the subway, recreate your actual experience on paper, choosing words and details that convey the impression you want your readers to have.

To describe something from memory, picture it in your mind. Then observe that image just as if you had the real object in front of you. Take notes on what you see in your mind's eye. Images you recall from memory may not be as vivid and clear as your direct observations, but you can begin to sharpen your recollections by paying close attention to your surroundings.

Descriptive details play an important role in bringing a narrative essay to life. Suppose you are writing an essay about a person. By choosing descriptive details carefully, you can make a point about the person or a place or show the relationship of person and place to the events explained in your essay. In the following paragraph from "Chinese Puzzle," an essay by Grace Ming-Yee Wai, the writer uses descriptive details to make a point about her father and to explain something significant she learned from the incident she describes in the paragraph.

> . . . My father was a loving and devoted son to my grandparents. He made sure they were happy and comfortable. He wanted them with us so he was assured of their well-being. My grandfather had fallen ill when I was around seven years old. The doctors thought he had cancer. Twenty years ago, that meant certain death. The night the diagnosis was given, I was alone with my parents after the store was closed. Dad was crying. I was frightened because I had never before seen him cry. Taking off his glasses and looking at me with red, teary eyes and unmistakable pain, he asked me, "Do you love your Ye-Ye?" It was difficult to speak to him when he seemed so vulnerable, but with all the courage I could muster and tears welling up in my eyes, I answered, "Yes." Mom was behind Dad comforting him. At

seven years of age, I was learning what it is to love your parents, and I was learning even Dads cry. Thankfully, my grandfather's cancer went into remission after treatment. . . .

In this paragraph, Wai explains how she felt—"I was frightened"—and how her father felt—he was "vulnerable" and he was experiencing "unmistakable pain." Sensory details of how Wai *feels* and what she *sees* and *hears* help you put yourself in her place that night her grandfather was diagnosed as having cancer. Seeing her dad cry and her mother comfort him, Wai learns to love her parents even more because for the first time she sees them as human and as sharing her emotions.

Exercise 8.6

Apply what you have learned about sensory details by doing this exercise with group members. First, review the group roles and responsibilities listed on the inside back cover of *The Confident Writer*. Next, choose any essay from Chapters 1 through 6 and scan it with group members to find details that appeal to your five senses. List your details on a chart like the one in Figure 8.2. Either make your own chart, or download a copy from *The Confident Writer* website. Before recording a detail on your chart, make sure that you have discussed it and that everyone agrees where it belongs. After completing your chart, discuss what purpose the details serve and whether

Figure 8.2 **Sensory Details**

SIGHT	SOUND	SMELL	TASTE	TOUCH

they are appropriate choices. Share your chart with the rest of the class. Evaluate your work as your instructor recommends, or go to the student website to download the group evaluation form.

Consider Your Audience and Purpose

Generally you have a choice of two purposes for describing anything:

- *Objective purpose:* to report information without bias or emotion

- *Subjective purpose:* to explain by expressing your feelings and impressions

Your purpose and audience are linked. For example, suppose your topic is a museum you have visited. You choose as your audience anyone who is planning a visit to the museum. Your purpose is to give an *objective* description of the building's layout, the types of exhibits presented, and their locations. On the other hand, suppose you were most impressed by the beauty of the museum's architecture and grounds. Your audience is someone who has never been there. Writing with a *subjective* purpose, you would choose details that will enable your reader to see the museum as you see it.

Use the *objective purpose* to describe a topic in an unemotional way without making a judgment about it. For example, perhaps you have done some research on mate selection in the United States, and you find out that couples whose marriages are successful have several characteristics in common. You might decide to write an essay informing readers what researchers have said these characteristics are. When writers describe objectively, they report only what they see, hear, smell, taste, and touch. They neither project their feelings onto the people and objects they describe nor interpret events and behaviors.

Use the *subjective purpose* to describe your feelings or impressions. For example, suppose you have recently emerged from a bad relationship, and you realize now that the person you were involved with was not the person you thought he or she was when you first met. You might decide to write an essay in which you describe the events that made you change your feelings about this person. When writers describe subjectively, they project their feelings onto what they experience through their senses, and they interpret events and behaviors in light of their own beliefs and values.

Your daily newspaper used to be a place that you could depend on for clear-cut examples of writing that meet either the objective purpose or the subjective purpose. For example, you could expect front-page news stories to report the facts objectively, without bias. On the other hand, you could expect editorials and letters from readers to contain details that would support their writers' opinions. Today, however, these distinctions may not be so clear. You may be more likely to find objective writing in documents, scholarly journals, some nonfiction books, and textbooks than in the daily newspaper.

☑ CONCEPT CHECK
To review audience and purpose, see Chapter 1.

[**Exercise 8.7**]　Following are three short excerpts. Decide whether the purpose in each one is *objective* or *subjective*. Be able to support your answer with evidence from each passage.

1. . . . At the end of our two-block alley was a small sandlot playground with　1
swings and slides well-shined down the middle with use. The play area was
bordered by wood-slat benches where old-country people sat cracking roasted
watermelon seeds with their golden teeth and scattering the husks to an
impatient gathering of gurgling pigeons. The best playground, however, was
the dark alley itself. It was crammed with daily mysteries and adventures. My
brothers and I would peer into the medicinal herb shop, watching old Li dole
out onto a stiff sheet of white paper the right amount of insect shells, saffron-
colored seeds, and pungent leaves for his ailing customers. It was said that he
once cured a woman dying of an ancestral curse that had eluded the best of
American doctors. Next to the pharmacy was a printer who specialized in gold-
embossed wedding invitations and festive red banners. . . .

From The Joy Luck Club, *by Amy Tan*

2. Carnivorous plants are those that get nourishment by trapping and digesting　1
insects. Specially modified flowers or leaves may produce an odor or have a
color that is attractive to insects. In some species a sticky coating on the
petals holds the insect in place while the flower closes around it, trapping it
inside the flower. The plant's juices contain a digestive acid.

Carnivorous plants grow in many parts of the world and come in many　2
varieties. One jungle species has a flower that is almost three feet in diameter.
Two carnivorous plants that grow in bogs in the northeastern part of the
United States are the *pitcher plant* and the *sundew.* These plants are easy
to recognize.

The pitcher plant looks exactly like a small pitcher that has a narrow neck　3
widening to a larger base. Mature plants can be 3 to 5 inches tall. The
"pitcher" is dark rusty red with darker vertical striations. It has a base of dark
green leaves.

The sundew has a flower that looks much like a daisy with shorter, fatter　4
petals. In the mature plant, the flower rises from a clump of dark greenish-
brown leaves on a stem about 10 to 12 inches tall. The stem curves down at
the top so that the flower hangs down.

3. In the West, in the blue mountains, there are creeks of grey water. They angle　1
out of the canyon, come across the brown scratched earth to the edge of the
desert and run into nothing. When these creeks are running they make a
terrific noise.

No one to my knowledge has ever counted the number, but I think there　2
are more than twenty; it is difficult to be precise. For example, some of the

creeks have been given names that, over the years, have had to be given up because a creek has run three or four times and then the channel has been abandoned.

You can easily find the old beds, where the dust has been washed out to reveal a level of rock rubble—cinnabar laced with mercury, fool's gold, clear quartz powder, and fire opal—but it is another thing to find one of the creeks, even when they are full. I have had some success by going at night and listening for the noise. . . .   3

From Desert Notes, Reflections in the Eye of a Raven, *by Barry Lopez*

Exercise 8.8

This exercise will help you understand the difference between the objective and subjective purposes of description. Remember that an objective description is free from judgment or personal opinion. When you describe something objectively, you relate only what anyone might observe directly, as in this example: *The sky is cloudy.* This sentence describes what any observer can see. When you describe something subjectively, you relate the feelings or thoughts that it provokes in you, as in this example: *The sky is gloomy.* This sentence describes a personal judgment or feeling about the sky's appearance.

Go to a website that contains photographs, such as *photovault.com,* or ask your instructor or librarian to suggest a URL for one. Then choose a photograph that appeals to you. Examine the photograph carefully, and then do items 1 through 4.

1. Divide a sheet of paper into two columns, and label the columns *Objective* and *Subjective.*

2. In the Objective column, list only what you see, for example, "two people" or "a blue chair."

3. In the Subjective column, list your impressions, for example, "two angry people" or "a soft, comfortable blue chair."

4. Using the details you have collected, do one of the following: write an objective description of what you see in the photograph, write a subjective description, or write a description that contains both objective and subjective details.

Student Voices: A Descriptive Essay

The author gives his impression of a storm, describing what happened and how he felt. As you read the essay, find as many sensory details as you can. For critical reading and thinking questions related to this essay, go to Chapter 8 Your Reflections on *The Confident Writer* website.

A Night to Remember
Steve Hackney

Foreboding, suggesting fear and danger, is the controlling idea.

To build background for his thesis, the author explains how he used to feel about storms.

1 I have always been intrigued by storms. The wind, lightning, and thunder stir my emotions to produce a foreboding curiosity. This feeling draws me near, but at the same time makes me wary of getting too close. My favorite place to watch storms is at the beach. I love to sit out on the balcony of the hotel room at night when a storm passes by. I can sit for hours and watch the blue fingers of lightning dive behind an invisible horizon against the black background of the night. I've often wondered how it would feel to be struck by lightning or what it would be like to experience a hurricane or tornado. Well, I've recently had the opportunity to be involved in some nasty weather. I had the misfortune of driving through the severe storm that ripped through Lake County in March of 1993. After experiencing something like that firsthand, my feelings about storms have definitely changed.

Good image

Thesis statement

2 To celebrate the beginning of the weekend, my fiancée and I had rented a couple of movies; we had spent most of the evening lying in front of the television. Because we had the VCR on, we were completely uninformed of the bad weather that was approaching.

3 Unaware of the warnings that had been issued by the local weather stations, I started home at about 11:30 P.M. There were no signs of bad weather other than a light drizzle, but that didn't seem to be anything to worry about. It appeared to be an ordinary Friday night, except for one thing: The streets were deserted. The night spots in downtown Mt. Dora usually attract quite a few patrons during the weekend, but not this night. There was no traffic, no pedestrians on the sidewalk, no one anywhere.

Spatial order in paragraph 4 helps readers visualize the scene and gives coherence to the details.

4 As I left the eerie streets of Mt. Dora and turned left onto Lakeshore Drive (the road runs along the shoreline of Lake Dora) the weather began to change dramatically. The wind began to blow fiercely, and the rain was getting harder with each passing second. Palm fronds were blowing across the road like leaves.

Eerie echoes foreboding in paragraph 1 and helps set the fearful mood.

The rain was now coming at me horizontally instead of vertically, blowing from left to right. Within a few minutes, I couldn't see the road directly in front of my car. The force of the rain felt and sounded like a hundred fire hoses aimed directly at the left side of my car. I slowed down to a literal crawl and tried to continue without driving into the lake or a ditch.

Time transitions

5   After a vain attempt to drive the remaining quarter of a mile to my house, I had to pull over. I couldn't see anything but water. The stretch of road that I was on is particularly close to the shoreline, and apparently the water from the lake was being blown across the road. The reality of what was really happening was beginning to set in, and I started to panic. I knew by the force of the wind that a tornado had to be close by. As I sat beside the road, my car was violently rocked back and forth like a rowboat in the middle of the ocean. Horrible images filled my mind. All I could think about was my car flipping over or a tree branch crashing through the window and hitting me in the head. I didn't know what to do other than pray, and I did. I kept saying over and over, "Please, God, don't let me die."

6   A few moments later, I began to think that if there was a tornado in the area, and it was coming my way, I didn't want to be around when it arrived. So, fearing for my life, I forced the car door open and started running. I ran down a side street to the front porch of the first house I came to. I rang the doorbell, but no one answered. I ran to a second house and, again, no answer. Finally, I ran across the street to a house with a light in the window and rang the doorbell. An elderly man answered the door and was kind enough to let me use his telephone. I called my parents to tell them where I was and that I was OK. I stood dripping wet on the man's porch until the rain died down. I then thanked him, ran back to my car, and proceeded to make my way home. When I arrived there, I considered myself lucky to be alive and without injury.

This use of dialogue clearly shows the author's fear.

Conclusion summarizes why the author's feelings have changed and explains why the experience was significant: He learned to respect and fear the power of storms.

7   Because of the events of that night and how I was rendered helpless by the forces of nature, my feelings about storms have changed. I'm still intrigued by their beauty, but now a different element of thinking comes into my mind: respect for their power and fear of their potential. I still like to watch the storms when I go to the beach, but only if I'm well out of their reach.

Think Through Your Topic

Remember that your reason for using either narration or description as your organizational pattern for an essay is that you think it is the best choice for your topic. Your topic drives your choice of pattern, not the other way around. For example, suppose your topic is "a person worthy of admiration." If you want to write about an event that shows this person's character, then narration would be a good pattern to use. But if you want readers to visualize the person and perhaps even respond emotionally to what you say about him or her, then description might be your choice. A combination of the two patterns might be even better. No matter what your topic is, think it through by answering ten questions to generate ideas.

Questions to Consider for Narration and Description

1. What is your topic, and why have you chosen it?
2. Is your purpose to relate an event or to create an impression?
3. If your topic is an event or a story, then what makes it significant?
4. If your topic is an impression or a feeling, then what is the controlling idea?
5. Is the topic something you know and care about?
6. Will the topic interest readers or seem important to them?
7. What is your central idea, thesis, or message for readers?
8. What point of view will you take?
9. What examples or sensory details will bring this topic to life?
10. How will dialogue add realism to your story or enliven your description?

Plan and Write Your Essay

Any prewriting strategy you have used successfully will work for planning either a narrative or descriptive essay. One strategy that works especially well for planning a narrative essay is to ask the questions journalists ask when they investigate a story. Answering these questions may sharpen your memory of an event and may remind you to include in your essay the basic information that will help your readers follow the story.

- *What* happened?
- *Who* was there?
- *When* did the event take place?
- *Where* did it happen?
- *Why* did it happen, or what caused it?
- *How* did it happen, or what were the details and circumstances?
- *What if it had not happened, or* what if *it had happened differently?*

Combining your answers to *why, how,* and *what if* questions may lead you to a discovery about the *significance* of the event if that is not already clear to you. Which prewriting strategy you settle on is less important, however, than the thought process you go through in choosing and in using it.

The difference between an effective description and an ineffective one lies in the details. Details that appeal to the five senses of sight, sound, taste, touch, and smell are the key to good description. To get the right amount and specificity of detail in your writing, use two strategies that will also help you plan your essay: 1) a three-level outline developed from a brainstorming list and 2) a coherence pattern.

The three-level outline begins with a main idea that is broken down into major details and minor details as in the outline for the essay on Ray, the resourceful roommate on pages 210–211. Remember that the controlling idea for the essay is Ray's resourcefulness, and all the details reflect this controlling idea.

Coherence patterns such as time order, emphatic order, and spatial order are helpful for planning because they give you a framework for thinking about

Figure 8.3   Maintaining Coherence in Description

EMPHATIC ORDER: TRANSITIONS	SPATIAL ORDER: TRANSITIONS
more, less	left, right
most, least	up, down
important	top, bottom
more or most important	above, beneath
less or least important	in front, behind
even more	sideways
more so	over, under
higher, highest	near, far
lower, lowest	inside, outside
primary	overhead, underfoot

and selecting appropriate details. Use spatial order for describing places. As you think of what to write, imagine yourself in the place. What do you see in front of you, in back, to the left, to the right, above your head, and beneath your feet? Use emphatic order for describing the behaviors or characteristics of a person. What are the person's qualities: a good sense of humor, generosity, tolerance for others' differences? What is the most important quality, and what specific actions or behaviors reveal this quality? Figure 8.3 lists transitions that will help you maintain coherence in your descriptive essay. Figure 8.4 is an overview of what to include in your narrative or descriptive essay.

Figure 8.4   **Narrating and Describing: An Overview**

PARTS	WHAT TO INCLUDE IN A NARRATIVE ESSAY	QUESTIONS TO ASK
Introduction	1. Topic 2. Significance 3. Context 4. Thesis	1. What is the story? 2. Why is it important to me? 3. What is my point of view? 4. What point do I want to make with this story?
Each body paragraph	1. Topic sentence 2. Major details 3. Minor details 4. Transitions	1. What is one major event in my story's development? 2. What are the most important details that will explain the event? 3. Can I add dialogue to my story? 4. What transitions should I use to help readers follow the sequence of events?
Conclusion	1. Restatement of thesis 2. Significance for readers	1. How can I make the same point in different words? 2. What will readers learn from my story?

PARTS	WHAT TO INCLUDE IN A DESCRIPTIVE ESSAY	QUESTIONS TO ASK
Introduction	1. Topic 2. Purpose 3. Context 4. Thesis	1. Is my topic a person, place, or object? 2. Is my purpose for writing objective or subjective? 3. What is my controlling idea? 4. What overall impression do I want to create?
Each body paragraph	1. Topic sentence 2. Major details 3. Minor details 4. Transitions	1. What is one aspect of my overall impression? 2. What major sensory details will support this impression? 3. What else can I add? 4. What transitions will keep my details coherent?
Conclusion	1. Final anecdote or example 2. Significance for readers	1. What brief story or example can I give to bring the person, place, or object to life for readers? 2. What will my description cause readers to think, feel, or understand?

≪ Topics for Writing ≫

1. **React to the Reading.** Using Langston Hughes's essay as a model, write about a time when you became disillusioned and tell what you learned from the experience. Using Steve Hackney's essay as a model, write about a storm or other disaster you survived.

2. **Use Your Experience.** Write about an important person in your life or a familiar place, object, or event. The following list may give you some suggestions:

   - A favorite possession
   - A teacher I will always remember
   - A place of interest in my hometown
   - An experience that changed my life
   - A place most people would (or would not) want to live
   - An impression people have about my college that may (or may not) be true

3. **Make a Real-World Connection.** Write about a hardship that someone you know has had to overcome. Tell this person's story, and explain what you learned from it.

4. **Go to the Web.** Write about a person whom you admire for his or her achievements in a field such as the arts, sports, science, business, or public service. Search the Web for information on this person that you can use in your essay. Google the person's name or ask your instructor or librarian to suggest a URL to use.

≪ Checklist for Revision ≫

Did you miss anything? Check off the following items as you revise and edit your essay.

Narration

- ❏ Does your thesis briefly state what story you are telling?
- ❏ Have you determined the significance of your story?
- ❏ Do the events follow a sequence that is marked by transitions?
- ❏ Do you have a consistent point of view?
- ❏ Have you included dialogue?

Description

- ❏ Is your topic a person, place, or object?
- ❏ Does your essay have a thesis and controlling idea?
- ❏ Do your details appeal to readers' five senses?

❑ Is your purpose either subjective or objective?

❑ Have you used a coherence pattern that is marked by transitions?

Narration and Description

❑ Does your essay have three parts?

❑ Do your body paragraphs have topic sentences?

❑ Does your introduction create a context for the thesis?

❑ Have you used an appropriate concluding device?

❑ Have you proofread your essay and corrected any errors?

⟨⟨ Your Discovery Journal ⟩⟩

It is not unusual for an employer to ask job applicants to describe their best quality or to think of a word that defines who they are.

How would you describe yourself to someone else? How do you think others would describe you? Is there a word, phrase, or controlling idea that expresses who you are?

Reflect on the following statement, and then complete it in your journal. As an additional option, you can do this activity online by going to *The Confident Writer* website.

If I had to describe myself in one word, it would be _____.

⟨⟨ Website Resources ⟩⟩

This chapter's resources include

▬ Chapter 8 Exercises

▬ Chapter 8 Quiz

▬ Downloadable Charts: *Sensory Details*

▬ Downloadable Charts: *Group Evaluation Form*

▬ Chapter 8 Your Reflections

▬ More Topics for Writing

▬ Chapter 8 Summary

To access these learning and study tools, go to *The Confident Writer* website.

(((*Confident writers are precise. They choose words*

carefully and express their ideas clearly so that

readers will understand.)))

Explaining a Process

What you already know about *process* analysis

o You have had experience with many ordinary processes such as learning to drive a car, registering for classes, or following a recipe.

o You can explain the steps involved in processes such as washing a load of laundry, changing the oil in your car, or ordering something from an online store.

o You may have had to learn a process on the job, such as how to use a cash register, stock inventory in a store, or enter data into or retrieve information from databases.

Your *goals* for this chapter

[1] Determine a purpose for writing about a process, and make your purpose clear to readers.

[2] Build background for your topic; explain your process in a real-world context that readers can relate to or apply.

[3] Ask questions to determine how much you know about a certain process and whether it is a good choice for your essay.

[4] Identify the steps of your process, organize and explain the steps, and make sure that your thesis statement clearly expresses your thoughts or feelings about the process.

As a parent, you may have assembled a child's swing set or a toy. As an employee, you may have had on-the-job training. As a college student in a biology course, you may have followed a lab procedure. No doubt you know how to prepare a simple meal. Were you ever asked to give someone directions to your home or to another destination? Do you know how to ride a bicycle? We take these processes for granted, but if you stop to think about any familiar process, you will realize that there is an expected outcome, a goal to reach, a reason behind the process, and steps to follow to complete it.

Even the courses you take explain processes. Algebra teaches procedures for solving problems. Biology examines the life processes of organisms. Your composition class explains how to write an essay.

Process is a pattern of thought and organization whereby the writer explains the steps or stages that lead to an outcome. In some processes a *sequence* of steps is essential. In others, sequence does not matter. However, all processes serve an underlying purpose for both the writer and the audience.

[First Thoughts]

To build background for reading, explore your thoughts about thunderstorms. Then answer the following questions, either on your own or in a group discussion:

1. What causes a thunderstorm?

2. What are some ways to protect yourself during a thunderstorm?

3. Read the title, the headnote, and the first two paragraphs of the following essay. Based on this preview, what do you think will follow?

[Word Alert]

Before reading, preview the following words and definitions. During your reading, use context clues and your dictionary to define any additional unfamiliar words.

stability (4)	state of calm
atmosphere (4)	surrounding mass of gases that envelops the earth and other celestial bodies
condensing (5)	changing from a gas to a liquid
adhere (5)	to stick

devastating (7)	destructive, overwhelming
havoc (10)	widespread destruction
lethal (18)	deadly

When the Big Clouds Gather

David H. Levy

David H. Levy is the science editor for *Parade* magazine. He is the author of eleven books, a noted lecturer, and the host of the popular radio show *Let's Talk Stars*. In this article from his column "Science on Parade," Levy explains how thunderstorms develop and what to do when the clouds gather.

☑ CONCEPT CHECK
What hazardous weather conditions are common where you live? What damage has resulted, and how can residents protect themselves?

1   It started with the sky darkening—fast, as though by a dimmer switch—and sudden gusts of wind on a recent evening in the Northeast. Instinctively, I raced into the house for safety as bolt after bolt of lightning flashed in the night sky, followed by deafening claps of thunder. When the rain poured, it came not down but across, straight toward the house. A huge bolt lit up the night like day, and I saw a tree split in two and crash to the ground less than 100 feet away.

2   Thunderstorms, among the most beautiful displays in Nature, are also a danger not to be taken lightly. Those who ignore the warning signs, or don't know what to do when they appear, put themselves in harm's way from lightning, high winds, hail and sudden flooding. While they can develop at any time, thunderstorms are most common between May and September in the U.S. The storm season varies with the region: In the desert Southwest, storms can develop almost daily from July to September but are virtually nonexistent the rest of the year. In general, the higher the temperature, the more often thunderstorms occur.

3   You usually will be safe to enjoy a storm's beauty and power inside a house or an office building. You're decidedly more at risk by a lake or on open ground. Do you know what to do if caught in a thunderstorm? Here is some basic science to explain these spectacular events and a set of guidelines to help you to protect yourself and your family.

Nature Rages to Restore Calm

4   Thunderstorms are Nature's way of maintaining stability in the atmosphere. The air above us is stable or balanced when heavier, cooler air is near the surface and lighter, warmer air is above it. Instability occurs when the air at the ground becomes hot and humid while the higher air is cool and dry. The atmosphere is then "upside down." It tries to restore stability through a process called *convection:* The warm, moist air rises, producing droplets of water that fall as rain in a thunderstorm, bringing cooler, drier air down with them. The air has become stable. The storm has done its job.

5   To understand how droplets form, it is helpful to look *inside* a thundercloud. Imagine a tiny spec of dust wandering about at the bottom of a rapidly

growing *cumulonimbus* (mountain-shaped) cloud. It is a humid day. The speck, carried along by winds, rises through the cloud into cooler and cooler air. The air is cooling so rapidly that the moisture in it is condensing. Particles of water adhere to the speck, making it heavier and heavier until—along with millions of similar droplets—it falls as rain. The droplets' high-speed movement through the cloud builds up an electric charge, released as lightning.

6   Simply put, lightning is an enormous electric spark. When you walk on a carpet, the friction you create builds up a static-electric charge in your body. If you then touch an object that has an opposite charge (a wall, a doorknob, a person), a spark jumps from you to that object, and you feel a shock.

7   Lightning is basically the same thing—but, on Nature's grander scale, it can be devastating. As water droplets race through the cloud, the friction they create builds up a huge static-electric charge—mainly negative at the bottom of the cloud, positive at the top. Much of a storm's lightning remains within the cloud, leaping the gap between top and bottom. But when an object on the ground, such as a building or a tree, becomes positively charged, the lightning sparks to the ground as a brilliant bolt.

8   When this happens, enormous heat is generated so that the air around the bolt virtually explodes—the sound of thunder. You hear the thunder *after* you see the lightning flash, because the speed of sound is much slower than that of light.

9   You can tell how close you are to a lightning flash by counting the seconds that pass between the lightning and the time you first hear thunder. Sound travels at 1100 feet a second. So, if the thunder began 5 seconds after the lightning, the strike was 5500 feet away (1100 feet x 5 seconds), or just over a mile. If the time interval was 15 seconds, then the lightning bolt was about 3 miles away.

Count the Hazards

10   As you read this article, an average of 1800 thunderstorms are creating havoc somewhere on Earth in one or more of the following ways:

11   *Lightning.* In a typical year, 73 people are killed and more than 300 injured by lightning. Lightning kills far more people than any other weather event, including tornadoes. A bolt of lightning can force an enormous amount of electricity through your body. Consider an electric shock in the home. Its 120 volts can cause severe injury. Compare that to the 15 *million* volts from a lightning bolt!

12   Although the overall odds of being struck by lightning in the U.S. are estimated at one in 615,000, the likelihood increases depending on where you are when a storm comes up. "Half the casualties of lightning occur during activities in open fields, such as soccer and baseball," warns Conrad Lautenbacher, administrator of the National Oceanic and Atmospheric Administration. "Parents and coaches have to know: If you hear thunder, get your children inside a substantial building. A vehicle with a metal roof and sides is a good second choice."

13   *High winds.* Strong winds are typical of thunderstorms, but some weather patterns produce a *microburst*—a violent, localized downdraft covering 2.5

How to Stay Safe

Thunderstorms arrive suddenly, with little warning except the darkening sky as the thundercloud approaches. If you see tall, puffy cumulus clouds growing and daylight rapidly dimming, observe these safety measures:

IF YOU'RE NEAR A HOUSE OR OTHER BUILDING . . .

- Make sure that all children are accounted for.

- Secure outdoor furniture.

- Go indoors. If the storm is severe, with frequent and close lightning bursts, head for a basement or a room in the middle of the house or other building.

- Keep away from objects that might conduct electricity (such as radiators, pipes, and metal door frames).

- Stay away from windows.

- Do not take a bath or shower during a storm. Water helps to conduct electricity, and walls don't always protect from the high energy of a lightning bolt.

- Do not get close to electrical appliances such as plug-in radios and TVs. Use battery-operated radios.

- Restrict all calls to cell phones.

IN AN OPEN FIELD OR ON A GOLF COURSE . . .

- If you feel your hair start to stand on end or your skin tingle, or if you hear crackling sounds, lightning may be about to strike you. Drop down quickly, bend forward, feet together, hands on knees. Do not lie flat: You want to make yourself as small as possible and have minimal contact with the ground.

- Don't stand on an apartment-house roof during a thunderstorm. (Last summer, a young man was fatally struck by lightning in New York City while doing just that.)

IF YOU'RE SWIMMING . . .

- Get out of the pool, lake or ocean at the first sign of lightning or thunder. Find indoor shelter or get into a car. Stay out of the water for at least 30 minutes without thunder.

- Stay away from metal fences or flagpoles.

IF SOMEONE IS STRUCK . . .

- Heart attacks are the usual cause of lightning fatalities. If breathing stops, seek medical help at once.

Source: Parade Magazine, May 18, 2003, p. 4.

miles or less, with winds up to 150 mph. Some, called "dry," microbursts, have little rain, as most of the water stays above 10,000 feet. Microbursts can blow down trees and rip manufactured homes off their foundations.

14   *Floods.* Slow-moving storms can produce sudden large torrents that flood streets. The enormous pressure of large amounts of water rushing through a low-lying area can move a car a mile or more.

15   *Hail.* If the humid air rises far enough and stays in the cloud long enough, the water droplets can freeze and grow and fall as hail. Hailstones can be as large as softballs—yet another reason to go indoors. In 1995, a hailstorm in Dallas damaged so many planes that some airlines temporarily lost portions of their fleets while repairs were made.

16   *Tornadoes.* Thunderstorms come in various sizes. A storm can grow from a single-cell storm—a small, solitary thundercloud—to a multicell cluster that covers a large area. "Supercell" storms are the most likely to produce tornadoes. They form when lower-atmosphere winds are moving at a radically different

speed and/or direction from ground winds, causing the whole system to rotate rapidly. Supercells are most common in the Midwest, where cold air rushing in from the North attacks warm and humid Southern air to produce incredibly tall, swirling clouds and violent winds that can toss a car and level a house.

Know How and When to Play It Safe

17 Weather forecasters issue thunderstorm warnings as if all storms are equally dangerous. One result is that many of us regard them as "crying wolf" and ignore the warnings. Often they'll say, "chance of thunderstorms," because it's hard to know precisely when and where a storm will burst—one can arrive suddenly, with little warning except the darkening sky as it approaches.

18 Outdoor activities are fun when it's fair but can be lethal in a thunderstorm. Golf, cycling and swimming expose us to metal and water, which conduct electricity. Continuing your fun in a storm is like inviting lightning to strike.

19 Prevention is much better than treating a victim. Get into the habit of observing the weather and paying attention to forecasts. And know what safety measures to take.

20 Like other grand spectacles of Nature, thunderstorms—at once extraordinarily beautiful, dangerous, and frightening—must be respected. A little knowledge about them can help you to protect yourself and those in your care when the big clouds gather.

⟨⟨ The Critical Reader ⟩⟩

[CENTRAL IDEA]

1. What is David H. Levy's thesis, and where is it stated?

2. Who is Levy's audience? How can you tell?

[EVIDENCE]

3. What are the hazards, or dangers, of thunderstorms?

4. Which paragraphs contain details that explain how thunderstorms develop?

5. According to the author, what are some steps you can take to protect yourself during thunderstorms?

[IMPLICATIONS]

6. Is the author's view of weather forecasters generally favorable or unfavorable? Using evidence from the article, explain your answer.

[WORD CHOICE]

7. Levy uses sensory details to help readers understand the power and destructiveness of thunderstorms. Which words or phrases create the clearest images for you, and why?

≪ The Critical Thinker ≫

To examine David H. Levy's essay in more depth, follow these suggestions for reflection, discussion, and writing. Then choose one of them as a topic for writing.

1. How does Levy's thesis statement relate to his purpose for writing?

2. What is Levy's tone? Find specific words and phrases that help you determine his tone,

3. In paragraph 2, the author describes thunderstorms as both "beautiful" and "a danger not to be taken lightly." What do you think is his meaning?

4. Based on the information you have gained from Levy's article, what tips would you give people for keeping safe during thunderstorms? In addition to the author's suggestions, are there others that you can suggest from your own experience?

Determine a Purpose for a Process

Goal 1

Determine a purpose for writing about a process, and make your purpose clear to readers.

Processes are of two kinds: *directional* or *informational*. A *directional process* explains how to do something. For example, recipes are directional processes; so are explanations of how to study for a test, the best way to wash a load of laundry, how to survive traveling with small children, and how to buy a house. In other words, after reading the explanation, you should be able to follow the steps and accomplish the task on your own. *Informational processes,* on the other hand, explain how things work or how something gets done. For example, an explanation of how potato chips are made is an informational process; so are explanations of how your state legislature passes laws and how a fetus develops in the womb. The outcome of these processes is not that you will be able to do them on your own

Products are manufactured according to a clearly established process in which workers have responsibilities to carry out and steps to follow.

Figure 9.1   The Connection Between Process and Purpose

TYPE OF PROCESS	PURPOSE	OUTCOME FOR READERS
Directional	To give directions that explain how to do something.	Readers will be able to follow your steps and complete the process on their own.
Informational	To provide information that explains how something works, gets made, or is accomplished	Readers will be able to understand the steps or stages in the process so that their knowledge of it is broadened.

but that you will improve your knowledge and understanding of the steps involved.

Both kinds of processes are closely connected to your purpose for writing. When you write about a process, one of the first things to consider is why you want to write about it. Do you want to teach your readers how to do something? Or do you want to broaden their understanding of how something works or how something is made or accomplished? The chart in Figure 9.1 summarizes the connection between process and purpose.

Exercise 9.1

Apply what you have learned so far about directional and informational processes by doing this exercise with group members. First, review the group roles and responsibilities listed on the inside back cover of *The Confident Writer*. Next, read and discuss the following list of common processes. Determine which processes are directional (D) and which are informational (I). Be able to support your answers when you share your results with the rest of the class. Then evaluate your group's discussion as your instructor recommends, or download the group evaluation form from *The Confident Writer* website.

_____ 1. How to build a fence

_____ 2. How to document a research paper

_____ 3. The life cycle of a gypsy moth

_____ 4. The making of a politician's image

_____ 5. How to give CPR (cardiopulmonary resuscitation)

_____ 6. Ways businesses have reduced energy consumption

_____ 7. How a newspaper is printed

_____ 8. A method for reducing boredom

_____ 9. How to prepare for the GRE (Graduate Record Examination)

_____ 10. How Congress spends your taxes

_____ 11. How to figure your income tax

Exercise 9.2 Look closely at the photo on page 230. What do you see? What process is taking place? Suppose you were to visit the place in the photo and watch the process firsthand. If you were then to write an essay about the process, would your explanation be informational or directional, and why?

Create a Context for a Process

Goal 2 Build background for your topic; explain your process in a real-world context that readers can relate to or apply.

Your decision to write about a process should follow directly from your experience and your audience's needs. Write about processes that you are familiar with through reading and observation or that you have actually done and think are worthwhile. Suppose you believe that everyone should know how to do CPR (cardiopulmonary resuscitation). Maybe you think this because you took a course in CPR and, by performing this simple maneuver, were able to prevent someone from choking to death. To establish a context for your process, you could begin your essay by briefly explaining what happened. From there, you could move to an explanation of the steps involved in performing CPR.

Whatever process you choose to explain, provide a *context* for that process by making clear to your readers why it is important to you and should be important to them as well. For example, tell your readers how you learned about the process, why you do it, or where you have seen it done. You can build readers' interest in *any* process by placing it in context and having a purpose for writing. Consider the following two introductory paragraphs written by college students. Both paragraphs create a context for the processes these students explain.

The following paragraph is from an essay by a student, Brandon Holland, titled "The Fundamentals of Catching in Baseball." As you read the paragraph, notice how the author arouses readers' interest by telling them that catching a baseball involves more than they may think it does. Also, look for an analogy: To what does the author compare catching?

> Catching is one of the most difficult positions to play in sports. It requires a great deal of thought, physical stress on the body, and coordination. Many people think that a catcher just catches the ball and throws it back to the pitcher. However, this is a terrible misconception! A catcher plays a much greater role beyond what most people are aware of. As a catcher, you have the responsibility of the secret service. You are responsible for taking the bullet, or the baseball, to protect the president, or the umpire. The catcher is also responsible for making quick decisions that determine the outcome of the entire game and must sacrifice his body on every play. It takes a very dedicated and mentally and physically strong individual to catch. . . .

The essay goes on to explain the requirements and responsibilities of catching.

The next paragraph is from an essay by a student, Jenna Nation, titled "How to Eat." As you read this paragraph, notice the author's tone. Notice how she appeals to her readers' experience as she creates the context for her process: how to eat with enjoyment.

☑ CONCEPT CHECK
Did you notice that Jenna Nation begins her introductory paragraph by asking a question? To review types of introductions, see Chapter 4. To review tone, see Chapter 6.

Eating is an activity that many people, for some reason or another, no longer enjoy with the same enthusiastic fervor of our ravenous forbears. Why do we as a society shun the joy of food? Perhaps it is the stinging pang a woman feels jabbing into her like a dull knife after she has eaten that particularly succulent New York–style cheesecake or the instant remorse a man endures after devouring a tasty pepperoni and sausage pizza. The media, through glossy computer-generated photos of twig-like models and bone-thin actresses, has helped deprive us of our love of such a wonderful event. We enjoy the food as we eat it, but the gut-wrenching guilt afterwards is far from wonderful. Well, I refuse to be a slave to this misguided experience. For those of you who have forgotten just how lovely this can be, fear not because there is still plenty of hope for you! One day, hopefully soon, you too will be able to once again satisfy your persistent craving for a chocolate cream pie with extra whipped cream and feel only the satisfaction of a fantastic dessert contentedly digesting in your stomach. Afterwards, you will not feel any guilt, regret, or remorse. Instead, you will have only an overwhelming sense of gratitude because you are not one of those starving children in some poverty-stricken third-world country your mother always told you about. . . .

The essay goes on to explain how to rid yourself of guilt so that you can enjoy eating again.

To write creatively about any process, build a context for the process in your introductory paragraph. Find some larger purpose for writing your essay. For example, reveal to your audience something they may not know about the process or about its meaning or importance.

Student Voices: A Process Essay

The author explains how to train a horse, a process that may be unfamiliar to you. As you read the essay, try to follow the steps of the process. For critical reading and thinking questions related to this essay, go to Chapter 9 Your Reflections on *The Confident Writer* website.

Horses
Sarah Coleman-Brantley

1   Because horses are intelligent, majestic creatures that are capable of thinking, reasoning, compromising, and making friends, working with horses has always been a very enjoyable experience for me. I especially enjoy training horses, but in order to be successful, one needs to know the correct process to train

a horse. When I trained my first horse, Fancypants, I used the following steps: approach/retreat, acceptance, and repetition.

2   The first step I used to train Fancypants is called approach/retreat. The purpose of this step is to establish a communication link between the horse and trainer and to establish who is the leader. To do this, I took Fancypants into a large round pen so that she would have enough room to run but could not get too far away from me. I then turned her loose, squared my shoulders up to her, and looked her straight in the eye. To a horse, this means "Get away from me. I'm mad." Fancypants kicked up her hind legs, slung dust everywhere, and took off in a run to the outer edge of the round pen. The whole time she ran around the pen I kept my shoulders squared up to her and stared straight at her. Fancypants ran as fast as she could around the pen for about four minutes. Even though she wanted to stop, I made her continue trotting around for about five more minutes by tossing a long rope out toward her but never hitting her with it. Since it was a very hot day, she was breathing quickly and heavily and sweating around her chest and flanks.

3   Once the approach/retreat step was in play, I then started looking for acceptance as the next step in her training. To let her know I was ready to reach a compromise, I dropped my gaze from her eyes down to her neck. Fancypants immediately went from a fast-paced trot to a slow, cautious walk. I had made the first move toward friendship; it was now her turn. She quickly decided she would rather be a friend than to have me as a threat. To let me know this, Fancypants lowered her head so that her lips were almost touching the dusty soil. When I turned my body about sixty degrees away from her so that she would know it was okay to come to me, Fancypants walked with her head still bowed down to the center of the round pen where I stood. She allowed me to saddle her up and put a bridle on her. So that she would know she had my trust and I would know I had hers, I ran my hands gently over her entire body. I started by rubbing between her ears and working my way down her sweaty neck. At the risk of being trampled or bitten, I continued to rub her legs, stomach, and back. I calmly placed one foot in the stirrup and slowly lifted myself into the saddle. Then Fancypants just started walking around the pen. I didn't want to push her too hard since it was only her first day, so I rode her back to the center of the pen, unsaddled her, and gave her a good bath and an extra carrot for dinner.

4   Although Fancypants had accepted me as a friend and rider, the training would have all been for nothing if I hadn't followed through with the final step: repetition. I rode Fancypants every day except Sundays for the next month. During the first week of training, I rode her only in the round pen. Once I was sure Fancypants felt comfortable with the new weight she was now carrying, we rode around in the two-acre pasture. Her training regressed a little once we started riding in an open field. With so much space around her, Fancypants acted as if she should be the one in charge of where we went.

However, after about a week and a half of reigning practice at a very slow pace, Fancypants began to understand where I wanted her to go. After Fancypants realized that I was still in control in an open area, we picked up the pace a little bit. By the end of the third week, Fancypants was behaving as if I had been riding her for years. She could stop and go on command, back up, and move forward at any pace. Even though she was performing very well at that time, I still continued to ride her routinely. Through practice and repetition, Fancypants learned what was expected of her.

5   I was very happy that Fancypants was easy to train. Through approach/retreat, acceptance, and repetition, Fancypants became a well-behaved, ridable horse.

[**Exercise 9.3**] Think of everything you have done over the past few days—at home, at work, or on campus—that involved the completion of a process. Make a list of these processes. Circle the one that you think might be most interesting to readers. Decide whether it is a directional or an informational process and what your purpose for writing about it would be. Share your results with the rest of the class.

Think Through Your Topic

Goal 3 Ask questions to determine how much you know about a certain process and whether it is a good choice for your essay.

The reason to use process as your organizational pattern for an essay is that you think it is the best choice for developing your topic. As Chapter 8 explains, your topic drives your choice of pattern, not the other way around. For example, suppose you want to explain to students how to register for classes without getting stressed. Because registration is a process, your organizational pattern is clear: Explain the steps involved in selecting courses and making up a schedule. No matter what you write about, the best topic is one that you know something about, one that allows you to draw from your experiences. Suppose you do want to write about a process. Think through your topic by answering ten questions to generate ideas.

Questions to Consider for Process

1. Is your topic a directional or informational process?

2. Is the process easy or difficult to perform or understand?

3. Can you explain it effectively in about 500 words, the average length of a short essay?

4. Why do you want to write about the process? Is it something you know about or do often?

5. Is the process interesting in itself? Will you be able to make it interesting for your readers?

6. What do you want your readers to be able to do or understand after reading your essay?

7. As you think about the possible steps of your process, what are a few that come to mind?

8. Does the process require any special equipment?

9. Do you need to define any special terms for your readers?

10. What larger meaning or significance for readers do you see in the process?

Plan and Write Your Essay

Goal 4 | **Identify the steps of your process, organize and explain the steps, and make sure that your thesis statement clearly expresses your thoughts or feelings about the process.**

Identifying, organizing, and explaining the steps of your process are not difficult tasks if you keep your audience in mind. If your purpose is to give directions, your steps must be clear enough so that readers can follow them to accomplish the task. If readers must have special tools or equipment to complete the process you describe, be sure to tell them exactly what they need. If your purpose is to give information, your steps or stages must be clear enough for readers to understand how the process works. If an understanding of the process requires the knowledge of special terms, be sure to define them the first time you mention them. For example, if you are writing about CPR, you have to assume that some readers may be unfamiliar with this process. One of your first tasks is to define *CPR* by telling what it is and what the letters mean.

Identify the Steps

If you have decided to write about a process, first brainstorm your topic to determine the steps involved. Narrow your list to three to five major steps. Following is a list of steps for the topic "how to set up a home office":

1. Decide how you will use the office.

2. Choose a place for the office.

3. Select the furniture you will need.

4. Arrange your equipment and supplies.

Next make an outline by expanding your list of major steps with supporting details. These will help you make the process clear to readers. Following is an expanded list of steps for the topic "how to set up a home office":

I. Decide how you will use the office:
   A. for study
   B. for job-related work
   C. for managing the household, paying bills, and so forth
II. Choose a place for the office:
   A. a spare bedroom
   B. an area of another room, such as the utility room, bedroom, or kitchen
   C. a portable office, such as a cart or table on wheels
   D. a closet that can be converted to an office space
III. Select the furniture you will need:
   A. desk or table
   B. chair
   C. lamp or light fixture
   D. bookcase
   E. file cabinet or file boxes
IV. Arrange your equipment and supplies:
   A. heavy equipment:
      1. computer and printer
      2. typewriter
      3. fax machine
      4. telephone
   B. supplies:
      1. paper, pens, pencils, paper clips, and so forth
      2. books and reference materials

Expanding your major steps with supporting details helps you identify any additional evidence needed to explain each step clearly and at the same time provides you with an outline to follow. Your list helps you keep your mind focused on the process so that when you are writing your rough draft, you will not leave anything out. Remember that any list or outline you begin with is not final. You may need to modify it as you think of new or better ideas.

Organize and Explain the Steps

Sequence is an appropriate coherence pattern to use with process. Even if the steps in a process do not have to be followed in order, your readers should be able to follow the development of your process from one step or stage to another. Transitional words and phrases can help you achieve coherence as you organize your steps into paragraphs. See Figure 9.2 on the following page for a list of some of the transitions that signal sequence.

Figure 9.2   **Transitions That Signal Sequence**

again	furthermore
also	last
and	later
before	meanwhile
begin by	moreover
begin with	next
besides	still
during	then
finally	too
first, second, etc.	when
following	while

After you have listed your steps and expanded them with details, read them over carefully to determine whether they are organized logically. If not, revise them to improve the sequence. Next, choose an appropriate transition to introduce each of your major steps. During your drafting process, combine each major step with its supporting details into a paragraph.

Following is a list of the major steps, with appropriate transitions underlined, for the process "how to set up a home office":

I.   The first step in setting up your home office is to decide how you will use your office.

II. The next step is to choose a place for the office that will be best suited to its use.

III. When you have found the right place for your home office, you are ready for the third step, which is to select the furniture you will need.

IV. The final step is to arrange your equipment and supplies in your new home office.

Each of the steps from the outline on page 237 has been expanded into a topic sentence. Suppose you were writing an essay on the topic "how to set up a home office." You could use these topic sentences to begin each of your body paragraphs. For your evidence, you could expand the details from the outline on page 237 into complete sentences, adding more details and examples where needed. Keep in mind that there are other transitions you could use and many ways to introduce major steps.

[Exercise 9.4] Choose a section of David H. Levy's chapter-opening essay and outline it, clearly showing the process that is explained, the major steps involved, and the details that support them. Then share your results with the rest of the class.

[Exercise 9.5] Review the student essay on pages 233-235. Then outline the essay. List substeps under the three major steps of the process. Then share your outline in a class discussion.

Write Your Thesis Statement

Your thesis statement should clearly indicate what process you are explaining and how you will develop it. For example, your thesis might specify the exact number of steps the reader will need to follow to complete the process. If the process occurs in several stages that have names, your thesis could briefly list the names of the stages. Following are two thesis statements; the first one numbers steps, and the second one names stages:

CONCEPT CHECK
To review how to write a thesis statement, see Chapter 4 for a detailed explanation.

1. To avoid the cost of having the oil changed in your car, follow my *five steps* for a quick, clean, and inexpensive oil change that you can do yourself.

2. Understanding the three stages of the memory process—*reception, retention,* and *recollection*—can help students make efficient use of their study time.

Each of these thesis statements also makes clear what the writer's purpose is. In the first one, the writer intends to tell readers how they can save money by doing their own oil changes. In the second statement, the writer wants to help students understand how their memory works so they can study efficiently. The next example is a possible thesis statement for the topic "how to set up a home office":

If having a convenient work space has always been a dream of yours, the four essentials of creating a home office can help you realize your dream.

This thesis statement makes clear that the writer will tell readers how to create a home office by following four essential steps.

When writing about processes, remember to first decide whether the process you have chosen is a *directional* or *informational* one. In your prewriting activities, ask the ten questions on pages 235–236. Concentrate on determining the major steps of the process. Then brainstorm for details that will explain the steps. Figure 9.3 on the following page is an overview of what to include in your process essay.

Figure 9.3   **Writing About a Process: An Overview**

PARTS	WHAT TO INCLUDE	QUESTIONS TO ASK
Introduction	1. Topic 2. Purpose 3. Context 4. Thesis	1. Is my process directional or informational? 2. What do I want readers to understand or be able to do? 3. What background do my readers need? 4. What is my point, and what do I think about the process?
Body paragraphs	1. Topic sentence 2. Major details 3. Minor details 4. Transitions	1. Should my topic sentence introduce the first step of the process or *be* the first step? (Your answer will depend on how many steps you have and how detailed your essay needs to be.) 2. What are the major steps of my process? 3. What minor details can I use to explain each step? 4. What transitions should I use to introduce each major step?
Conclusion	1. Summary of steps 2. Significance for readers	1. In a nutshell, what are the steps of the process? 2. What makes this process important or useful?

Exercise 9.6   For tips on how to improve your paragraphing skills and use of transitions, visit a college or university website, using *paragraph* and *transitions* as search words. Download an exercise or other useful information to share with the class. Your instructor or a librarian can help you with search words and URLs.

≪ Topics for Writing ≫

1. **React to the Reading.** Using Levy's chapter-opening essay as a model, explain how to prepare for a tornado, hurricane, or other severe weather condition. Using Coleman's essay as a model, write about a process such as training a dog, teaching a child to read, or a similar process.

2. **Use Your Experience.** Write about a process with which you are familiar or one that you have watched being done. The following list may give you some suggestions:

   - How to reduce stress
   - How to break a habit
   - How the people of a certain country celebrate a wedding or other event
   - How you made an important decision or solved a problem
   - How to adjust to life in a new town

3. **Make a Real-World Connection.** Write about a process you have studied in one of your courses, or write about another college- or work-related process. Choose from the following list, or make up your own topic.

College:
- How to prepare for a test
- How to adjust to college life
- How to improve your grade in a course
- How to apply for a student loan or campus job
- How a student athlete prepares for a game or event

Work:
- How to write a résumé
- How to apply for a job
- How to perform a specific task at work
- How to make a presentation
- How to get along with coworkers
- How a company provides a product or performs a service

4. **Go to the Web.** Is there a process that you would like to write about, but you would need more information to do so? Research the topic on the Internet. Your instructor or a librarian may suggest sites to search and appropriate search words to use.

≪ Checklist for Revision ≫

Did you miss anything? Check off the following items as you revise and edit your essay.

- ❏ Do you clearly state what the process is?
- ❏ Do you have a purpose for writing about the process?
- ❏ Does your introduction create a context for explaining the process?
- ❏ Does your thesis statement express a thought or feeling about the process?
- ❏ Do the steps of the process stand out?
- ❏ Do you introduce major steps with appropriate transitions?
- ❏ Do you explain each step in sufficient detail?
- ❏ Does your concluding paragraph restate the thesis or explain the significance of the process?
- ❏ Have you proofread your essay and corrected all errors?

‹‹ Your Discovery Journal ››

Reflect on your understanding of the difference between directional and informational processes by completing the following statements. Then give one example of each type of process.

As an additional option, you can do this activity online by going to *The Confident Writer* website.

> *In an* informational *process analysis of a topic, the purpose is to* _____.
>
> *In a* directional *process analysis of a topic, the purpose is to* _____.

‹‹ Website Resources ››

This chapter's resources include

- Chapter 9 Exercises
- Chapter 9 Quiz
- Downloadable Charts: *Group Evaluation Form*
- Chapter 9 Your Reflections
- More Topics for Writing
- Chapter 9 Summary

To access these learning and study tools, go to *The Confident Writer* website.

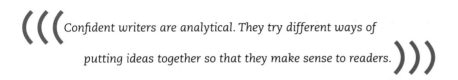

(((Confident writers are analytical. They try different ways of

putting ideas together so that they make sense to readers.)))

Choosing Classification or Division

What you already know about *classifying* and dividing

o You can easily identify the three parts of an essay.

o You know how to find an item in a store by looking in the section where it belongs.

o You are familiar with each part of your campus, and you know the types of students who attend your college.

Your *goals* for this chapter

[1] Understand the meaning, purpose, and process of classification, and be able to use this organizational pattern in creative and meaningful ways.

[2] Understand the meaning, purpose, and process of division, and be able to use this organizational pattern in creative and meaningful ways.

[3] Considering your topic and purpose, determine whether classification or division is an effective organizational pattern for your essay.

[4] Write a thesis statement that lists your topic's categories or parts, and support your thesis with well-chosen details.

Shopping in an unfamiliar store is easy because items are arranged in sections according to type. In a supermarket, for example, you expect to find yogurt with dairy products and lettuce with fresh produce. *Classification* is the system that helps you find items that are sorted into convenient categories.

Have you ever taken an appliance apart or assembled a piece of furniture? All things are made up of parts. *Division* is the system that helps you identify the parts and determine how they connect.

To help you see the difference between classification and division, think of flowers. A flower can be *classified* as one of several types: a rose or an orchid, for example. A flower can also be *divided* into several parts: The stem and the petals are the two with which you are most familiar.

Classification and division systems not only help us create order in our lives but also help writers organize details in meaningful ways. For example, writers choose classification when they want to sort and group items into convenient categories for discussion. Writers choose division when they want to analyze a whole object, system, or idea by looking at its parts.

This chapter explains how you can use classification and division to organize your ideas.

[First Thoughts]

To build background for reading, explore your thoughts about intelligence. Then answer the questions, either on your own or in a group discussion:

1. What does the word *intelligence* mean to you? What examples can you give?

2. Can people be "smart" in some ways and not in others? What examples can you give?

3. Read the title, the headnote, and the first two paragraphs of the excerpt. Based on this preview, what do you think will follow?

[Word Alert]

Before reading, preview the following words and definitions. During your reading, use context clues and your dictionary to define any additional unfamiliar words.

unique (2)	one of a kind
spectrum (2)	range
conscientious (9)	thorough

symbols (4, 13)	ideas or objects that represent other things
intently (13)	with deep concentration
persistent (13)	refusing to give up
tycoons (14)	wealthy and powerful businesspeople
merits (14)	earned value

The Different Ways of Being Smart

Sara D. Gilbert

In this excerpt from Chapter 5 of Sara D. Gilbert's *Using Your Head, The Different Ways of Being Smart,* Gilbert categorizes types of intelligence. Her thesis, or central idea, is that there are many kinds of intelligence and that each of us is "smart" in one or more ways. As you read the excerpt, try to discover how each paragraph supports its own main idea and how all the paragraphs together support Gilbert's central idea.

1   Book smarts, art smarts, body smarts, street smarts, and people smarts: These . . . labels . . . describe the various forms of intelligence and their use. As you might imagine, psychologists and other researchers into the nature of intelligence have come up with more formal terms for the types that they have isolated. One set of labels in common use is: convergent, divergent, assimilating, and accommodating. The converger and assimilator are like our book-smart person; the diverger, like our art-smart; and the accommodator, like our street-smart and people-smart. . . .

2   Whatever categorization we use, we will find some overlap within any individual. In fact, there are probably as many answers to the question "What are the different ways of being smart?" as there are people in the universe, because each of us is unique. We can't be typecast; we each have a wide spectrum of special talents.

3   Still, you probably know well at least one person whose talents generally fall into each of our categories. Keep those people in mind as you read through the detailed descriptions of them. . . .

4   At first it might seem that each of those types must call on very different sorts of abilities to be smart in his or her own ways. But in fact, each of the categories of intelligence on our list must use the same ingredients . . . learning ability, memory, speed, judgment, problem-solving skill, good use of language and other symbols, and creativity. Also, the thought processes that go on inside the heads of people with those varying kinds of smarts include the same steps: planning, perceiving, imaging, remembering, feeling, and acting.

5   Intelligence expresses itself in different forms, in part because of the differing physical qualities born and built into each person's body and brain, and in part because of the values and motivations that each person has learned.

6   However, the fact that each kind of smarts makes use of the same steps means that anyone can learn or develop skills in any or all of the categories. . . . Let's take a closer look at the many ways of being smart.

7   A *book-smart* person is one who tends to do well in school, to score high on tests, including intelligence tests. He or she is likely to be well-organized, to go about solving problems in a logical, step-by-step fashion, and to have a highly developed language ability. Another label for a book-smart person is "intellectual," meaning someone who uses the mind more to *know* than to feel or to control, and a book-smart person is especially proud of having knowledge. That knowledge may range from literature through science to math, but it is probable that it is concentrated in one area. Research shows that different knowledge areas occupy different clusters in the brain, so someone whose connections for complicated calculations are highly developed may have less development in the areas controlling speech and writing.

8   Although as we've said, current research indicates that learning centers may be scattered throughout both hemispheres of the brain, the activities of the "logical" left side are probably most important in the lives of book-smart people. Book-smart people may also be creative: many mathematical or scientific problems could not be solved, for instance, without creative insights, but the primary focus of a book-smart person is the increase of knowledge.

9   *Art-smart* people, on the other hand, rely primarily on creativity. They create music, paintings, sculpture, plays, photographs, or other forms of art often without being able to explain why or how they chose a particular form or design. They are said to be "right-brained" people, because it appears that the control centers for such skills as touch perception and intuition—the formation of ideas without the use of words—lie in the right hemisphere. Artistic people tend to take in knowledge more often by seeing, hearing, and feeling than by conscientious reading and memorizing.

10   An art-smart person may not do too well in school, not because he or she is not bright, but because of an approach to problem solving that does not fit in well with the formats usually used by teachers and tests. A book-smart person might approach a problem on a math test logically, working step-by-step toward the right answer, while an art-smart person may simply "know" the answer without being able to demonstrate the calculations involved. On a social studies exam, the book-smart person will carefully recount all the facts, while the more artistic one may weave stories and fantasies using the facts only as a base. In both cases, it's a good bet that the book-smart student will get the higher grade.

11   People who are serious about becoming artists, of course, may need to absorb a great deal of "book knowledge" in order to develop a solid background for their skills. There are other overlaps, as well: People with great musical ability, for instance, also tend to be skilled at mathematics, perhaps because of brain-cell interactions that are common to both processes. And in order to make use of any talent, art-smart people must have good body control as well.

12   The people we're calling *body smart* have a lot of that kind of body control. Most of them start out with bodies that are well put together for some kind of athletics—they may have inherited good muscular development for a sport

like football, or loose and limber joints for gymnastic-style athletics. Or they may be people whose hands are naturally well coordinated for performing intricate tasks.

13   But although the physical basis for their talent may come from their genes and from especially sensitive brain centers for motor control, to make use of their "natural" skills they must be able to observe accurately—to figure out how a move is made or an object is constructed—and they must think about how to do it themselves. This thinking involves a complex use of symbols that enables the brain to "tell" another part of itself what to do. In other situations, such as school, a body-smart person is probably best able to learn through some physical technique: In studying for an exam, for instance, he or she will retain information by saying it out loud, acting out the facts, or counting them off with finger taps. Although athletes or the manually talented are often teased as being "dumb" in schoolwork, that is not necessarily an accurate picture. To be good in using physical talents, a person must put in a lot of practice, be able to concentrate intently, and be stubbornly persistent in achieving a goal. And those qualities of will and self-control can also be put to good use in more "intellectual" achievements.

14   Persistence is also an important quality of *street-smart* people. They are the ones who are able to see difficulties as challenges, to turn almost any situation to advantage for themselves. As young people, they are the ones who are able to make the most money doing odd jobs, or who can get free tickets to a concert that others believe is completely sold out. As adults, they are the business tycoons, for instance, or the personalities who shoot to stardom no matter how much or little talent they have. A street-smart student may do well in the school subjects that he or she knows count for the most and will all but ignore the rest. When taking exams, street-smart people are likely to get better grades than their knowledge merits because they can "psych out" the test, and because, when facing a problem or question they can't answer, they are skilled at putting on the paper something that looks good.

15   To be street smart in these ways—to be able to achieve highly individualistic goals and to be able to get around obstacles that totally stump others—a person must draw upon a wide scope of mental powers. It takes excellent problem-solving ability, creative thought, good planning and goal setting, accurate perception, persistent effort, skill with language, quick thinking, and a strong sense of intuition.

16   Intuition plays a major role in *people smarts* as well. This kind of intelligence allows a person to sense what others are thinking, feeling, wanting, and planning. Although we might tend to put this sort of skill down as basic "instinct," it actually relies on higher activities of the brain. People smarts rely on very accurate and quick perceptions of clues and relationships that escape the notice of many, and they include the ability to analyze the information taken in. A people-smart student can do well in school simply by dealing with individual

teachers in the most productive way: Some can be charmed, some respond well to special requests for help, some reward hard work no matter what the results, and so forth. The people-smart student figures out easily what is the best approach to take. People with these talents also achieve well in other activities, of course—they become the leaders in clubs, and organizations, and they are able to win important individuals, like potential employers, over to their side. They would probably be typed as right-brained people, like artists, but their skill with language, both spoken and unspoken, is one that draws heavily on the left side.

17   Have you been able to compare these types with people you know in your class, family, or neighborhood? Of course, no individual is actually a type: People with any one of the kind of smarts that we've described also have some of the others. . . .

‹‹ The Critical Reader ››

[CENTRAL IDEA]

1. According to Gilbert, what are the many ways of being smart?

2. Who do you think is Gilbert's audience? What details in the excerpt help you determine the audience?

[EVIDENCE]

3. List the examples Gilbert uses to explain each type of "smarts."

4. How do you think this evidence supports Gilbert's central idea that there are many kinds of intelligence and that each of us is "smart" in one or more ways?

[IMPLICATIONS]

5. An *inference* is an educated guess based on your experience and on the knowledge that is available to you. Based on Gilbert's statement "Anyone can learn or develop skills in any or all of the categories," what inference can you make about a person who says, "I can't learn math"?

6. After reading the excerpt, what inferences can you make about intelligence tests and their ability to determine how "smart" a person is?

[WORD CHOICE]

7. Instead of using the psychological terms *convergent, divergent, assimilating,* and *accommodating,* Gilbert makes up her own terms for the categories of intelligence she describes. Why do you think she does this? What do her word choices tell you about her audience and her purpose?

⟨⟨ The Critical Thinker ⟩⟩

To examine Sara D. Gilbert's essay in more depth follow these suggestions for reflection, discussion, and writing.

1. Which one of Gilbert's categories plays the strongest role in your own thinking and learning? Use evidence from the essay to explain your answer.

2. Based on your understanding of Gilbert's categories, explain how a certain public figure, such as a well-known athlete, entertainer, or politician, displays one or more of Gilbert's categories of intelligence.

3. In paragraph 6, Gilbert says, "However, the fact that each kind of smarts makes use of the same steps means that anyone can learn or develop skills in any or all of the categories." Explain what you think this statement means. To what "steps" does Gilbert refer? Give one example of something you have learned how to do that required you to use a type of "smarts" that may not be your strongest category. Then explain what the experience taught you.

4. Do you think that Gilbert's categories describe the full range of intelligence? Do you think the categories are limiting? What other categories of intelligence can you add to Gilbert's types?

[Exercise 10.1]

For another perspective on Gilbert's topic, find and read an article on Howard Gardner's theory of multiple intelligences. Use your college library's online resources to find and access an appropriate article. A librarian can help you with your search. After reading the article, write answers to the following questions to share in a class discussion:

1. Who is Howard Gardner?

2. In your own words, what is Gardner's theory of multiple intelligences?

3. How many types of intelligence does Gardner define, and what are they?

4. What relationship do you see between Gilbert's "smarts" and Gardner's "intelligences"?

5. What have you learned about yourself from these authors' theories?

How to Use Classification

Goal 1
Understand the meaning, purpose, and process of classification, and be able to use this organizational pattern in creative and meaningful ways.

Classification is a sorting system that groups items according to what they have in common—their *shared characteristics*. For example, you could classify college students by age, race, sex, or national origin. You could also classify them as state residents or out-of-state residents; commuters or dormitory dwellers; and part-time or full-time attendees. Other categories might be the degree or job certification they are seeking, their major field of interest, the organizations they belong to, and their grade point averages. You could even classify students according to social habits and study habits. For example, some students belong to fraternities or sororities, some are independents, and some form social groups based on shared interests. Some students do nothing but study, some rarely study at all, and others strike a balance between studying and socializing. You can probably think of several other categories that include you and the other students you know.

[Exercise 10.2] Each list of items belongs to a different category. Read the list and decide what the items have in common. Use your dictionary to look up any unfamiliar words. Cross out any items that do not belong. Then in the blank space above each list, write the name of a category that correctly classifies the items. The first one is done as an example.

1. _Mythical creatures_

   leprechaun
   werewolf
   witch
   vampire
   unicorn

2. _____

   ice cream
   bread
   cake
   pudding
   pie

3. _____

   dinner fork
   spatula
   knife
   spoon
   salad fork

4. _____

   sneakers
   boots
   sandals
   slippers
   socks

5. _____

   mosquito
   hornet
   yellow jacket
   ladybug
   bee

6. _____

   violin
   cello
   trumpet
   harp
   viola

7. _____

   Monopoly
   badminton
   checkers
   chess
   Parchesi

9. _____

   tiger
   hyena
   leopard
   lion
   cheetah

8. _____

   orchid
   daffodil
   fern
   rose
   lily

10. _____

   Jimmy Carter
   George W. Bush
   Al Gore
   Bill Clinton
   Ronald Reagan

[**Exercise 10.3**] List three to five items that can be included in each of the following categories. Share your results with the rest of the class.

1. Team sports

2. Types of fish that are good for eating

3. Office equipment

4. Unusual pets

5. Games for children

Determine a Purpose for Classification

Choosing classification, as with choosing any organizational pattern, depends on your purpose for writing. Sara D. Gilbert's purpose is to empower readers with the knowledge that there are different ways of being smart. Gilbert's categories and explanations make intelligence, which is a complicated subject, easy for anyone to understand.

Two different students writing about the topic "types of university professors" might come up with entirely different categories based upon their purpose for writing. One student might write an informative article for the college newspaper to explain to first-year students what their professors' titles mean. This student's categories would be "assistant professor," "associate professor," and "professor." Another student might write an equally informative but humorous essay about types of professors based on their teaching styles. This student's categories might be "the dictator," "the calculator," and "the communicator."

Both students' writing purposes are influenced by their audiences. The student writing about professors' titles assumes that his audience, first-year

✅ CONCEPT CHECK
What examples of classification are you familiar with from your courses or from work?

How many categories of items do you see in this photograph?

college students, may be confused by the titles, so he provides information to clear up the confusion. The student writing about types of professors assumes that many of her readers are experienced students who have encountered professors like the ones she writes about and will therefore appreciate her humor.

[Exercise 10.4]

This exercise takes a visual approach to classification. Carefully examine the photograph above. Look at each item pictured and determine what kind or type of item it is. Sort the items into categories. Name your categories, and set up your paper in columns—one for each category. Then list each item in the appropriate column.

Sara D. Gilbert did not set out to write a classification essay. Instead, her topic, purpose, and audience probably determined the organizational pattern she would use. She wanted readers to understand that there are different ways of being smart. She knew that her audience would be more likely to understand her theory of intelligence if she made it clear and uncomplicated. Finally, she probably hoped that readers would be able to identify their own type of smarts. Thus, the fact that Gilbert sees intelligence as not one thing but different types of abilities and preferences made classification a good choice.

Suppose you attend a country festival and craft show, and one of the entertainers is a spoon player. You have never seen a pair of spoons used as a musical instrument, and this demonstration gives you an idea for a humorous essay about uses of silverware other than as eating utensils. You define as your audience the general public, who you assume believes forks and knives are good only for negotiating the food on their plates. You decide that your topic will be "the little-known uses of silverware," and you come up with these three categories: *musical instruments, unusual jewelry,* and *wind chimes and other crafts.* Your purpose is to inform your audience of these uses.

Understand the Process of Classification

If you choose classification as your organizational pattern, you begin with two or more things and sort them into *categories* of similar *types* or *kinds* of items. The following example classifies some of the items for sale in a college bookstore according to their type.

Classification is a useful pattern for explaining a complex subject. For example, in the chapter-opening essay, Sara D. Gilbert uses classification to explain several types of intelligence. In the essay on pages 87–90, Stephen King uses classification to explain the kinds of questions readers ask. Textbooks also contain examples of classification. In a psychology text, you may read about Abraham Maslow's categories of human needs. Linnea's classification of animal and plant species is a common topic covered in biology textbooks.

Whether you choose classification as an organizational pattern for an essay depends on your topic, purpose, and audience. If you do choose classification, name your categories and make sure that each one is different from the others. Sort items into your categories based on their shared characteristics.

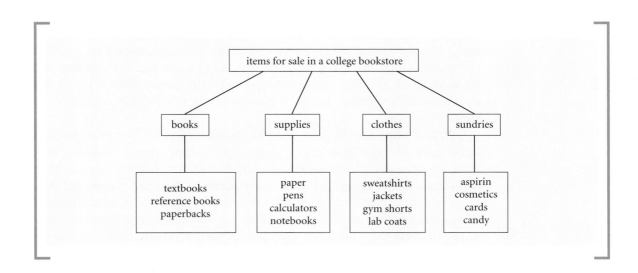

[**Exercise 10.5**]

Apply what you have learned about classification by doing this exercise with group members. First, review the group roles and responsibilities listed on the inside back cover of *The Confident Writer*. Next, discuss the following topics. Select one topic and determine a purpose for writing about it. Classify your topic into three or more categories. When you are finished, share your results with the rest of the class. Then evaluate your group's performance, as your instructor recommends, or go to *The Confident Writer* website to download the group evaluation form.

- Types of talk show hosts
- The CDs or DVDs you own
- Pressures college students face
- Kinds of magazines
- Summer jobs for students
- Types of students on your campus

How to Use Division

Goal 2 Understand the meaning, purpose, and process of division, and be able to use this organizational pattern in creative and meaningful ways.

Like classification, *division* is a useful pattern for explaining a complex subject. But unlike classification, which sorts many items into different categories, *division* deals with one item and the relationships among its parts. For example, a chemist uses division to analyze a solution such as a soft drink or a liquid detergent to determine what ingredients it contains. A movie critic's evaluation of a film relies on division. The critic analyzes the film's components, such as the actors' performances, the script, the camera work, and special effects. The film's overall effectiveness and appeal to viewers depend upon how well these components work together. Suppose you want to write an essay on job success. What qualities do employers expect? Punctuality, personal responsibility, interpersonal effectiveness, and ability to communicate are a few of the qualities that make a good employee. As you can see, the solution and its ingredients, the film and its components, the employee and his or her qualities—all are connected by a part-to-whole relationship, which is the basis of division.

Writers often use division and classification together. For example, you can classify undergraduate degree programs into four types: associate of arts, associate of science, bachelor of arts, and bachelor of science. You can then divide each degree program into its components of required courses and electives. You can write about friends by first classifying them as acquaintances, fair-weather friends, or close friends. Next, you can identify a friend of yours as one of these three types, for example, a close friend. Then you can use division to analyze each personal quality that makes this person a close friend.

As with classification, whether you choose division as an organizational pattern for an essay depends on your topic, purpose, and audience. If you do choose division, state your topic clearly, analyze each of its parts, and explain how they function for the good of the whole.

[**Exercise 10.6**] Beside each topic, write C if it suggests classification. Write D if it suggests division.

_____ 1. The qualities to look for in a mate

_____ 2. The characteristics of a good news reporter

_____ 3. Types of automobile drivers

_____ 4. The stages of grief

_____ 5. Careers in the field of sports

_____ 6. The components of an automobile engine

_____ 7. Social mistakes you do not want to make

_____ 8. A typical day in your life

_____ 9. The parts of a computer

_____ 10. Kinds of bicycles and their uses

Determine a Purpose for Division

To understand the purpose of division, think about a car's sound system. To operate the sound system, you must understand each of its parts and their functions. In your car's manual, you may find a diagram of the sound system with each part identified by name and function. Your textbooks provide other examples. In a biology text, you may find a chapter on the human digestive system. Your understanding of how the whole system works depends upon your knowledge of its parts and their functions. The purpose of division is to analyze each part of a complex whole so that the function or significance of the whole is clear to readers.

☑ CONCEPT CHECK
What are the qualities you look for in a good friend?

In the following paragraph, the author's purpose is to inform readers about the parts of a golf club:

A golf club consists of several parts, each one of which has a specific function. The grip is the part of the club that a golfer grasps in his or her hands to take a swing. The shaft extends from the grip to the club head. The shaft can be flexible or stiff, and it can be made from a variety of materials, depending on the golfer's needs. For example, flexible shafts are for golfers who do not swing fast but who want more distance. Stiff shafts are for those who have a fast swing but who want more control. Tiger Woods uses clubs with extra stiff shafts. The club head has several parts, the most important of which are the hosel and the face. The hosel is a tubular part of the club head into which the shaft is inserted. The face of the club head is the part that meets the ball during the golf swing. The face sits at different angles for different clubs. The angle of the face determines the height and the spin of the golf ball when it is hit. In conclusion, selecting the right club may improve your game.

In this paragraph, a golf club is divided into parts and the functions of each part are explained. The significance of this analysis is that all golf clubs consist of the same basic parts, but not all clubs are alike. By knowing how each part of a club functions, golfers can make better use of their clubs and can choose clubs that are appropriate to the way they play the game.

[Exercise 10.7] Select a topic from the ones you identified as division topics in Exercise 10.6, or make up your own topic. As in the following example, state a purpose or reason for writing about your topic.

Topic: the components of a successful party

Purpose: to help readers plan and put together a successful party

Understand the Process of Division

Remember that division is about a part-to-whole relationship. Division differs from classification just as the parts of an apple (peeling, core, seeds) differ from the types of apples (Macintosh, Cortland, Granny Smith). Division provides a way to think about a subject by breaking it down into parts so that you can better understand the subject as a whole. Suppose you have visited a museum of natural history, and you think that readers would like to know what the museum contains that might interest them. A good way to describe the museum as a whole is to divide it into parts, or sections, and explain what each one contains. For example, suppose the museum is a four-story building. You could write about what a visitor would find on each floor. You could plan your essay by making a diagram like the one on the opposite page.

You could also use an informal outline to plan your essay, as in the following example:

Thesis: Each floor of the City Museum of Natural History contains something of interest to visitors.
First Floor: Lobby

• gift shop
• cafeteria

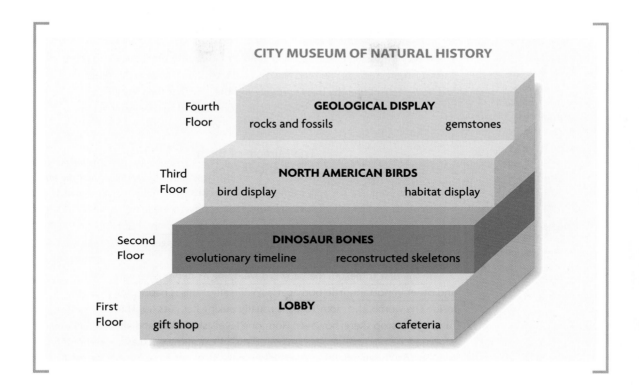

CITY MUSEUM OF NATURAL HISTORY

Fourth Floor — **GEOLOGICAL DISPLAY** — rocks and fossils — gemstones

Third Floor — **NORTH AMERICAN BIRDS** — bird display — habitat display

Second Floor — **DINOSAUR BONES** — evolutionary timeline — reconstructed skeletons

First Floor — **LOBBY** — gift shop — cafeteria

Second Floor: Dinosaur bones

- evolutionary timeline
- reconstructed skeletons

Third Floor: North American birds

- bird display
- habitat display

Fourth Floor: Geological display

- rocks and fossils
- gemstones

Whether you use a diagram or an outline for planning, remember that the purpose of division is to explain how parts are related to a whole. For example, knowing the parts of a golf club helps golfers choose the right club for the right purpose. Knowing the parts of a museum helps visitors find the displays that interest them.

Student Voices: A Division Essay

The author of this humorous essay divides a nine-month pregnancy into three parts, or trimesters. As you read the essay, identify the trimesters of pregnancy and how each affects the baby's growth and the way that the mother-to-be feels. For critical reading and thinking questions related to this essay, go to Chapter 10 Your Reflections on *The Confident Writer* website.

The Miracle of Birth
Heather Artley

Thesis statement

1 A woman is pregnant for approximately nine months. That nine-month period is divided into stages called trimesters, *tri* meaning three. Many women have said that they loved being pregnant, but I like to refer to the trimesters as the puking and crying stage, the fat stage, and the always-having-to-pee stage.

The introduction states the topic (pregnancy) and divides it into three parts (trimesters). The trimesters (stages) are named.

topic sentence

2   In the first trimester, the baby is developing its nervous system and other important little body parts. While all of this is happening inside the womb, the mom-to-be is usually puking her guts up. The fun doesn't stop there, however. Hormone levels skyrocket, and all of a sudden, mom-to-be is crying over the slightest thing, such as a McDonald's commercial that she thinks is cute or sweet.

Details explain events of first trimester.

topic sentence

3   The second trimester is usually slightly gentler on one's stomach. That may be because it has now doubled in size, along with mom's butt and thighs. The baby is growing faster now, and the vital organs are developing. The baby is beginning to do somersaults, and suddenly there is a new stabbing sensation, almost as if the baby is using mom's ribs for parallel bars. Comfort is now a thing of the past.

Details explain events of second trimester.

topic sentence

4   The third trimester never goes by fast enough. For some odd reason, sleep is completely out of the question in the last stage of pregnancy. Perhaps the lack of sleep is due to the up-and-coming gymnast in mom's womb or the five hundred trips to the bathroom in one night. The many sleepless nights may also be attributed to the anticipation of not having to pee five hundred times a night or having a waist again. The baby is now gaining about a pound a week, and all the intricate fine-tunings of development are happening to the major organs, hair, and skin.

Details explain events of third trimester.

The author does a good job of naming parts, providing some interesting details, and maintaining her humorous tone throughout. However, the introduction and body paragraphs would benefit from the addition of more details.

Tired expressions weaken conclusion (see Chapter 6).

5   Pregnancy is a wonderful experience as long as puking, gaining forty to sixty pounds, and peeing five hundred times a night do not bother the mom-to-be. To me, pregnancy was a bummer, but as the old saying goes, "No pain, no gain." The end definitely justifies the means, and now that I can control my bladder and have most of my waist back, the fun really starts.

Think Through Your Topic

Goal 3 Considering your topic and purpose, determine whether classification or division is an effective organizational pattern for your essay.

Remember that whether you use classification or division, there are certain fundamentals to keep in mind. First of all, both patterns simplify complex ideas. Classification starts with many things and sorts them into categories. Division starts with one thing and breaks it down into its parts. Second, both patterns require that you have a purpose for classifying or dividing. The categories or parts must be useful, clearly defined, and distinct from each other. Third, both patterns have a controlling idea: In classification, the controlling idea is the number or name of the categories. In division, the controlling idea is the relationship of the parts to the whole, including an explanation of what each part is and how it functions. Finally, as with any pattern, detailed examples and explanations are your cornerstone of development. Suppose you do decide that classification or division would be the best organizational pattern for your topic and purpose. Think through your topic by answering ten questions to generate ideas.

Questions to Consider for Classification and Division

CLASSIFICATION

1. Is your topic a group of ideas or items—such as types of movies, pressures students face, or styles of dress—that you can sort into categories?

2. What is your purpose for writing, and how will your classification help readers to understand or be able to do something?

3. How many categories will you have, what will you name each category, and why have you chosen these names?

4. Is each category distinct from the others so that your details and explanations do not overlap?

DIVISION

5. Is your topic one big idea or object that can be divided into smaller parts, sections, or stages?

6. What is your purpose for using this division, and what do you want readers to know about the relationship of the parts to the whole?

7. What are the parts, how many are there, and what is the function of each one?

8. What details can you use to explain each part's function and importance?

CLASSIFICATION AND DIVISION

9. Why is your topic important to you, and what significance does it have for your audience?

10. What overall point (thesis) will tie your classification or division together?

Plan and Write Your Essay

Goal 4

Write a thesis statement that lists your topic's categories or parts, and support your thesis with well-chosen details.

Having a central idea or thesis is important no matter what organizational pattern you choose for your essay. However, if you have chosen classification or division as your organizational pattern, then a well-written thesis statement can be especially helpful. Because the thesis will name your categories (classification) or parts (division), it is also a blueprint for the rest of the essay. For example, if your topic is "three types of students who attend your college," then you know that you will need to have at least three body paragraphs—one to explain each of your types. If your topic is "the five parts of plate presentation for a gourmet meal," then you will probably have at least five body paragraphs.

Once you have selected your categories or parts and have a working thesis, then use a prewriting strategy such as brainstorming to generate the details for your topic sentences and body paragraphs. As with any other topic or choice of pattern, consider your purpose, audience, and tone, and select appropriate devices for your introduction and conclusion.

State Your Thesis

The thesis statement for your essay should make clear what your topic is and how you plan to *classify* or *divide* it. The thesis may also indicate your purpose. In any case, your introductory paragraph should clearly state or imply your purpose, audience, and controlling idea if the thesis does not. Following is a possible thesis statement for an essay on folk art that is organized by classification.

> Silverware crafts, aluminum-can crafts, and glassware crafts make amusing gifts and conversation pieces for collectors.

CONCEPT CHECK
Review thesis statement (Chapter 4) and support (Chapter 5) as needed.

The thesis specifies three categories of crafts: silverware crafts, aluminum-can crafts, and glassware crafts. Now read the following introductory paragraph.

> If you are like me, you probably think knives, forks, and spoons are useful only for negotiating the food from your plate to your mouth. Unless you are convinced of

the need to recycle disposable items, you probably throw empty cans, bottles, and jars into the trash. Folk art has far more interesting uses for these items than the ones for which they were intended. Silverware crafts, aluminum-can crafts, and glassware crafts make amusing gifts and conversation pieces for collectors.

The writer's purpose is to inform readers of three unusual types of crafts that make use of unlikely objects. She assumes that her audience consists of people like her who would normally throw these items away or send them to the recycling bin.

Following are two thesis statements for two different essays that are organized by division.

1. A well-written paragraph has three parts: the topic sentence, the support sentences, and the concluding sentence.

2. Two important components of any successful college orientation program are self-management techniques and academic skills development.

In the first sentence, the topic is *a well-written paragraph,* and the purpose is to inform readers about the parts that make up such a paragraph. In the second sentence, the topic is *a successful college orientation program,* and the purpose is to inform readers about two of its components. Both sentences suggest a part-to-whole relationship. For example, each sentence in a paragraph determines how the paragraph functions as a whole. The components of self-management and academic skills determine the success of a college orientation program as a whole.

[**Exercise 10.8**] In the next three excerpts, identify the following: topic, purpose, and pattern (classification or division).

1. Although a computer is a complicated piece of machinery, it has three basic parts: *input device, processor,* and *output device.* The input device consists of a keyboard, mouse, or modem. Input devices allow you to enter, access, and send information. The processor is the part of the computer that you cannot see. Inside the computer is the hard disk, an electronic memory and storage system. The words you type on the keyboard are processed through the system and converted into a special electronic language that can be saved and stored. The output device consists of a screen and printer. The screen allows you to see the information that you have either entered or accessed. Whatever you enter shows up on the screen. Similarly, when you want to get information out of the computer, you call up the file on screen. To get a copy of your file on paper, you then use the printer.

2. Stress is a problem for many first-year college students, especially those who are living on campus, away from home for the first time. The pressures these students face come from three main sources: academic life, family demands,

and personal stressors. These pressures can be overwhelming unless students get help early in their college careers.

The pressures of academic life include difficult courses, the large amount of required reading, the unfamiliarity of course material, the stepped-up pace of instruction, and the need to make good grades to maintain a scholarship. Adjusting to living with a roommate and dealing with loneliness are additional pressures of academic life.

Family demands are another kind of pressure. These demands include parents' expectations. Students living at home are often expected to work to defray expenses and to do their share of household chores. These demands cut into their study time, creating more stress. Married students and single mothers may have spouses and children competing for their time.

Personal stressors may include poor time management, insufficient background for a course, weak study skills, and lack of self-motivation. However, students can overcome all three kinds of pressure if they seek help. On any college campus there are services available to help students at risk, and people who want them to succeed.

3. We all listen to music according to our separate capacities. But, for the sake of analysis, the whole listening process may become clearer if we break it up into its component parts, so to speak. In a certain sense we all listen to music on three separate planes. For lack of a better terminology, one might name these: (1) the sensuous plane, (2) the expressive plane, (3) the sheerly musical plane. The only advantage to be gained from mechanically splitting up the listening process into these hypothetical planes is the clearer view to be had of the way in which we listen. . . .

From "What to Listen for in Music" by Aaron Copland

Support Your Thesis

Suppose your topic is "the functions of memory" and your purpose is to describe the functions and explain how they work. You begin by naming the functions: *sensory memory, short-term memory,* and *long-term memory.* The evidence you select to accomplish your purpose consists of *how long* each function lasts, *what kind of information* each function is responsible for, and *what role* each function plays in the memory process as a whole. Notice that in this example, the parts and evidence are clearly differentiated.

Generally speaking, whether classification or division is your pattern of choice, the parts or categories you identify should be distinct from one another. Moreover, you should avoid any repetition or overlapping of supporting details. Suppose you are writing about inexpensive ways to exercise. Your categories are mall walking, neighborhood walking, and living room aerobics. As you brainstorm for evidence, you realize that your two walking categories

Figure 10.1   Transitions That Signal Classification and Division Relationships

types	categories	parts
kinds	groups	components
divided	broken into	one type, another type, . . .

overlap. Except for place, the details you use to explain these categories will be the same. To solve this problem, you create another category and name it "power walking." Then you add one more category: community games. You now have three distinct categories, and the details you use to explain them are less likely to overlap.

Remember that effective transitions can help readers follow your ideas. For example, how do you know that Sarah D. Gilbert plans to classify the different ways of being smart? Paragraph 1 begins with her list of "smarts," and Gilbert tells her audience that these are the various forms of intelligence. From this point on, you can anticipate that Gilbert will explain each type of intelligence. The last sentence of paragraph 2 provides a clue to her classification's significance—that each of us has "a wide spectrum of talents." In other words, we are all intelligent in different ways, and this is not only useful but also empowering information.

Figure 10.1 lists signal words and transitions you can use to achieve effective organization and coherence. Figure 10.2 is an overview of what to include in your essay if classification or division is your organizational pattern.

Figure 10.2   Classifying or Dividing: An Overview

PARTS	WHAT TO INCLUDE IN A CLASSIFICATION ESSAY	QUESTIONS TO ASK
Introduction	1. topic	1. What people, ideas, or objects will I sort into categories?
	2. purpose	2. What is the purpose behind my classification?
	3. controlling idea	3. What are the categories or types?
	4. thesis	4. What is the point of my classification?
Each body paragraph	1. topic sentence	1. What is one category?
	2. major details	2. What are the most important details that will explain the items in this category?
	3. minor details	3. What other details can I add?
	4. transitions	4. What transitions will connect my ideas?
Conclusion	1. concluding device	1. Should I restate the thesis or choose another way to conclude?
	2. significance for readers	2. What will readers gain from my classification?

Figure 10.2   continued

PARTS	WHAT TO INCLUDE IN A DIVISION ESSAY	QUESTIONS TO ASK
Introduction	1. topic	1. What single object or idea will I divide into parts?
	2. purpose	2. What is the purpose behind my division?
	3. context	3. What are the parts and functions?
	4. thesis	4. What is the point of my division?
Each body paragraph	1. topic sentence	1. What is one part?
	2. major details	2. What are the most important details that will explain this part and its function?
	3. minor details	3. What other details can I add?
	4. transitions	4. What transitions will connect my ideas?
Conclusion	1. concluding device	1. Should I relate an anecdote or choose another way to conclude?
	2. significance for readers	2. What will readers gain from my division?

≪ Topics for Writing ≫

1. **React to the Reading.** Using Gilbert's different ways of being smart as a guide, write about your own type of intelligence and what it enables you to accomplish.

2. **Use Your Experience.** Choose a topic from the following list that you can relate to your own experience, or make up your own topic:

   - My monthly budget
   - TV programs
   - Qualities that make a good president
   - The people at work
   - My ideal mate
   - Automobile drivers
   - Types of teachers
   - My neighborhood

3. **Make a Real-World Connection.** What examples of classification or division do you find in your daily life on campus, at work, or at home? For instance, items for sale in a college bookstore are classified according to type. A closet at home may be divided into sections, or the types of customers you deal with at work may fit into certain categories. Choose a real-world example of classification or division as your topic for an essay.

4. **Go to the Web.** For additional topic suggestions, go to *The Confident Writer* website.

⟪ Checklist for Revision ⟫

Did you miss anything? Check off the following items as you revise and edit your essay.

- ❏ Is your topic a group of items (classification) or a single item (division)?
- ❏ Are your purpose and audience clearly indicated?
- ❏ Have you introduced your topic effectively?
- ❏ Does your thesis state your categories or parts?
- ❏ Does each body paragraph have a topic sentence?
- ❏ Do you have enough evidence to explain each category or part?
- ❏ Are your categories or parts distinct so that there is no overlapping?
- ❏ Do you use transitions to maintain coherence?
- ❏ Do you have an effective conclusion?
- ❏ Have you proofread your essay and corrected errors?

⟪ Your Discovery Journal ⟫

Stereotyping is a form of classification. Stereotypes are opinions formed about individuals based on their membership in a group. Have you ever been the victim of stereotyping? Have you ever been guilty of stereotyping a person only to find out later that the person was very different from what you had expected? Reflect on these questions by completing the following statement for your journal.

As an additional option, you can do this activity online by going to *The Confident Writer* website.

> *One thing I have learned about the effects of classifying people according to stereotypes is that* _____.

⟪ Website Resources ⟫

This chapter's resources include

- Chapter 10 Exercises
- Chapter 10 Quiz
- Downloadable Charts: *Group Evaluation Form*
- Chapter 10 Your Reflections
- More Topics for Writing
- Chapter 10 Summary

To access these learning and study tools, go to *The Confident Writer* website.

CHAPTER

11

(((*Confident writers are open-minded. They may*

have an opinion on a topic, but they want

their readers to know all the pros and cons.)))

Comparing and Contrasting

What you already know about *comparing* and contrasting

- When you shop at a supermarket, you compare prices and contrast ingredients on the labels of different items.
- To explain why you prefer one restaurant over another, you discuss their similarities and differences.
- When choosing a college, you may have considered the advantages and disadvantages of commuting from home versus living on campus.

Your *goals* for this chapter

[1] Choose subjects that have something in common. Compare and contrast them with a purpose, and write a thesis statement that provides a pattern that you can follow.

[2] Write about your subjects one at a time or both at the same time, based on their points of comparison.

[3] Determine whether comparison and/or contrast is an effective organizational pattern for your essay, based on your topic and purpose.

[4] Know what strategies to use and the problems to avoid in planning and writing your essay.

266

When you compare and contrast any two subjects—such as cars, movies, instructors, or courses—you examine their similarities and differences. If your comparison is a good one, there will be a reason behind it that makes the comparison both interesting and significant. For example, you might compare the location, monthly rent, and amenities of two apartments near your campus. Your purpose is to determine which one is best for you. To choose a part-time job, you would compare hours, salary, and requirements.

Comparing and contrasting are so much a part of daily living that you may not realize how often you use them. Whether you are choosing a job, selecting courses, or deciding which friends to invite to a party, you are probably making comparisons. When you describe a friend, family member, or mate, you may compare or contrast his or her qualities with your own or someone else's.

Like narration, description, and the other organizational patterns explained in this book, comparison and contrast is another choice for you to consider when you are deciding how to analyze a topic and organize your support of a central idea or thesis. This pattern works best for comparing *two* items, and you can use it for writing compositions, for responding to questions on essay tests, and for other writing tasks as well.

[First Thoughts]

To build background for reading, explore your thoughts about eating in restaurants. Then answer the following questions, either on your own or in a group discussion.

1. What would you be most likely to order for breakfast, and why?

2. What is your favorite restaurant, and how does it compare to others like it?

3. Read the title, headnote, and first one or two paragraphs of the following essay. Based on this preview, what do you think will follow?

[Word Alert]

Before reading, preview the following words and definitions. During your reading, use context clues and your dictionary to define any additional unfamiliar words.

comb-over (1,19)	hair grown long and combed over to one side to hide baldness
brogues (7)	strong oxford shoes

inkblot test (8)	Used figuratively here, the Rorschach or Inkblot Test is a measure of a person's emotional state based on his or her interpretation of a series of standard inkblots.
retro-chic (18)	a trendy style based on the reinvention or reinterpretation of a past style
grime (17, 21)	black dirt or soot clinging to a surface
vestiges (23)	visible traces or remnants

The Inkblot Test

Robb Walsh

Robb Walsh has published cookbooks and reviewed restaurants for the *Houston Press*, the *Austin Chronicle,* and other publications. The following essay is from Walsh's book *Are You Really Going to Eat That? Reflections of a Culinary Thrill Seeker.* The essay originally appeared in the *Houston Press* in 2001.

1   There are eight customers in the Triple A Restaurant at 10:30 in the morning. All of them are men, and four sport comb-overs. The wood-grain Formica on the tables and the orange vinyl on the chairs are a little worn. There is a picture of a 1935 high school football team hanging on one wall. My waitress is named Betty; she grew up in the Heights and has been working at Triple A for eighteen years.

2   I am interested in a menu item that occupies almost half the page: "Two Farm Fresh Eggs (Any Style) with . . ." The "with" options include a pork chop, a breakfast steak, chicken-fried steak with cream gravy, and bacon or ham or choice of sausage. The sausage choices constitute another sublist. All of the above includes grits or country-style potatoes and toast or biscuits. Betty describes the three kinds of sausage available: The home-made pan style is a free-form patty that's been spiced up hot; the country sausage is a big link like kielbasa; and the little links are the regular kind. I order two eggs with chicken-fried steak and hash browns and biscuits. And I get a side order of that home-made sausage, just out of curiosity.

3   "How do you want your eggs?" Betty asks.

4   "Over easy and greasy," I smile.

5   "It's going to take a while," she says. "We batter the chicken-fried steak from scratch. It's not the frozen kind."

6   Neither are the crunchy potatoes; they are big pieces of fresh spuds fried crisp. The eggs are just right. The chicken-fried steak is piping hot with a wrinkly brown crust and a peppery tan cream gravy on the side. The biscuits are average. The biggest problem with Triple A's breakfast is the vehicle on which it is served: The oval platters are too small for the portions. I ended up eating from three plates. I split my biscuits on the right-hand plate and pour a little cream gravy on them, while I eat the eggs, potatoes, and chicken-fried steak from the middle plate. From the left, I sample the homemade sausage, which is extremely spicy and fried extra brown.

7   Betty is gabbing with the other waitresses, and it takes a lot of gesturing to get my coffee refilled. But it's a sunny day outside, and from the window by my booth I can see the farmer's market next door. I also see an old black shoeshine man working on Triple A's front porch. His customer is sitting against the wall, so I can't see his face, just his brown brogues. The shoeshine man is spreading the polish with his fingers. I linger over my coffee until 11:20 and leave just as the lunch crowd arrives.

8   If the scene above were an inkblot test, how would you characterize it? Inviting? Depressing? Boring? Charming?

9   Before you answer, consider the following inkblot:

10   At 11 in the morning, almost all the tables are occupied at Century Diner on the corner of Main Street and Texas Avenue. There are some young, hip guys lingering over books and magazines, and a lot of downtown business folks in nice clothes eating lunch.

11   The vinyl booths by the window are two-tone, pastel green and off-white. The tables are covered with brand-new Formica in a bright pattern of circles and shapes, a design that was called "modern" forty years ago. The waiters wear black-and-white bowling shirts with slogans such as "Something Superior for Your Interior" on the back. The menu is sprinkled with little nuggets about old diner lingo, such as the fact that "Adam and Eve on a raft" once meant ham and eggs on toast.

12   But ham and eggs on toast is not on the menu. Instead, the place offers a contemporary take on diner food, including "The Total New Yorker," a bagel with Nova Scotia salmon and cream cheese, and "The Health Kick," an egg-white omelet. Although two eggs with ham, bacon, or sausage aren't offered, the menu does feature "Eggs N' Hash," two eggs with hash browns and New York–style corned-beef hash.

13   My waiter is a young guy with dyed black hair. He's too busy to chat, so I don't get his name. I order two eggs. They don't have hash browns at lunch so I settle for french fries. The waiter doesn't know what the breakfast meats are, but he checks. I order the sausage and a side of biscuits and gravy.

14   "How do you want your eggs?" he asks.

15   "Over easy and greasy," I smile.

16   Coffee comes in a little stainless-steel Thermos, which is a nice touch. It reminds me of the little glass "bottle" you used to get at coffee shops in the 1960s. The eggs are just right. The french fries are excellent. The link sausage is precisely what you'd expect. The biscuits are huge, and the gravy has lots of bacon pieces in it. Unfortunately, it has been spooned over the top of unsplit biscuits. I try to break them up to soak up some of the gravy.

17   At a table just across the divide from mine, two men and a woman in conservative business suits are gossiping about somebody's chances in some election. The conversation is spirited, and the woman's eyes sparkle as she laughs at

one of the men's observations. I can't hear what he said, but it must have been pretty funny. I pour myself some more coffee and copy down this quote from the big shiny menu: "'The character of a diner builds up the way grime does'— Douglas Yorke."

18   My own reactions to these diner-shaped inkblots are not hard to predict. Breakfast at Triple A puts me in a warm and wonderful mood. And the retro-chic at Century Diner feels phony. But I'm pretty much alone in this opinion.

19   One friend calls the breakfast at Triple A "a heart attack on a plate." Another finds the dark wood paneling, worn-out furniture, and fat old guys with comb-overs "depressing." And she thinks the Century's decor and waiters' costumes are "precious."

20   What does the inkblot test tell you?

21   The same restaurant can feel entirely different to you and me. I can walk into a truck stop alone and feel right at home. But a beautiful young woman walking by herself might feel differently. My mother is obsessive about cleanliness; she'd rather eat at McDonald's than at a place with character if there's the threat of grime. And then there are deeper prejudices.

22   When I moved to Austin from Connecticut to start school at UT (the University of Texas), I was seventeen years old, 2,000 miles away from my parents, and high on my newfound freedom. I drove my motorcycle all over town discovering funky places to eat. I loved little luncheonettes run by crazy old ladies, drugstore soda fountains, and old urban institutions like the Southern Dinette on East 11th Street in the heart of the black east side.

23   Why did I love these places? It wasn't always about the food. I was also seeking a level of comfort. As a newcomer, I was fascinated by the characters in these old places and by the vestiges of a disappearing Texas. As a long-haired geek from the East, I was scared of the rednecks and fraternity boys who prowled the trendy campus hangouts. Maybe I ate in eccentric dives and places on the wrong side of the tracks because I felt like an outcast myself.

24   Sometimes friends who grew up in Texas, people who are concerned with healthy diets and whose families struggled with poverty in their childhood, don't find these funky joints nearly as endearing as I do. In another's eyes, these places are outdated, high-cholesterol slop houses, full not of colorful characters but of boring old farts. I understand these biases, and I want to be honest about my own.

25   It's still not always about the food with me. Sometimes I think a restaurant review needs to stick closely to the subject at hand. But in other cases, I'm more interested in food as a reflection of culture, and so it is with this case. There are some differences in the food at Triple A and Century Diner. But having breakfast at an old diner one morning and a new retro diner the next brings up intriguing questions.

26　　Like, do you prefer sanitized imitations of old institutions to grimy old institutions themselves? And why does a retro-chic diner in the oldest part of Houston get its history lessons (and breakfast dishes) from New York? Does the architectural preservation downtown make any sense absent some cultural preservation?

27　　Several letters to the editor lately have complained about my ramblings—that my restaurant reviews are too personal and not focused enough on food. To this charge I proudly plead guilty.

28　　When I began reviewing at the *Austin Chronicle* in 1991, I was influenced by the very personal narratives of food writer John Thorne. Thorne's own inspiration was Mark Zanger, who under the pseudonym Robert Nadeau reviewed restaurants for the *Boston Phoenix* in the late 1970s. "He was teaching himself eating and drinking and simultaneously wondering out loud what he should be making of it, gnawing away at all pat assumptions," wrote Thorne. "He taught me that honesty means nothing if there's no real risk to it, no genuine self-examination."

29　　Lofty aspirations for a restaurant reviewer, no doubt, but at least it's a worthy goal. In that spirit, I offer you this nonreview. And I invite you to visit Triple A and Century Diner for some genuine self-examination of your own. Which one do *you* like better?

‹‹ The Critical Reader ››

[CENTRAL IDEA]

1. What is the author's thesis, and where it it stated?

2. What is the author's purpose?

[EVIDENCE]

3. In what ways do the restaurants differ?

4. In paragraphs 4 and 15, why does the author repeat the way he likes his eggs: "over easy and greasy"?

[IMPLICATIONS]

5. Based on the author's description, which restaurant do you prefer, Triple A or Century Diner, and why?

[WORD CHOICE]

6. Explain the choice of the term *inkblot test* as it is used in the title and in paragraph 9.

‹‹ The Critical Thinker ››

To examine Robb Walsh's essay in more depth, follow these suggestions for reflection, discussion, and writing.

1. Read Walsh's descriptions of each restaurant's atmosphere and food again. Which details create the clearest images in your mind? Which descriptive words or phrases seem most effective, and why? Do you know of any restaurants that would fit into Walsh's two categories?

2. What is your opinion of restaurant critics? Do you read restaurant reviews? Would you go to either of the restaurants Walsh describes? Why, or why not?

3. In paragraph 1, Walsh explains where Betty grew up and that she has been a waitress at Triple A for eighteen years. In paragraph 15, Walsh describes the waiter at Century Diner as a "young guy" with "dyed black hair." What purpose do these details serve?

4. Write a review of a restaurant you like. Describe its food, atmosphere, waitstaff, and customers.

How to Compare and Contrast

Goal 1

Choose subjects that have something in common. Compare and contrast them with a purpose, and write a thesis statement that provides a pattern that you can follow.

When you *compare* two subjects, you examine their similarities, the characteristics that make them alike. When you *contrast* two subjects, you examine their differences, the characteristics that set them apart. Since it is difficult to do one without the other, you usually examine both the similarities and the differences between subjects when you are comparing them. In fact, the word *compare* often implies *contrast* as well.

As an organizational pattern, comparison and contrast is also useful for examining the advantages and disadvantages of choosing one object, idea, or action over another. Similarly, if you want to discuss the pros and cons of nationalizing health care or the arguments for and against electing a certain candidate, your organizational pattern will be comparison and contrast. To use the pattern effectively, follow these four steps:

1. Choose an appropriate topic.

2. Determine your purpose.

3. Let your thesis be your template.

Choose an Appropriate Topic

Your topic should consist of two subjects for comparison that have something in common. Choose subjects that belong to the same category or class of things. For example, suppose the topic is "movies." You could approach this topic in a number of ways. For example, you could begin by narrowing your topic to "romantic comedies," "action films," or "animated features." Then you could select two movies of the type you want to compare. Or you might take a different tactic. Instead of comparing two movies, you might decide to contrast two different roles that a favorite actor of yours has played. How you limit the topic is your choice, but the subjects of your comparison should be of the same class. For example, the author of "The Inkblot Test" compares two restaurants of the same type.

[**Exercise 11.1**]   Read the following list of topics. Decide how you might limit each topic. Make sure that the subjects of your comparison are of the same class. Share your results with classmates. The first one is done as an example.

> two athletes: ~~Venus and Serena Williams~~ Tiger Woods and Jack Nicklaus
>
> two candidates' views on the same issue
>
> two college campuses
>
> two stores of the same type
>
> two places to visit
>
> two subjects of your choice

Determine Your Purpose

☑ **CONCEPT CHECK**
For more information on purpose, see Chapter 1.

Suppose the topic you have chosen is "two jobs I have had." Why do you want to compare two different jobs? What do you want to say about them? Was one easier or more challenging than the other? Did you like one more than the other? Perhaps you just want to explain the similarities and differences between the two jobs without making a judgment about either of them. Suppose you decide that you will compare two jobs you had at two different fast-food restaurants. Though the restaurants were of the same type, perhaps there was a great difference in how they were managed. Generally speaking, there are two major purposes for comparing and contrasting subjects:

1. To identify and explain the similarities and/or differences that clearly distinguish between one subject and another of its class

2. To identify and explain the similarities and/or differences between two subjects to show that one has advantages over the other or to make some other value judgment.

The first purpose is informational. You simply want readers to know how the two subjects compare. You are not making a judgment about the subjects; you leave that for your readers. The second purpose contains an element of persuasion. You want readers to understand or react to your own views or values about one or both subjects. For example, if you want to explain all the ways in which your jobs at two fast-food restaurants were different or similar, you have selected the first purpose. If you want to explain why you liked one job better than the other, you have selected the second purpose. First, decide how your subjects are related: their basis for comparison. Then determine your purpose for writing about them. Figure 11.1 lists five topics, the relationship between the subjects to be compared, and two different purposes for the comparison.

Figure 11.1   Comparing and Contrasting Subjects

SUBJECTS	RELATIONSHIP	PURPOSE #1	PURPOSE #2
Two DVD players	Same system, different brands	To explain their similarities and differences	To explain why you would rather own one than the other
Two apartment complexes	Two places to live	To show how they differ and explain what each offers	To explain the advantages of one over the other as a place to live
Two candidates running for office	Different parties, same issues	To compare each person's position on the issues	To show which candidate would do a better job
Two jobs	Both fast-food restaurants	To compare and contrast both restaurants' characteristics	To explain why one is a better workplace
Two basketball players	Same team, different styles of play	To explain differences between the players' styles	To show how each contributes to the team's success

[**Exercise 11.2**] Following is a list of essay topics that suggest the first purpose of comparing and contrasting: *to clearly identify and distinguish between two subjects.* Rewrite each topic so that it implies the second purpose and adds a *judgment* about the subjects. The first one is done as an example. Share your results with the rest of the class.

1. To explain how two TV sitcoms appeal to different audiences: To explain why one TV sitcom is more popular than another

2. To describe two neighborhoods

3. To explain the differences between two comedians' styles

4. To discuss two different places to live

5. To explain your performance in two different courses you took last semester

6. To distinguish between two automobiles made by the same manufacturer.

Let Your Thesis Be Your Template

A good thesis statement provides a *template,* or pattern, to follow in writing your essay. Your thesis statement should make clear to your readers *why* you are writing about the two subjects you have chosen (purpose) and *how* you plan to compare and contrast them (parts). Imagine that for your psychology class, you must write an essay exam in which you compare Sigmund Freud's and Carl Jung's theories of personality. The audience for your essay is your psychology professor, and your purpose is to demonstrate your understanding of the two theories. You decide to write a purpose 1 comparison since all you want to do is identify and distinguish between the theories, not make any judgments about them. Your opinion is that the theories differ in two important ways. The parts of your thesis are your two points of comparison: how the two men define the components of personality and how the personality develops. To write your thesis statement, do three things.

1. State your topic and purpose:

to compare the personality theories of Freud and Jung and to show that they differ in two major ways

2. State the terms of comparison:

components of personality
development of personality

3. Combine topic, purpose, and terms of comparison into one complete sentence that is free of grammatical errors:

Sigmund Freud and Carl Jung, two influential theorists, describe personality differently in terms of its components and its development.

There are other effective ways to write a thesis statement, but combining topic, purpose, and points of comparison into one sentence is a reliable method. Also, this type of thesis statement sets up the essay for you. You know what to discuss first and second. You can conclude your essay by making some implications for the reader. For example, picking up on the word *influential* in the thesis statement in this example, you might briefly explain one or two ways in which Freud's and Jung's theories have influenced the development of modern psychology. Now try the following exercise.

[**Exercise 11.3**] Select a topic from the list in Exercise 11.1, or make up your own topic. Write a thesis statement that sets up the pattern for your comparison. Follow the three steps below for writing your thesis statement.

1. State your topic and purpose.

2. State the terms of comparison.

3. Combine topic, purpose, and terms of comparison into one complete sentence that is free of grammatical errors.

Choose a Method of Analysis

Goal 2

Write about your subjects one at a time or both at the same time, based on their points of comparison.

☑ **CONCEPT CHECK**

Can you see how the two ways to analyze your topic correspond to the objective and subjective purposes for description explained in Chapter 6?

A thesis statement that includes your topic, suggests your purpose, and briefly states the points of comparison will help you determine what evidence to use to support your thesis. The next step is to organize the evidence so that your essay develops logically and flows smoothly.

When you compare two items, there are two ways you can organize the evidence. You can say all you want to about first one subject, then the other. This is called a *subject-by-subject* comparison, and it works best if you are doing a brief comparison of two subjects. You can also organize your essay by points of comparison. Under each point, you discuss first one subject, then the other. This is called a *point-by-point* comparison, and it works best if you have a great deal to say about both your subjects.

To do either kind of comparison, you must first decide what your points of comparison are. Whatever you say about one subject, you should also say about the other. For example, if a point of difference between you and your sister is the kind of leisure-time activities you prefer, then you should explain which activities you enjoy and which activities your sister prefers. The following example will help you see the difference between a *subject-by-subject* comparison and a *point-by-point* comparison.

Suppose you decide to write an essay comparing yourself to your older sister. You want to write this essay because people have always assumed that you and your sister are alike. However, people's expectations of you seem to be based on your sister's personality and the choices she has made. You want to set the record straight. Your thesis comes easily: "My relatives expected me to pursue a career in healthcare like Alice did, but if they really knew how different my sister and I are, they would not be surprised that I chose differently." You have decided that your points of comparison will be *personality traits, study habits, personal preferences,* and *goals,* but you are not sure how to organize your essay.

If you organize your details *subject by subject,* you will discuss your differences and Alice's differences separately. It does not matter whose personality traits, study habits, personal preferences, and goals you discuss first. In the process of planning, drafting, and revising your essay, you may decide which order seems to work best. Figure 11.2 shows an example of a subject-by-subject outline.

If you organize the same details *point by point,* you will discuss how you and Alice differ in each of the traits, habits, preferences, and goals you have chosen. Your outline might look like the one in Figure 11.3, page 279.

Figure 11.2 A Subject-by-Subject Outline

I. Subject: Self
- A. Personality traits
  1. Introverted, self-motivated
  2. Artistic
  3. Need to do things my way
- B. Study habits
  1. Procrastinator
  2. Avoid difficult tasks
  3. Choose courses according to preference
- C. Personal preferences
  1. Want to be my own boss
  2. Enjoy drawing, painting, various crafts, visiting galleries and museums
  3. Like change, hate routine
- D. Goals
  1. Career goal: to work at a job I like that has potential for making a lot of money (interior design)
  2. Life goals: to have privacy, create beautiful surroundings, have leisure time to travel

Figure 11.2   A Subject-by-Subject Outline (continued)

II. Subject: Alice

   A. Personality traits

      1. Extroverted, other-motivated

      2. Analytical

      3. Needs directions, rules

   B. Study habits

      1. Never procrastinates

      2. Finds difficult tasks challenging

      3. Chooses courses according to need

   C. Personal preferences

      1. Would prefer to work for someone

      2. Enjoys the outdoors, physical activity, sports

      3. Hates change, prefers routine

   D. Goals

      1. Career goal: to work at a job that lets her help people and that she feels is important (nursing)

      2. Life goals: to fulfill her lifelong ambition of becoming a nurse, to be respected in her field, to have a comfortable and secure life

You could use either one of these outlines to write an effective comparison and contrast essay. Whether you prefer to discuss your subjects one at a time or point by point is your choice as a writer. Be willing to experiment with both methods of organizing an essay. In the process you may decide that one of them works better for you.

[Exercise 11.4]

Apply what you have learned about comparing and contrasting by doing this visual exercise with group members. First, review the list of group roles and responsibilities listed on the inside back cover. Next, complete the activity that follows and share your results with the rest of the class. Then evaluate your group's performance as your instructor recommends, or download the group evaluation form at *The Confident Writer* website.

1. Examine the photographs on page 280, paying careful attention to every detail.

2. Compare and contrast what you see in the photos, and make a list of the similarities and differences.

3. Make a judgment about the photos: Which one does your group prefer, and why?

Figure 11.3   A Point-by-Point Outline

I. Personality traits
   A. Sociability
      1. Alice is extroverted, other-motivated.
      2. I am introverted, self-motivated.
   B. Creativity
      1. Alice is analytical.
      2. I am creative.
   C. Independence
      1. Alice needs directions, rules.
      2. I need to do things my way.
II. Study habits
   A. Procrastination
      1. Alice never procrastinates.
      2. I do procrastinate.
   B. Facing difficult tasks
      1. Alice finds difficult tasks challenging.
      2. I avoid difficult tasks.
   C. Course selection
      1. Alice chooses courses according to need.
      2. I choose courses according to preference.
III. Personal preferences
   A. Jobs
      1. Alice would prefer to work for someone.
      2. I want to be my own boss.
   B. Activities
      1. Alice enjoys the outdoors, physical activity, sports.
      2. I enjoy drawing, painting, various crafts, visiting galleries and museums.
   C. Change
      1. Alice hates change, likes routine.
      2. I like change, hate routine.
IV. Goals
   A. Career
      1. Alice wants to work at a job that lets her help people and that she feels is important (nursing).
      2. I want to work at a job I like that has a potential for making a lot of money (interior design).
   B. Life
      1. Alice wants to fulfill her lifelong ambition of becoming a nurse, to be respected in her field, and to have a comfortable and secure life.
      2. I want to have privacy, create beautiful surroundings, and have leisure time to travel.

What do a room's furnishings tell you about its owners?

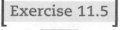

This exercise will help you become aware of the ways to use comparison and contrast. First, read through the transitions for comparison and contrast listed in Figure 11.4. Then listen for these signal words in a lecture or class discussion in one of your courses. Write down the signal words that you hear, and briefly explain the context in which they are used. Share your list in a class discussion. Also, remember to use transitions to help readers follow the ideas in your comparison and contrast essay.

Figure 11.4   Transitions That Signal Comparison or Contrast

TRANSITIONS FOR COMPARISON	TRANSITIONS FOR CONTRAST
like	unlike
similar	different
similarities	differences
similarly	on the contrary
in comparison	in contrast
both	neither
in common	differs from
also	however
share	instead of
too	on the other hand

Using a point-by-point analysis, the author explains her choice of a college. As you read the essay, determine what her points of comparison are. For critical reading and thinking questions related to this essay, go to Chapter 11 Your Reflections on *The Confident Writer* website.

University of Arkansas Versus Arkansas Tech University
Alexandra Stowe

1   Deciding where to attend college is a very difficult decision to make. I narrowed my decision down to the University of Arkansas in Fayetteville and Arkansas Tech University in Russellville. They both offer many of the same majors, but they differ in location, size of facility and student body, and price. Students choosing between these two schools should be aware of these differences so that they can select the right college.

Topic: two universities

Thesis

Points of comparison

2   The University of Arkansas is located in Fayetteville, Arkansas, which is in the northwest corner of the state. Fayetteville has many rolling hills, and students who are not used to hills will at first have a difficult time getting around town. However, Fayetteville has a lot to offer students. There is a large variety of activities for students to choose from both on and off campus. There are many parks, a large shopping mall, three multiplex movie theaters, a drive-in movie theater, the Walton Arts Center, and a wide variety of restaurants.

Point of comparison: location

3   Campus size can have a big impact on one's choice of school. At the University of Arkansas, the classrooms are a considerable distance from dorms and parking lots. The long walk to class might be considered good exercise, but it could also be a detriment if a student is running behind for class. The University of Arkansas has a transit system because of its size. Buses run, but sometimes waiting for a bus can take longer than walking to class. The University of Arkansas has approximately 16,000 students in attendance. Because of this number of students, the class sizes are larger, and there is not much individual attention given to students.

Point of comparison: size and student body (U. of Arkansas)

4   Receiving individual attention is not an issue at Arkansas Tech University. With a little over 5,500 students in attendance, there are smaller class sizes and more individual attention given to each student. The dorms and parking lots are next door or within a close walking distance to the classrooms. A student living in a residence hall can leave for class five minutes before class starts and still make it on time. There is not a transit

Point of comparison: size and student body (U. of Arkansas Tech)

system at Arkansas Tech University because there is not yet a need for one to be implemented. Since Arkansas Tech is small, a student is likely to experience a community feeling while on campus.

5   Price can greatly influence one's choice of a college. The University of Arkansas, compared with other large colleges, has a very reasonable cost. Since it has very high fees, there are many activities that the University of Arkansas can provide for its students. The University of Arkansas's estimated cost for attendance of one semester is approximately $3,000, not including room and board. On the other hand, Arkansas Tech is more affordable than the University of Arkansas. The fees at Arkansas Tech are significantly lower than the University of Arkansas. Arkansas Tech's estimated cost for attendance for one semester is $1,900, excluding room and board.

Point of comparison: price

6   The University of Arkansas and Arkansas Tech University both provide a good education. Deciding between them will come down to personal preference and affordability.

The conclusion would benefit from examples that explain what the author means by "a good education."

Think Through Your Topic

Goal 3
Determine whether comparison and/or contrast is an effective organizational pattern for your essay, based on your topic and purpose.

Students sometimes confuse comparison and contrast with classification. That is because some comparison may be involved in differentiating among the items to be classified. Remember that a good writer will often combine patterns if doing so suits his or her purpose. Simply put, comparison and contrast are best used when your purpose is to examine two subjects of the same type or class in depth. If you do select comparison and/or contrast as your organizational pattern for an essay, think through your topic by answering ten questions to generate ideas.

Questions to Consider for Comparison and Contrast

1. What are the two subjects that you want to compare or contrast?
2. Are your two subjects members of the same class of things or ideas?
3. Why have you chosen these two subjects?
4. Do you want to distinguish between your subjects without expressing an opinion (Purpose 1)?

5. Do you want to make a value judgment about your subjects (Purpose 2)?

6. What similarities do your subjects share?

7. How do your subjects differ?

8. What will be your points of comparison?

9. How many points of comparison will you have?

10. What will be your overall point or thesis, and why should readers be interested in it?

Plan and Write Your Essay

Goal 4 Know what strategies to use and the problems to avoid in planning and writing your essay.

First, choose subjects that have something in common. Next, decide whether your purpose is to differentiate between subjects or to make a judgment about them. Then write a working thesis statement that sets up the pattern for your essay. To brainstorm your topic, divide a sheet of paper into two columns. Write one of your subjects at the top of each column. Then list similarities and differences under separate headings in each column. These will become your points of comparison. The more complete your list, the more potential details you will have for your essay. Also, the number of details will help you decide whether to do a subject-by-subject or point-by-point analysis. For example, if you have only a few similarities and differences, you may be able to do a subject-by-subject analysis with one well-developed paragraph for each of your subjects. If you have many points of comparison, then a point-by-point analysis might work best for you. Tie your essay together with creative introductory and concluding paragraphs.

To make your essay interesting for readers, avoid these three common problems that students often make when comparing two subjects:

- **Pointless comparison.** Remember that your purpose may be to convince your readers that one item is better than another or has advantages over the other. On the other hand, perhaps you merely wish to inform readers about your subjects' similarities and differences. Unless you engage readers by telling them what they can hope to learn from your comparison, their reaction to your thesis may be "So what?" To avoid a pointless comparison, write for a specific audience. For example, in her essay about the two universities, Alexandra Stowe makes clear that she is writing for students who may be considering whether to attend the University of Arkansas or Arkansas Tech University.

- **Unclear or indistinct points of comparison.** State your points of comparison clearly so that each one is distinct and there is no overlapping. Do not make the mistake of explaining one point in great detail and skimping on the details for your other points. Make sure that you have sufficient details for all points of comparison.

- **Choppy sentences.** Unless you use transitions effectively, your readers may feel that you are jumping from point to point in a distracting way. Connect your ideas with transitions such as those listed in Figure 11.4 so that they flow smoothly.

Figure 11.5 is an overview of what to include in your comparison and contrast essay.

Figure 11.5   Comparing and Contrasting: An Overview

PARTS	WHAT TO INCLUDE	QUESTIONS TO ASK
Introduction	1. Topic 2. Purpose 3. Context 4. Thesis	1. Is my topic two subjects of the same class? 2. What do I want to explain or to make a judgment about? 3. What introductory device will I use? 4. Does my thesis clearly state the topic, purpose, and points of comparison?
Body paragraphs (subject-by-subject)	1. Topic sentence 2. Major details 3. Minor details 4. Transitions	1. Which subject will I examine first? 2. What are my major points of comparison? 3. What minor details will explain each point? 4. What transitions should I use to introduce each major point of comparison?
Body paragraphs (point-by-point)	1. Topic sentence 2. Major details 3. Minor details 4. Transitions	1. Which point of comparison will I examine first? 2. What will I say about each subject? 3. What additional details can I add? 4. What transitions will help readers move from one subject to the other as I explain each point?
Conclusion	1. Concluding device 2. Significance for readers	1. Should I summarize the points of comparison or use some other device? 2. What makes my comparison of the subjects useful or important?

≪ Topics for Writing ≫

1. **React to the Reading.** Write a critical review of your college's food service. Using Robb Walsh's essay as a model, compare two similar meals you have eaten and rate them for your readers. If you are a commuter and do not use your college's food service, then write about two restaurant meals instead.

2. **Use Your Experience.** Choose one of the following topics that will allow you to apply what you have learned from experience:
   - Two books
   - Two items of clothing
   - You and a friend or a relative
   - Two places you have lived
   - Two musicians or two music groups
   - Two colleges or universities
   - Bosses versus employees
   - Teachers versus students
   - Children versus parents
   - Two subjects of your choice

3. **Make a Real-World Connection.** Comparison and contrast provide a useful pattern for academic writing. For example, you could use information learned in a humanities course as the evidence for writing an essay that compares two styles of architecture, two styles of painting, or two philosophers' definitions of art or education. Using the information you have learned in one of your courses, write an essay in which you compare or contrast two subjects of your choice.

4. **Go to the Web.** Compare the information found on two blogs or websites of the same type. Let your interest be your guide when choosing sites to compare. Your instructor or librarian can make suggestions if you have trouble choosing sites.

≪ Checklist for Revision ≫

Did you miss anything? Check off the following items as you revise and edit your essay.

- ❏ Do your subjects for comparison belong to the same class of things?

- ❏ Is it clear to readers that your purpose is either to distinguish between subjects or to make a judgment about them?

- ❏ Does your introduction create a context for your comparison?

- ❏ Does your thesis statement provide a template in which topic, purpose, and points of comparison are clearly stated?

❑ Have you done a subject-by-subject or point-by-point analysis?

❑ Are your paragraphs detailed enough to develop the thesis?

❑ Have you chosen transitions that help your readers follow your analysis?

❑ Does your essay have an appropriate conclusion?

❑ Have you proofread your essay and corrected all errors?

≪ Your Discovery Journal ≫

Think about the writing skills you are developing. Compare the skills you now possess with those you hope to have in the future. What are your strong points? What needs improvement? Reflect on these questions by completing the following statements for your journal.

As an additional option, do journal activities online by going to *The Confident Writer* website.

One of my strengths in writing is _____.

One thing that I would like to change about my writing is _____.

≪ Website Resources ≫

This chapter's resources include

▬ Chapter 11 Exercises

▬ Chapter 11 Quiz

▬ Downloadable Charts: *Group Evaluation Form*

▬ Chapter 11 Your Reflections

▬ More Topics for Writing

▬ Chapter 11 Summary

To access these learning and study tools, go to *The Confident Writer* website.

(((*Confident writers are critical. They are critical*

thinkers who form their own opinions, but

they are also respectful of opposing viewpoints.)))

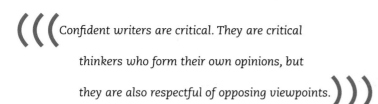

Explaining Causes and Effects

What you already know about *cause* and effect

- You know that when your car's gas gauge is nearing the empty mark, you should fill up.

- When you express an opinion and explain the reasons why you think that way, you are explaining causes.

- If you do not study for an exam, and you earn a poor grade, you know what effect this grade will have on your average in the course.

Your *goals* for this chapter

[1] To alert your audience that a cause-and-effect analysis follows, choose among three signals.

[2] Choose between two basic methods for developing your essay: One focuses on causes; the other focuses on effects.

[3] Determine whether cause-and-effect analysis is an appropriate organizational pattern for your essay, based on your topic and purpose.

[4] Follow a five-step plan to write your cause-and-effect essay and to avoid common problems in logic.

At least once each day you probably ask the question "Why?" You want to know what *causes* people to think or act the way they do. You seek the *reasons* behind events and their outcomes.

Causes lead to *effects*. An *effect* is a *result* of some action. For example, suppose you have a leaky roof. You examine the roof, and you see that some shingles have come loose. Now you know *why* your roof leaks. The loose shingles are the *cause,* and the leaky roof is the *effect.* Some cause-and-effect relationships, like the loose shingles that cause the roof to leak, are easy to recognize. Idea relationships are a different matter. Many questions arise whose answers we can only determine by making *inferences,* or educated guesses, based on past observations and prior knowledge. For example, the causes of poverty, homelessness, drug addiction, teen suicide, and crime are not so easy to pinpoint. People may have strong opinions about these issues, but opinions are inferences, not facts.

Writing about causes and effects takes critical thinking, an open mind, and a willingness to question your own and others' viewpoints. Your courses provide many exciting opportunities to observe causes and effects in action. A significant part of what you learn in any course is a habit of thinking that involves examining causes and their effects.

[First Thoughts]

To build background for reading, explore your thoughts about global warming. Then answer the following questions, either on your own or in a group discussion.

1. Based on what you have read or heard, what is global warming?

2. Are you concerned about global warming? Why, or why not?

3. Read the title, headnote, and first one or two paragraphs of the following essay. Based on this preview, what do you think will follow?

[Word Alert]

Before reading, preview the following words and definitions. During your reading, use context clues and your dictionary to define any additional unfamiliar words.

greenhouse gases (1)	carbon dioxide from the burning of fossil fuels and methane from other sources
fossil fuels (2)	coal, oil, and natural gas

climatologist (3)	one who studies climate and its effects
Niño cycle, El Niño (4, 8)	a warming of the ocean surface, off the western coast of South America, in four- to twelve-year cycles, that affects the weather
thermodynamics (8)	a branch of physics that deals with the relationship between heat and other forms of energy
anthropogenic (8)	of or relating to the origin and development of humans
oscillations (12)	variations between alternate extremes within a defined time period

What Is Causing Global Warming?

Sharon Begley and Andrew Murr

Sharon Begley, Senior Editor at *Newsweek,* writes on science and the environment. Andrew Murr has written articles and books on a variety of topics. This article appeared in *Newsweek,* July 2/July 9, 2007.

1   When 600 climate scientists from 40 countries reported in February that there was, for the first time, "unequivocal" evidence that the world is warming and greater than 90 percent certainty that man-made greenhouse gases have caused most of the warming since 1950, at least one expert demurred. "We're going to see a big debate on it going forward," said Vice President Dick Cheney. By "it," he meant "the extent to which [the warming] is part of a normal cycle versus the extent to which it's caused by man."

2   There is no denying the intuitive appeal of the idea that climate change is natural. After all, local temperatures can rise or fall by 40 degrees from one day to the next; violent storms can barrel in over the course of only minutes. It's little surprise, then, that many laypeople look at much tinier and subtler changes—the 1 degree Fahrenheit increase in global mean temperature since the 1970s, say—and figure those, too, could well be natural. As for 11 of the 12 hottest years on record occurring in the last 12? Well, everyone has experienced a run of statistics-defying weather. Besides, some signs of climate change are undeniably the work of Mother Nature's whims and not man's "addiction" (as President Bush called it) to fossil fuels, at least in part. For instance, glaciers in East Africa, including Mount Kilimanjaro, began shrinking around 1880—well before the greenhouse effect ramped up. And the 1936 heat wave is still the worst many American cities ever experienced, never mind the (globally) record-setting 1990s. No wonder that, in the *Newsweek* Poll, only 17 percent of those surveyed correctly absolved a hotter sun of responsibility for recent global warming.

3   That impression is at odds with the science, however. As the February report from the Intergovernmental Panel on Climate Change concluded, greenhouse gases have caused most of the recent warming. "Without greenhouse

gases and other [man-made] forcings," says climatologist Gabriele Hegerl of Duke University, an author of the report, "we cannot really explain the observed climate changes."

4   Climatologists did not reach that conclusion lightly. They know full well that climate change can arise from any of three basic causes. One is what they call "internal, natural variability" (a fancy name for "s——t happens," climate-wise). Because there is as much randomness in climate as there is in a roulette wheel, droughts and heat waves and killer storms are to be expected, just like a run of events or reds in Las Vegas. Around 1880, for instance, atmospheric circulation over the Indian Ocean strengthened in such a way that less rain and snow fell on East Africa, including Kilimanjaro, finds glaciologist Stefan Hastenrath of the University of Wisconsin. No one knows why the circulation changed. But the result of this natural hiccup was glacial retreat that has gotten worse through the decades. Changes in the Niño cycle can also reflect internal, natural variability. A second cause of climate change, "natural external forcings," refers to random, or at least hard-to-predict, shifts in outside influences, such as more heat coming from the sun or from Earth's core.

5   And then there is the hand of man.

6   The first hint that natural variation fails to explain recent climate change comes from the climate version of noticing that the roulette ball has clattered into an even number three times in a row. That is, you compare seemingly weird weather to what has come before to see if it might not be as strange as it seems. (The chance of three evens in a row in roulette is about 1 in 8, so when it happens you don't automatically conclude the wheel is rigged.) When scientists measured a rise in Earth's average temperature of 1 degree F over the past 50 years, they therefore scurried to the record books, both man's and nature's—that is, to historical weather archives as well as tree rings and ice cores that preserve records of ancient temperatures—to search for precedents.

7   That's when the roulette wheel started to look rigged. The temperature increase since the 1950s "is not like anything seen in the paleoclimate data," says atmospheric scientist Joyce Penner of the University of Michigan. "It's very clear that the last 50 years are very unusual." Temperatures in the Northern Hemisphere during the second half of the 20th century were even farther out of line with natural variability. They are warmer than during "any other 50-year period in the last 500 years," found the IPCC report, "and it is likely that this was the warmest period in the past [1,300 years]."

8   The case for natural variability founders on another shoal. When natural cycles such as El Niño cause unusual warming, they also cause unusual cooling. One place heats up and another gets a chill, as if Peter were robbed of heat to warm Paul. The result is no net global change. To warm both Peter and Paul in a closed system violates the laws of thermodynamics. But according to the latest IPCC report, which assesses hundreds of climate studies, temperatures have risen on every continent except one (there are not enough data from Antarctica

to draw a conclusion about its climate history). "You can detect an anthropogenic imprint on all continents where we have adequate observations," says Francis Zwiers, director of the Climate Research Division of Environment Canada, a government agency, who is also an author of the IPCC report. Peter and Paul both got warmer. Or, as the IPCC put it, "No known mode of internal variability leads to such widespread, near universal warming as has been observed in the past few decades. Although modes of internal variability such as El Niño can lead to global average warming for limited periods of time, such warming is regionally variable, with some areas of cooling."

9   The conclusion that observed climate change is our fault rests on the pattern of warming, too. As it happens, "human and natural factors that affect climate have unique signatures," says climatologist Ben Santer of Lawrence Livermore National Laboratory, part of the U.S. Department of Energy. The clearest signature is differences in the warming of different layers of the atmosphere. According to satellites and weather balloons, the lower atmosphere, or troposphere, has warmed; the upper atmosphere, or stratosphere, has cooled. That's not what a hotter sun would do. "If you increase output from the sun, you increase the amount of energy that arrives at the top of Earth's atmosphere," says Santer. "And you get heating throughout the whole column. Have we observed anything like that? The answer is a very clear no." Greenhouse gases such as carbon dioxide from the burning of coal, oil and natural gas and methane from, among other surprising sources, rice fields (where bacteria thriving in the submerged paddies release this and other gases) act from the bottom up. That is, they warm the troposphere and cool the stratosphere by trapping heat waves wafting off the planet's surface. The warm troposphere and cool stratosphere "is entirely consistent with our best understanding of how temperatures would change with an increase in greenhouse gases," says Santer.

10   Another problem for the blame-the-sun idea is that the climate balance sheet doesn't, well, balance. Solar output rises and falls over an 11-year cycle. The high point in the cycle raises surface temperatures 0.2 degree F, at most—much less than the increase that has been measured between the late 1800s and now.

11   More recent changes are even tougher to blame on a hotter sun. From 1955 to 2000, the world's oceans warmed .7 degree F, Tim Barnett of Scripps Institution of Oceanography and colleagues reported in 2005. That may seem small, but the immensity of the oceans means the amount of heat required to warm them even a little is enormous. In the same period, the sun has increased its energy output less than 0.1 percent, according to satellite measurements. That's not nothing, but it's not enough to explain the warmer seas. The extra solar output can no more account for that than holding a candle under a pot can account for boiling a gallon of water. Extra heat pouring out of the planet's core could warm the oceans, except for one problem: it would heat the oceans from the bottom up. In fact, the greatest warming is at the waters' surface. "And if it were

12   natural variability, then a couple of oceans might warm but others would cool, and the net would be zero," says Barnett. "All the oceans are warming, and for that you need a net heat source. We've ruled out everything but greenhouse gases."

One by one, climatologists have gone through the signs of climate change and exonerated both natural variability and natural outside sources as the main culprits. Extremely warm summers, such as the 2003 European heat wave that killed thousands of people? A human fingerprint. Glacial retreat? Ditto, though it is partly natural. Stronger tropical storms, such as Katrina? Possibly our fault, though on this one the evidence is murkier. Heavy precipitation that alternates with dry spells so that when it rains it pours? That also conforms to models of man-made climate change. And neither natural variability nor more solar heat can explain the warmer surface waters in the hurricane breeding grounds of the Atlantic and Pacific, which have heated up .5 to 1 degree since 1906. Natural oscillations have never been that great, says Santer. And extra solar heat "is way, way too small, an order of magnitude too small."

13   This is not to say that every sign of climate change reflects the heat-trapping effects of the gases we spew out of our utility plants, cars and planes. Increases in the sun's output were probably responsible for the warming that occurred in the early 20th century. And natural variability explains some sea-level rise and loss of arctic sea ice. Undoubtedly, other natural explanations for climate change will pop up; one currently getting some buzz (as well as lots of criticism) is that changes in the sun's output alter the barrage of cosmic rays that strike Earth, producing fewer clouds and therefore a warmer world.

14   But that raises a question for those who emphasize nature's contributions to global warming and other aspects of climate change. Let's suppose that those are nudging the climate toward worse storms and more droughts and more heat waves, just as greenhouse gases are. In that case, you'd think the world would want to control the causes of global warming that it can. At last check, no one had figured out how to turn down the sun.

⟨⟨ The Critical Reader ⟩⟩

[CENTRAL IDEA]

1. What is the authors' central idea?
2. What is the authors' purpose?

[EVIDENCE]

3. Where in the essay do the authors state the possible causes of global warming?
4. What purpose do the details in paragraph 2 serve?
5. The belief that climate change is our fault is based on what, according to these authors?

[**IMPLICATIONS**]

6. Do you find the authors' thesis and evidence convincing? Why, or why not?

[**WORD CHOICE**]

7. The authors use several scientific terms associated with climate in this essay, some of which are listed in Word Alert. The use of scientific or technical terms can help or hinder readers, depending on their familiarity with the subject. In your opinion, do the authors do a good job of making the information on global warming accessible for readers? Explain your answer.

≪ The Critical Thinker ≫

To examine Begley and Murr's essay in more depth, follow these suggestions for reflection, discussion, and writing.

1. How important is the issue of global warming to you? For example, among the other issues that concern you, where does global warming rank?

2. In this brief article, the authors discuss causes of global warming and some of its effects. Based on what you have learned from this article and from other sources, what are some practical things people can do to reduce greenhouse gases and global warming?

3. In paragraphs 6 and 7, the authors use the analogy of roulette to explain why climate change is not the result of natural variation. Do you find this analogy helpful? Why, or why not?

4. What initiatives are in place on your campus or in your community to address the issue of global warming?

Signal Your Readers for Cause and Effect

Goal 1

To alert your audience that a cause-and-effect analysis follows, choose among three signals.

✓ **CONCEPT CHECK**
To review all the ways to introduce a thesis, see Chapter 4.

Recognizing the cause-and-effect pattern in others' writing and being able to use the pattern in your own writing depend upon your understanding of three common signals of causes and effects:

1. The question/answer signal

2. The act/consequence signal

3. The probability signal

The presence of these signals in introductory paragraphs, in thesis statements, and in topic sentences of paragraphs alerts you that causes or effects will follow. Using the signals in your own writing will let your readers know what to expect.

The Question/Answer Signal

As explained in Chapter 4, asking a question in an introductory paragraph is one of the devices writers use to build your interest in reading. The question may signal either a cause or an effect. Writers may state a question directly:

> Why do most Americans avoid sitting next to strangers in a theater when most Europeans will do just the opposite?

Or they may state the question indirectly:

> Many observers have wondered why Americans avoid sitting next to strangers in a theater while Europeans will do just the opposite.

An answer to either question would explain the reasons that Americans and Europeans differ in how close they are willing to sit to strangers. Direct or indirect questions in the title, introduction, thesis statement, or topic sentences of paragraphs are signals of cause and effect. Some signal words to look for are *why, reason, cause, result,* and *because.*

In this excerpt from an essay by George Gallup Jr., "The Faltering Family," Gallup asks a question that the rest of the essay answers. The question and the answer are underlined and annotated.

1   In a recent Sunday school class in a United Methodist Church in the Northeast, a group of eight- to ten-year-olds were in a deep discussion with their two teachers. When asked to choose which of ten stated possibilities they most feared happening, their response was unanimous. All the children most dreaded a divorce between their parents.

2   Later, as the teachers, a man and a woman in their late thirties, reflected on the lesson, they both agreed they'd been shocked at the response. When they were the same age as their students, they said, the possibility of their parents' being divorced never entered their heads. Yet in just one generation, children seemed to feel much less security in their family ties. . . .

✓ CONCEPT CHECK
When asking a question in your writing, always frame it within a context that introduces and explains or answers it.

3   What are the pressures that have emerged in the past twenty years that cause long-standing family bonds to be broken?   *Question*

4   Many now agree that the sexual revolution of the 1960s worked a profound change on our society's family values and personal relationships. Certainly, the seeds of upheaval were present before that critical decade. But a major change that occurred in the mid-sixties was an explicit widespread rejection of the common values about sexual and family relationships that most Americans in the past had held up as an ideal. . . .   *Answer*

    Answer

The effects of Hurricane Katrina raised questions about our ability to respond quickly after a disaster.

Gallup's essay goes on to explain four pressures that have caused the rejection of traditional family values: alternative lifestyles that have led to an increase in one-parent families; a change in our attitudes concerning sexual morality; the economic necessity for women to work outside the home; and the acceptance of feminist philosophy. Gallup analyzes the *effect* of the breakdown of family values by explaining the four pressures as possible *causes*.

[**Exercise 12.1**]   Review Begley and Murr's chapter-opening essay. Where in the essay do they state questions and answer them? What are the questions and answers? What purpose do they serve? Share your findings with the rest of the class.

[**Exercise 12.2**]

Look at the photograph above. What questions arise in your mind as you view the damage pictured in the photograph? Have you survived a hurricane, tornado, or other storm? What can people do to protect themselves when hurricane warnings are issued? Write a paragraph in which you ask and answer a question based on Hurricane Katrina and its aftermath.

The Act/Consequence Signal

Scientists, journalists, historians, and others often write about actions and consequences. Consequences are the *results* of certain actions or *causes*. The assassination of John F. Kennedy in 1963 was a consequence that has aroused controversy for decades. That he died from gunshot wounds is unquestioned. But who fired the gun? Was there more than one killer? The question of who committed the action that resulted in the consequence of Kennedy's death is still being debated. One argument goes like this: If there were one gunman, one gun, and one bullet, then there would not be three bullet wounds. This argument suggests that the consequence—three bullet wounds—could not be the result of one person firing one bullet. The act/consequence signal of cause and effect is easy to spot by the signal words *if . . . then*. Note in the following examples, however, that the same act/consequence relationship may be signaled by *if* alone, without the word *then* preceding the consequence statement.

> *If* you do not brush and floss your teeth regularly, you may develop gingivitis or gum disease.
> *If* you want people to treat you with respect, you must show them respect as well.
> *If* you had not run that stop sign, you might have avoided the accident.

Some *if . . . then* relationships can be proven true—for example, the statement "If you do not water your houseplants, they will die" is verified by experience because you know that plants need water to survive. But the statement "If Bernard Bluff is elected president, there will be an end to the current economic crunch" can probably never be proven. Even if Bluff were elected, and even if the economy were to improve, there would still be differences of opinion concerning which actions resulted in an improved economy. Perhaps factors other than Bluff's election were at work. Therefore, when writing about causes and effects, keep in mind that an action may have consequences, and a consequence may be the result of several actions. Only through careful selection of evidence can you increase the likelihood that your *if . . . then* statement and its development will convince readers.

In the following excerpt from "Why Reading Aloud Makes Learning Fun," an article by Jim Trelease, the thesis is underlined, the *if . . . then* statement is bracketed, and the effects of reading to your children are annotated in the margin.

Thesis *Act/consequence signal*	1 It's really never too early to start reading to a child. [If a child is old enough to talk to—and parents talk to their children from Day 1—then he or she is old enough to be read to.] It doesn't matter that infants can't understand the words; the English language inside the covers of books is frequently a whole lot more organized, colorful and coherent than "koochie, koochie, koochie." Setting even a tiny child
Effect	in front of a book and reading to him or her is intellectual stimulation.

Effect   2   A visual competency is developing, too, because the child is being taught to focus attention on a picture on a page. This visual literacy is just as important as print literacy, and it is usually achieved before print literacy. At 18 months old, a child can identify a picture of a puppy and understand the word—and that's long before he can read it. . . .

Effects   3   Next to hugging your child, reading aloud is probably the longest-lasting experience that you can put into your child's life. You will savor it long after he or she has grown up. Reading aloud is important for all the reasons that talking to

Effects   children is important—to inspire them, to guide them, to educate them, to bond with them and to communicate your feelings, hopes and fears. You are giving children a piece of your mind and a piece of your time. They're more interested, really, in you than they are in the story—at least in the beginning. But it is not just you who are communicating but the author and illustrator. These are people who, in some cases, lived hundreds of years ago. So reading becomes a way to

Effect   eavesdrop on history.

Effects   4   Reading aloud to children on a routine basis improves their reading, writing, speaking, listening, and imagining skills. And it improves their attitudes toward learning. Today attitude is the major stumbling block to literacy achievement. But what we do in this culture is teach children how to read first; then we try to get them interested in it. That's putting the cart before the horse. Reading aloud is

Source that supports the thesis   the primary focus for the national report *Becoming a Nation of Readers.* The first conclusion these people drew after two solid years of looking over all the research was: If you want to build readers, read aloud to children early and often. Much the same conclusion was reached in another national study, released in late

Source that supports the thesis   February, called *What Works: Research About Teaching and Learning.* . . .

Trelease goes on to say that too many children have a "workbook mentality" about reading, meaning they associate it with unpleasant schoolwork instead of regarding it positively as a leisure activity. He also sees a connection between the high percentage (75 percent) of boys in remedial classes and the lack of male involvement in their intellectual growth. He concludes that fathers, as well as mothers, should read to their children.

[Exercise 12.3]   Skim Begley and Murr's essay on pages 289–292 to find an *if . . . then* statement (remember, the word *then* may not always precede the consequence part of the statement). Determine what is the act and what is the consequence. Share your results with the rest of the class.

[Exercise 12.4]   To help yourself think about causes and effects that operate in your life, make up three to five *if . . . then* statements like those on page 296. Select the best one of your statements, and list the evidence you could use to support it if you were to develop it into an essay.

The Probability Signal

From time to time you may have wondered what would happen if you took a certain action or made a certain choice. *Probability* means *likelihood*. What is the probability that a seven will come up with any given roll of the dice? What is the likelihood that you will make an A on your next test, that you will get the job you want, or that airline rates will go down before you decide to take your next trip? Scientists deal in probabilities every time they conduct experiments. Researchers are trying to find cures for diseases that have eluded them, and so they keep asking "What if." What if we add this chemical, or that one? When you experiment with new study techniques, you are testing probabilities. You are looking for the cause that will produce the desired result. Words and terms that signal probable cause-and-effect relationships are *probable, possible, likely, unlikely, may, might, perhaps,* and *what if.* The future tense is a probability signal also. Whenever writers predict causes or effects by explaining what people *will do* or what actions or events *will* take place, they are suggesting probable outcomes.

The following short passage describes a study in which a University of Kentucky researcher observed frog embryos to see what would happen to the ones attacked by predators. Probability signals are underlined.

PREMATURE EJECTION

1 When the going gets tough, some frog embryos get going. A new study shows that a red-eyed tree frog embryo <u>will</u> hatch early if attacked.

2 Red-eyed tree frogs are found in tropical rain forests from Mexico to Panama, and females lay masses of gelatinous eggs in plants over water. The eggs usually hatch around seven days later, and the tadpoles drop into the water. Karen Warkentin, a biologist at the University of Kentucky, observed clutches of frog eggs at ponds in Panama and noted the response to predators. When a wasp landed on the clutch and tried to bite open one of the eggs, the embryo frequently popped out and got away from its enemy.

3 "It's a pretty effective way to escape," says Warkentin, noting that nearly 90 percent of the early-hatching embryos survived the attack.

4 Not all embryos are capable of such a response. Warkentin notes: they <u>must be</u> at least four days old. Still, the ability of some unborn creatures to sense danger and take action is significant.

5 "People have not thought about embryos as actively making decisions or responding to their environment," says Warkentin. "This tells us that embryos, at least in some cases, are not as helpless as we thought."

from National Wildlife, *February/March 2001*

According to Warkentin's research, frog embryos will hatch early if they are in danger. The significance of this finding is that it will affect the way we think about all embryos in the future. For example, if frog embryos can sense danger and take evasive action, then they may be able to respond to the environment in other ways as well. Moreover, Warkentin's findings may lead to similar research using the embryos of other species.

[**Exercise 12.5**]

Apply what you have learned about cause-and-effect signals by doing this exercise with group members. First, review group roles and responsibilities listed on the inside back cover. Next, complete the activity that follows and share your results with the rest of the class. Then evaluate your group's performance as your instructor recommends, or go to *The Confident Writer* website and download the group evaluation form.

1. Identify and discuss a problem on your campus, such as inadequate parking, binge drinking at social events, cheating, sexual harassment, or some other issue that everyone in your group thinks is important.

2. State your problem, in writing, as a question such as "Why do students cheat?" Doing this will help you determine your problem's *causes.*

3. State your problem as an action that has consequences, using the *if . . . then* format. For example, "If students cheat, then everyone is hurt in the following ways." Doing this will help you determine your problem's *effects.*

4. Using the probability signal, write a sentence in which you state a desired solution to your problem. For example, "Cheating is everyone's problem, and we will have to work together to find a solution."

5. Choose either statement 2, 3, or 4 to develop more fully. For example, if you choose statement 2, answer your question by listing the causes. If you choose statement 3, list your problem's consequences. If you choose statement 4, list the steps involved in finding a solution to your problem.

6. Share your completed statement and list in a whole-class discussion that focuses on ways to use the three signals in thinking and writing about causes and effects.

How to Explain Causes and Effects

Goal 2
Choose between two basic methods for developing your essay: One focuses on causes; the other focuses on effects.

Just because two events are closely connected in time, it does not mean that one causes the other or that one is the result of the other. A classic example goes like this: An airplane crashes. It is later determined that several people on board had been eating dill pickles moments before the crash. Other airplane crashes are studied, and the same effect is observed: People eat pickles; planes go down. Therefore, eating dill pickles causes airplanes to crash. The example may sound silly, but it makes a point. We have a tendency to look for cause and effect in what may be a coincidence.

Most issues or problems are too complex to have a single cause, and the effects we attribute to a certain cause may not follow logically. What are the reasons that led to your choice of a college? When you make a low score on a test, do you know why? What are your dreams for the future, and what chain of events will you have to set in motion for those dreams to become reality? Cause and effect are not only the components of an organizational pattern for writing, but they are also a habit of thought that can help you gain control of your writing and your life.

To write about the causes of a problem or the effects of an issue, or any other topic that examines causes and effects, develop your thesis by using one of the two methods diagrammed and explained next.

Method 1: Several Causes, One Effect

Explain several *causes* that result in a single *effect*. The organizational pattern of an essay developed from the thesis statement "I live in Sweetwater because life in this small town embodies several of America's traditional values" might look like this:

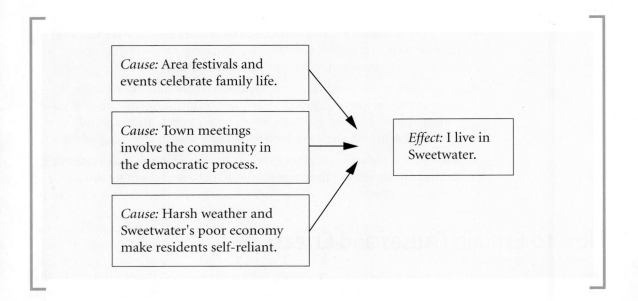

One paragraph could be devoted to explaining each of the three causes. In the first paragraph, for example, you could describe one or more festivals or events and tell *how* they celebrate family life.

Method 2: Several Effects, One Cause

Explain several *effects* of a single *cause*. The organizational pattern of an essay developed from the thesis statement "The move to Sweetwater will result in positive changes for my family" might look like this:

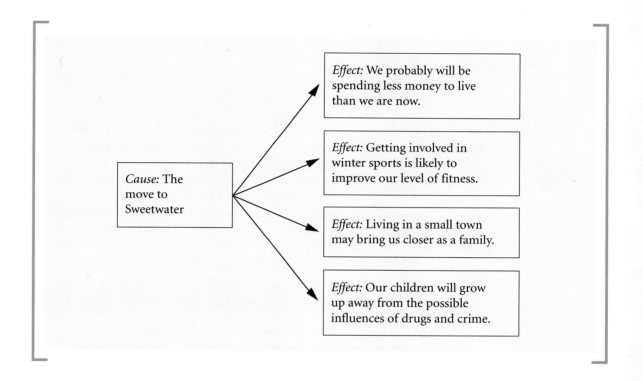

You could devote one paragraph to explaining each of the four effects. In the first body paragraph, for example, you could compare and contrast what it costs to live where you are living now with what it will cost you to live in Sweetwater.

To achieve coherence within and between paragraphs of your essay, use transitional words and phrases that signal cause-and-effect relationships, such as those listed in Figure 12.1 on page 302. Choosing appropriate signal words will help readers follow your ideas.

Figure 12.1   Transitions That Signal Cause-and-Effect Relationships

affect	for	solution
as a result	if . . . then	so
because	in order to	so that
cause	problem	then
consequently	reason	therefore
due to	result	
effect	since	

Exercise 12.6

Facts and figures can be convincing details to use when explaining causes and effects. For example, what percentage of college students are binge drinkers? What percentage of college students have been involved in alcohol-related accidents or deaths? What are the factors that put students at risk for becoming alcoholics? What are some guidelines for drinking responsibly? To answer these questions, use a search engine such as Google and type "binge drinking," "students," "alcohol abuse" in its dialog box. These words will turn up a list of sites for you to browse. For best results, click on sites affiliated with a college or a well-known organization.

Student Voices: A Cause-and-Effect Essay

The author asks and answers a question that may help to explain the anticonservative bias she has observed on her campus. As you read the essay, look for other signals of cause and effect. For critical reading and thinking questions related to this essay, go to *The Confident Writer* website.

Anticonservative Bias
Andrena Woodhams

1   Nowadays it seems that part of the college experience is the suffering of criticism, ridicule and various disparaging remarks toward President Bush and his administration. So common is the occurrence that you may be asking yourself why I think it's even worthy of remarking upon. What you may not have considered is the overwhelming dominance of left-wing liberalism and the virtual absence of conservative voices in higher education. [This ethos masks a serious reality: that the "diversity" so prized by modern academia seems to mean in practice "politically correct" as in the "save the whales, redistribute income and make special allowances for favored minorities" sense rather than

The introduction builds background and helps to frame the question.

Thesis

the truly wide variety of opinions that span the sociopolitical spectrum of turn-of-the-twenty-first-century America.⌋ How much of this problem lies in the unacknowledged bias of our professors?

The author asks a question.

2   On numerous occasions, I've observed firsthand the ridicule that we conservative students are subjected to upon offering a viewpoint other than the professor's. As a result, we coast through class, keeping our heads down; the opinions of students who disagree with a professor rarely can be voiced because such students feel forced to keep their mouths shut for a good grade's consideration.

The transition signals that the effects of anticonservative bias follow.

3   What student who cares about his or her academic standing dares contradict a professor utterly convinced of one perspective? Maybe if I didn't want to get into law school, I would have the courage to risk a real debate!

4   Rollins's mission statement declares that its continuing priorities include "diversity among students, staff, and faculty."

5   The Rollins College Code of Student Rights and Responsibilities prohibits "conduct which prevents free academic interaction and opportunities or which creates an intimidating, hostile, or offensive study or work environment." The areas covered by this policy are "age, race, ethnicity, gender, sexual orientation, religion, or disability." So how come this policy doesn't extend to political affiliation?

The author questions a stated policy.

6   There can be no true intellectual diversity in higher education until both conservatives and liberals can feel equally comfortable about expressing their opinions. Until we realize the weakness of the present situation, students are only getting half an education—even at $34,000 or more per year.

Conclusion points to the future.

7   Student Republicans, Libertarians, and rugged individualists, throw off your chains!

The author issues a call to action.

Think Through Your Topic

Goal 3 **Determine whether cause-and-effect analysis is an appropriate organizational pattern for your essay, based on your topic and purpose.**

Writing that is done primarily to fulfill an assignment lacks purpose and personality. Choose topics that interest you; write about issues on which you have a strong opinion. Perhaps there is a problem that you are struggling with, a difficult decision that you must make, or a question that needs an answer. For topics such as these, cause-and-effect analysis may work especially well as your organizational pattern. Whatever topic you choose, think it through by answering ten questions to generate ideas.

Questions to Consider for Cause and Effect

1. Is your topic an issue, a problem, a decision, or a question that both interests and concerns you?

2. Will your topic also engage your audience?

3. What is your purpose? Why do you want to write about this topic?

4. What is your thesis or central idea? What do you want to say about your topic?

5. How will you introduce your thesis?

6. What causes or effects will you identify?

7. What details will you choose to explain them?

8. Will you use the question/answer, act/consequence, or probability signal to alert readers that a cause-and-effect analysis follows?

9. Will you use Method 1 or Method 2 to analyze your topic?

10. What will readers learn from your essay?

Plan and Write Your Essay

Goal 4 *Follow a five-step plan to write your cause-and-effect essay and to avoid common problems in logic.*

If you think a topic you have chosen would benefit from a cause-and-effect pattern of organization, *the first step* in planning your essay is to brainstorm your topic, using the three signals as a guide:

1. *The question/answer signal:* Does your topic enable you to answer a question that has significance for both you and your readers? George Gallup Jr., for example, asks the question "What are the pressures that have emerged in the past twenty years that cause long-standing family bonds to be broken?" The question is significant to anyone who is concerned about the high divorce rate in America and the effects of divorce on children.

2. *The act/consequence signal:* Does your topic enable you to explain an action and its consequences? Several famous people have written articles and books about their drug addictions and how they overcame them. Some describe the act of taking drugs (cause) and the consequences, such as lost jobs and loss of self-respect (effects). Others explain how the consequences of taking drugs (cause) led them to take an action such as entering a drug rehabilitation program (effect).

3. *The probability signal:* Does your topic enable you to make a prediction about the future? For example, Warkentin's study suggests that biologists and others may have to change the way they think about an embryo's ability to respond to its environment. You could write an essay about a discov-

ery that changed people's thinking or actions. You could also write an essay in which you predict what you will be doing in five or ten years based on the preparations you are making now.

The second step in planning your essay is to decide on a purpose for writing and determine your audience's needs. Suppose you choose as your topic "What causes math anxiety," and your purpose is to help readers identify the causes so they can overcome them. In addition to explaining the causes, you may also need to examine the effects of math anxiety so that readers will have a clear idea of why they should be concerned. Your audience may include readers who are math anxious and who already have a built-in interest in your topic. Your audience may also include readers who have never heard of math anxiety but who may be interested in learning about it since it may affect their friends and their children.

The third step in planning your essay is to write a thesis statement that will control the development of your essay. Again, you can use the three signals as a guide. Remember to remain flexible in your choice of a thesis so that you can revise or rewrite it as needed. Following are examples of three possible thesis statements for an essay on the topic "Where I Live and Why." The cause and effect parts of each statement are labeled in parentheses.

The question/answer signal:	I live in Sweetwater (effect) because life in this small town embodies several of America's traditional values. (cause)
The act/consequence signal:	If you are seeking the pleasures of a coastal New England town (cause), then, like me, you might choose Sweetwater as your ideal place to live. (effect)
The probability signal:	The move to Sweetwater (cause) will result in positive changes for my family. (effects)

The fourth step in planning your essay is to select and organize your evidence to support your thesis. Though you can choose from among many ways to organize your essay, you may want to start by using one of the two methods diagrammed on pages 300–301.

The fifth step is to make sure that you avoid the logical fallacies that can undermine your essay's effectiveness. A *logical fallacy* is false reasoning that can cause you to make assumptions or draw conclusions that do not follow from the evidence. False reasoning can make you see connections where none exist. Watch out for these fallacies as you plan and write your essay.

- **Oversimplification:** As mentioned before, many issues and problems are quite complex and may have several causes or effects. Global warming, for example, may be the result of both human activity and natural causes. Your own biases can cloud your thinking so that you fail to mention opposing viewpoints. If you hold strong opinions, you may have to work at seeing the other side. You may have to work at looking for multiple causes or effects when one cause seems to predominate.

- **Post Hoc:** This fallacy is the result of thinking that because two events are connected in time that one must be the cause of the other. The conclusion, explained earlier in this chapter, that dill pickles cause airplane crashes is an example of the post hoc fallacy. Coincidence may sometimes masquerade as a causal connection. Showing a logical connection between events and their causes requires facts, and other provable evidence.

- **Circular Reasoning:** Circular reasoning is a fallacy that results when the stated cause and effect are the same or nearly the same. One student who was living with three other students in a dorm room designed for two wrote this as the thesis statement for an essay: "The overcrowded conditions on our campus are the result of an enrollment number that has outpaced the space available." Basically, this sentence says that the campus is overcrowded as a result of overcrowding. A better thesis would be "Because of overcrowding on our campus, residence halls are filled past capacity, parking is hard to find, and scheduling classes is difficult when courses have already been filled." This sentence states the problem (overcrowding) and several effects. From here, the student can offer possible solutions, but the circular statement leads only to a dead end.

Figure 12.2 is an overview of what to include in your cause-and-effect essay.

Figure 12.2 Cause and Effect: An Overview

PARTS	WHAT TO INCLUDE	QUESTIONS TO ASK
Introduction	1. topic 2. purpose 3. context 4. thesis	1. Is my topic an issue, problem, decision, or question that concerns me? 2. Which one of the three cause-and-effect signals will I use? 3. What background information will my readers need? 4. Does my thesis clearly state my topic and purpose?
Body paragraphs	1. topic sentence 2. choice of details 3. method of analysis 4. transitions	1. Which cause or effect will I explain first? 2. What major and minor details will convince my readers? 3. Is *method 1* or *method 2* the best way to analyze my topic? 4. What transitions will I choose to make sure that my discussion flows smoothly?
Conclusion	1. concluding device 2. significance for readers	1. Should I restate my thesis or use another device? 2. What can I add to my conclusion that will help my readers understand the value of my analysis?

≪ Topics for Writing ≫

1. **React to the Reading.** Either write an essay on global warming in which you answer one of the questions in The Critical Thinker, or write your response to the student essay on anticonservative bias on college campuses.

2. **Use Your Experience.** Write about a topic that is of major concern to you. Choose a topic from the following list, or make up your own topic.

   - An important decision that you made and its consequences
   - Your reasons for choosing a college
   - The best piece of advice you ever received
   - A favorite possession
   - An accident or other disaster
   - A place that has meaning for you or your family
   - An issue or matter of controversy
   - A trend or a fashion
   - Living in or visiting another country
   - A person who is a hero in your eyes

3. **Make a Real-World Connection.** Write about the reasons that motivated your choice of a major or career. Include in your essay your expectations for the future.

4. **Go to the Web.** Google an issue raised in the chapter-opening essay, such as greenhouse gases, climate change, or the retreat of the glaciers. Find an article on the topic and write a review of it. Or go to *The Confident Writer* website and choose another topic for writing.

≪ Checklist for Revision ≫

Did you miss anything? Check off the following items as you revise and edit your essay.

- ❏ Is your topic appropriate for a cause-and-effect essay?
- ❏ Does your introductory paragraph contain one of the three signals for cause and effect: question/answer, act/consequence, or probability?
- ❏ Does your thesis statement include your topic and purpose?
- ❏ Have you done a method 1 or method 2 analysis of your topic?
- ❏ Do your paragraphs have topic sentences?
- ❏ Are your paragraphs detailed enough to develop the thesis?
- ❏ Have you chosen transitions that will help your readers follow your analysis?

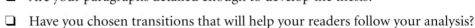

❑   Do you conclude with an appropriate device and a statement of your topic's significance for readers?

❑   Have you proofread your essay and corrected all errors?

≪ Your Discovery Journal ≫

Think about an ongoing problem you have, either with your writing skills or with a skill required in one of your other courses. What is the problem, what are its causes, and what can you do to solve the problem? To answer these questions, complete the following reflective statements.

As an additional option, you can do this activity online by going to *The Confident Writer* website.

> *A problem I have is* _____.
>
> *One possible cause of the problem is* _____.
>
> *One way to solve my problem might be to* _____.

≪ Website Resources ≫

This chapter's resources include

- Chapter 12 Exercises
- Chapter 12 Quiz
- Downloadable Charts: *Group Evaluation Form*
- Chapter 12 Your Reflections
- More Topics for Writing
- Chapter 12 Summary

To access these learning and study tools, go to *The Confident Writer* website.

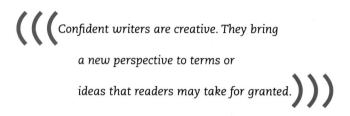

(((Confident writers are creative. They bring

a new perspective to terms or

ideas that readers may take for granted.)))

Using Definition

What you already know about *definition*

- o You know that someone who asks, "What do you mean?" may be seeking a definition.

- o You know that the words you choose can arouse either positive or negative feelings in others.

- o You probably have had the experience of being misunderstood because you did not choose your words carefully.

Your *goals* for this chapter

[1] Choose among giving examples, making comparisons, tracing a history, narrating events, or using negation to write definitions that are precise and useful.

[2] Determine whether definition is an appropriate organizational pattern for your essay, based on your topic and purpose.

[3] Choose appropriate strategies and avoid common problems when planning and writing your definition essay.

Writing often involves defining words or terms so that readers know exactly what you mean by them. Definitions are useful for explaining the meaning of a word or term that readers may be unfamiliar with or may misunderstand. Perhaps you want to redefine a word by explaining what it means to you, or you may need to clarify a term that has more than one meaning. Two types of definitions are useful in your writing: *simple definitions* and *extended definitions*. A simple definition is one that can be stated in a few words—for example, a simple definition of *fitness* is "a state of physical health, resulting from exercise and proper nutrition." You can slip a simple definition into a paragraph to define a term that may be unfamiliar to your audience.

You can find simple definitions in the dictionary, but rather than copy dictionary definitions, try to define terms in your own words. Use the dictionary to verify meanings and make corrections as needed.

An *extended definition,* on the other hand, is longer, usually a paragraph or more, and can become the basis of a whole essay. As an organizational pattern, *definition* helps you explain the meaning of words, terms, or abstract ideas, such as *generosity* or *success,* with the goal of giving your readers new insights into terms or ideas they take for granted.

[First Thoughts]

To build background for reading, explore your thoughts about families and family values. Then answer the questions, either on your own or in a group discussion:

1. What does the word *family* mean to you?

2. What does the phrase *family values* mean to you?

3. Read the title, the headnote, and the first two paragraphs of the following essay. Based on this preview, what do you think will follow?

[Word Alert]

Before reading, preview the following words and definitions. During reading, use context clues and your dictionary to define any additional unfamiliar words.

incriminating (4)	accusing, implicating, faulting
ministered (4)	took care of

righteous (6)	morally upright, just
encrusted (7)	caked with, covered
factoring out (8)	excluding, ignoring
deprived (11)	kept from owning or enjoying

The Perfect Family

Alice Hoffman

Alice Hoffman is the author of thirteen novels, a book of short stories, and three children's books. Her essays have appeared in numerous magazines, newspapers, and anthologies. Her screenplay *Independence Day* was made into a hit movie. In this essay, Hoffman challenges our ideas about family: what it means and how it has changed.

1   When I was growing up in the 50's, there was only one sort of family, the one we watched on television every day. Right in front of us, in black and white, was everything we needed to know about family values: the neat patch of lawn, the apple tree, the mother who never once raised her voice, the three lovely children: a Princess, a Kitten, a Bud[1] and, always, the father who knew best.

2   People stayed married forever back then, and roses grew by the front door. We had glass bottles filled with lightning bugs and brand-new swing sets in the backyard, and softball games at dusk. We had summer nights that lasted forever and well-balanced meals, three times a day, in our identical houses, on our identical streets. There was only one small bargain we had to make to exist in this world: we were never to ask questions, never to think about people who didn't have as much or who were different in any way. We ignored desperate marriages and piercing loneliness. And we were never, ever, to wonder what might be hidden from view, behind the unlocked doors, in the privacy of our neighbors' bedrooms and knotty-pine-paneled dens.

3   This was a bargain my own mother could not make. Having once believed that her life would sort itself out to be like the television shows we watched, only real and in color, she'd been left to care for her children on her own, at a time when divorce was so uncommon I did not meet another child of divorced parents until 10 years later, when I went off to college.

4   Back then, it almost made sense when one of my best friends was not allowed to come to my house; her parents did not approve of divorce or my mother's life style. My mother, after all, had a job and a boyfriend and, perhaps even more incriminating, she was the one who took the silver-colored trash cans out to the curb on Monday nights. She did so faithfully, on evenings when she had already balanced the checkbook and paid the bills and ministered to sore throats and made certain we'd had dinner; but all up and down

[1]*Princess, Kitten, and Bud are characters from* Father Knows Best, *a family sitcom that aired from 1954–1962.*

the street everybody knew the truth: taking out the trash was clearly a job for fathers.

5   When I was 10, my mother began to work for the Department of Social Services, a world in which the simple rules of the suburbs did not apply. She counseled young unwed mothers, girls and women who were not allowed to make their own choices, most of whom had not been allowed to finish high school or stay in their own homes, none of whom had been allowed to decide not to continue their pregnancies. Later, my mother placed most of these babies in foster care, and still later, she moved to the protective-services department, investigating charges of abuse and neglect, often having to search a child's back and legs for bruises or welts.

6   She would have found some on my friend, left there by her righteous father, the one who wouldn't allow her to visit our home but blackened her eye when, a few years later, he discovered that she was dating a boy he didn't approve of. But none of his neighbors had dared to report him. They would never have imagined that someone like my friend's father, whose trash cans were always tidily placed at the curb, whose lawn was always well cared for, might need watching.

7   To my mother, abuse was a clear-cut issue, if reported and found, but neglect was more of a judgment call. It was, in effect, passing judgment on the nature of love. If my father had not sent the child-support checks on time, if my mother hadn't been white and college-educated, it could have easily been us in one of those apartments she visited, where the heat didn't work on the coldest days, and the dirt was so encrusted you could mop all day and still be called a poor housekeeper, and there was often nothing more for dinner than Frosted Flakes and milk, or, if it was toward the end of the month, the cereal might be served with tap water. Would that have meant my mother loved her children any less, that we were less of a family?

8   My mother never once judged who was a fit mother on the basis of a clean floor, or an unbalanced meal, or a boyfriend who sometimes spent the night. But back then, there were good citizens who were only too ready to set their standards for women and children, factoring out poverty or exhaustion or simply a different set of beliefs.

9   There are always those who are ready to deal out judgment with the ready fist of the righteous. I know this because before the age of 10 I was one of the righteous, too. I believed that mothers were meant to stay home and fathers should carry out the trash on Monday nights. I believed that parents could create a domestic life that was the next best thing to heaven, if they just tried. That is what I'd been told, that in the best of all worlds we would live identical lives in identical houses.

10   It's a simple view of the world, too simple even for childhood. Certainly, it's a vision that is much too limited for the lives we live now, when only one in 19 families are made up of a wage-earner father, a mother who doesn't work outside the home and two or more children. And even long ago, when I was growing up, we paid too high a price when we cut ourselves off from the rest of the

A promotional portrait of the cast of the 1965 televion series Father Knows Best. *Clockwise from lower left: Billy Gray, Elinor Donahue, Robert Young, Jane Wyatt, and Lauren Chapin.*

world. We ourselves did not dare to be different. In the safety we created, we became trapped.

11   There are still places where softball games are played at dusk and roses grow by the front door. There are families with sons named Bud, with kind and generous fathers, and mothers who put up strawberry preserves every June and always have time to sing lullabies. But do these families love their children any more than the single mother who works all day? Are their lullabies any sweeter? If I felt deprived as a child, it was only when our family was measured against some notion of what we were supposed to be. The truth of it was, we lacked for little.

12   And now that I have children of my own, and am exhausted at the end of the day in which I've probably failed in a hundred different ways, I am amazed that women alone can manage. That they do, in spite of everything, is a simple fact. They rise from sleep in the middle of the night when their children call out to them. They rush for the cough syrup and cold washcloths and keep watch till dawn. These are real family values, the same ones we knew when we were children. As far as we were concerned our mother could cure a fever with a kiss. This may be the only thing we ever need to know about love. The rest, no one can judge.

≪ The Critical Reader ≫

[CENTRAL IDEA]

1. What is Alice Hoffman's thesis? Is it stated or implied?

[EVIDENCE]

2. How does Hoffman describe the typical family of the 1950s when she was growing up?

3. In what way was Hoffman's family not typical?

4. What is Hoffman's idea of family?

[IMPLICATIONS]

5. Using evidence from the essay, what do you think is Hoffman's attitude toward mothers and fathers and their place, or role, in the family?

[WORD CHOICE]

6. Hoffman makes use of repeated words and phrases throughout the essay: *righteous* is used once in paragraph 6 and twice in paragraph 9. *Judgment* is used twice in paragraph 7 and once in paragraph 9. *Judged* is used in paragraph 8, and the essay ends on the word *judge*. What do you think is the significance of these word choices in relation to the author's thesis and to the title?

≪ The Critical Thinker ≫

To examine Alice Hoffman's essay in more depth, follow these suggestions for reflection, discussion, and writing. Then choose one of them as a topic for writing.

1. What do you think is Hoffman's meaning in the first sentence of paragraph 3: "This was a bargain my own mother could not make," and what purpose does this sentence serve?

2. Why was one of Hoffman's best friends not allowed to come to her house, and in what way did that almost make sense, as she says in paragraph 4?

3. Who is Hoffman's audience, and what is her tone? Use evidence from the essay to explain your answer.

4. What are your hopes for your own family? Will your family values differ from or be similar to the family in which you grew up?

How to Write an Extended Definition

Goal 1

Choose among giving examples, making comparisons, tracing a history, narrating events, or using negation to write definitions that are precise and useful.

Definitions should be linked to purpose and audience. For example, many writers define terms to call the reader's attention to a problem or an issue. *Burnout* is a term coined by social scientists in the 1970s to describe the psychological state of workers who had grown tired of their jobs to the point that they could no longer function successfully. Once the problem had a name, employers could begin to seek solutions. Companies today offer incentives and develop programs to help employees overcome burnout or avoid it altogether.

The homeless is another term that calls our attention to a lingering social problem. Defining a group of people living without work and without homes keeps them visible so they cannot be ignored. Those who write about the homeless do so with the purpose of moving readers to do something about the plight of these people.

When you use definition in your writing, decide first what your purpose is and what your audience's beliefs and expectations are. For example, Alice Hoffman assumes that her readers are familiar with the ongoing debate about family values in the United States. Her purpose is to broaden the definition of family and to suggest that the perfect family does not exist. Much of her essay defines *family* and *family values* by contrasting real families with ideal families.

To write an extended definition, one that provides a lengthy explanation of the meaning of a word or term, you can choose from five common methods:

1. Give examples.

2. Make comparisons.

3. Trace history.

4. Narrate events.

5. Define by negation.

Give Examples

Examples illustrate what you mean by creating clear and vivid images in the reader's mind. Examples can come from personal experiences, observations, reading, and research. When you define a term by using examples, you explain it by describing it in a graphic way. The following excerpt from Art Carey's *The United States of Incompetence* defines *work*.

■ **CONCEPT CHECK**
What is your definition of *work*? What examples would you choose to explain the term?

The excerpt begins by defining *work* as a four-letter word, thereby implying that work is dirty. The author further defines *work* by giving several brief examples that show what people think about work. Next are several examples of workers that illustrate ways people avoid work. The rest of the chapter from which this excerpt comes continues to define Americans' attitudes toward work and how these attitudes have changed. Carey also defines *work* as "a necessary evil," and "a terrible drudgery." In addition, he uses examples to illustrate situations in which people's work habits reveal how they feel about their jobs.

> The United States used to be famous for hard work. Now, *work* has become a four-letter word. Many Americans—whether stuck on an assembly line or in the ranks of middle management—consider work tedious, unsatisfying, a necessary evil that earns the paycheck and buys the food. In a society that idolizes wealth and worships leisure, work is the terrible drudgery that stands between the average American schmo and the weekend. *TGIF! It's Miller Time!*

The output of a factory is halved on Mondays as many workers call in "sick."

Four men from the highway department stand around a pothole, laughing and drinking coffee. Everyone seems to be supervising; no one seems to be working.

A sanitation crew squanders the afternoon in a bar when they're supposed to be picking up trash.

A policeman spends the bulk of his shift flirting with waitresses and napping in his squad car instead of patrolling the streets.

A high-salaried executive whiles away the morning making personal phone calls and reading the paper rather than tending to business. . . .

Defining a word or term depends on a clear understanding of what it means. Exercise 13.1 takes you through three steps to accurate definitions.

[Exercise 13.1] Select any five words or terms from the following list and experiment with three-step defining: First, define the word or term in your own words. Second, give one or more synonyms for the word or term, and verify your definition and synonyms with the dictionary. Finally, write two graphic examples to illustrate your definition of the word. See the sample answer following the list. Share your results with the rest of the class.

poverty	prejudice	basketball fan
hobby	depression	pessimist
tightwad	optimist	slob
friend	leisure	art

Sample Answer:

Term:	Self-control
Definition:	Self-control is a quality of people who are able to set standards for themselves and live by them.
Synonym:	Self-discipline
Example #1:	A student who refuses to binge drink even though his or her friends are doing it has self-control.
Example #2:	A person who is able to lose weight and keep it off has self-control.

Make Comparisons

Another way to define a term is to compare or contrast it with one you think the reader already knows. To explain what *test anxiety* is, you can compare it with the stress a person might feel in any anxiety-provoking situation. Both types of stress can cause similar symptoms: sweaty palms, rapid pulse, nausea, feelings of helplessness, and other physical or mental responses. The difference is that common stress can have any number of causes, but test anxiety occurs only in relation to taking tests or thinking about them. The following paragraph from the first chapter of Michael Korda's book *Success!* defines *success* by comparing it to a journey:

> Try to think of success as a journey, an adventure, not a specific destination. Your goals may change during the course of that journey, and your original ambitions may be superseded by different, larger ones. Success will certainly bring you the material things you want, and a good, healthy appetite for the comforts and luxuries of life is an excellent road to success, but basically you'll know you have reached your goal when you have gone that one step further, in wealth, fame or achievement, than you ever dreamed was possible.

Defining by comparison is also useful for explaining a complex term: one that has more than one meaning or one that can be applied to different categories of people or items. *Mental retardation,* for example, is difficult to define because there are different types of mental retardation.

In the following excerpt, the author defines two categories of mental retardation. The excerpt is from Sallie Tisdale's article "Neither Morons Nor Imbeciles Nor Idiots, In the Company of the Mentally Retarded" that appeared in *Harper's* magazine, June 1990:

> There are two widely accepted categories of retardation: organic and nonorganic. Organic retardation has more than 250 known causes, among them Down syndrome and other chromosomal disorders, metabolic imbalances, tumors, brain malformations, and trauma. But researchers in the field commonly hold that only about 20 percent of all the people called retarded have an organic problem.
>
> The remaining 80 percent are affected by nonorganic retardation—retardation caused by, say, parental neglect or abuse, or by a baby's having eaten lead paint—and there is nothing physiologically wrong with them. Almost all the people classified as mentally retarded are considered to be nonorganically retarded. One of the more controversial questions in the field of mental retardation right now is whether the nonorganically retarded are—or should be labeled—retarded at all. . . .

Sallie Tisdale's purpose in the essay is to convince readers that we need a more descriptive definition of mental retardation. The excerpt above comes near

✓ CONCEPT CHECK

Can you see how the patterns of comparison and contrast and definition can work together? For more information on comparison and contrast, see Chapter 11.

the beginning of the essay, where Tisdale illustrates the complexity of the term and shows why traditional definitions of *mental retardation* are inadequate.

[Exercise 13.2] Add a comparison to the examples you wrote for the words or terms you defined in Exercise 13.1.

Sample Answer:

Term:	Self-control
Definition:	Self-control is a quality of people who are able to set standards for themselves and live by them.
Synonym:	Self-discipline
Example #1:	A student who refuses to binge drink even though his or her friends are doing it has self-control.
Example #2:	A person who is able to lose weight and keep it off has self-control.
Comparison:	Self-control is like self-motivation. It is something you have to do for yourself; no one can do it for you.

Trace a History

Sometimes it is helpful to show that a word or term you are defining has roots in the past. For example, *rock and roll,* as defined by experts in the subject, is a term coined in the 1950s to mean a type of music that combines jazz, blues, and country rhythms. As new trends in popular music have developed, writers have defined and explained them in terms of their roots in the rock music of the 1950s. When you show how the definition of a word or term has connections to the past, you are tracing its history.

[Exercise 13.3] Read the following excerpt from "Why People Are Rude," an essay by David A. Wiessler. In this essay, Wiessler defines *rudeness* both by using examples and by placing it in a historical context. Find and underline the part of the excerpt that defines by tracing the history.

1 Rudeness is becoming a common occurrence in American life. If you don't like it, lump it. Or mind your own business. Or get out of the way.

2   That is the kind of talk and attitude that's cropping up more often in almost every public experience—on the highways, in theater lines, over the telephone, on public transit. The examples are almost endless: . . .

3   An Atlanta newsstand operator is unable to wait on his customers because passers-by shout at him for directions, information, or change without waiting their turns.

4   A woman stands in a Washington, D.C., supermarket line while her children do the shopping. When the cart is full, she has the children wheel it to the front of the line where she is standing ahead of everyone else.

5   What's behind such incidents? Some experts say the trend began in the 1960's when traditional values and manners came under fire. Others blame the fast-paced American lifestyle for creating a society that has little time any more to be polite.

6   This is particularly true in big cities, where people are surrounded by strangers. "In a small town, the person to whom you are rude is more likely to be someone you are going to see again tomorrow," observed psychologist Stanley Milgram at the Graduate Center of the City University of New York. "In the city, it is very unlikely you will ever again encounter someone with whom you have a minor conflict. . . ."

Narrate Events

Another way to define is to relate a brief story or incident that illustrates or reveals the meaning of a term as you see it. Suppose you want to define the word *responsibility*. Perhaps this word has a special meaning for you because you remember when you first understood what it means to be responsible. You decide to write an essay using as your extended definition the narration of an event in your life that made you become a responsible person.

The following excerpt is from Chapter 4 of *Emotional Intelligence* by Daniel Goleman. The author defines the term *self-awareness* first by narrating an incident that reveals this quality, then by contrasting it with the psychological terms *metacognition* and *metamood*.

1   A belligerent samurai, an old Japanese tale goes, once challenged a Zen master to explain the concept of heaven and hell. But the monk replied with scorn, "You're nothing but a lout—I can't waste my time with the likes of you!"

2   His very honor attacked, the samurai flew into a rage and, pulling his sword from its scabbard, yelled, "I could kill you for your impertinence."

3   "That," the monk calmly replied, "is hell."

4   Startled at seeing the truth in what the master pointed out about the fury that had him in its grip, the samurai calmed down, sheathed his sword, and bowed, thanking the monk for the insight.

5   "And that," said the monk, "is heaven."

6   The sudden awakening of the samurai to his own agitated state illustrates the crucial difference between being caught up in a feeling and becoming aware that you are being swept away by it. Socrates's injunction "Know thyself" speaks to this keynote of emotional intelligence: awareness of one's own feelings as they occur.

7   It might seem at first glance that our feelings are obvious; more thoughtful reflection reminds us of times we have been all too oblivious to what we really felt about something, or awoke to these feelings late in the game. Psychologists use the rather ponderous term *metacognition* to refer to an awareness of thought process, and *metamood* to mean awareness of one's own emotions. I prefer the term *self-awareness,* in the sense of an ongoing attention to one's internal states. In this self-reflexive awareness mind observes and investigates experience itself, including the emotions. . . .

[Exercise 13.4]   What does the term *good friend* mean to you? Write a paragraph in which you define the meaning of this term by narrating an incident. For example, what happened? Who was involved? What did your friend do to demonstrate that he or she was a good friend? Your paragraph should answer these questions.

[Exercise 13.5]

Your college courses all have what we call *terms of the discipline:* specialized words or terms that professionals in a field use. Examples from your writing class include *thesis statement, coherence,* and *audience.* Mastery of a subject depends on a full understanding of the terms used to discuss it. Do you have a method for learning the special terms associated with the subjects you are taking? If not, try this one. Write terms and definitions on note cards. Write the term on one side and its definition on the other side. Under the definition, write a sentence that contains the term. Periodically review your note cards by looking at each word, reciting its definition, and then turning the card over to check yourself. Select some terms to learn and try out the method.

Define by Negation

As explained in previous sections, definitions can take many forms. First of all, you can define an object by telling what it *is*—the class of things to which it belongs. For example, a *kiwi* is a type of fruit known as a berry. Second, you can define an object by comparing it with other members of its class. For example, a *kiwi* is green and fleshy inside like a grape, has a taste similar to that of a strawberry, and is about the size and shape of a large Italian tomato. Unlike these more familiar berries, however, a kiwi has a fuzzy brown inedible skin. Third, you can define an object by tracing its history. For example, the subtropical *kiwi* was originally available in the United States only as an imported luxury fruit, but now it is cultivated and marketed here. Fourth, you can define by narrating an incident, as in this brief passage:

I remember the first time I saw a kiwi. It looked like a fuzzy brown egg. A friend showed me how to eat it by cutting it in half and scooping out the flesh with a spoon. "Don't eat the skin," he said. The flavor was sweet and familiar, a combination of strawberry and banana.

Finally, you can define an object by *negation,* which is an explanation of what the object *is not.* For example, a *kiwi* is not an aggregate fruit like a raspberry, not a single-seed fruit like a plum or a cherry, and not a segmented fruit like an orange. The fuzz on the kiwi's skin is neither soft nor stiff, but somewhere in between. In the following passage, *bagel* is defined mainly by negation:

> A bagel is not a dinner roll, not a sweet roll, not a bun, nor a biscuit. It looks like a donut, but it is not. It is as hard as a sourdough roll, chewy as a French roll, but it is neither of these. It is not confined to any one use, such as a breakfast food, lunch treat, or dessert snack. Though made of the same basic ingredients, not all bagels are alike. Round, chewy, and with a hole in the middle, a bagel is a type of hard bread that comes in many flavors and can be enjoyed any time of day.

[Exercise 13.6] Apply what you have learned about the common methods of definition by doing this exercise with group members. First, review the group roles and responsibilities listed on the inside back cover. Next, complete the activity that follows and share your results with the rest of the class. Then evaluate your group's performance as your instructor recommends, or download the group evaluation form at *The Confident Writer* website.

1. Review and discuss Alice Hoffman's essay on pages 311–313.

2. List several examples the author uses to define *family.*

3. Explain where and how the author uses comparison to define *family.*

4. Explain where and how the author defines *family* by tracing its history.

5. List one or more of the incidents the author narrates to expand her definition of *family.*

6. Explain where and how the author defines *family* or *family values* by negation.

[Exercise 13.7] Whether you are writing a simple definition or an extended definition, verify all definitions with a dictionary. Even if your definition is a personal one—for example, what *success* means to you—keep your readers' assumptions in mind by also acknowledging the term's conventional meaning. However, the dictionary is only the beginning. For historical background on a term or idea, encyclopedias and other reference works can be a big help. For example, to find the meaning of the Greek word *hubris*, the poetical term *sonnet*, or the anatomical term *cranium*, you could turn to an online dictionary or encyclopedia. Browse some sites that your instructor or a librarian has suggested to find definitions of a term or idea that you want to write about. Then share your results with the rest of the class.

Student Voices: A Definition Essay

What does *sportsmanship* mean to you? Read this essay to learn one student's definition of this term. For critical reading and thinking questions related to this essay, go to Chapter 13 Your Reflections on *The Confident Writer* website.

Sportsmanship: How to Win and Lose Gracefully
Aric Mitchell

1   When Opie Taylor on the old *Andy Griffith Show* failed to win a local track and field competition, he refused to congratulate those who did and chose a life of absolute hatefulness and misery until his father, Sheriff Andy Taylor, straightened him out and put an end to the boy's foolishness. What Opie was displaying was a poor form of the idea of sportsmanship. *Sportsmanship, very simply, is the way we react to our status of achieving goals or how we behave toward winning or losing.*

The author begins with an example and a brief definition of the term sportsmanship.

Thesis

2   The connotation of the word usually means how we react positively toward an outcome, but in actuality, there are two types of sportsmanship: poor sportsmanship and good sportsmanship. Good sportsmanship is the idea that we accept whatever happens to us in a manner of goodwill, while poor sportsmanship means just the opposite.

The term is defined by comparison: good and poor sportsmanship are contrasted.

3   The only publicly acceptable form of sportsmanship is the good kind. From childhood, we are taught to be good sports. The idea is not too hard to practice while things are going one's way. No one ever had a hard time exhibiting good sportsmanship after winning a football or basketball game. However, the idea becomes complex when things are not going one's way. When the football game is won by the other team or that game-winning three-pointer does not go through the net, the process of being a good sport becomes one of the hardest struggles life has to offer. It is times like these that character is built—or lost.

Sportsmanship is a test of character.

4   Trying to find a reason for losing and laying the blame for an ill-fated outcome on someone else's shoulders are poor displays of sportsmanship. These behaviors build just as much character as the act of admitting defeat and congratulating the other team, but the type of character built is what distinguishes

Negation: The author explains what is not sportsmanship.

the two. Displays of poor sportsmanship turn a competitor into what society has coined the "sore loser." Sore losers have bad reputations for their behavior towards losing, and their reactions often bring more harm than good to the way others feel about them, but sore losers are not alone in the world of poor sportsmanship. Sore winners also exist.

5   *Sore winners* can be defined in many ways, but the easiest way to describe them is with the word *gloater*. These people cannot leave well enough alone. They are not happy with just defeating their opponent; they must also flaunt their victory. They give too much of the credit for winning to their own skill and not enough to opportunity or luck. The only thankfulness they ever show is to themselves, and they build poor relationships with those around them.

A synonym is offered.

6   The sportsmanship litmus test is something we take every time we compete in something. Whether it is in a football game, in a basketball game, or against the rest of the class for the highest grade, we are proving what kind of "sports" we are. What kind of a sport are you? The next time you play ping-pong, or pool, or volleyball, or poker, keep these things in mind. Your character might just depend on it.

The author points to the future by challenging readers to test their sportsmanship.

Think Through Your Topic

Goal 2 Determine whether definition is an appropriate organizational pattern for your essay, based on your topic and purpose.

Whether you define a term like *sportsmanship* or a concept like *global warming*, your objective is to clarify the term's meaning. You also need to have a firm grasp on your audience's assumptions and understand how the general public defines the term or idea. To think through your topic, answer ten questions to generate ideas.

Questions to Consider for Definition

1. Is your topic a term whose definition most people take for granted such as *freedom*, a specialized or technical term such as *interest rate*, or an abstract idea such as *success*?

2. What are your audience's assumptions about your topic?

3. What is your purpose? Why do you want to define this term?

4. What is your thesis or central idea? Why is the term important to you?

5. How will you introduce your term and your thesis?

6. What examples can you use to define your term?

7. What comparisons can you make that will help your readers understand?

8. Do you need to trace your term's history or to narrate an incident that reveals its meaning?

9. Can you show what your term means by explaining what it does not mean?

10. What conclusion can you offer readers about your term's importance or usefulness to them?

Plan and Write Your Essay

Goal 3 Choose appropriate strategies and avoid common problems when planning and writing your definition essay.

The following suggestions may help you plan and write an effective essay in which you want to define a word or term.

Define with a Purpose

Determine a *purpose* for writing by asking yourself *what* you want to define and *why.* Do you want to define an unfamiliar term or a term that is easily misunderstood or confused with another? Do you want to redefine a word or clarify a term that has one or more meanings? Make your purpose clear in the introduction to your essay.

Understand Your Audience

Decide who your *audience* is. Also, determine what your audience's experiences might be concerning the word or term you define. If your definition of *freedom,* for example, is different from what you think most people mean by this term, begin by summarizing the popular definition before explaining how yours is different from it. If the subject you have chosen is a technical one— for example, "the advantages of using a spreadsheet"—then define *spreadsheet* and any other technical terms for uninitiated readers.

Limit Your Topic

If you decide to write a personal definition of an abstract term, such as *success* or *heroes,* make sure your topic is narrow enough to be specific. For example,

☑ **CONCEPT CHECK**
For more information on audience and purpose, see Chapter 2. Limiting topics is explained in Chapter 1.

heroes is too broad a topic. If you write about heroes, limit your discussion either to a specific kind of hero or to your beliefs and values concerning heroes. You could write about a war hero, such as General Norman Schwarzkopf of Desert Storm; a fictional hero, such as Batman or Cat Woman; a historical figure, such as Sir Thomas More or Joan of Arc; or an everyday hero, such as Christa McAuliffe, Concord, New Hampshire's teacher in space who died in the 1986 *Challenger* explosion. In your essay, limit your topic even further to explain exactly what makes the person or fictional character heroic or not heroic according to your definition.

On the other hand, instead of writing about one particular hero, you might decide to define the qualities of heroism using several people as examples. You could even write an essay explaining how the popular notion of what a hero is has changed, or whether there *are* any heroes today. After limiting your topic, write a thesis statement as in the following example:

> An everyday hero is one who overcomes hardship to be successful and whose success inspires others.

Support Your Thesis

Thoroughly explain your definition using one or more of the five common methods explained in this chapter: define by giving examples, by making comparisons, by tracing history, by narrating incidents, or by negation.

Use Transitions

One way to make a smooth transition between paragraphs is to repeat a word from the last sentence of a paragraph in the first sentence of the following paragraph. In addition to repetition, use the transitions listed in Figure 13.1.

Figure 13.1 Transitions That Signal Definition

GIVING EXAMPLES	MAKING COMPARISONS	TRACING HISTORY	NARRATING INCIDENTS	DEFINING BY NEGATION
for example	to compare	in the past	before, after	in contrast
for instance	in common	historically	first, second, etc.	neither, nor
to define	a synonym for	looking back	soon, next, then	unlike
means	like	tracing	finally, at last	not

Avoid Two Common Problems

Clarity is the watchword of writing good definitions. Use examples and make comparisons that are specific. Avoid vague generalities. For example, describing a classroom as "friendly" only goes so far. Each member of your audience may have a different concept of what a friendly classroom is. What does *friendly* mean to you? Does it have something to do with the atmosphere, the furnishings, the way the instructor teaches, or the way students respond? If you include concrete details, readers will be better able to relate your definition to their own understanding of the term.

When using definition, or any other pattern for that matter, avoid the use of tired expressions. One such expression to avoid is "Webster says . . ." followed by a verbatim dictionary definition of your term. It is tempting to begin a definition essay this way because it seems so simple and direct. It is also boring. If you think a standard definition is required for clarity, then find a creative way to frame it within your paragraph so that it is part of a seamless explanation.

Figure 13.2 is an overview of what to include in your definition essay.

Figure 13.2   Definition: An Overview

PARTS	WHAT TO INCLUDE	QUESTIONS TO ASK
Introduction	1. topic 2. purpose 3. context 4. thesis	1. What word, term, or idea do I want to define? 2. What purpose will my definition serve? 3. Does my introduction include a simple definition of the term and provide background for my readers? 4. Does my thesis state my topic and purpose?
Body paragraphs	1. topic sentence 2. major details 3. minor details 4. transitions	1. Does each body paragraph have a topic sentence? 2. Do I define my term in as many ways as possible: by tracing a history, providing examples and comparisons, narrating an incident, or defining by negation? 3. Are my details specific and free of tired expressions? 4. What transitions will I choose to make sure that my sentences flow smoothly?
Conclusion	1. concluding device 2. significance for readers	1. Should I point to the future or use another concluding device? 2. What can I add to my conclusion that will be meaningful to readers?

⟨⟨ Topics for Writing ⟩⟩

1. **React to the Reading.** Using the chapter-opening essay or the student essay as a springboard for ideas, write your own definition of *family* or *sportsmanship*.

2. **Use Your Experience.** Define a term or idea that is important to you and that you think will interest readers. Choose a topic from the following list, or make up your own topic.

   - Good (or bad) manners
   - A good (or bad) friend
   - A good (or poor) teacher
   - Success or failure
   - A type of music, painting, book, or movie
   - A term or expression your family uses
   - The perfect vacation
   - A quality such as honesty, generosity, or sense of humor
   - An attitude such as optimism, pessimism, or futurism
   - A hero

3. **Make a Real-World Connection.** Choose one of the following topics:

   - A scientific or technical term
   - A term or concept from one of your courses
   - A slang term or popular expression
   - A workplace term

4. **Go to the Web.** Choose a topic from *The Confident Writer* website.

⟨⟨ Checklist for Revision ⟩⟩

Did you miss anything? Check off the following items as you revise and edit your essay.

- ❑ Is your topic appropriate for a definition essay?
- ❑ Does your introductory paragraph contain a brief definition of the term you have chosen?
- ❑ Are your purpose and audience clearly stated or implied?
- ❑ Does your thesis statement include your topic and purpose?
- ❑ Do your paragraphs have topic sentences?
- ❑ Have you defined your term in several ways?

❏   Are your details specific, and are your transitions appropriate?

❏   Is your conclusion effective?

❏   Have you proofread your essay and corrected all errors?

≪ Your Discovery Journal ≫

Reflect on your personal qualities as a student. What is one word that defines your behavior or describes what you are like as a student? Answer this question by completing and explaining the following statement.

As an additional option, you can do this activity online by going to *The Confident Writer* website.

The word that best defines me as a student is _____.

≪ Website Resources ≫

This chapter's resources include

- Chapter 13 Exercises
- Chapter 13 Quiz
- Downloadable Charts: *Group Evaluation Form*
- Chapter 13 Your Reflections
- More Topics for Writing
- Chapter 13 Summary

To access these learning and study tools, go to *The Confident Writer* website.

(((*Confident writers are persuasive. They have the*

power to influence others and broaden their views.)))

Arguing Persuasively

What you already know about *arguing* persuasively

- You are aware of topics or issues such as global warming, the controversy surrounding athletes' use of steroids, and the high cost of health care.

- Like most people, you probably believe that everyone has a right to an opinion, but you may also recognize that some opinions are better informed than others.

- No doubt you have influenced the decisions of others, and others have influenced your decisions.

Your *goals* for this chapter

[1] Know what the four elements of argument are, and be able to use them effectively.

[2] Avoid making the common errors in reasoning that can weaken an argument.

[3] Determine whether your topic is an appropriate issue for argumentation.

[4] Use appropriate strategies for planning your argument and writing your essay.

No matter what you write, it is important to have a purpose for writing. Of the two basic purposes, to inform or to persuade, your purpose in making an argument will always be to persuade your readers to think, feel, or act in a way that you think they should. *Argumentation* is an *attitude* toward your subject rather than an organizational pattern, such as narration or cause and effect. When you argue for or against something that you think is important, you are taking a position on an issue. To argue effectively so that you will convince readers, support your position with evidence and use sound logic in doing so. To organize your evidence in an argumentative essay, you can choose any pattern or combination of patterns to fulfill your purpose and develop your thesis.

On any issue, people will disagree, and their opinions can be strongly held, especially if the issue calls into question their values or beliefs. An effective argument not only states the author's position but also addresses opposing viewpoints and accounts for the audience's assumptions and concerns. This chapter explains how to develop a powerful and persuasive argument.

[First Thoughts]

To build background for reading, explore your thoughts about camera phones and Internet sites such as YouTube and MySpace. Then answer the following questions, either on your own or in a group discussion.

1. What is your opinion of sites such as YouTube?

2. Have you or anyone you know ever been the victim of camera-phone surveillance? Explain what happened.

3. Read the title, headnote, and first one or two paragraphs of the following essay. Based on this preview, what do you think will follow?

[Word Alert]

Before reading, preview the following words and definitions. During your reading, use context clues and your dictionary to define any additional unfamiliar words.

transparency (1)	ease of detection, obviousness, clarity
cognizant (2)	aware, conscious of, knowing

Orwellian (3)	of or relating to George Orwell, British author of the novel *Animal Farm* and the famous essay "Politics and the English Language." The term evokes the concept of a totalitarian society in which people are kept under surveillance and behaviors unfriendly to the state are punished.
Taliban, Hamas (6)	terrorist organizations
depredations (6)	acts of plunder, damage, or destruction
Hugo Chavez (7)	Venezuelan dictator
twit (9)	an annoying person
Alderaan, Death Star (9)	from the *Star Wars* series of films

The World is Watching, and No One Cares

Joe Queenan

Joe Queenan is a prolific writer whose articles have appeared in publications such as *Barron's,* the *New York Times Book Review,* the *Guardian,* and *Newsweek.*

1   In the audaciously predictable style for which he is famous, New York Times columnist Thomas Friedman recently rhapsodized about the many ways in which "transparency" is making our "global discussion . . . so much richer."

2   The theory was that the 24-7 surveillance wrought by camera phones, blogs, YouTube, Facebook and MySpace have turned all of us into public figures. Because everything we say or do is now apt to turn up on the Internet—potentially with humiliating results—we must live our lives more judiciously, cognizant that in the new "transparent" age, there is nowhere to hide.

3   Not long ago, such a society would have been deemed an Orwellian nightmare, a living hell where the brain police spied on everyone. But somehow Friedman has gotten it into his head that although surveillance is a bad idea when the government does it, it is just peachy keen when done by amateurs.

4   I'm not so sure. It seems to me that if YouTube had been around when George Washington failed to prevent his American Indian allies from butchering unarmed French prisoners (and thereby started the French and Indian War), his career could have been ruined at the start, paving the way for some circumspect scoundrel like Aaron Burr or Benedict Arnold to sabotage the republic before it even got off the ground.

5   If camera phones had been widely available in the 1930s, shots of FDR's wheelchair would have been posted all over the Internet, and Roosevelt might very well have lost the 1936 election to one of the gutless clowns the Republicans regularly ran against him.

6   Friedman's argument that "the whole world is watching"—thereby compelling mankind to be on its best behavior—ignores reality. The Taliban is simply not concerned that some blogger, hammering away at his laptop in his mommy's basement, doesn't approve of its activities. Hamas is not worried about having its latest depredations captured on cell phone cameras.

7   Hugo Chavez doesn't care how many videos poking fun at him are posted on YouTube—he's still going to silence the media, suppress the opposition and wreck Venezuela's economy. By the looks of it, Chavez feels the same way about blogs: Sticks and stones may break his bones, but words will never hurt him.

8   Friedman suggests that the "digital footprint" young people leave on My-Space and Facebook means—and he doesn't seem to think this is necessarily bad—that it will be extremely difficult for them to recover from the mistakes of their youth. Deceitful resumes, compromising photos, ill-advised confessions of sexual predilections could all come back to haunt them. But this assumes that some future version of American society actually will hold people accountable for their bozolike past behavior.

9   Get real. When the 35-year-old twit who once posted a video of himself mooning Dick Cheney applies for a job with the International Monetary Fund, the 36-year-old interviewing him for the position will be the guy who once blogged about imprisoning George Bush on the planet Alderaan and getting the Death Star to destroy the State Department. That's not a digital footprint. It's a digital handshake.

10   The one seemingly valid point that Friedman makes is that transparency will force corporations to be on their best behavior. But even this is a flawed assumption. Camera phones and YouTube videos are useful when depicting pollution or botched surgical procedures. But transparency doesn't work well in the bond market or the private equity field because finance is an abstraction and cell phone cameras cannot capture the invisible. You cannot post a picture of a hyped stock. You cannot post a video of a rigged initial public offering. You cannot depict felonious stock market activity on MySpace unless some white-collar crook agrees to be videotaped.

11   The weapons of transparency might be good at embarrassing people, but this approach only works with people who worry about being embarrassed. The Mafia doesn't. Osama bin Laden doesn't. The guy who's going to key your car tonight just because you stole his parking space doesn't. And the woman who conceivably might confront you with your quasi-pornogaphic, falsehood-swollen online profile 10 years from now isn't going to because she's the gal who once posted a video of herself puking her guts all over her wedding cake.

12   In a society in which everyone has decided to immortalize their stupidity, being an idiot isn't going to hurt anyone's career. The new "transparency" is just like the old television: The whole world might be watching, but nobody seems to be paying much attention.

‹‹ The Critical Reader ››

[CENTRAL IDEA]

1. What is the author's central idea?

2. What is the author's purpose?

[EVIDENCE]

3. Does the author agree or disagree with Friedman that it will be difficult for people to recover from a "digital footprint" made in their youth?

4. What organizational pattern does the author use in paragraphs 4 and 5?

5. The author says that Friedman makes one seemingly valid point about the "new transparency." What is that point?

[IMPLICATIONS]

6. In paragraph 11 the author provides several examples of the type of people who would not be embarrassed by seeing images of themselves in compromising situations that were posted on the Internet. Give two examples of people that you think would be embarrassed.

[WORD CHOICE]

7. The author's use of words such as *bozolike* (paragraph 8), *twit* (paragraph 9), and *stupidity* and *idiot* (paragraph 12) serves what purpose?

‹‹ The Critical Thinker ››

To examine Joe Queenan's essay in more depth, follow these suggestions for reflection, discussion, and writing.

1. Would you be embarrassed if someone photographed or videotaped you without your knowledge and then posted the images on the Internet? Explain why, or why not.

2. One of the issues Queenan touches on in this essay is privacy. How much privacy do Americans have today? Is privacy a concern for you? Do you think people have less privacy today than they did in the past?

3. Read again the first sentence of paragraph 6. Is it unrealistic to think that people will behave better if they think someone is watching? What about public behavior and the whole idea of good manners? Do you think people behave better or worse than they did when you were young? What examples can you offer?

4. Write a paragraph or short essay in which you answer either question 1 or 2 from First Thoughts.

Understand the Elements of Argument

Know what the four elements of argument are, and be able to use them effectively.

A good argument consists of four elements. An *issue* or concern such as the need to find alternative energy sources forms the basis of the argument. The *claim* is the writer's stated position on the issue. The writer then supports the claim and defends his or her position with *evidence* consisting of facts and other details. A persuasive argument will also address and answer *opposing claims*. To construct an effective argument, follow these four steps:

1. Choose an issue.
2. State your claim.
3. Support your claim.
4. Acknowledge opposing claims.

Choose an Issue

An *issue* is *a matter of public concern.* Gun control, abortion, affordable health care, and affirmative action are issues. An issue can be a problem that needs a solution or a question that requires an answer. Issues are often controversial; where issues are involved, people take sides. Those who favor nationalizing health care and those who do not are engaged in an ongoing argument about this issue. Pro-choice and pro-life groups debate with considerable heat the issue of abortion. Issues such as these are never resolved easily because people hold tenaciously to their opinions. If resolution does come, both sides must be willing to compromise. Some issues are of greater public concern than others, and people differ on what they think are the most important issues facing us today.

[**Exercise 14.1**] Following is a list of issues for you and a partner to consider. Each of you should first think about the issues and then arrange them in their order of importance to you. Read each other's lists, and then talk about the issues. Choose one issue that you think public officials should expend the most energy trying to resolve. Share your results with the rest of the class.

- Criminals' rights versus victims' rights
- Discrimination in the workplace against minorities, women, the aged, and the physically impaired
- Illegal drug trafficking and drug use
- Displays of racial intolerance, such as swastikas, burning crosses, and hate speech

- Athletic programs and problems
- Public mistrust of government
- Affordable health care for all
- The role of the United Nations

To define an issue suitable for writing an argumentative essay, first decide what is important to you. What are some of your social or private concerns? What matters of public concern do you talk or argue about with your friends and family? Issues can be the problems that affect a large segment of the public, such as those listed in Exercise 14.1, or they may affect a smaller, more narrowly defined public.

If you do not want to write about an issue that has a broad appeal, perhaps you can think of an issue that has a narrower, more personal appeal. For example, what matters of concern have caused arguments and differences of opinion on your campus, in your workplace, or in your family? Divorce is a personal issue many people face, and so is the problem of having to put a family member in a nursing home. One student defined the issue of inadequate police protection of residents in his neighborhood. Almost any subject might become the source of an issue from which you could construct a persuasive argument.

[Exercise 14.2] Think about any discussions you have had during the past week; what were they about? What matters of public concern are being debated in the news, and which of these issues are important to you? What have you read lately that has caused you to agree or disagree with the author? After thinking about and answering these questions, define three or more issues that are important to you.

State Your Claim

A *claim* is either an *assertion,* or statement, of what you believe to be true, or a *demand* that something be done. "He injured me with his car" is an assertion. "He ought to pay my medical bills" is a demand. Both of these claims require proof if the injured person expects to convince a court that he or she was injured and should get paid. A *claim* is different from an *issue,* in that an issue is a matter of public concern or controversy, such as "gun control," but a claim is your position on the issue, the assertion or demand you make, such as "Instead of passing new gun control legislation, we should do a better job of enforcing our existing laws." Many statements of claims will either include words such as *ought to, should, need,* and *must* or imply the idea that something should or ought to be done. Suppose you want to write about the issue

Some issues inspire protest both from those who support them and those who oppose them.

of cheating on your campus. What claim can you make about this problem? Following is a list of possible claims about the issue of cheating:

The student government should establish an honor court to deal with cheating. (demand)

We should re-examine our college's policy on cheating. (demand)

The reasons why college students cheat are more alarming than the cheating itself. (assertion)

Finding a solution to cheating is everyone's responsibility. (assertion)

In the first paragraph of Rachel I. Barnes's essay below, the issue is whether to keep or abolish the electoral college. *Note:* The claim is underlined.

SO YOU WANT TO THROW OUT THE ELECTORAL COLLEGE?

Our presidential election system dates back to the founding fathers who established the Electoral College. Since that time scholars and others have wondered how willingly Americans would accept a president who lost the popular vote but won the electoral vote. On two notable occasions, we were put to the test: In 1888, Benjamin Harrison, a Republican, ran against Grover Cleveland, the Democratic incumbent. Although Harrison lost the popular vote, he beat Cleveland in the electoral vote to become president of a nation that largely accepted his win without complaint. Similarly, in the election of 2000, Republican George W. Bush lost the popular vote by a slim margin to Democrat Al Gore. However, Bush beat Gore in the electoral vote, a win that did not set well with many voters for two reasons. First, it seemed unfair that one state, Florida, could throw the election to a candidate who lost the popular vote. Second, Democrats questioned the legitimacy of the vote, calling for a recount that prolonged the election and led to legal wrangling on both sides. In the aftermath, Democrats and Republicans agreed on one point: that election reforms were needed. Proposals have included everything from requests for uniform election laws to abolition of the Electoral College. My own view is that we should think long and hard before scrapping a system that has failed to elect the majority candidate only once in recent memory.

The claim is stated as a demand.

[Exercise 14.3] Review Joe Queenan's chapter-opening essay, and then come up with your own definition of the issue and statement of the claim. Decide whether the claim is an assertion or a demand. Share your answers with the rest of the class.

To make a claim about an issue, ask yourself, what can or should be done about this? What can I or anyone do? Should state or local government, police, individual citizens, or special groups take action? A statement that answers one or more of these questions is your claim.

[Exercise 14.4] Select three issues either from the list in Exercise 14.1 or from your list in Exercise 14.2 and make a claim about them. State your claim in a complete sentence.

Support Your Claim

To convince readers, your argument needs to be well thought out and logical. Your support should include each of the following:

1. Hard evidence (rational appeals)
2. Soft evidence (emotional appeals)

Hard evidence includes facts, examples, and authoritative opinion, and it makes a *rational appeal* to readers to use their reasoning powers. A nonsmoking ad on television that uses facts such as the percentage of smokers who die from heart and lung diseases is using hard evidence to get smokers to think about their chances of survival if they do not give up their habit. Suppose you want to argue that the salaries and benefits of nursing home health care workers are too low. You could support your claim with hard evidence such as the high turnover in personnel due to job dissatisfaction, the shortage of health care workers willing to work in nursing homes, and the number of employees who barely meet minimum qualifications for employment.

Soft evidence includes moral considerations, common-sense observations, personal opinions, and social values. It makes an *emotional appeal* to readers to listen to their hearts and consciences. Soft evidence can often be more powerful and persuasive than hard evidence. A nonsmoking ad on television that uses social values and common sense might show attractive young people making such statements as "Even a smart guy looks dumb with a cigarette hanging out of his mouth" or "I'm not interested in kissing a woman who has smoker's breath." An antidrug ad that uses a moral consideration to make an emotional appeal might show a teenage boy hanging out with some children in a schoolyard; they are laughing and seem to be having a good time. A voice-over says, "This young man is making a living by hooking his friends on crack cocaine. He gives them the first few hits for free, then raises the price when they're hooked. He says, 'This stuff won't hurt you; trust me.' Of course he'd never use crack himself; he's too smart." The moral consideration in this ad is trust. A friend is trustworthy; he or she will not lie to you. The ad's claim is that someone who tries to sell you drugs is not your friend.

Emotional appeals are often characterized by emotionally charged language, words and phrases that are carefully selected for their positive or negative connotations and for their power to evoke readers' feelings. Phrases such as "open-door policy," "equal access," and "equal opportunity" evoke our feelings against discrimination. Words such as *bigot, privileged class, elitist,* and *good ol' boy* appeal to our prejudices. If you write an essay in which you make a claim in favor of a trade agreement between the United States and another country, you might include emotionally charged phrases such as "free trade" and "free market economy." But if your claim is against a trade agreement, you might choose phrases such as "fewer American jobs" or "cheap labor." The words you select should reinforce your claim.

Following are paragraphs 5–8 from Rachel I. Barnes's essay "So You Want to Throw Out the Electoral College?" These paragraphs explain why the author is against abolishing the Electoral College. The excerpt is annotated to show how the argument develops: Key ideas are underlined to make the author's claims and reasons stand out.

✔ CONCEPT CHECK
The tone of your argument can be persuasive. Your choice of words can have a powerful effect on readers. For more information on tone, see Chapter 6.

Claim

Reasons that support the claim

5 Despite critic's claims, the Electoral College is fundamentally more democratic than a one-person-one-vote system. For example, if the president were elected by popular vote, candidates would restrict their campaigning to the most densely populated states, ignoring the small states. Because of the Electoral College, candidates are forced to campaign throughout the country. This, in turn, insures that the smaller states' interests are protected and that everyone—not just the voters in large urban areas—has a say in who gets elected. Minorities have made significant political gains as a result of forming huge voting blocs, particularly in northern states. In a one-person-one-vote system, these blocs would lose some of their power.

Claim

6   Far from discouraging people from voting, the 2000 election proves that every vote does count. If registered Republicans who did not vote in this election had voted for Bush, he would have won the popular vote and the election

Reasons that support the claim

without recounts and controversy. If more registered Democrats in Florida or in some of the other states that Bush carried had voted for Gore, then he would have been the winner. In either case, the number of people who vote in an election can be the deciding factor.

Claim

Reasons that support the claim

7   Abolishing the Electoral College would not be easy. It would take a constitutional amendment—something that has been tried and failed. Senator John F. Kennedy, who later became president, argued against a direct popular election proposal in the fifties. During both the Nixon and Carter administrations, Congress rejected proposals for a direct popular election. Because small states benefit from the Electoral College, their senators are unlikely to vote for its abolition.

Claim

8   Probably the best reasons to keep the Electoral College lie in the lessons learned from the Florida debacle. Remember that only once in recent years has a candidate who lost the popular vote won the electoral vote. Also, the 2000 election was our closest ever: Statisticians called it a tie, giving each candidate

Reasons that support the claim

49 percent of the popular vote. Many voters claimed a lack of excitement for either Bush or Gore and this may account for the fact that neither candidate emerged as a clear favorite nationwide. Finally, do not underestimate the fact that Bush carried the majority of the small states, which comprise a huge geographical area of the country. In this election, the Electoral College worked in their favor. In the previous two elections, other parts of the country stood to gain more from a Clinton win. Thus you could say that the Electoral College is a leveling factor, enabling all of the people to be represented some of the time. This is its greatest benefit and one that should guarantee its survival.

[Exercise 14.5] Either on your own or in a small group discussion, find examples of hard and soft evidence in Joe Queenan's essay on pages 331–332.

Acknowledge Opposing Claims

If all you do is make a claim and support it, your argument will be one-sided and therefore unconvincing. A persuasive argument will acknowledge differing opinions and answer opposing claims. For example, abortion is an issue that has been analyzed to near-exhaustion in the press and on television with no resolution in sight. Most people have chosen a side and consider themselves either pro-choice or pro-life. Whatever side you are on, your defense of your position will be weak unless you acknowledge what people on the other side think and the arguments they use to support their position.

Rachel I. Barnes answers opposing claims in paragraphs 2, 3, and 4 of her essay "So You Want to Throw Out the Electoral College?". The opposing claims are underlined and Barnes's answers are bracketed. Both claims and answers are annotated in the margin.

Claim

2   Critics of the system call it outdated. They see the Electoral College as an indirect voting system rather than the direct "one person, one vote" principle of majority rule on which our system of government is based. For example, when voters cast their ballots, they are not voting for the candidate of their choice; instead, they are voting for a slate of electors pledged to that candidate. [Although voters indirectly elect the president through their electors, each voter's vote "counts" in the sense that it helps determine for whom the electors vote.] There are 538 electors in all: Each state gets one elector for each of its senators and representatives, and Washington D.C. gets three electors. To win in the Electoral College, a candidate must get a majority of the votes. What makes it possible for a candidate to lose the popular vote and win the electoral vote is the winner-take-all rule followed by many states. According to this rule, a candidate who wins a state's popular vote gets all its electoral votes. [So, again, each person's vote in a particular state contributes toward a candidate's loss or victory in that state.] Although it may not be unconstitutional for an elector to break his or her pledge to vote for a candidate, that almost never happens. What happened in the 2000 election is that Bush lost the popular vote nationwide, but he carried more states than Gore did. As a result, the total number of electoral votes in the states Bush carried, including Florida, proved greater than the total number of electoral votes in the states Gore carried.

Answer

Answer

Claim

3   Critics also point out that only 50 percent of registered voters voted in the 2000 election. Many voters believe that their vote does not count, and the 2000 election proved them

Answer

right, according to the critics. [However, pollsters have always complained about low voter turnout even in elections where a candidate won the popular vote and the electoral vote by huge margins. So it would seem that whether we retain or abolish the Electoral College, we might still have low voter turnout.]

Claim

4   Critics say that Americans want the Electoral College abolished, according to polls such as the Hart/Teeter poll of November 2000, which showed 57 percent of voters favoring election of the president by a popular vote. [However, poll

Answer

results are merely a barometer of the people's feelings at a given time and should not be the basis on which important issues having far-reaching consequences are decided.]

[Exercise 14.6] Review Joe Queenan's essay, and decide whether he answers opposing claims. If you think he does, list the claims and answers on a sheet of notebook paper, or annotate them in the margin. Share your results with the rest of the class.

[Exercise 14.7]

No matter what issue you choose to write about—whether it is a social, environmental, political, cultural, or other issue that matters to you—your argument will be strengthened by evidence that includes facts and figures and expert opinion. Online newspapers, magazines, and topical websites provide a wealth of information.

Choose an issue or topic that interests you, or select an issue either from the list in Exercise 14.1 or from Topics for Writing on page 348. To gather information about your topic, go to a topical site or a news site such as *www.nytimes.com*. Your instructor or librarian can help you find sites that address your topic. Look for articles or essays on opposing points of view. Then list what you think is the most important evidence on both sides. Share your issue and evidence in a class discussion, or use it as your instructor directs.

Develop Your Argument Logically

Goal 2
Avoid making the common errors in reasoning that can weaken an argument.

A logical argument is based on sound reasoning. Your reasoning will be sound if you have enough evidence to support your claim, if you answer opposing claims, and if you avoid the common fallacies that make an argument invalid. A *fallacy* is an error in reasoning. Fallacies fall into two categories: those that ignore issues and those that oversimplify issues.

Fallacies that ignore an issue distract your attention from the argument. For example, in recent elections, candidates have been criticized for attacking each other's character instead of debating the issues that concern voters.

☑ CONCEPT CHECK
See also Chapter 13
for an additional
explanation of
oversimplification,
post hoc, and circular
reasoning.

Writers may resort to emotional appeals when the facts alone are not convincing or when they think that by arousing your fears, they can distract you from any rational attacks on their claims. Fallacies that oversimplify issues may present only one side of an argument, ignoring its complexity. Or they may reduce an argument to a choice between two opposing sides when many other options may be valid. Both types of fallacies—those that ignore issues and those that oversimplify issues—are often the result of poor thinking habits, such as jumping to conclusions before considering the evidence or rejecting evidence that does not support your opinion.

During your revision process, examine your evidence carefully for any fallacies that may weaken your argument. Then add whatever details are necessary to adequately support your claim. Figure 14.1 below and Figure 14.2 on page 343 list common fallacies with definitions, examples, and explanations of the thinking errors behind each fallacy.

Figure 14.1   Common Fallacies That Ignore Issues

FALLACY	DEFINITION	EXAMPLE	REASONING ERROR
Argument to the Person*	An attack on the person instead of the argument	Calling someone a "racist" when race has nothing to do with the issue	Emotional words detract from the argument.
Argument to the People**	An appeal to people's emotions instead of to reason	Predicting dire consequences of an action without offering facts to support your claim	Predictions do not mean anything without facts to back them up.
Begging the Question	Stating an opinion as if it were a fact	A city council member saying "Orlando is a beautiful city, as anyone can see."	Beauty is a matter of opinion.
Circular Reasoning	Restating a claim as part of the evidence	Saying that the roads are crowded because there are too many cars on the roads	*Why* are the roads crowded? *Why* are there too many cars? The conditions are not explained.
Non Sequitur	A conclusion that does not follow from the facts given	Concluding that someone who is a good teacher would also be a good department chair	Being a good teacher does not necessarily make one a good leader.
Red Herring	Changing the subject; distracting readers from the issue	Answering "I'm for family values" to the question "What is your stand on gun control?"	Family values and gun control are two different issues.

*Argument to the person is also called *argumentum ad hominem*.

**Argument to the people is also called *argumentum ad populem*.

[**Exercise 14.8**]

Apply what you have learned about fallacies that ignore or oversimplify issues by doing this exercise with group members. First, review the group roles and responsibilities listed on the inside back cover. Next, complete the activity that follows and share your results with the rest of the class. Then evaluate your group's performance as your instructor recommends, or go to *The Confident Writer* website and download the group evaluation form.

Each of the following items is a fallacy. Read and discuss each fallacy, decide which fallacy it is, and explain the error in reasoning that led to the fallacy. Use Figures 14.1 and 14.2 as a resource. The first item is done as an example.

1. Everybody knows you can't get drunk on only one drink.
   The fallacy is begging the question. You can get drunk on one drink if the alcohol content is high enough. To say that "everybody knows" does not make a statement a fact.

2. You don't want to buy that dress; only a redneck would wear something like that.

3. The clerk was rude to me in that store, so I'll never go back.

4. "America: Love it or leave it."

Figure 14.2 Common Fallacies That Oversimplify Issues

FALLACY	DEFINITION	EXAMPLE	REASONING ERROR
Bandwagon	An argument based on the idea that "everybody does it" or wants it	A teenager saying "Why can't I stay out past 10:00 P.M.? All my friends do."	The teenager's parents make the rules, not friends or their parents.
Either-or	Reducing an issue to only two sides	Reducing the abortion issue to pro-choice or pro-life	There are other possible positions to take on this issue.
Faulty Analogy	An inappropriate or inaccurate comparison	A parent saying, "When I was your age I walked five miles to school in the snow, so why do you need a car?"	The conditions that existed when the parent was young are not the same as today's conditions.
Post Hoc (Faulty Cause and Effect)	Believing that because one event follows another, the first event must be the cause of the other	Someone saying, "I left my window open last night, so now I have a cold."	Leaving the window open does not cause a cold; germs do.
Hasty Generalization	A conclusion drawn from insufficient evidence at hand	Concluding that blind dates are a waste of time based on one bad experience	One bad experience on a blind date does not prove that all blind dates are bad.

5. The outsourcing of American jobs will only result in weakening our economy.

6. Since we are both the same size and that shirt looks nice on you, I know it will look the same on me.

7. Ray is on academic probation, but his hours at work have changed, so he'll do better in school now.

8. Everyone else is going to that new movie, so I will too.

9. Jay's girlfriend says, "Where were you last night?" Jay answers, "I sure am glad to see you."

10. Parents should prevent their children from watching violent TV programs because such programs are forceful and extreme.

11. I knew that question would be on the test because I didn't study for it.

Exercise 14.9 The first passage below is from "The World Is Watching and No One Cares" on pages 331–332. The second passage is from "So You Want to Throw Out the Electoral College?" on pages 326–341. The third passage is from "The Perfect Family" on pages 311–313. Read each passage. Decide whether you agree or disagree with the claim stated, and be able to explain why. Next, determine whether the passage contains a fallacy. Share your answers in a class discussion.

1. "In a society in which everyone has decided to immortalize their stupidity, being an idiot isn't going to hurt anyone's career." (paragraph 12)

2. "Because small states benefit from the Electoral College, their senators are unlikely to vote for its abolition." (paragraph 7)

3. "There are always those who are ready to deal out judgment with the ready fist of the righteous." (paragraph 9)

Exercise 14.10 Try your hand at spotting fallacies. Watch several commercials on television, and take notes on what you hear. Write down any statements that contain fallacies. Identify the fallacies by name and explain what makes them false. Be prepared to share your results in a class discussion.

Student Voices: An Argumentative Essay

What would you do if you were standing in a line and the young man in front of you punched his girlfriend? Read the following essay to find out what the author did when confronted with this situation. Tara L. Tedrow attends Wake Forest University in North Carolina. Her essay appeared in an Orlando newspaper. For critical reading and thinking questions related to this essay, go to Chapter 14 Your Reflections on *The Confident Writer* website.

Everyone's Business
Tara L. Tedrow

1   Orlando's theme parks have year-round rides and attractions to scare visitors. [Sometimes the scariest thing can be what happens to the person next to you in a line and what your reaction is.]

Introductory statement builds interest.

2   My friends and I decided to venture about thirty miles away from our university and head to a locally famous haunted house. Driving down the dark mountain roads set the mood, and the old house at the end of a dirt-path entrance was even more frightening. We were all set to get the bejesus scared out of us when, while we were standing in line, a real-life horror happened.

Paragraphs 2–6 relate an anecdote that serves as evidence to support the claim.

3   The young couple in jeans and baseball caps in front of us started to argue. It didn't faze us, for almost everyone gets into an argument at some point. Then the guy punched his girlfriend in the face. Her knees went limp, and she fell. Her nose was bleeding and she was crying. He picked her up and said, "That's for botherin' me."

4   Appalled, I took a step forward and told him to leave her alone. To my surprise, I was told to mind my own business—not by the guy who turned his fist toward me, but by the girl.

5   [No one in the line said anything to the bully boyfriend, but a couple of guys cat-called me to "butt out" and said, "It's not your problem."] Everyone else around me just turned away, not wanting to get involved. The guy chuckled, telling me to kiss off while his girlfriend wiped her bloody nose.

opposing claim

6   I went to one of the guards who worked there to complain about what the guy had done and was told, ["Honey, that sort of thing is none of our business and not yours either."] There was not a police officer in sight to ask for help.

opposing claim

7   To hear someone tell me that a girl's being victimized was none of my business outraged me, as did the apathy and the silent acceptance and cowardice of the crowd over what had happened. [Violence, both domestic and public, needs to be curbed. Action needs to be taken; people need to stand up and

The author's claims and anecdote answer the opposing claims.

become advocates for those who are victims. Neighbors, friends, family, and random onlookers cannot stay silent in the face of such deplorable actions.]

The author issues a warning in her conclusion.

8 While I can only pray that the girl has enough sense to leave such a monster, I do hope that, after all of the decades of struggle by the women's movement, we don't passively allow a generation of young women to emerge thinking that abuse is acceptable.

Think Through Your Topic

Goal 3 Determine whether your topic is an appropriate issue for argumentation.

An issue is appropriate for argumentation if it is one that you care about and if you have a definite opinion to express about it. If you do not clearly define the issue for readers and make your position apparent, then the argument will not be convincing. You also need to have a firm grasp on your audience's assumptions about the issue and what the opposing viewpoints are. These rules apply whether the issue is one of general concern, such as domestic violence, or one of local concern, such as parking on your campus. To think through your topic, answer ten questions to generate ideas.

Questions to Consider for Argumentation

1. In one word or a short phrase, what is the issue?
2. Is the issue something that is of major concern or importance to you?
3. Does the issue have general appeal, or is it of local concern?
4. What is your position on the issue?
5. Why do you hold this position? What are your reasons for doing so?
6. What are the opposing viewpoints?
7. What is the strongest argument in favor of your position?
8. Who will be the audience for your essay?
9. Is your audience more likely to agree or disagree with your position on the issue?
10. How should you introduce the issue so that readers will be interested?

Plan and Write Your Essay

Goal 4
Use appropriate strategies for planning your argument and writing your essay.

Remember that argumentation is not a pattern in itself; it is an attitude you take toward your topic. The essential parts of your argument are your issue, your claim, your evidence to support your claim, and your answers to the opposing viewpoints. How you structure the argument around these four elements is up to you. For example, in the chapter-opening essay, Joe Queenan combines the patterns of *comparison and contrast* and *cause and effect*. In "Everyone's Business," Tara L. Tedrow uses *narration* to build her argument. To build your argument, let the four essentials be your guide.

- **The issue.** What is your issue? Is it a matter of national concern or more local concern, such as a workplace issue or campus issue? Your issue is also the topic of your essay. Your thesis statement should clearly state what the issue is and what your claim is.

- **Your claim.** Your claim is your position on an issue, and your position is a reflection of your values. What is your position? Why is the issue important to you? Are you for it or against it? Your answers to these questions will help you determine your position. Also, what is your purpose in writing about the issue? Is your claim an assertion or a demand? Do you simply want readers to know that a problem exists, or do you want them to take action? Your purpose should also take into account your readers' assumptions and values.

- **Support for your claim.** What evidence will best support your claim? The best arguments strike a balance between hard evidence (rational appeals) and soft evidence (emotional appeals). An argument that is strictly an emotional appeal will insult the intelligence of readers who might otherwise be convinced if you present them with some facts, statistics, and authoritative opinions. On the other hand, a strictly rational argument may ignore readers' attitudes and values. Reinforce your position with language carefully chosen for its effect. Select words whose connotations and tone support your argument.

- **Answer opposing claims.** Who is the audience for your essay? What positions are they likely to hold on your issue? How will you answer the audience's claims if they differ from yours? Those who agree with you will automatically be on your side. Those who oppose you will have to be convinced. Decide in advance what the opposing viewpoints will be and determine how you will answer them.

Like any other essay, your argumentation essay will have an introduction, a body, and a conclusion. The transitions you use to achieve coherence within and between paragraphs will depend on your organizational pattern. Figure 14.3 on the following page is an overview of what to include in the three parts of your essay.

Figure 14.3   Arguing Persuasively: An Overview

PARTS	WHAT TO INCLUDE	QUESTIONS TO ASK
Introduction	1. topic 2. purpose 3. context 4. thesis	1. What is my issue? 2. What is my claim, and is it an assertion or a demand? 3. Is my issue of general or local concern, and how will I introduce the issue to my audience? 4. What is my central idea—the claim that I want to make about the issue?
Body paragraphs	1. topic sentence 2. details 3. organization and logic 4. transitions	1. Does each body paragraph have a topic sentence that relates to my thesis? 2. Do my major and minor details consist of hard and soft evidence to support my claim and to answer the opposing claims? 3. What organizational pattern will I use, and how can I avoid the common fallacies in reasoning? 4. What transitions will I choose to make sure that my argument flows smoothly?
Conclusion	1. concluding device 2. significance for readers	1. Should I summarize my claim and evidence, or should I use another concluding device? 2. Do I want my readers to take action or simply to agree with my position, and in either case, what will they gain by doing so?

14

‹‹ Topics for Writing ››

1. **React to the Reading.** Joe Queenan's issue is "the new transparency," which is made possible by the use of camera phones and Internet sites such as YouTube. Tara L. Tedrow's issue is domestic violence as a problem that should concern everyone. If one of these issues interests you, write an essay in which you either support or challenge the author's viewpoint.

2. **Use Your Experience.** Write about an issue that is important to you, preferably one with which you have had some direct experience. Choose a topic from the following list, or make up your own topic.

   - Stem-cell research, genetic engineering, or cloning
   - Global warming or another environmental issue
   - The benefits or drawbacks of living together before marriage
   - Gay marriage (in favor of or opposed to)

- Whether candidates' private lives influence their performance in office
- Nationalized health care (for or against)
- The use of public protest
- Racial profiling

3. **Make a Real-World Connection.** Choose as your issue a campus problem such as lack of parking space or overcrowded housing, or take a position on a work-related issue.

4. **Go to the Web.** Choose a topic from *The Confident Writer* website.

≪ Checklist for Revision ≫

Did you miss anything? Check off the following items as you revise and edit your essay.

- ❑ Is your topic an issue that is appropriate for argument?
- ❑ Do you have a clearly stated thesis?
- ❑ Is your claim an assertion or a demand?
- ❑ Are your audience and purpose obvious?
- ❑ Have you introduced your thesis in an interesting way?
- ❑ Is your claim supported by enough evidence to be convincing?
- ❑ Have you answered opposing claims?
- ❑ Are your claim and evidence logically organized and fallacy free?
- ❑ Does the tone of your essay suit your purpose?
- ❑ Do you have an effective conclusion that emphasizes the significance of your argument for readers?
- ❑ Have you proofread your essay and corrected all errors?

≪ Your Discovery Journal ≫

Reflect on your progress as a writer. What have you learned this term that will help you write effectively in the future? Which of your skills still need improvement? To answer these questions, complete the following statements.

As an additional option, you can do this activity online by going to *The Confident Writer* website.

My greatest strength as a writer is _____.

One skill I need to improve is _____.

≪ **Website Resources** ≫

This chapter's resources include

- Chapter 14 Exercises
- Chapter 14 Quiz
- Downloadable Charts: *Group Evaluation Form*
- Chapter 14 Your Reflections
- More Topics for Writing
- Chapter 14 Summary

To access these learning and study tools, go to *The Confident Writer* website.

More Choices:
A Collection of Readings

[First Thoughts]

To build background for reading, explore your thoughts about prejudice or discrimination. Then answer the following questions, either on your own or in a group discussion:

1. What evidence of discrimination do you see today? Who is discriminated against, and in what way?

2. What action can you take in support of those who are discriminated against?

3. Read the title, the headnote, and the first two paragraphs of the reading selection. Based on this preview, what do you think will follow?

Selection 1

My Name Is Margaret

Maya Angelou

Maya Angelou is an author, performer, composer, and singer. In this selection from her autobiographical novel, *I Know Why the Caged Bird Sings*, Angelou narrates an experience that reflects on the importance of her name to her identity. Angelou was born Marguerite Johnson in 1928.

1   Recently a white woman from Texas, who would quickly describe herself as a liberal, asked me about my hometown. When I told her that in Stamps my grandmother had owned the only Negro general merchandise store since the turn of the century, she exclaimed, "Why, you were a debutante." Ridiculous and even ludicrous. But Negro girls in small Southern towns, whether poverty-stricken or just munching along on a few of life's necessities, were given as extensive and irrelevant preparations for adulthood as rich white girls shown in magazines. Admittedly the training was not the same. While white girls learned to waltz and sit gracefully with a tea cup balanced on their knees, we were lagging behind, learning the mid-Victorian values with very little money to indulge them. (Come and see Edna Lomax spending the money she made picking cotton on five balls of ecru tatting thread. Her fingers are bound to snag the work and she'll have to repeat the stitches time and time again. But she knows that when she buys the thread.)

2   We were required to embroider and I had trunkfuls of colorful dishtowels, pillowcases, runners and handkerchiefs to my credit. I mastered the art of crocheting and tatting, and there was a lifetime's supply of dainty doilies that would never be used in sacheted dresser drawers. It went without saying that all girls could iron and wash, but the finer touches around the home, like setting a table with real silver, baking roasts and cooking vegetables without meat, had to be learned elsewhere. Usually at the source of those habits. During my tenth year, a white woman's kitchen became my finishing school.

3   Mrs. Viola Cullinan was a plump woman who lived in a three-bedroom house somewhere behind the post office. She was singularly unattractive until she smiled, and then the lines around her eyes and mouth which made her look

perpetually dirty disappeared, and her face looked like the mask of an impish elf. She usually rested her smile until late afternoon when her women friends dropped in and Miss Glory, the cook, served them cold drinks on the closed-in porch.

4   The exactness of her house was inhuman. This glass went here and only here. That cup had its place and it was an act of impudent rebellion to place it anywhere else. At twelve o'clock the table was set. At 12:15 Mrs. Cullinan sat down to dinner (whether her husband had arrived or not). At 12:16 Miss Glory brought out the food.

5   It took me a week to learn the difference between a salad plate, a bread plate and a dessert plate.

6   Mrs. Cullinan kept up the tradition of her wealthy parents. She was from Virginia. Miss Glory, who was a descendant of slaves that had worked for the Cullinans, told me her history. She had married beneath her (according to Miss Glory). Her husband's family hadn't had their money very long and what they had "didn't 'mount to much."

7   As ugly as she was, I thought privately, she was lucky to get a husband above or beneath her station. But Miss Glory wouldn't let me say a thing against her mistress. She was very patient with me, however, over the housework. She explained the dishware, silverware and servants' bells.

8   The large round bowl in which soup was served wasn't a soup bowl, it was a tureen. There were goblets, sherbet glasses, ice cream glasses, wine glasses, green glass coffee cups with matching saucers, and water glasses. I had a glass to drink from, and it sat with Miss Glory's on a separate shelf from the others. Soup spoons, gravy boat, butter knives, salad forks and carving platter were additions to my vocabulary and in fact almost represented a new language. I was fascinated with the novelty, with the fluttering Mrs. Cullinan and her Alice-in-Wonderland house.

9   Her husband remains, in my memory, undefined. I lumped him with all the other white men that I had ever seen and tried not to see.

10   On our way home one evening, Miss Glory told me that Mrs. Cullinan couldn't have children. She said that she was too delicate-boned. It was hard to imagine bones at all under those layers of fat. Miss Glory went on to say that the doctor had taken out all her lady organs. I reasoned that a pig's organs included the lungs, heart and liver, so if Mrs. Cullinan was walking around without those essentials, it explained why she drank alcohol out of unmarked bottles. She was keeping herself embalmed.

11   When I spoke to Bailey about it, he agreed that I was right, but he also informed me that Mr. Cullinan had two daughters by a colored lady and that I knew them very well. He added that the girls were the spitting image of their father. I was unable to remember what he looked like, although I had just left him a few hours before, but I thought of the Coleman girls. They were very light-skinned and certainly didn't look very much like their mother (no one ever mentioned Mr. Coleman).

12   My pity for Mrs. Cullinan preceded me the next morning like the Cheshire cat's smile. Those girls who could have been her daughters, were beautiful. They didn't have to straighten their hair. Even when they were caught in the rain, their braids still hung down straight like tamed snakes. Their mouths were pouty little cupid's bows. Mrs. Cullinan didn't know what she missed. Or maybe she did. Poor Mrs. Cullinan.

13   For weeks after, I arrived early, left late and tried very hard to make up for her barrenness. If she had had her own children, she wouldn't have had to ask me to run a thousand errands from her back door to the back door of her friends. Poor old Mrs. Cullinan.

14   Then one evening Miss Glory told me to serve the ladies on the porch. After I set the tray down and turned toward the kitchen, one of the women asked, "What's your name, girl?" It was the speckled-faced one. Mrs. Cullinan said, "She doesn't talk much. Her name's Margaret."

15   "Is she dumb?"

16   "No. As I understand it, she can talk when she wants to but she's usually quiet as a little mouse. Aren't you, Margaret?"

17   I smiled at her. Poor thing. No organs and couldn't even pronounce my name correctly.

18   "She's a sweet little thing, though."

19   "Well, that may be, but the name's too long. I'd never bother myself. I'd call her Mary if I was you."

20   I fumed into the kitchen. That horrible woman would never have the chance to call me Mary because if I was starving I'd never work for her. I decided I wouldn't pee on her if her heart was on fire. Giggles drifted in off the porch and into Miss Glory's pots. I wondered what they could be laughing about.

21   Whitefolks were so strange. Could they be talking about me? Everybody knew that they stuck together better than the Negroes did. It was possible that Mrs. Cullinan had friends in St. Louis who heard about a girl from Stamps being in court and wrote to tell her. Maybe she knew about Mr. Freeman.

22   My lunch was in my mouth a second time and I went outside and relieved myself on the bed of four-o'clocks. Miss Glory thought I might be coming down with something and told me to go on home, that Momma would give me some herb tea, and she'd explain to her mistress.

23   I realized how foolish I was being before I reached the pond. Of course Mrs. Cullinan didn't know. Otherwise she wouldn't have given me the two nice dresses that Momma cut down, and she certainly wouldn't have called me a "sweet little thing." My stomach felt fine, and I didn't mention anything to Momma.

24   That evening I decided to write a poem on being white, fat, old and without children. It was going to be a tragic ballad. I would have to watch her carefully to capture the essence of her loneliness and pain.

25   The very next day, she called me by the wrong name. Miss Glory and I were washing up the lunch dishes when Mrs. Cullinan came to the doorway. "Mary?"

26   Miss Glory asked, "Who?"

27   Mrs. Cullinan, sagging a little, knew and I knew. "I want Mary to go down to Mrs. Randall's and take her some soup. She's not been feeling well for a few days."

28   Miss Glory's face was a wonder to me. "You mean Margaret, ma'am. Her name's Margaret."

29   "That's too long. She's Mary from now on. Heat that soup from last night and put it in the china tureen and, Mary, I want you to carry it carefully."

30   Every person I knew had a hellish horror of being "called out of his name." It was a dangerous practice to call a Negro anything that could be loosely construed as insulting because of the centuries of their having been called niggers, jigs, dinges, blackbirds, crows, boots and spooks.

31   Miss Glory had a fleeting second of feeling sorry for me. Then as she handed me the hot tureen she said, "Don't mind, don't pay that no mind. Sticks and stones may break your bones, but words . . . You know, I been working for her for twenty years."

32   She held the back door open for me. "Twenty years. I wasn't much older than you. My name used to be Hallelujah. That's what Ma named me, but my mistress give me 'Glory,' and it stuck. I likes it better too."

33   I was in the little path that ran behind the houses when Miss Glory shouted, "It's shorter too."

34   For a few seconds it was a tossup over whether I would laugh (imagine being named Hallelujah) or cry (imagine letting some white woman rename you for her convenience). My anger saved me from either outburst. I had to quit the job, but the problem was going to be how to do it. Momma wouldn't allow me to quit for just any reason.

35   "She's a peach. That woman is a real peach." Mrs. Randall's maid was talking as she took the soup from me, and I wondered what her name used to be and what she answered to now.

36   For a week I looked into Mrs. Cullinan's face as she called me Mary. She ignored my coming late and leaving early. Miss Glory was a little annoyed because I had begun to leave egg yolk on the dishes and wasn't putting much heart in polishing the silver. I hoped that she would complain to our boss, but she didn't.

37   Then Bailey solved my dilemma. He had me describe the contents of the cupboard and the particular plates she liked best. Her favorite piece was a casserole shaped like a fish and the green glass coffee cups. I kept his instructions in mind, so on the next day when Miss Glory was hanging out clothes and I had again been told to serve the old biddies on the porch, I dropped the empty serving tray. When I heard Mrs. Cullinan scream, "Mary!" I picked up the casserole and two of the green glass cups in readiness. As she rounded the kitchen door I let them fall on the tiled floor.

38   I could never absolutely describe to Bailey what happened next, because each time I got to the part where she fell on the floor and screwed up her ugly

39   face to cry, we burst out laughing. She actually wobbled around on the floor and picked up shards of the cups and cried, "Oh, Momma. Oh, dear Gawd. It's Momma's china from Virginia. Oh, Momma, I sorry."

39   Miss Glory came running in from the yard and the women from the porch crowded around. Miss Glory was almost as broken up as her mistress. "You mean to say she broke our Virginia dishes? What we gone do?"

40   Mrs. Cullinan cried louder, "That clumsy nigger. Clumsy little black nigger."

41   Old speckled-face leaned down and asked, "Who did it, Viola? Was it Mary? Who did it?"

42   Everything was happening so fast I can't remember whether her action preceded her words, but I know that Mrs. Cullinan said, "Her name's Margaret, goddamn it, her name's Margaret!" And she threw a wedge of the broken plate at me. It could have been the hysteria which put her aim off, but the flying crockery caught Miss Glory right over her ear and she started screaming.

43

44   I left the front door wide open so all the neighbors could hear.

Mrs. Cullinan was right about one thing. My name wasn't Mary.

Suggestions for Reflection, Discussion, and Writing

1. What is the author's attitude toward Mrs. Cullinan? Cite specific details that reveal her attitude. How do these details contribute to the tone of the essay as a whole?

2. One characteristic of narration is the focus on a significant event. What event is explained, and what is its impact on Margaret?

3. Do you know someone who, like the woman from Texas in Angelou's essay, describes himself or herself as a liberal but whose actions indicate differently? Do you know someone who doesn't think he or she is prejudiced, but who really is? Write an essay about a way in which people who think they are not prejudiced may discriminate against others.

[First Thoughts]

To build background for reading, explore your thoughts about America's future leaders. Then answer the following questions, either on your own or in a group discussion:

1. What are the qualities that make a good leader?

2. Do you see yourself as one of tomorrow's leaders? Why, or why not?

3. Read the title, the headnote, and the first two paragraphs of the reading selection. Based on this preview, what do you think will follow?

Selection 2

David Porter, a columnist for the *Orlando Sentinel*, writes on social and political issues. In this essay, he asks us to consider the fact that today's young people are tomorrow's leaders.

Open the Door Wide for Leaders of Tomorrow

David Porter

1   Somewhere in America today, a future president of the United States may be preparing for a physics exam, serving a hamburger in a fast-food restaurant or planning a Saturday-night date.

2   The person who will be sworn in as the president of the United States in 2037 is a teenager, or a young adult, who is walking among us right now.

3   How are we—mature adults, parents, voters and taxpayers—shaping the worldview of that future president?

4   What condition will this country be in by the time that president takes over the Oval Office?

5   I'm the product of a generation that saw one president gunned down on a public street and another president forced to resign in disgrace. Those events affected the way many people around the world looked at America. I still remember the air-raid drills when I was in grammar school. We were taught that the Russians might launch a thermonuclear war at any time. The civil-rights movement and the antiwar activism of the Vietnam era taught me that it was possible for Americans to confront our government and demand changes.

6   It's clear that those events helped to shape the leadership philosophies of President George W. Bush and former President Bill Clinton. They are like me: products of parents who lived through the Depression and World War II. Yet the relevance of those experiences are lost on my 14-year-old daughter and many of her peers.

7   She says her generation can do better. I believe her. Demographic forces that are evident today certainly will change the face of this nation's leadership elite. A woman in charge of the Oval Office? Count on it happening—perhaps more than once—during the next 30 years. The same goes for a non-white president. Haven't you noticed the browning of America's complexion? Issues that we spend so much time on, such as same-sex marriage, will seem silly to the leadership class of 2037.

8   Some people will say that such leadership changes will spell doom for this nation. Yet America will not be able to maintain its greatness if Americans are unable, or unwilling, to embrace this change.

9   The challenge for my generation is to prepare our children to lead. So we have got to do better.

10   It's crucial to put our nation in order. Our failure to figure out how to ensure that all Americans—regardless of income—can get the health care they need is an international embarrassment.

11   This nation's standard of living will collapse unless we embrace a sensible energy policy that stresses conservation, renewable energy and new energy technologies.

12   Building better international relations also is crucial. Spiritually and financially, the United States can't afford to remain on a war footing for the next 30 years. It is absolutely critical to resolve the hostilities in the Middle East and nurture emerging nations in Africa and Asia.

13   The most important step is to open the door wide for young people to bring them into business, politics and government. They require more than show and tell. We've got to be willing to listen and try their ideas. We can't afford to treat them as know-nothing kids.

14   They are our future.

15   They are America.

Suggestions for Reflection, Discussion, and Writing

1. Who is the author's audience, and how does he appeal to their interests?

2. The author says that his daughter thinks her generation can do a better job of running the country, and that he agrees with her. What are his stated reasons?

3. In paragraphs 9–12 the author explains the challenges for the leaders of 2037. Do you agree or disagree with the author? What issues do you think are the most important challenges for tomorrow's leaders? Write an essay in which you answer these questions.

[First Thoughts]

To build background for reading, explore your thoughts about today's youth culture. Then answer the questions, either on your own or in a group discussion.

1. What does the phrase *youth culture* mean to you?

2. How would you define *maturity* as opposed to *adolescence*?

3. Read the title, the headnote, and the first two paragraphs of the reading selection. Based on this preview, what do you think will follow?

Selection 3

The Perpetual Adolescent

Joseph Epstein's writing has appeared in publications such as the *New Yorker*, the *Atlantic Monthly*, *Commentary*, and others. For many years, he was the editor of the *American Scholar*. His books include *Envy*, *Snobbery: The American Version*, and *Friendship: An Exposé*.

Joseph Epstein

1   Whenever anyone under the age of 50 sees old newsreel film of Joe DiMaggio's 56-game hitting streak of 1941, he is almost certain to be brought up by the fact that nearly everyone in the male-dominated crowds—in New York, Boston, Chicago, Detroit, Cleveland—seems to be wearing a suit and a fedora or other serious adult hat. The people in those earlier baseball crowds, though watching a boyish game, nonetheless had a radically different conception of themselves than most Americans do now. A major depression was ending, a world war was on. Even though they were watching an entertainment that took most of them back to their boyhoods, they thought of themselves as adults, no longer kids, but grown-ups, adults, men.

2   How different from today, when a good part of the crowd at any ballgame, no matter what the age, is wearing jeans and team caps and T-shirts; and let us not neglect those (one hopes) benign maniacs who paint their faces in home-team colors or spell out, on their bare chests, the letters of the names of star players: S-O-S-A.

3   Part of the explanation for the suits at the ballpark in DiMaggio's day is that in the 1940s and even '50s there weren't a lot of sport, or leisure, or casual clothes around. Unless one lived at what H. L. Mencken called "the country-club stage of culture"—unless, that is, one golfed, played tennis, or sailed—one was likely to own only the clothes one worked in or better. Far from casual Fridays, in those years there weren't even casual Sundays. Wearing one's "Sunday best," a cliché of the time, meant wearing the good clothes one reserved for church.

4   Dressing down may first have set in on the West Coast, where a certain informality was thought to be a new way of life. In the 1960s, in universities casual dress became absolutely *de rigueur* among younger faculty, who, in their ardor to destroy any evidence of their being implicated in evil hierarchy, wished not merely to seem in no wise different from their students but, more important, to seem always young; and the quickest path to youthfulness was teaching in jeans, T-shirts, and the rest of it.

5   This informality has now been institutionalized. Few are the restaurants that could any longer hope to stay in business if they required men to wear a jacket and tie. Today one sees men wearing baseball caps—some worn backwards—while eating indoors in quite good restaurants. In an episode of *The Sopranos*, Tony Soprano, the mafia don, representing life of a different day, finds this so outrages his sense of decorum that, in a restaurant he frequents, he asks a man, in a quiet but entirely menacing way, to remove his goddamn hat.

6   Life in that different day was felt to observe the human equivalent of the Aristotelian unities: to have, like a good drama, a beginning, middle, and end.

Each part, it was understood, had its own advantages and detractions, but the middle—adulthood—was the lengthiest and most earnest part, where everything serious happened and much was at stake. To violate the boundaries of any of the three divisions of life was to go against what was natural and thereby to appear unseemly, to put one's world somehow out of joint, to be, let us face it, a touch, and perhaps more than a touch, grotesque.

7   Today, of course, all this has been shattered. The ideal almost everywhere is to seem young for as long as possible. The health clubs and endemic workout clothes, the enormous increase in cosmetic surgery (for women and men), the special youth-oriented television programming and moviemaking, all these are merely the more obvious signs of the triumph of youth culture. When I say youth culture, I do not mean merely that the young today are transcendent, the group most admired among the various age groups in American society, but that youth is no longer viewed as a transitory state, through which one passes on the way from childhood to adulthood, but an aspiration, a vaunted condition in which, if one can only arrange it, to settle in perpetuity.

8   This phenomenon is not something that happened just last night; it has been underway for decades. Nor is it something that can be changed even by an event as cataclysmic as that of September 11, which at first was thought to be so sobering as to tear away all shreds of American innocence. As a generalization, it allows for a wide variety of exceptions. There still are adults in America; if names are wanted, I would set out those of Alan Greenspan, Jeane Kirkpatrick, Robert Rubin, Warren Buffett, Sol Linowitz, and many more. But such men and women, actual grown-ups, now begin to appear a bit anomalous; they no longer seem representative of the larger culture.

9   The shift into youth culture began in earnest, I suspect, during the 10 or so years following 1951, the year of the publication of *Catcher in the Rye*. Salinger's novel exalts the purity of youth and locates the enemy—a clear case of Us versus Them—in those who committed the sin of having grown older, which includes Holden Caulfield's pain-in-the-neck parents, his brother (the sellout screenwriter), and just about everyone else who has passed beyond adolescence and had the rather poor taste to remain alive.

10   The case for the exaltation of the young is made in Wordsworth's "Intimation of Immortality," with its idea that human beings are born with great wisdom from which life in society weans them slowly but inexorably. Plato promulgated this same idea long before: For him we all had wisdom in the womb, but it was torn from us at the exact point that we came into the world. Rousseau gave it a French twist, arguing that human beings are splendid all-round specimens— noble savages, really—with life out in society turning us mean and loutish, which is another way of saying that the older we are, the worse we get. We are talking about romanticism here, friend, which never favors the mature, let alone the aged.

11   The triumph of youth culture has conquered perhaps nowhere more completely than in the United States. The John F. Kennedy administration, with its

emphasis on youthfulness, beginning with its young president—the first president routinely not to wear a serious hat—gave it its first public prominence. Soon after the assassination of Kennedy, the Free Speech Movement, which spearheaded the student revolution, positively enshrined the young. Like Yeats's Byzantium, the sixties utopia posited by the student radicals was "no country for old men" or women. One of the many tenets in its credo—soon to become a cliché, but no less significant for that—was that no one over 30 was to be trusted. (If you were part of that movement and 21 years old in 1965, you are 60 today. Good morning, Sunshine.)

12   Music was a key element in the advance of youth culture. The dividing moment here is the advent of Elvis. On one side were those who thought Elvis an amusing and largely freakish phenomenon—a bit of a joke—and on the other, those who took him dead seriously as a figure of youthful rebellion, the musical equivalent of James Dean in the movie *Rebel Without a Cause,* another early winning entry in the glorification-of-youth sweepstakes then forming. Rock 'n' roll presented a vinyl curtain, with those committed to retaining their youth on one side, those wanting to claim adulthood on the other. The Beatles, despite the very real charms of their non-druggie music, solidified things. So much of hard rock 'n' roll came down to nothing more than a way of saying bugger off to adult culture.

13   Reinforcement for these notions—they were not yet so coherent as to qualify as ideas—was to be found in the movies. Movies for some years now have been made not only increasingly for the young but by the young. I once worked on a movie script with a producer who one day announced to me that it was his birthday. When I wished him happy returns of the day, he replied that it wasn't so happy for him; he was turning 41, an uncomfortably old age in Hollywood for someone who hadn't many big success-scalps on his belt.

14   Robert Redford, though now in his mid-sixties, remains essentially a guy in jeans, a handsome graduate student with wrinkles. Paul Newman, now in his late seventies, seems uncomfortable in a suit. Hugh Grant, the English actor, may be said to be professionally boyish, and in a recent role, in the movie *About a Boy,* is described in the *New York Times* as a character who "surrounds himself with gadgets, videos, CDs, and other toys" and who "is doing everything in his power to avoid growing up." The actor Jim Carrey, who is 42, not long ago said of the movie *The Majestic,* in which he stars, "It's about manhood. It's about adulthood," as if italicizing the rarity of such movies. He then went on to speak about himself in standard self-absorbed adolescent fashion: "You've got that hole you're left with by whatever your parents couldn't give you." Poor baby.

15   Jim Carrey's roles in movies resemble nothing so much as comic-book characters come to life. And why, just now, does so much of contemporary entertainment come in the form of animation or comic-book cartooning? Such television shows as *The Simpsons* and *King of the Hill,* the occasional back page in the *New York Times Book Review* or the *New Yorker* and the comic-book novel, all seem to feel that the animated cartoon and comic-book formats are

very much of the moment. They are of course right, at least if you think of your audience as adolescent, or, more precisely, as being unwilling quite to detach themselves from their adolescence.

16   Recent history has seemed to be on the side of keeping people from growing up by supplying only a paucity of stern tests of the kind out of which adulthood is usually formed. We shall never have another presidential candidate tested by the Depression or by his experience in World War II. These were events that proved crucibles for the formation of adult character, not to say manliness. Henceforth all future presidential—and congressional—candidates will come with a shortage of what used to pass for significant experience. Crises for future politicians will doubtless be about having to rethink their lives when they didn't get into Brown or found themselves unequipped emotionally for Stanford Business School.

17   Corporate talent these days feels no weightier. Pictures of heads of corporations in polo shirts with designer logos in the business section of the *New York Times,* fresh from yet another ephemeral merger, or acquiring an enormous raise after their company has recorded another losing year, do not inspire confidence. "The trouble with Enron," said an employee of the company in the aftermath of that corporation's appalling debacle, "is that there weren't any grown-ups."

18   The increasing affluence the United States enjoyed after World War II, extending into the current day, also contributed heavily to forming the character I've come to think of as the perpetual American adolescent. Earlier, with less money around, people were forced to get serious, to grow up—and fast. How quickly the Depression generation was required to mature! How many stories one used to hear about older brothers going to work at 18 or earlier so that a younger brother might be allowed to go to college, or simply to help keep the family afloat! With lots of money around, certain kinds of pressure were removed. More and more people nowadays are working, as earlier generations were not, with a strong safety net of money under them. All options opened, they now swim in what Kierkegaard called "a sea of possibilities," and one of these possibilities in America is to refuse to grow up for a longer period than has been permitted any other people in history.

19   All this is reinforced by the play of market forces, which strongly encourage the mythical dream of perpetual youthfulness. The promise behind 95 percent of all advertising is that of recaptured youth, whose deeper promise is lots more sex yet to go. The ads for the $5,000 wristwatch, the $80,000 car, the khakis, the vodka, the pharmaceuticals to regrow hair and recapture ardor, all whisper display me, drive me, wear me, drink me, swallow me, and you stop the clock—youth, Baby, is yours.

20   The whole sweep of advertising, which is to say of market, culture since soon after World War II has been continuously to lower the criteria of youthfulness while extending the possibility for seeming youthful to older and older

people. To make the very young seem older—all those 10- and 12-year-old Britney Spears and Jennifer Lopez imitators, who already know more about brand-name logos than I do about English literature—is another part of the job. It's not a conspiracy, mind you, not six or eight international ad agencies meeting in secret to call the shots, but the dynamics of marketing itself, finding a way to make it more profitable all around by convincing the young that they can seem older and the old that they can seem a lot younger. Never before has it been more difficult to obey the injunction to act one's age.

21   Two of the great television sitcom successes of recent years, *Seinfeld* and *Friends,* though each is different in its comic tone, are united by the theme of the permanent adolescent loose in the big city. One takes the characters in *Seinfeld* to be in their middle to late thirties, those in *Friends* in their late twenties to early thirties. Charming though they may be, both sets of characters are oddly stunted. They aren't quite anywhere and don't seem to be headed anywhere, either. Time is suspended for them. Aimless and shameless, they are in the grip of the everyday *Sturm und Drang* of adolescent self-absorption. Outside their rather temporary-looking apartments, they scarcely exist. Personal relations provide the full drama of their lives. Growth and development aren't part of the deal. They are still, somehow, in spirit, locked in a high school of the mind, eating dry cereal, watching a vast quantity of television, hoping to make ecstatic sexual scores. Apart from the high sheen of the writing and the comic skill of the casts, I wonder if what really attracts people to these shows—*Friends* still, *Seinfeld* in its reruns—isn't the underlying identification with the characters because of the audience's own longing for a perpetual adolescence, cut loose, free of responsibility, without the real pressures that life, that messy business, always exerts.

22   Time for the perpetual adolescents is curiously static. They are in no great hurry: to succeed, to get work, to lay down achievements. Perhaps this is partly because longevity has increased in recent decades—if one doesn't make it to 90 nowadays, one feels slightly cheated—but more likely it is that time doesn't seem to the perpetual adolescent the excruciatingly finite matter, the precious commodity, it indubitably is. For the perpetual adolescent, time is almost endlessly expandable. Why not go to law school in one's late thirties, or take the premed requirements in one's early forties, or wait even later than that to have children? Time enough to toss away one's twenties, maybe even one's thirties; 40 is soon enough to get serious about life; maybe 50, when you think about it, is the best time really to get going in earnest.

23   The old hunger for life, the eagerness to get into the fray, has been replaced by an odd patience that often looks more like passivity. In the 1950s, people commonly married in their twenties, which may or may not have been a good thing, but marriage did prove a forcing house into adulthood, for men and women, especially where children issued from the marriage, which they usually did fairly quickly. I had two sons by the time I was 26, which, among other things, made it

impossible, either physically or spiritually, for me to join the general youth movement of the 1960s, even though I still qualified by age. It also required me to find a vocation. By 30, one was supposed to be settled in life: wife, children, house, job—"the full catastrophe," as Zorba the Greek liked to say. But it was also a useful catastrophe. Today most people feel that they can wait to get serious about life. Until then one is feeling one's way, still deciding, shopping around, contributing to the formation of a new psychological type: the passive-nonaggressive.

24   Not everywhere is nonaggression the psychological mode of choice. One hears about the young men and women working the 14-hour days at low six-figure jobs in front-line law firms; others sacrificing to get into MBA programs, for the single purpose of an early financial score. But even here one senses an adolescent spirit to the proceedings. The old model for ambition was solid hard work that paid off over time. One began at a low wage, worked one's way up through genuine accomplishment, grew wealthier as one grew older, and, with luck, retired with a sense of financial security and pleasure in one's achievement. But the new American ambition model features the kid multimillionaire—the young man or woman who breaks the bank not long out of college. An element of adolescent impatience enters in here—I want it, *now!*—and also an element of continued youthfulness.

25   The model of the type may be the professional athlete. "The growth of professional basketball over the past twenty-odd years, from a relatively minor spectator sport to a mass-cultural phenomenon," notes Rebecca Mead, in the *New Yorker,* "is an example of the way in which all of American culture is increasingly geared to the tastes of teenage boys." Mead writes this in an article about Shaquille O'Neal, the 32-year-old center for the Los Angeles Lakers, who earns, with endorsements, 30-odd million dollars a year and lives the life of the most privileged possible junior high school boy: enjoying food fights, go-carts, motorcycles, the run of high rides at amusement parks. It may be a wonderful, but it's also a strange life.

26   And yet what is so wrong about any of this? If one wants to dress like a kid, spin around the office on a scooter, not make up one's mind about what work one wants to do until one is 40, be noncommittal in one's relationships—what, really, are the consequences? I happen to think that the consequences are genuine, and fairly serious.

27   "Obviously it is normal to think of oneself as younger than one is," W. H. Auden, a younger son, told Robert Craft, "but fatal to want to be younger." I'm not sure about fatal, but it is at a minimum degrading for a culture at large to want to be younger. The tone of national life is lowered, made less rich. The first thing lowered is expectations, intellectual and otherwise. To begin with education, one wonders if the dumbing down of culture one used to hear so much about and which continues isn't connected to the rise of the perpetual adolescent.

28   Consider contemporary journalism, which tends to play everything to lower and lower common denominators. Why does the *New York Times,* with its pretensions to being our national newspaper, choose to put on its front pages stories about Gennifer Flowers's career as a chanteuse in New Orleans, the firing of NFL coaches, the retirement of Yves Saint Laurent, the canceling of the singer Mariah Carey's recording contract? Slow-news days is a charitable guess; a lowered standard of the significant is a more realistic one. Since the advent of its new publisher, a man of the baby boomer generation, an aura of juvenilia clings to the paper. Frank Rich and Maureen Dowd, two of the paper's most-read columnists, seem not so much the type of the bright college student but of the sassy high-school student—the clever, provocative editor of the school paper out to shock the principal—even though both are in their early fifties.

29   Television comes closer and closer to being a wholly adolescent form of communication. Clicking the remote from major network news shows, one slides smoothly from superficiality to triviality. When Tom Brokaw announces that some subject will be covered "In Depth," what he really means is that roughly 90 seconds, perhaps two minutes, will be devoted to it. It's scarcely original to note that much of contemporary journalism, print and electronic, is pitched to the short attention span, the soundbite, photo-op, quickie take, the deep distaste for complexity—in short, so much is pitched to the adolescent temperament.

30   Political correctness and so many of the political fashions of our day—from academic feminism to cultural studies to queer theory—could only be perpetrated on adolescent minds: minds, that is, that are trained to search out one thing and one thing only: Is my teacher, or this politician, or that public spokesman, saying something that is likely to be offensive to me or members of any other victim group? Only an adolescent would find it worthwhile to devote his or her attention chiefly to the hunting of offenses, the possibility of slights, real and imagined.

31   Self-esteem, of which one currently hears so much, is at bottom another essentially adolescent notion. The great psychological sin of our day is to violate the self-esteem of adolescents of all ages. One might have thought that such self-esteem as any of us is likely to command would be in place by the age of 18. (And what is the point of having all that much self-esteem anyhow, since its logical culminating point can only be smug complacence?) Even in nursing homes, apparently, patients must be guarded against a feeling of their lowered consequence in the world. Self-esteem has become a womb to tomb matter, so that, in contemporary America, the inner and the outer child can finally be made one in the form of the perpetual adolescent.

32   The coarsening of American culture seems part of the adolescent phenomenon. Television commercials have gotten grosser and grosser. The level of profanity on prime-time television shows has risen greatly over the years. Flicks known to their audiences as "gross-out movies," featuring the slimy and hideous,

are part of the regular film menu. Florence King, writing about this phenomenon in her column in the *National Review,* noted: "Since arrested development is as American as apple pie, it is easy to identify the subconscious motivation of the adult male Ughs who produce all these revolting movies and commercials." What makes these things possible is what is known as "niche programming," or the aiming of entertainment at quite specific segments of the audience— African Americans, or teenagers, or the educated classes, or the beer brutes. But increasingly, apparently, we are all being forced into that largest of niches, the American adolescent mentality.

33   Consider now what must be taken as the most consequential adolescent act in American history during the past half century: the Bill Clinton–Monica Lewinsky relationship. I hesitate to call it an affair, because an affair implies a certain adult style: the good hotel room, the bottle of excellent wine, the peignoir, the Sulka pajamas. With Bill and Monica, you had instead the pizza, the canoodling under the desk, the cigar business, even the whole thing going without consummation. No matter what one's politics, one has to admit that our great national scandal was pure high school.

34   In a 1959 review of Iona and Peter Opie's *The Lore and Language of School Children,* the poet Philip Larkin revealed first sensing a sharp waning of his interest in Christianity when he read the Bible verse that promises one will return to one's childish state upon entry into Heaven. Larkin wanted nothing more to do with being a child or with the company of children. He looked forward to "money, keys, wallets, letters, books, long-playing records, drinks, the opposite sex, and other solaces of adulthood."

35   I wanted these things, too, and as soon as possible. From roughly the age of 14, I wanted to stay out all night, to dress like Fred Astaire, to drink and smoke cigarettes with the elegance of William Powell, to have the company of serious women like Susan Hayward and Ingrid Bergman. As I grew older, I sadly began to realize it wasn't going to happen, at least not in the way I had hoped. What happened instead was the triumph of youth culture, with its adoration of youth, in and for itself, and as a time in one's life of purity and goodness always in danger of being despoiled by the corruption of growing older, which is also to say, of "growing up."

36   At a certain point in American life, the young ceased to be viewed as a transient class and youth as a phase of life through which everyone soon passed. Instead, youthfulness was vaunted and carried a special moral status. Adolescence triumphed, becoming a permanent condition. As one grew older, one was presented with two choices, to seem an old fogey for attempting to live according to one's own standard of adulthood, or to go with the flow and adapt some variant of pulling one's long gray hair back into a ponytail, struggling into the spandex shorts, working on those abs, and ending one's days among the Rip Van With-Its. Not, I think, a handsome set of alternatives.

37   The greatest sins, Santayana thought, are those that set out to strangle human nature. This is of course what is being done in cultivating perpetual adolescence, while putting off maturity for as long as possible. Maturity provides a more articulated sense of the ebb and flow, the ups and downs, of life, a more subtly reticulated graph of human possibility. Above all, it values a clear and fit conception of reality. Maturity is ever cognizant that the clock is running, life is finite, and among the greatest mistakes is to believe otherwise. Maturity doesn't exclude playfulness or high humor. Far from it. The mature understand that the bitterest joke of all is that the quickest way to grow old lies in the hopeless attempt to stay forever young.

Suggestions for Reflection, Discussion, and Writing

1. How does the author define *youth culture*, and when did the youth culture begin?

2. Explain what the author means by this statement from paragraph 20: "Never before has it been more difficult to obey the injunction to act one's age." (An *injunction* is an order or command.)

3. Epstein's perpetual adolescent is the "kid multimillionaire" or the "professional basketball player" who never grows up. In paragraph 26 Epstein asks, "And yet what is so wrong about any of this?" How and where does Epstein answer this question, and do you agree or disagree with him?

[First Thoughts]

To build background for reading, explore your thoughts about the pronunciation of a name and its effects. Then answer the questions, either on your own or in a group discussion.

1. Has anyone ever mispronounced your name? How did that make you feel, or how do you think you would feel if someone did?

2. In your opinion, should immigrants who plan to live and work in the United States learn English?

3. Read the title, the headnote, and the first two paragraphs of the reading selection. Based on this preview, what do you think will follow?

Selection 4

Leave Your Name at the Border

Manuel Muñoz is the award-winning author of *Zigzagger* and *The Faith Healer of Olive Avenue*. His writing has appeared in many journals, and his stories have aired on National Public Radio.

Manuel Muñoz

1 At the Fresno airport, as I made my way to the gate, I heard a name over the intercom. The way the name was pronounced by the gate agent made me want to see what she looked like. That is, I wanted to see whether she was Mexican. Around Fresno, identity politics rarely deepen into exacting terms, so to say "Mexican" means, essentially, "not white." The slivered self-identifications Chicano, Hispanic, Mexican-American and Latino are not part of everyday life in the Valley. You're either Mexican or you're not. If someone wants to know if you were born in Mexico, they'll ask. Then you're From Over There—de allá. And leave it at that.

2 The gate agent, it turned out, was Mexican. Well-coiffed, in her 30s, she wore foundation that was several shades lighter than the rest of her skin. It was the kind of makeup job I've learned to silently identify at the mall when I'm with my mother, who will say nothing about it until we're back in the car. Then she'll stretch her neck like an ostrich and point to the darkness of her own skin, wondering aloud why women try to camouflage who they are.

3 I watched the Mexican gate agent busy herself at the counter, professional and studied. Once again, she picked up the microphone and, with authority, announced the name of the missing customer: "Eugenio Reyes, please come to the front desk."

4 You can probably guess how she said it. Her Anglicized pronunciation wouldn't be unusual in a place like California's Central Valley. I didn't have a Mexican name there either: I was an instruction guide.

5 When people ask me where I'm from, I say Fresno because I don't expect them to know little Dinuba. Fresno is a booming city of nearly 500,000 these days, with a diversity—white, Mexican, African-American, Armenian, Hmong and Middle Eastern people are all well represented—that shouldn't surprise anyone. It's in the small towns like Dinuba that surround Fresno that the awareness of cultural difference is stripped down to the interactions between the only two groups that tend to live there: whites and Mexicans. When you hear a Mexican name spoken in these towns, regardless of the speaker's background, it's no wonder that there's an "English way of pronouncing it."

6 I was born in 1972, part of a generation that learned both English and Spanish. Many of my cousins and siblings are bilingual, serving as translators for those in the family whose English is barely functional. Others have no way of following the Spanish banter at family gatherings. You can tell who falls into which group: Estella, Eric, Delia, Dubina, Melanie.

7 It's intriguing to watch "American" names begin to dominate among my nieces and nephews and second cousins, as well as with the children of my

hometown friends. I am not surprised to meet five-year-old Brandon or Kaitlyn. Hardly anyone questions the incongruity of matching these names with last names like Trujillo or Zepeda. The English-only way of life partly explains the quiet erasure of cultural difference that assimilation has attempted to accomplish. A name like Kaitlyn Zepeda doesn't completely obscure her ethnicity, but the half-step of her name, as a gesture, is almost understandable.

8   Spanish was and still is viewed with suspicion: always the language of the vilified illegal immigrant, it segregated schoolchildren into English-only and bilingual programs; it defined you, above all else, as part of a lower class. Learning English, though, brought its own complications with identity. It was simultaneously the language of the white population and a path toward the richer, expansive identity of "American." But it took getting out of the Valley for me to understand that "white" and "American" were two very different things.

9   Something as simple as saying our names "in English" was our unwittingly complicit gesture of trying to blend in. Pronouncing Mexican names correctly was never encouraged. Names like Daniel, Olivia and Marco slipped right into the mutability of the English language.

10   I remember a school ceremony at which the mathematics teacher, a white man, announced the names of Mexican students correctly and caused some confusion, if not embarrassment. Years later we recognized that he spoke in deference to our Spanish-speaking parents in the audience, caring teacher that he was.

11   These were difficult names for a non-Spanish speaker: Araceli, Nadira, Luis (a beautiful name when you glide the *u* and the *i* as you're supposed to). We had been accustomed to having our birth names altered for convenience. Concepción was Connie. Ramón was Raymond. My cousin Esperanza was Hope—but her name was pronounced "Hopie" because any Spanish speaker would automatically pronounce the *e* at the end.

12   Ours, then, were names that stood as barriers to a complete embrace of an American identity, simply because their pronunciations required a slip into Spanish, the otherness that assimilation was supposed to erase. What to do with names like Amado, Lucio or Élida? There are no English "equivalents," no answer when white teachers asked, "What does your name mean?" when what they really wanted to know was "What's the English one?" So what you heard was a name butchered beyond recognition, a pronunciation that pointed the finger at the Spanish language as the source of clunky sound and ugly rhythm.

13   My stepfather, from Ojos de Agua, Mexico, jokes when I ask him about the names of Mexicans born here. He deliberately stumbles over pronunciations, imitating our elders who have difficulty with Bradley and Madelyn. "Ashley Sánchez. ¿Tú crees?" He wonders aloud what has happened to the "nombres del rancho"—traditional Mexican names that are hardly given anymore to children born in the States: Heraclio, Madaleno, Otilia, Dominga.

14   My stepfather's experience with the Anglicization of his name—Antonio to Tony—ties into something bigger than learning English. For him, the erasure of

his name was about deference and subservience. Becoming Tony gave him a measure of access as he struggled to learn English and get more fieldwork.

15   This isn't to say that my stepfather welcomed the change, only that he could not put up much resistance. Not changing put him at risk of being passed over for work. English was a world of power and decisions, of smooth, uninterrupted negotiation. There was no time to search for the right word while a shop clerk waited for him to come up with the English name of the correct part needed out in the field. Clear communication meant you could go unsupervised, or that you were even able to read instructions directly off a piece of paper. Every gesture made toward convincing an employer that English was on its way to being mastered had the potential to make a season of fieldwork profitable.

16   It's curious that many of us growing up in Dinuba adhered to the same rules. Although as children of farm workers we worked in the fields at an early age, we'd also had the opportunity to stay in one town long enough to finish school. Most of us had learned English early and splintered off into a dual existence of English at school, Spanish at home. But instead of recognizing the need for fluency in both languages, we turned it into a peculiar kind of battle. English was for public display. Spanish was for privacy—and privacy quickly turned to shame.

17   The corrosive effect of assimilation is the displacement of one culture over another, the inability to sustain more than one way of being. It isn't a code word for racial and ethnic acculturation only. It applies to needing and wanting to belong, of seeing from the outside and wondering how to get in and then, once inside, realizing there are always those still on the fringe.

18   When I went to college on the East Coast, I was confronted for the first time by people who said my name correctly without prompting; if they stumbled, there was a quick apology and an honest plea to help with the pronunciation. But introducing myself was painful: already shy, I avoided meeting people because I didn't want to say my name, felt burdened by my own history. I knew that my small-town upbringing and its limitations on Spanish would not have been tolerated by any of the students of color who had grown up in large cities, in places where the sheer force of their native languages made them dominant in their neighborhoods.

19   It didn't take long for me to assert the power of code-switching in public, the transferring of words from one language to another, regardless of who might be listening. I was learning that the English language composed new meanings when its constrictions were ignored, crossed over or crossed out. Language is all about manipulation, or not listening to the rules.

20   When I come back to Dinuba, I have a hard time hearing my name said incorrectly, but I have an even harder time beginning a conversation with others about why the pronunciation of our names matters. Leaving a small town requires an embrace of a larger point of view, but a town like Dinuba remains forever embedded in an either/or way of life. My stepfather still answers to Tony and, as the United States–born children grow older, their Anglicized names be-

gin to signify who does and who does not "belong"—who was born here and who is de allá.

21   My name is Manuel. To this day, most people cannot say it correctly, the way it was intended to be said. But I can live with that because I love the alliteration of my full name. It wasn't the name my mother, Esmeralda, was going to give me. At the last minute, my father named me after an uncle I would never meet. My name was to have been Ricardo. Growing up in Dinuba, I'm certain I would have become Ricky or even Richard, and the journey toward the discovery of the English language's extraordinary power in even the most ordinary of circumstances would probably have gone unlearned.

22   I count on a collective sense of cultural loss to once again swing the names back to our native language. The Mexican gate agent announced Eugenio Reyes, but I never got a chance to see who appeared. I pictured an older man, cowboy hat in hand, but I made the assumption on his name alone, the clash of privileges I imagined between someone de allá and a Mexican woman with a good job in the United States. Would she speak to him in Spanish? Or would she raise her voice to him as if he were hard of hearing?

23   But who was I to imagine this man being from anywhere, based on his name alone? At a place of arrivals and departures, it sank into me that the currency of our names is a stroke of luck: because mine was not an easy name, it forced me to consider how language would rule me if I allowed it. Yet I discovered that only by leaving. My stepfather must live in the Valley, a place that does not allow that choice, every day. And Eugenio Reyes—I do not know if he was coming or going.

Suggestions for Reflection, Discussion, and Writing

1. What is in a name? Why is the pronunciation of his name important to this author?

2. In paragraph 17, what does the author mean by "the corrosive effect of assimilation"? First, look up the definitions of *corrosive* and *assimilation*. Next, read the author's explanation in paragraph 17. Then, using examples of your own, explain the author's meaning.

3. Do you agree or disagree with the author's statement in paragraph 19: "Language is all about manipulation or not listening to the rules"? Write a paragraph in which you explain your answer.

[First Thoughts]

To build background for reading, explore your thoughts about Islam. Then answer the questions, either on your own or in a group discussion.

1. What do you know about the religion of Islam and Islamic beliefs?

2. Are you, or is anyone you know, a follower of Islam? Explain your answer.

3. Read the title, the headnote, and the first two paragraphs of the reading selection. Based on this preview, what do you think will follow?

Selection 5

Yes, I Follow Islam, But I'm Not a Terrorist

Nada El Sawy

Nada El Sawy is a resident of New York City. She wrote this essay for *Newsweek*'s "My Turn" column in October 2001.

1   As an Egyptian-American and a Muslim, I've always been dismayed by the way Islam has been generally misrepresented in the media and misunderstood by most Americans. Since the tragic events of Sept. 11, Islam has been in the spotlight, and though leaders such as President George W. Bush and New York Mayor Rudolph Giuliani have made a concerted effort to distinguish it from terrorism, some people still aren't getting the message.

2   I am a graduate student in journalism, often assigned to write articles about current events. The day after the terrorist attacks I headed out to Brooklyn to cover a story about an Islamic school that had been pelted with rocks and bloody pork chops in the hours after the World Trade Center towers collapsed. Whoever committed this act knew enough about Islam to know that pork is forbidden, but apparently little else about Islamic beliefs. "I wish people would stop calling us terrorists," one sixth grader told me.

3   When I read about Osama bin Laden or groups like the Egyptian Islamic Jihad, I want to tell them, "You're giving Islam a bad name!" I want to show people that the religion I know is one that calls for patience, harmony and understanding.

4   Islam may be the world's second largest religion, but in the United States, home to about 6 million of its followers, it remains a mystery. Americans seem to believe that backpacking through Europe or keeping up with the news gives them an understanding of everything about the cultures, religions and traditions that differ from their own. While I'm heartened by the sincere curiosity of some, like the stylist who asked me about my beliefs as he trimmed my hair, most people still have a long way to go.

5   I have yet to meet anyone—who isn't either especially well read, a religion major or a Muslim—who can accurately describe Islamic beliefs. Many people

find it fascinating that I worship Allah without understanding that "Allah" is simply the Arabic word for God. Muslims use the word only because the universal teachings of Islam have been preserved in the Arabic language.

6   I can recall a Thanksgiving dinner with family friends several years ago when the host offered a small prayer. As we all held hands, he started with the customary thanks for the food, family and friends. Then he proceeded to say, "And thank you to God—or whoever else you choose to worship, may it be Allah . . . " He meant well, but I remember flinching. He and his family had traveled to the Middle East, taken pictures of Muslims praying, read about the cultures they were visiting, but none of it had led to a clear understanding of Islam.

7   I'm not surprised when classmates confront me with the charge that Muslims around the world are killing in the name of religion. I'm careful not to mention the many Muslims who have been killed in places like Kosovo, Indonesia and Palestine. I don't want to respond with that kind of foolish rebuttal because I abhor the senseless murder of all human beings.

8   The truth is, fanaticism can spring from misguided excess in any religion, and Muslims who kill in the name of their beliefs are not true Muslims. Aggression is not a tenet of our religion, but rather something that is condemned except in self-defense. The Quran states: "Fight in the cause of Allah those who fight you, but commit no aggression; for Allah loves not transgressors" (al-Baqarah 2:190).

9   If few people understand that Islam is a peaceful religion, even fewer know how beautiful it can be. When I studied in Cairo during my junior year of college, my grandmother had a religion teacher come to her house every week to teach us the Quran. Hearing him chant the verses was like listening to breathtaking music. There is also an element of poetry in a Muslim's everyday life. One says "Allah" or "ma sha'a Allah"("As God wills") upon seeing something beautiful, like a sunset or a newborn baby. Whenever family members or friends part, one says, "La il-lah illa Allah" ("there is only one God") and the other responds, "Muhammad rasoul Allah" ("Muhammad is God's prophet").

10   To me, informing people about these wonderful aspects of Islam is a pleasure, not a burden. There are signs that Americans may be ready to learn. I was moved recently when I saw a woman on the subway reading a book about Islam to her young daughter. She explained that she was teaching herself, as well as her daughter. If more people take that approach, there will come a day when fanaticism is no longer equated with faith, and Muslims aren't seen as terrorists but as human beings.

Suggestions for Reflection, Discussion, and Writing

1. The author says that most Americans have little understanding of Islam. What did you learn about this religion from reading El Sawy's essay that you did not already know?

2. The author distinguishes between her Muslim faith and a misguided fanaticism. What is her explanation?

3. Write about the events of September 11th and its effects on you and those close to you. To what extent have these events influenced your perceptions of Islam and the Middle East?

[First Thoughts]

To build background for reading, explore your thoughts about today's media. Then answer the questions, either on your own or in a group discussion.

1. What is your main source of news: network TV, cable TV news shows, newspapers, magazines, or the Internet?

2. Do you think that the variety of today's news outlets is a good or a bad thing? Explain your answer.

3. Read the title, the headnote, and the first two paragraphs of the reading selection. Based on this preview, what do you think will follow?

Selection 6

The Real Media Divide

Markus Prior

Markus Prior is an assistant professor of politics and public affairs at Princeton University's Woodrow Wilson School. He is the author of the recent book *Post-Broadcast Democracy: How Media Choice Increases Inequality in Political Involvement and Polarizes Elections.* The following essay originally appeared in the *Washington Post* on July 16, 2007.

1   Today's news world is a political junkie's oyster. Cable TV offers CNN, Fox News, MSNBC and C-SPAN. The *Washington Post,* BBC online, The Note and many, many more news websites are only a click away. But that's where they remain for many Americans. Decades into the "information age," the public is as uninformed as before the rise of cable television and the Internet.

2   Greater access to media, ironically, has reduced the share of Americans who are politically informed. The most significant effect of more media choice is not the wider dissemination of political news but mounting inequality in political involvement. Some people follow news more closely than in the past, but many others avoid it altogether.

3   Now that Americans can choose among countless channels and websites, the role of motivation is key. Many people's reasons for watching television or surfing the Web do not include learning about politics. Today's media users seek out the content they really like. Unfortunately for a political system that benefits from an informed citizenry, few people really like the news.

4   Consider the broadcast networks' desperate struggle to hold on to an ever-shrinking news audience. The problem is not that shallow, loud or negative cov-

erage of politics causes viewers to tune out in disgust. It's that for many people shallow, loud entertainment offers greater satisfaction, and it always has. Now, such entertainment is available around the clock and in unprecedented variety. Television viewers have not abandoned the evening news out of frustration—they just found something more enjoyable. Even Katie Couric can't stanch that trend.

5   The flip side of the entertainment fan who doesn't have to watch the news is the news junkie who now can follow it constantly. A relatively small segment of the population—my own research indicates it's less than a fifth—specializes in news content. But such people consume so much of it that the total amount of time Americans spend watching, reading and listening to news has not declined even though many people have tuned out.

6   The new fault line of civic involvement is between news junkies and entertainment fans. Entertainment fans are abandoning news and politics not because it has become harder to be involved but because they have decided to devote their time to content that promises greater immediate gratification. As a result, they learn less about politics and are less likely to vote at a time when news junkies are becoming even more engaged. Unlike most forms of inequality, this rising divergence in political involvement is a result of voluntary consumption decisions. Making sure everybody has access to media won't fix the problem—it is exactly the cause.

7   When media users get what they want all the time, does anyone get hurt? Well, yes. The expansion of news choices has many worried about partisan bias. Such worries are overstated. Fox New's Bill O'Reilly preaches mostly to the converted; there have always been passionate conservatives, and exposure to one-sided media will hardly make them more conservative. Plus, a little O'Reilly doesn't harm anybody. The danger lies not in larger audiences for politically biased news outlets per se but in exclusive exposure to outlets all biased in the same direction. But many Fox News viewers also watch CNN and MSNBC.

8   More troubling is that entertainment fans reduce the political representation of their interests when they avoid news and cut down on their political participation. Politicians pay more attention to voters than to nonvoters, so the views of these less-involved entertainment fans may not be reflected in political outcomes as much as they were in the past.

9   Greater media choice is both gratifying and a powerful political asset for those people who read op-eds and then move on to NPR, Instapundit and Wolf Blitzer. It is more treacherous for entertainment fans. Happy as they are with a remote control in one hand and a computer mouse in the other, they never consciously weigh the pleasure of constant entertainment against the cost of leaving politics to news junkies and politicians. The danger is not that they are seduced by the views of Ann Coulter or Arianna Huffington but that they don't know who such people are. And not that they cast more ideologically extreme votes but that they no longer vote at all.

Suggestions for Reflection, Discussion, and Writing

1. Markus Prior says that many people avoid the news, that few people really like the news, and that greater media choice has led to a less informed citizenry and fewer citizens who vote. What is your reaction to these claims? Do you agree or disagree, and why?

2 The author contrasts "entertainment fans" with "news junkies." Where in the essay does he make this comparison? In your own words, what is the difference between these types of media consumers? Which type are you?

3. Write a paragraph in which you answer these two questions: What is your favorite news source, and what do you like about it? To what extent does your involvement (or lack of involvement) with the news influence your voting habits?

[First Thoughts]

To build background for reading, explore your thoughts about where you go when you want to "get away from it all." Then answer the questions, either on your own or in a group discussion.

1. Where do you go to take a break from home, work, or classes?

2. Think ahead to a time when you will retire from working: What do you think you might want to do then?

3. Read the title, the headnote, and the first two paragraphs of the reading selection. Based on this preview, what do you think will follow?

Selection 7

Where to Now?

William Raspberry

William Raspberry was a longtime member of the *Washington Post* Writers Group until he retired in 2005. He is a celebrated author whose column has appeared in newspapers throughout the country since 1966. He teaches at Duke University.

1 The beginning of the week usually finds me in Durham, NC, preparing for the classes I teach at Duke University. But this was fall break, and I didn't have to make the trip.

2 Instead—almost without thinking about it—I dressed and headed for the *Washington Post,* where I busied myself with various journalistic chores.

3 And then it hit me: Where will I go next fall break—and spring break, and all those other free-from-school times? What will I do to get out of the house?

4   At the end of this month, I'll be retiring from the newspaper where I've worked for more than 43 years, and I had already been going through the process of redefining my existence without the *Post*. But this was a new worry: How does a retired guy get out of the house.

5   Let me be clear: This is not a commentary on my marriage. I've enjoyed 39 years with a wonderful woman, and I'd happily sign up for as many more. No, the getting-out-of-the-house quandary is as much about her as me. You may have seen the story by my *Post* colleague Anthony Faiola concerning a new disorder being treated by Japanese mental-health therapists: RHS, or retired husband syndrome.

6   Apparently, Japanese wives have grown used to playing something of a servant's role to their husbands—making their dinner when they come home from work, seeing to their well-being and so on.

7   But listen to one desperate Japanese housewife's reaction to her husband's beaming announcement that he was retiring.

8   "'This is it,' I remember thinking. "I am going to have to divorce him now.' It was bad enough that I had to wait on him when he came home from work. But having him around the house all the time was more than I could possibly bear.

9   I don't consider myself a particularly high-maintenance husband, but Sondra can't possibly cherish the prospect of having both a lot less income and a lot more husband invading the space she surely must think of as primarily hers.

10   But how to save her sanity—and mine?

11   One helpful friend to whom I put the dilemma pointed me to Ray Oldenburg's 16-year-old book, *The Great Good Place,* wherein he laments the loss of what he calls "third places" in American life. The first place, of course, is home; the second is work. Third places, in Oldenburg's taxonomy, are those informal gathering spots where one finds not just escape but camaraderie, conversation, friendly argument and pleasant conversation with regulars.

12   I read his description of—his paean to—third places, and I think of old-time barbershops, where barbering was largely a backdrop for an informal social life; of chess players in the city park, where the only admission ticket is a delight in the game and where opponents need know little more about you than your first name; and of small-town diners where regulars dawdle for hours over coffee and pie.

13   But all these are Norman Rockwell vignettes. Barbershops, even if they haven't gone unisex, are unmistakably about business these days, and I wouldn't urge you to dawdle too long without spending money at Starbucks. Commercialization and suburbanization are crushing the life out of third places.

14   At least in America. Irish pubs, German *biergartens,* Moroccan tea shops, French neighborhood cafes—all are hangouts of regulars who seem to check their titles and status at the door. Or at any rate, *potential* regulars, for, as Oldenburg points out, admittance may be free, but "membership" happens only after the regulars get to know and trust you.

15   *The Great Good Place* argues that third places build community, social capital and civic solidarity. Perhaps, but my immediate worry is that they won't be there for *me* when I need them.

16   I suppose a case could be made for the gym as a latter-day third place. Likewise the beauty salon or the sports bar. But listen to Oldenburg:

17   "The lure of a third place depends only secondarily upon seating capacity, variety of beverages served . . . or other features. What attracts the regular visitor to a third place is supplied not by management but by fellow customers. . . . It is the regulars who give the place its character and who assure that on any given visit some of the gang will be there."

18   And that describes perfectly the newsroom of the *Washington Post,* except that it was—and is—a *job* site. I need a new third place.

Suggestions for Reflection, Discussion, and Writing

1. In this essay, Raspberry refers to Oldenburg's book about *third places.* Basically, a *third place* is an informal gathering place where regulars meet and enjoy each other's company. What are some of Raspberry's examples of third places? What is your own example of a third place?

2. The first half of the essay (paragraphs 1–10) is about Raspberry's retirement. The second half of the essay is about *third places*. Why do you think Raspberry structured the essay this way?

3. Write a paragraph or short essay about a place where you spend time that qualifies as a third place, based on Oldenburg's description of one in paragraph 16–17.

[First Thoughts]

To build background for reading, explore your thoughts about women being required to register for the draft. Then answer the following questions, either on your own or in a group discussion:

1. Should women as well as men be required to register for the draft? Why, or why not?

2. What is your opinion about the role of women in the military?

3. Read the title, the headnote, and the first two paragraphs of the reading selection. Based on this preview, what do you think will follow?

Selection 8

Uncle Sam and Aunt Samantha

Anna Quindlen is a
Pulitzer Prize–winning
journalist and best-selling
author. Her work has
appeared in newspapers
and magazines. Currently,
she writes for *Newsweek*'s
"Last Word" column, in
which the following
essay appeared. *Blessings*
is the most recent of
Quindlen's many books.

Anna Quindlen

1   One out of every five new recruits in the United States military is female.

2   The Marines gave the Combat Action Ribbon for service in the Persian Gulf to 23 women.

3   Two female soldiers were killed in the bombing of the USS Cole.

4   The Selective Service registers for the draft all male citizens between the ages of 18 and 25.

5   What's wrong with this picture?

6   As Americans read and realize that the lives of most women in this country are as different from those of Afghan women as a Cunard cruise is from maximum-security lockdown, there has nonetheless been little attention paid to one persistent gender inequity in U.S. public policy. An astonishing anachronism, really: while women are represented today in virtually all fields, including the armed forces, only men are required to register for the military draft that would be used in the event of a national-security crisis.

7   Since the nation is as close to such a crisis as it has been in more than 60 years, it's a good moment to consider how the draft wound up in this particular time warp. It's not the time warp of the Taliban, certainly, stuck in the worst part of the 13th century, forbidding women to attend school or hold jobs or even reveal their arms, forcing them into sex and marriage. Our own time warp is several decades old. The last time the draft was considered seriously was 20 years ago, when registration with the Selective Service was restored by Jimmy Carter after the Soviet invasion of, yep, Afghanistan. The president, as well as the Army chief of staff, asked at the time for the registration of women as well as men.

8   Amid a welter of arguments—women interfere with esprit de corps, women don't have the physical strength, women prisoners could be sexually assaulted, women soldiers would distract male soldiers from their mission—Congress shot down the notion of gender-blind registration. So did the Supreme Court, ruling that since women were forbidden to serve in combat positions and the purpose of the draft was to create a combat-ready force, it made sense not to register them.

9   But that was then, and this is now. Women have indeed served in combat positions, in the Balkans and the Middle East. More than 40,000 managed to serve in the Persian Gulf without destroying unit cohesion or failing because of upper-body strength. Some are even now taking out targets in Afghanistan from fighter jets, and apparently without any male soldier's falling prey to some predicted excess of chivalry or lust.

10   Talk about cognitive dissonance. All these military personnel, male and female alike, have come of age at a time when a significant level of parity was

taken for granted. Yet they are supposed to accept that only males will be required to defend their country in a time of national emergency. This is insulting to men. And it is insulting to women. Caroline Forell, an expert on women's legal rights and a professor at the University of Oregon School of Law, puts it bluntly: "Failing to require this of women makes us lesser citizens."

11   Neither the left nor the right has been particularly inclined to consider this issue judiciously. Many feminists came from the antiwar movement and have let their distaste for the military in general and the draft in particular mute their response. In 1980 NOW released a resolution that buried support for the registration of women beneath opposition to the draft, despite the fact that the draft had been redesigned to eliminate the vexing inequities of Vietnam, when the sons of the working class served and the sons of the Ivy League did not. Conservatives, meanwhile, used an equal-opportunity draft as the linchpin of opposition to the Equal Rights Amendment, along with the terrifying specter of unisex bathrooms. (I have seen the urinal, and it is benign.) The legislative director of the right-wing group Concerned Women for America once defended the existing regulations by saying that most women "don't want to be included in the draft." All those young men who went to Canada during Vietnam and those who today register with fear and trembling in the face of the Trade Center devastation might be amazed to discover that lack of desire is an affirmative defense.

12   Parents face a series of unique new challenges in this more egalitarian world, not the least of which would be sending a daughter off to war. But parents all over this country are doing that right now, with daughters who enlisted; some have even expressed surprise that young women, in this day and age, are not required to register alongside their brothers and friends. While all involved in this debate over the years have invoked the assumed opposition of the people, even 10 years ago more than half of all Americans polled believed women should be made eligible for the draft. Besides, this is not about comfort but about fairness. My son has to register with the Selective Service this year, and if his sister does not when she turns 18, it makes a mockery not only of the standards of this household but of the standards of this nation.

13   It is possible in Afghanistan for women to be treated like little more than fecund pack animals precisely because gender fear and ignorance and hatred have been codified and permitted to hold sway. In this country, largely because of the concerted efforts of those allied with the women's movement over a century of struggle, much of that bigotry has been beaten back, even buried. Yet in improbable places the creaky old ways surface, the ways suggesting that we women were made of finer stuff. The finer stuff was usually porcelain, decorative and on the shelf, suitable for meals and show. Happily, the finer stuff has been transmuted into the right stuff. But with rights come responsibilities, as teachers like to tell their students. This is a responsibility that should fall equally upon all, male and female alike. If the empirical evidence is considered rationally, if the decision is divested of outmoded stereotypes, that's the only possible conclusion to be reached.

Suggestions for Reflection, Discussion, and Writing

1. The author's issue is whether women should be required to register for the draft. Her claim is that they should. What evidence does she provide to support her claim?

2. Does the author state opposing claims? If so, how does she answer them?

3. If you had a son or daughter who was pursuing a career in military service, would you be for or against that choice, and why? Write an essay in which you explain your answer.

[First Thoughts]

To build background for reading, explore your thoughts about your grandparents. Then answer the following questions, either on your own or in a group discussion:

1. When you think of your grandparents, what are the first details that come to mind?

2. What are the advantages and disadvantages of living with grandparents or other close relatives?

3. Read the title, the headnote, and the first two paragraphs of the reading selection. Based on this preview, what do you think will follow?

Selection 9

A Present for Popo

Elizabeth Wong

Elizabeth Wong, a Chinese-American, was born and raised in San Francisco. She is an award-winning playwright and television screenwriter. In the 1990s, she wrote a column for the *Los Angeles Times*, in which the following essay appeared.

1 When my Popo opened a Christmas gift, she would shake it, smell it, listen to it. She would size it up. She would open it nimbly, with all enthusiasm and delight, and even though the mittens were ugly or the blouse too small or the card obviously homemade, she would coo over it as if it were the baby Jesus.

2 Despite that, buying a gift for my grandmother was always problematic. Being in her late 80s, Popo didn't seem to need any more sweaters or handbags. No books certainly, as she only knew six words of English. Cosmetics might be a good idea, for she was just a wee bit vain.

3 But, ultimately, nothing worked. "No place to put anything anyway," she used to tell me in Chinese. For in the last few years of her life, Popo had a bed in a room in a house in San Gabriel owned by one of her sons. All her belongings, her money, her very life was now co-opted and controlled by her sons and

their wives. Popo's daughters had little power in this matter. This was a traditional Chinese family.

4   For you see, Popo had begun to forget things. Ask her about something that happened 20 years ago, and she could recount the details in the heartbeat of a New York minute. But it was those niggling little everyday matters that became so troubling. She would forget to take her heart medicine. She would forget where she put her handbag. She would forget she talked to you just moments before. She would count the few dollars in her billfold, over and over again. She would ask me for the millionth time, "So when are you going to get married?" For her own good, the family decided she should give up her beloved one-room Chinatown flat. Popo herself recognized she might be a danger to herself. "I think your grandmother is going crazy," she would say.

5   That little flat was a bothersome place, but Popo loved it. Her window had a vew of several import–export shops below, not to mention the grotesque plastic hanging lanterns and that nasty loudspeaker serenading tourists with 18 hours of top-40 popular hits.

6   My brother Will and I used to stand under her balcony on Mei Ling Way, shouting up, "Grandmother on the Third Floor! Grandmother on the Third Floor!" Simultaneously, the wrinkled faces of a half-dozen grannies would come to the balcony and proudly claim us: "These are my grandchildren coming to take me to *dim sum*." Her neighbors would cluck and sigh, "You have such good grandchildren. Not like mine."

7   In that cramped room of Popo's, I could see past Christmas presents. A full-wall collage of family photos that my mother and I made together and presented one year with lots of fanfare. Popo had attached additional snapshots by way of paper clips and Scotch tape. And there, on the window sill, a little terrarium to which Popo had tied a small ribbon. "For good luck," as she gleefully pointed out the sprouting buds. "See, it's having babies."

8   Also, there were the utility shelves on the wall, groaning from a wide assortment of junk, stuff and whatnot. Popo was fond of salvaging discarded things. After my brother had installed the shelving, she did a little jig, then took a whisk broom and lightly swept away any naughty spirits that might be lurking on the walls. "Shoo, shoo, shoo, away with you, Mischievous Ones!" That apartment was her independence, and her pioneer spirit was everywhere in it.

9   Popo was my mother's mother, but she was also a second mother to me. Her death was a great blow. The last time I saw her was Christmas, 1990, when she looked hale and hearty. I thought she would live forever. Last October, at 91, she had her final heart attack. The next time I saw her, it was at her funeral.

10   An open casket, and there she was, with a shiny new penny poised between her lips, a silenced warrior woman. Her sons and daughters placed colorful pieces of cloth in her casket. They burned incense and paper money. A small marching band led a New Orleans–like procession through the streets of Chinatown. Popo's picture, larger than life, in a flatbed truck to survey the world of her adopted country.

11	This little 4-foot, 9-inch woman had been the glue of our family. She wasn't perfect, she wasn't even nice, but she learned from her mistakes, and, ultimately, she forgave herself for being human. It is a lesson of forgiveness that seems to have eluded her own sons and daughters.
12	And now she is gone. And with her—the tenuous, cohesive ties of blood and duty that bound us to family. My mother predicted that once the distribution of what was left of Popo's estate took place, no further words would be exchanged between Popo's children. She was right.
13	But this year, six of the 27 grandchildren and two of the 18 great-grandchildren came together for a holiday feast of honey-baked ham and mashed potatoes. Not a gigantic family reunion. But I think, for now, it's the one yuletide present my grandmother might have truly enjoyed.
14	Merry Christmas, Popo!

Suggestions for Reflection, Discussion, and Writing

1. Find and underline the details in the essay that describe Popo's one-room flat and her possessions. What do these details tell you about Popo?

2. The words *present* or *gift* and *Christmas* are repeated throughout the essay. How do these ideas act as coherence devices? Before answering this question, you may want to review "coherence" in Chapter 3.

3. In this essay, Wong reflects on her grandmother's character and what it taught her. For example, she says in paragraph 8, "That apartment was her independence, and her pioneer spirit was everywhere in it." Write a descriptive essay about one of your relatives, someone who made an impression on you or taught you an important skill or lesson.

[First Thoughts]

To build background for reading, explore your thoughts about racial oppression. Then answer the questions, either on your own or in a group discussion.

1. What do you know or what have you read about Martin Luther King Jr.?

2. What do you know about the civil rights movement of the 1950s and 1960s?

3. Read the title, the headnote, and the first two paragraphs of the reading selection. Based on this preview, what do you think will follow?

Selection 10

The Ways of Meeting Oppression

Martin Luther King Jr.

Martin Luther King Jr. was a minister and leader of the civil rights movement during the 1950s and 1960s. A martyr for his cause, King was assassinated on April 4, 1968, at the age of thirty-nine. The following essay is from his book *Stride Toward Freedom*. King's appeals for racial justice and equality still inspire us today.

1   Oppressed people deal with their oppression in three characteristic ways. One way is acquiescence: The oppressed resign themselves to their doom. They tacitly adjust themselves to oppression, and thereby become conditioned to it. In every movement toward freedom some of the oppressed prefer to remain oppressed. Almost 2,800 years ago Moses set out to lead the children of Israel from the slavery of Egypt to the freedom of the promised land. He soon discovered that slaves do not always welcome their deliverers. They become accustomed to being slaves. They would rather bear those ills they have, as Shakespeare pointed out, then flee to others that they know not of. They prefer the "fleshpots of Egypt" to the ordeals of emancipation.

2   There is such a thing as the freedom of exhaustion. Some people are so worn down by the yoke of oppression that they give up. A few years ago in the slum areas of Atlanta, a negro guitarist used to sing almost daily: "Been down so long that down don't bother me." This is the type of negative freedom and resignation that often engulfs the life of the oppressed.

3   But this is not the way out. To accept passively an unjust system is to cooperate with that system; thereby the oppressed become as evil as the oppressor. Noncooperation with evil is as much a moral obligation as is cooperation with good. The oppressed must never allow the conscience of the oppressor to slumber. Religion reminds every man that he is his brother's keeper. To accept injustice or segregation passively is to say to the oppressor that his actions are morally right. It is a way of allowing his conscience to fall asleep. At this moment the oppressed fails to be his brother's keeper. So acquiescence—while often the easier way—is not the moral way. It is the way of the coward. The Negro cannot win the respect of his oppressor by acquiescing; he merely increases the oppressor's arrogance and contempt. Acquiescence is interpreted as proof of the Negro's inferiority. The Negro cannot win the respect of the white people of the South or the peoples of the world if he is willing to sell the future of his children for his personal and immediate comfort and safety.

4   A second way that oppressed people sometimes deal with oppression is to resort to physical violence and corroding hatred. Violence often brings about momentary results. Nations have frequently won their independence in battle. But in spite of temporary victories, violence never brings permanent peace. It solves no social problem; it merely creates new and more complicated ones.

5   Violence as a way of achieving racial justice is both impractical and immoral. It is impractical because it is a descending spiral ending in destruction for all. The old law of an eye for an eye leaves everybody blind. It is immoral because it seeks to humiliate the opponent rather than win his understanding; it

seeks to annihilate rather than to convert. Violence is immoral because it thrives on hatred rather than love. It destroys community and makes brotherhood impossible. It leaves society in monologue rather than dialogue. Violence ends by defeating itself. It creates bitterness in the survivors and brutality n the destroyers. A voice echoes through time saying to every potential Peter, "Put up your sword." History is cluttered with the wreckage of nations that failed to follow this command.

6   If the American Negro and other victims of oppression succumb to the temptation of using violence in the struggle for freedom, future generations will be the recipients of a desolate night of bitterness, and our chief legacy to them will be an endless reign of meaningless chaos. Violence is not the way.

7   The third way open to oppressed people in their quest for freedom is the way of nonviolent resistance. Like the synthesis in Hegelian philosophy, the principle of nonviolent resistance seeks to reconcile the truths of two opposites—the acquiescence and violence—while avoiding the extremes and immoralities of both. The nonviolent resister agrees with the person who acquiesces that one should not be physically aggressive toward his opponent; but he balances the equation by agreeing with the person of violence that evil must be resisted. He avoids the nonresistance of the former and the violent resistance of the latter. With nonviolent resistance, no individual or group need submit to any wrong, nor need anyone resort to violence in order to right a wrong.

8   It seems to me that this is the method that must guide the actions of the Negro in the present crisis in race relations. Through nonviolent resistance the Negro will be able to rise to the noble height of opposing the unjust system while loving the perpetrators of the system. The Negro must work passionately and unrelentingly for full stature as a citizen, but he must not use inferior methods to gain it. He must never come to terms with falsehood, malice, hate, or destruction.

9   Nonviolent resistance makes it possible for the Negro to remain in the South and struggle for his rights. The Negro's problem will not be solved by running away. He cannot listen to the glib suggestion of those who would urge him to migrate en masse to other sections of the country. By grasping his great opportunity in the South, he can make a lasting contribution to the moral strength of the nation and set a sublime example of courage for generations yet unborn.

10   By nonviolent resistance, the Negro can also enlist all men of good will in his struggle for equality. The problem is not a purely racial one, with Negroes set against whites. In the end, it is not a struggle between people at all, but a tension between justice and injustice. Nonviolent resistance is not aimed against oppressors but against oppression. Under its banner consciences, not racial groups, are enlisted.

Suggestions for Reflection, Discussion, and Writing

1. Which sentence states King's thesis? Find the sentence, and then restate the thesis in your own words.

2. What are King's ways of meeting oppression? How many are there, and what are their advantages and disadvantages?

3. Martin Luther King Jr. argued for nonviolent protest because he believed that violence was only a temporary solution to what would be a long struggle. Do you agree or disagree with him? Write a paragraph in which you explain your answer.

The Selective Writer: A Brief Handbook

Unit 4 is about *grammar*. If you are like many students, the mention of that word may cause you to have visions of difficult terms, confusing rules, and papers marked in red. However, grammar is more than a set of rules to be followed or broken. It is a system that describes how language works—how we use words and sentences to construct meaning and express our ideas.

Without question, grammar can be complicated, but it has its practical side. By understanding just a few basics, you can begin to eliminate surface errors and improve your writing. The ability to communicate in clear, correct language is an asset not only in college but also in the workplace. Employers in every field value effective communication skills, and most require job applicants to have them.

Unit 4 does not cover every aspect of grammar. It focuses instead on the skills you need now and the problems that are most likely to trouble you as a beginning writer. To get the most you can out of Unit 4, think of grammar as another facet of the writing process. For example, Units 1 and 2 describe writing as a series of choices you make about your purpose, audience, thesis, evidence, and organization. Grammar introduces another set of choices about what words to use, how to put them together in sentences, how to connect ideas, and how to correct errors. The more choices you have as a writer, the more selective you can be.

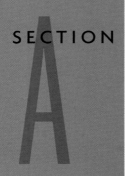
Basic Choices:
The Parts of Speech

A review of the parts of speech will prepare you for the rest of the topics covered in Unit 4. Words are the most basic units of meaning. Each word in a sentence functions as one of eight parts of speech: *nouns, pronouns, verbs, adjectives, adverbs, prepositions, conjunctions,* and *interjections.* How a word is used determines what part of speech it is. Knowing the parts of speech and how they function helps you to select the right words and put them together correctly. During the revision process, if you can identify the parts of speech within a sentence that is giving you difficulty, you may be able to figure out what is wrong and improve your sentence by making better choices.

A.1 Nouns

You learned long ago that a noun is the name of a person, place, or thing. Nouns also name ideas. See the following chart for examples.

Nouns can change their gender (actor, actress) and number (dog, dogs). Nouns have a *subjective case,* meaning they refer to the person, place, thing, or idea itself, as in "Harry." Nouns also have a *possessive case,* meaning they suggest ownership, as in "Harry's."

Nouns are classified into five categories. (1) *Proper names* are specific and are always capitalized, as in *General Colin Powell, Lake Michigan,* and *AT&T.* (2) *Common nouns* are general and are not capitalized, as in *teachers, country,* and *cookware.* (3) *Collective nouns* refer to groups, such as *team, squad, club,* and *committee.* (4) *Abstract nouns* name ideas, such as *kindness, humor,* and *respect.* (5) *Concrete nouns* name things you can experience through your five senses, such as *cookie, music,* and *fragrance.* Read the following two sentences in which the nouns are labeled.

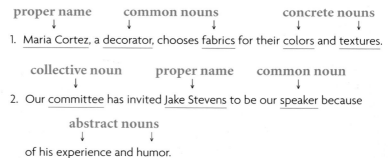

proper name   common nouns   concrete nouns

1. Maria Cortez, a decorator, chooses fabrics for their colors and textures.

collective noun   proper name   common noun

2. Our committee has invited Jake Stevens to be our speaker because

abstract nouns

of his experience and humor.

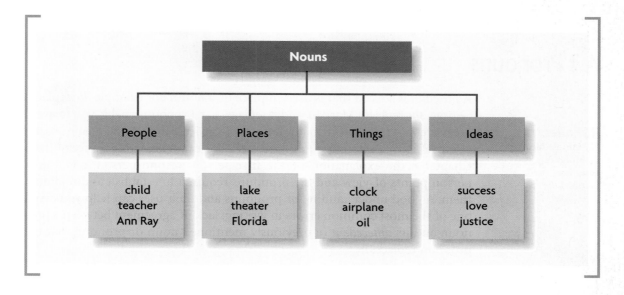

Why is it important to know that nouns have gender, number, case, and categories? These qualities of nouns are essential to your understanding of other grammatical concepts covered in Unit 4. For example, number is an essential part of subject-verb agreement. Case and number are essential parts of pronoun-antecedent agreement. Knowing the gender and categories of nouns can help you make more precise, accurate, and effective word choices and may also help you determine the reasoning behind an author's word choices.

[Exercise 1] Use what you have learned about the categories of nouns to complete the following sentences. The first one is done as an example.

1. I am a member of the chess _____*club*_____. (collective noun)
2. Adam's _*justice*_ is a quality I admire. (abstract noun)
3. _*Madrid*_ is a place I enjoy visiting. (proper name)
4. My desk is littered with _*pencils*_, _*pens*_, and _*papers*_. (common nouns)
5. For holiday dinners, we often serve _*hot-dogs*_ and _*hamburgueses*_. (concrete nouns)
6. Ed is captain of the football _*team*_. (collective noun)

[Exercise 2]

Examine a paragraph from one of your returned papers. Identify and circle all the nouns in the paragraph. Determine the category of each noun and decide whether your choices could be improved. Compare your results with those of a partner.

A.2 Pronouns

✓ CONCEPT CHECK
For more information on pronoun-antecedent agreement, see Section D.1.

A *pronoun* is a word that is used in place of a noun. For example, *he* replaces George, *she* replaces Mary Jo, and *it* replaces car. Pronouns enable you to avoid excessive repetition of the names of people, places, and things. Pronouns are also useful in maintaining point of view. For example, you may recall from Chapter 8 the explanation of the first-person, second-person, and third-person points of view and the pronouns required to establish and maintain them. A good understanding of pronouns and their uses can help you avoid one of the most common errors in writing: lack of agreement between a pronoun and its *antecedent* (a previously mentioned noun or pronoun that the pronoun replaces).

Characteristics of Pronouns

The four characteristics of pronouns are *person, gender, number,* and *case.* For example, the pronoun *she* is a third-person pronoun, it expresses the female gender, and it refers to one person. As you can see, *person* identifies the pronoun, *gender* describes the sex of the pronoun, and *number* classifies the pronoun as singular or plural. A pronoun's case indicates how it is used in a sentence, as in the following examples.

- She threw the ball.
- She threw it.
- She threw his ball over the fence.

In the first sentence, *she* is in the *subjective case* because *she* is the subject of the sentence: the one who performs an action. In the second sentence, *it* is in the *objective case* because this pronoun receives the verb's action. In the third sentence, *his* is in the *possessive case* because this pronoun indicates ownership.

Types of Pronouns

To select the right pronoun, ask yourself two questions: (1) What is the pronoun's case or function in the sentence? (2) What are the person, gender, and number of the noun or pronoun (antecedent) that the pronoun either refers to or replaces? In addition, being able to identify a pronoun's type may aid your selection. Pronouns are classified into eight types: *personal, possessive, demonstrative, reflexive, intensive, interrogative, relative,* and *indefinite.* Figure A-2.1, page 392, lists the types of pronouns with explanations, examples, and uses.

[**Exercise 3**] To check your understanding of pronouns, read the following paragraph and answer the questions that follow it. Use Figure A-2.1 as a reference.

(1) Ellen wanted to do something different, so she decided to ask a friend to go with her to Busch Gardens. (2) Ellen's friend, Soo Yin, asked, "What is there to do at Busch Gardens?" (3) Ellen told her that the attraction had rides, jungle animals, food, and souvenirs. (4) "Those should be enough to keep us entertained," said Soo Yin. (5) "In fact," she said, "I'm always ready to do whatever comes along." (6) When they arrived at the gate, they saw some friends. (7) Ellen and Soo Yin decided to join them. (8) Then Soo Yin remembered that she had left her sweater in the car. (9) The air was a little chilly, and Ellen said, "Would you bring mine too?" (10) In a few minutes they caught up with the rest of the group, and everyone had a good time. (11) Ellen herself was glad she had suggested the trip.

1. List the personal pronouns in sentence 1.

2. Identify the interrogative pronoun in sentence 2.

3. To what group of words does *that* refer in sentence 3?

4. What kind of pronoun is *those* in sentence 4, and to what does it refer?

5. What are the antecedents of *she* (sentence 5), *they* (sentence 6), and *them* (sentence 7)?

6. Find the relative pronoun in sentence 5.

7. Find the possessive pronouns in sentences 8 and 9.

Figure A-2.1 Types of Pronouns

PRONOUN TYPE	EXPLANATION	EXAMPLES	USE
Personal	They replace nouns that name people or things.	I, you, he, she, it, we, they, me, him, her, us, them	Susan, the gift is perfect. I sent you a note about it.
Possessive	These pronouns show ownership.	my, mine, your, yours, his, hers, its, our, ours, their, theirs	This gift is yours. The other one is mine.
Demonstrative	They refer to certain people or things.	this, that, these, those	Whose book is this? (This refers to book.)
Reflexive	They indicate the subject (person or thing) acting on, by, or for itself.	myself, yourself, himself, herself, itself, ourselves, yourselves, themselves	John cut himself a piece of cake.
Intensive	The intensive pronoun is a reflexive pronoun used for emphasis.	any reflexive pronoun with its antecedent in the same sentence	Stephen King himself spoke at our convention.
Interrogative	These pronouns are for asking questions.	who, whom, whoever, whomever, what, which, whose	Which one should I open first?
Relative	The relative pronouns are the same as the interrogatives but are used to relate groups of words to a noun or pronoun.	For people: who, whom, whoever, whomever, whose; For things: that, what, which, whatever	Where is the present that you gave me? Joe invited Carlos, who is my best friend.
Indefinite*	These pronouns have no antecedents but refer to people or things in general.	someone, many, few, another, everything, any, neither, most, something, all, both	I would love to date him, but I belong to another.

*For a more complete list of examples, see Figure D-1.2, page 451.

8. What is the indefinite pronoun in sentence 10?

9. What kind of pronoun is *herself* in sentence 11?

10. In which sentence do you find a second-person pronoun, and what is the pronoun?

A.3 Verbs

A *verb* is a word that expresses an action or a state of being. For example, *walk* is an action. You can visualize someone walking. On the other hand, *feel* and *seem* are verbs that describe states of being or conditions, as in these sentences:

- The child <u>seems</u> happy.
- I <u>feel</u> tired today.

Notice the words on either side of the verbs in these sentences. The noun *child* and the pronoun *I* tell you whose condition is being described. The words *happy* and *tired* tell you what each condition is.

Types of Verbs

Verbs like *walk* are called <u>*action verbs*</u>. Verbs like *seem* and *feel* are called <u>*linking verbs*</u> because they link, or connect, the noun or pronoun with the words that describe it. In addition to action verbs and linking verbs, there are <u>*helping verbs*</u>, which are also called *auxiliary verbs*.

Helping verbs have two functions: Used with a main verb, a helping verb can express tense (the time an action or condition occurs) or form a question, as in the following examples:

- I <u>have</u> mailed the letter. (a past action)
- <u>Have</u> you mailed the letter? (a question)

To be complete, a sentence must have at least one verb. Leaving out the verb can result in a *fragment*, or incomplete sentence, one of the common types of errors students make. Therefore, it is important to recognize verbs. Figure A-3.1 lists the three types of verbs and a few examples of each.

Figure A-3.1 Types of Verbs

Action verbs	walk, run, see, fly, put, sit, catch, follow, flow, sing, dictate, deliver
Linking verbs	all forms of *to be* (is, am, are, was, were, be, being, been), become, feel, grow, look, remain, seem
Helping verbs	all forms of *to be,* have, has, had, do, does, did, can, could, may, might, must, shall, should, will, would

Verb Tense

Tense refers to the time period a verb represents, such as past, present, or future. Figure A-3.2 on page 395 gives examples of all the verb tenses. You do not need to memorize the grammatical terms for the tenses. They are listed here only to help you see that all the tenses except the simple present, past, and future require some form of the verbs *to be* or *to have* as helping verbs that precede the main verb.

A verb can be *regular* or *irregular*. *Regular verbs* form the past tense and the past participle—the form of the verb used with auxiliary verbs in the present perfect, past perfect, and future perfect tenses—by adding *-d* or *-ed* to the simple verb form:

Simple Verb	Simple Past Tense	Past Participle
expire	expir<u>ed</u>	expir<u>ed</u>
offend	offend<u>ed</u>	offend<u>ed</u>

Irregular verbs do not form the simple past tense and the past participle by adding *-d* or *-ed*. Instead, they change their spelling, often by changing an internal vowel:

Simple Verb	Simple Past Tense	Past Participle
f<u>ee</u>l	f<u>e</u>lt	f<u>e</u>lt
r<u>i</u>ng	r<u>a</u>ng	r<u>u</u>ng
br<u>i</u>ng	br<u>ough</u>t	br<u>ough</u>t

Figure A-3.3 on page 396 lists some common irregular verbs with their simple past and past-participle forms.

[**Exercise 4**] In each of the following sentences, the verb is in the present tense. First, circle the verb in each sentence. Then rewrite the sentence in the tense indicated in parentheses. Use Figures A-3.2 and A-3.3 as needed for reference. The first sentence is done as an example.

1. I ⟨take⟩ the math test. (simple future)

   I will take the math test next week.

2. The sculptor molds statues out of clay. (simple past)

3. The plane arrives at 8:00 P.M. (present progressive)

4. The Stuart Gallery shows the work of local artists. (present perfect)

5. Stephen King writes *Misery*. (past perfect)

6. The secretary types the letter. (past perfect progressive)

7. I lie on the couch in the afternoon. (simple past)

Figure A-3.2 Verb Tenses

TENSE	EXAMPLE (REGULAR VERBS)
Simple present	I *applaud.*
Simple past	I *applauded* yesterday.
Simple future	I *will applaud* this afternoon.
Present perfect	I *have applauded* before.
Past perfect	I *had applauded* for several days.
Future perfect	By tomorrow I *will have applauded* for twenty-two hours.
Present progressive	I *am applauding* now.
Past progressive	I *was applauding* last week.
Future progressive	I *will be applauding* when I go on vacation next month.
Present perfect progressive	I *have been applauding* all night.
Past perfect progressive	Before we left the theater, I *had been applauding* the actors.
Future perfect progressive	By the time you leave the theater, I *will have been applauding* for several minutes.

8. The photographer develops his own film. (past progressive)

9. My sister goes to church each Sunday. (simple future)

10. We choose only the ripest pears. (future progressive)

[**Exercise 5**] In the following paragraph, fill in the past tense form of the verb in parentheses.

1 I _____ (write) a letter to my cousin last week asking her to come for a visit. 2 When she arrived, the sun was shining, and we _____ (hope) the weather would stay nice. 3 The next day, however, clouds _____ (begin) to form. 4 Then we _____ (hear) on the radio that a hurricane was coming. 5 We headed to the store and _____ (buy) bottled water and batteries. 6 When the rain _____ (start), we were watching TV. 7 After a few minutes, the electricity _____ (go) off. 8 We _____ (have) no power for several hours. 9 After the storm _____ (pass), we checked the house for damage. 10 We were surprised that only a few roofing shingles _____ (blow) off in the high wind.

Figure A-3.3 Some Common Irregular Verbs

SIMPLE VERB	SIMPLE PAST TENSE	PAST PARTICIPLE
arise	arose	arisen
become	became	become
begin	began	begun
blow	blew	blown
break	broke	broken
build	built	built
choose	chose	chosen
cost	cost	cost
do	did	done
draw	drew	drawn
drink	drank	drunk
eat	ate	eaten
feed	fed	fed
fight	fought	fought
fly	flew	flown
give	gave	given
have	had	had
hold	held	held
keep	kept	kept
know	knew	known
lay (to place)	laid	laid
lead	led	led
lie (to recline)	lay	lain
ride	rode	ridden
see	saw	seen
shake	shook	shaken
steal	stole	stolen
take	took	taken

A.4 Adjectives and Adverbs

Adjectives modify, or change, the meanings of nouns and pronouns by explaining what kind, which one, how many, or whose. Read the following sentences from Langston Hughes's "Salvation," and notice what the adjectives in bold type tell you about the words they modify.

What kind?	"The preacher preached a **wonderful rhythmical** sermon, all moans and shouts and lonely cries and dire pictures of hell. . . ."
Which one?	"**That** night, for the last time in my life but one—for I was a big boy twelve years old—I cried."
How many?	"And **some** of them jumped up and went to Jesus right away. But **most** of us just sat there."
Whose?	"**My** aunt told me that when you were saved you saw a light, and something happened to you inside!"

Adverbs modify the meaning of verbs, adjectives, and other adverbs by explaining how, when, where, how often, or to what extent. Notice how Langston Hughes uses the following adverbs in "Salvation."

How?	"So I sat there **calmly** in the hot, crowded church, waiting for Jesus to come to me."
When?	"Then just **before** the revival ended, they held a special meeting for children. . . ."
Where?	"And he held out his arms to all of us young sinners **there** on the mourner's bench."
How often?	"I began to be ashamed of myself, holding everything up **so long.**"
To what extent?	". . . I didn't believe there was a Jesus **any more,** since he didn't come to help me."

Suppose you want to make a judgment that one job is more interesting than another, or one boss is easier to work with than another, or a decision to change jobs was the hardest one you have ever made. To write about these judgments, you will use *degrees of comparison.* Adjectives and adverbs have three degrees of comparison: positive, comparative, and superlative:

Positive	To make no comparison	The job is *hard.*
Comparative	To compare two things: use *-er, more,* or *less*	This job is *harder* than that one. My job is *more* difficult than yours.
Superlative	To compare three or more things: use *-est, most,* or *least*	This is the *easiest* job I have ever had. This job is the *least* difficult one.

Now practice using adjectives, adverbs, and degrees of comparison by completing the next two exercises.

[Exercise 6] Read the following paragraph. Fill in the blanks with the proper adjectives and comparative forms. Choose from the list below:

dusty	darkest	bright	sharper	paler
youngest	quiet	narrow	healthiest	unfortunate
scariest	palest	musty	small	

Count Dracula lived in a 1 _____, _____ castle in a 2 _____ town in Hungary called Transylvania. Dracula was the 3 _____ vampire of them all. During the day, he slept in his 4 _____ box of earth because he could not stand the 5 _____ sunlight. At night he would roam the village looking for his most 6 _____ victims, the 7 _____ and 8 _____ women, who would become his brides. He would drink their blood by piercing two 9 _____ holes in their necks with fangs 10 _____ than steel. He might visit the same victim several nights in a row. The morning after the first bite, she would be drained of color. The next morning someone might say to her, "You have a 11 _____ face than usual." When the victim died from the loss of blood, someone would be sure to say, "That is the 12 _____ face I've ever seen." Of course the story of Count Dracula is only a legend, so you need not be afraid to go out even on the 13 _____ night.

[Exercise 7] Read the following paragraph. Fill in the blanks with the proper adverbs and comparative forms. Choose from the list below:

slowly	carelessly	more easily	regularly
usually	carefully	more efficiently	lately
really	harder	extremely	

Andrea 1 _____ did well in math, but 2 _____ she was having trouble in her algebra class. She had not done the homework 3 _____, so she was getting behind. Algebra was not an easy course for her. Maybe she needed to learn how to study 4 _____. Then she could do her homework 5 _____ and start to make better grades. Her instructor suggested that she work 6 _____ and 7 _____ when doing practice problems and proofread her work. He suggested that Andrea's errors came from working 8 _____. "You are 9 _____ quiet in class; perhaps you need to ask more questions," he said. "Well, there are some things I don't 10 _____ understand," Andrea answered. She decided to try 11 _____ to get over her fear of speaking in class.

Figure A-4.1 Comparison of Irregular Adjectives and Adverbs

POSITIVE	COMPARATIVE	SUPERLATIVE
bad	worse	worst
good	better	best
little	less	least
many	more	most
much	more	most
some	more	most

Irregular Adjectives and Adverbs

Some adjectives and adverbs are *irregular;* that is, their comparative and superlative degrees are not formed in the usual way. Figure A-4.1 above lists the comparative and superlative degrees of some common irregular adjectives and adverbs. Words that have no comparative degrees are *unique, dead,* and *perfect.* Something that is unique is one of a kind. Since it takes two to make a comparison, it is not possible for something that is one of a kind to be more or less unique. Similarly, it is not correct to say *this is the most perfect day I have ever seen.* The day is either perfect or not perfect; there is no degree of perfection. You may have heard the cliché "deader than a doornail." Not only is it a worn-out phrase, it is also illogical. Dead is dead; whatever is not dead is alive.

[**Exercise 8**] Examine a piece of your own writing, either an essay that has been marked and returned to you or some work in progress. Underline all the adjectives and adverbs in one of your paragraphs. Correct any comparative forms that you have used incorrectly. Substitute better, more precise, or more interesting adjectives and adverbs for the ones you have underlined.

[**Exercise 9**] Read the following paragraph and edit it for incorrect use of adjectives and adverbs.

It is more easier to flunk a course than to pass it if you remember three things: attendance, grades, and social life. First of all, when you wake up in the morning, just stay in bed. Something is sure to happen in class that will ruin your day. Since it is most beneficial to stay home or go to the beach than to attend class, your absence will put you more farther along the road to failure. Also, forget grades.

Grades make you sweat. Getting good grades takes more harder work than making F's. You can make an F without any effort at all. Finally, everyone needs a social life. That is the most importantest reason for attending college in the first place. There is a newest saying that applies here: Pass up a party and pass a test. Of course, if you insist on being a confident, successful student, just ignore everything I have said.

A.5 Prepositions

A *preposition* is one of many common words such as *in, out, over, under, beside,* or *within.* A *prepositional phrase* is a group of words that consists of a preposition plus its *object* (noun or pronoun). Prepositions and prepositional phrases link the object to the rest of the sentence. Prepositions have three characteristics.

1. They show relationships of time, space, direction, and condition.

>   prep. object
> The art festival occurs <u>in</u> the <u>spring</u>. (time)

>   prep. object
> You can sit <u>between</u> <u>us</u>. (space)

>   prep.   object
> He sunk the ball <u>through</u> the <u>hoop</u>. (direction)

>   prep. object
> I like all vegetables <u>except</u> <u>broccoli</u>. (condition)

2. A preposition usually comes before its object, as in the example sentences just given. However, in some sentences the preposition follows the object, as in the next two sentences.

> object   prep.
> <u>Love</u> is something I cannot do <u>without</u>.

> object prep.
> Would you please let the <u>cat</u> <u>in</u>?

3. Prepositions that consist of more than one word are called *compound prepositions.* See Figure A-5.1 on page 401 for a list of some common and compound prepositions.

>   compound prep. object
> The game was called <u>because of</u> <u>rain</u>. (condition)

[**Exercise 10**] Underline prepositional phrases and label prepositions and objects in the following sentences. In addition, explain the relationship each preposition or prepositional phrase suggests. The first one is done as an example.

                                                prep.   **object**

1. Some people like rare steak, but Lee is repelled by a cold red center.

    The prepositional phrase explains what Lee would be repelled by.

2. I do not like to see too much food heaped on my plate.

3. You will probably find your lost keys lying somewhere around the house.

4. Some hard candies are soft on the inside.

5. This fragrance reminds me of my grandmother's garden.

6. I found the receipt folded between the pages of the book I was reading.

7. You can find almost anything you want at the new supermarket.

8. This chocolate syrup tastes good over ice cream.

9. Don is well respected by his coworkers.

10. As far as I'm concerned, sunflower seeds are for the birds.

Figure A-5.1 Prepositions

COMMON PREPOSITIONS

against	beyond	off	toward
along	by	on	under
among	despite	onto	underneath
around	down	out	until
at	during	outside	up
before	except	over	upon
behind	for	past	with
below	from	since	within
beneath	in	through	without
beside	near	till	
between	of	to	

COMPOUND PREPOSITIONS

according to	due to	instead of
aside from	in addition to	on account of
as of	in front of	out of
as well as	in place of	prior to
because of	in regard to	with regard to
by means of	in spite of	with respect to

A.6 Conjunctions

A *conjunction* connects words, phrases, or clauses. A *phrase* is a group of words that lacks a subject, a predicate (verb plus auxiliaries), or both. A *clause* is a group of words that contains a subject and a predicate. Clauses, phrases, and the uses of conjunctions are explained in greater detail in Section B. For now, let's review three types of conjunctions that provide you with numerous choices for connecting your ideas: *coordinating, correlative,* and *subordinating.*

The *coordinating conjunctions* are easy to remember because there are only seven: *for, and, nor, but, or, yet,* and *so.* The acronym FANBOYS, made from their first letters, will help you remember them. These conjunctions connect words or word groups of the same kind, for example, two nouns, two verbs, or two *independent clauses* (word groups that contain a subject and a predicate and that can stand alone as complete in themselves). Coordinating conjunctions express relationships of addition, contrast, cause, effect, choice, and negative choice. To learn more about combining sentences with coordination, see Figure B-4.1 on page 415.

> We walk <u>and</u> swim each morning before breakfast. (*And* joins two verbs and relates them by *addition.*)
>
> You can take biology <u>or</u> physics to complete your program. (*Or* joins two nouns and relates them by *choice.*)
>
> I would like to go to the movies with you, <u>but</u> I have to study. (*But* joins two independent clauses and relates them by *contrast.*)

✔ CONCEPT CHECK
To learn more about correlation, see pages 452–453.

The *correlative conjunctions* work in pairs to link parts of a sentence that are alike. Some common correlative conjunctions are *either . . . or, neither . . . nor, both . . . and, not only . . . but also,* and *whether . . . or.*

> College graduates who can speak <u>both</u> English <u>and</u> another language may have an edge in tomorrow's workplace.
>
> <u>Either</u> I have gained weight, <u>or</u> this shirt has shrunk.

✔ CONCEPT CHECK
Sentence combining with subordination is explained in section B.5.

The *subordinating conjunctions* introduce *dependent clauses* (those that cannot stand alone as sentences) and connect clauses. Subordinating conjunctions include such words as *after, because, that, if, although,* and *where.* Subordinating conjunctions express relationships of time, cause, effect, condition, contrast, location, and choice.

> <u>Although</u> I want to go to the party, I have studying to do. (The clauses are related by *contrast.*)
>
> You can usually find a fast-food restaurant <u>wherever</u> you travel in the United States. (The clauses are related by *location.*)

A.7 Interjections

An *interjection* is a word or expression that indicates surprise or another strong emotion. When it stands alone, the interjection is punctuated with an exclamation point. Within a sentence, an interjection is set off by one or more commas. In formal writing, you should use interjections sparingly, if at all.

> Wow! You look great.
> Oh, it's you.
> So, what else is new?
> Hooray! I got an A on the test.
> Well, I expected as much.

[Exercise 11] In the following paragraph, identify the part of speech for each numbered and underlined word. Choose from noun, pronoun, verb, adjective, adverb, preposition, conjunction, or interjection.

Savannah, Georgia, is a great place to spend a weekend. Several hotels and inns along[1] the river offer tourists many opportunities for shopping and dining. Whether you[2] want a quick snack or a leisurely meal, you can find a restaurant to suit your budget. The riverfront shops offer everything from the usual t-shirts to the unusual custom kites and handcrafted[3] candles. If you have a sweet tooth, try[4] a pecan praline from one of several candy stores. Back at your hotel, step out on[5] the balcony to watch the huge oil tankers and barges slowly[6] navigate the river. If outdoor activities are your passion[7], rent a bicycle and pedal around Savannah's quaint squares or spend a day at the beach. If tours turn you on, visit historic[8] mansions or the low country. Fans of John Berendt's bestseller *Midnight in the Garden of Good and Evil* will enjoy a tour that explores the book's points of interest. As one traveler remarked, "Oh[9], I've been here eleven times, and[10] I still haven't seen it all."

Sentence Effectiveness Choices

A *sentence* is a group of words that starts with a capital letter and ends with a period, question mark, or exclamation point. A sentence is a basic unit of meaning that contains a subject and a predicate. A sentence is an *independent clause* that can stand alone as a unit of meaning. A sentence is a group of words, complete in itself, that needs no further explanation. These definitions describe the parts and functions of a sentence. You can also define a sentence by purpose and type.

Three things determine the effectiveness of your sentences: (1) the way you put together the parts of a sentence, (2) your choice of sentence types that can add interest and variety to your writing, and (3) your identification and elimination of surface errors that interfere with communication.

B.1 Sentence Parts, Purposes, and Types

A sentence has two basic parts: the *subject* and the *predicate*. To be complete, a sentence must have at least one subject and one predicate. The *subject* tells who or what the sentence is about. A sentence may have a *simple subject* (one) or a *compound subject* (more than one). The simple subject plus its modifiers is called the *complete subject*. The *predicate* tells what the subject is doing, what is happening to the subject, or what state of being the subject is in. The predicate contains one or more verbs and may include auxiliary (helping) verbs such as *has* or *have*. The *simple predicate* consists of the main verb plus auxiliaries. The *compound predicate* consists of two or more verbs joined by a conjunction.

In the following example sentences, subjects and predicates are underlined and annotated.

simple   simple
  sub.   pred.
  Jade laughed.

compound   simple
    sub.   pred.
Jade and Jake were laughing.

compound   compound
    sub.   pred.
Jade and Jake laughed and talked incessantly.

    complete   simple
      sub.   pred.
The happy young couple decided to buy a house.

Purposes of Sentences

Sentences are classified according to purpose as indicated in Figure B-1.1 on the following page.

[**Exercise 12**] Underline and label the subjects **(s)** and predicates **(p)** in each of the following sentences.

1. Diana Ross and the Supremes performed throughout the United States and the world.

2. Today many fans of Elvis Presley still celebrate his birthday on January 8.

3. Every generation has its own music.

4. Music brings people together and gives them something in common to share.

Figure B-1.1 Purposes of the Sentence

PURPOSE	EXPLANATION	EXAMPLE
Declarative	To make a statement	Tennis is a popular sport.
Interrogative	To ask a question	Do you play tennis?
Imperative	To make a request or give a command	Wear proper clothing on the court.
Exclamatory	To express strong feeling	What a great serve!

5. However, generations can be torn apart by differences of opinion concerning music.

6. Music appreciation courses explore different types of music and teach students how to evaluate them.

7. Many World War II generation parents cannot understand their children's music.

8. Similarly, their children often do not respond to music from the big band era.

9. Country music, on the other hand, has enjoyed a cross-generational appeal.

10. Who knows what the next musical trend will be?

Types of Sentences

Sentences are made up of *clauses* and *phrases* (word groups). Clauses can be *independent* or *dependent*. An independent clause contains a subject and a predicate and can stand alone as a unit of meaning. A dependent clause also contains a subject and a predicate, but it cannot stand alone. It must be connected to an independent clause to make complete sense. A *phrase* is a group of words that does not contain a subject and a predicate. The number of clauses and how they are connected determines the sentence type. There are four types of sentences: *simple, compound, complex,* and *compound-complex.*

Simple Sentence This type of sentence has one independent clause that contains at least one subject and one predicate. It may also contain one or more phrases.

s   p
Snow melts.
independent clause

                         s   compound pred.
In mud season, the snow melts and becomes slushy and dirty.
      phrase   **independent clause**

Compound Sentence This type of sentence has at least two independent clauses but no dependent clauses. The clauses can be joined in three ways: with a comma plus a coordinating conjunction (*and, but, nor, or, for, so,* or *yet*), with a semicolon and no conjunction, or with a semicolon plus a conjunctive adverb (such as *however, next,* or *instead*) followed by a comma. For more on compound sentences, see sections B.4, B.6, and C.5.

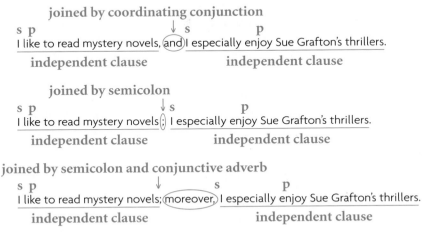

Complex Sentence This type of sentence has one independent clause and one or more dependent clauses. In a complex sentence, a subordinating conjunction (such as *after, although,* or *since*) or a relative pronoun (such as *who, whom, that,* or *what*) is used to connect clauses. For more on complex sentences, see sections B.5 and B.6.

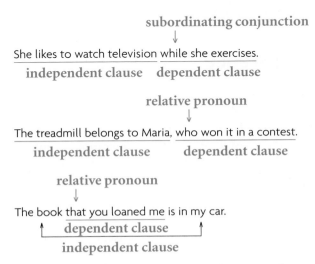

Compound-Complex Sentence This type of sentence has at least two independent clauses and one or more dependent clauses.

subordinating conjunction   coordinating conjunction
↓   ↓
While my father was in the hospital, he quit smoking, and he lost several pounds.
dependent clause   independent clause   independent clause

[**Exercise 13**] Apply what you have learned about independent and dependent clauses and sentence types. Combine each pair of sentences into one sentence. The first one is done as an example.

1. The forecast is for warm dry weather.
   I think I will go to the beach.

   The forecast is for warm dry weather, so I think I will go

   to the beach.

2. Terry sings in the church choir.
   Terry plays a clarinet in the university band.

3. My car has 50,000 miles on it.
   My car is in perfect shape.

4. Chris fought learning to use a computer.
   Chris couldn't get along without one now.

5. The concert was canceled.
   Hundreds of angry fans protested.

6. I am definitely not a morning person.
   Eight A.M. classes are not for me.

B.2 Eliminating Sentence Fragments

Clear and complete sentences are essential to good writing. Complete sentences communicate ideas effectively; incomplete sentences do not. Being able to recognize an incomplete sentence and knowing how to correct it will make you a more confident writer. An incomplete sentence is called a *fragment* because it is only part of an idea and is not complete in itself. Read the following fragment:

Because I could not get up this morning.

This fragment is a dependent clause. By itself, it does not express a complete thought. If you were to walk up to a friend of yours and say, "Because I couldn't get up this morning," your friend would probably look puzzled and say something like "So?" or "Because of what?" Your friend would be left hanging because you had not completed your thought. To complete the thought, you must connect the fragment to an independent clause.

dependent clause   independent clause
Because I could not get up this morning, I was late for work.

independent clause   dependent clause
I missed breakfast because I could not get up this morning.

Three features make a sentence complete: a *subject,* a *verb (predicate),* and a *complete thought.* If one or more of these elements is missing, a fragment results. Remember that the *subject* tells *who* or *what* the sentence is about. The *verb* tells what the subject is doing or what the subject's state of being is. A thought is *complete* if it communicates an idea that needs no further explanation.

Relative pronouns such as *who, which, that,* and *what* and subordinating conjunctions such as *because, although,* and *while* often appear at the beginning of a dependent clause and serve to connect it to an independent clause. When you edit your essays, reread any sentence that begins with one of these words to check it for completeness. See the following examples:

What the dentist told me.

This is a dependent clause beginning with a relative pronoun, and it is a fragment.

What the dentist told me is to floss every day.

What the dentist told me is a dependent clause that acts as the *subject* of an independent clause, so the sentence is complete.

Although I am very tired.

A dependent clause that begins with a subordinating conjunction is a fragment.

Although I am very tired, I will go to the movie with you.

The dependent clause *although I am very tired* is now connected to an independent clause, so the sentence is complete.

Another way to correct dependent clause fragments such as the ones in these examples is to remove the relative pronoun or subordinating conjunction if the group of words that follows can stand by itself as a sentence:

A
~~That~~ a great place to take children is Disney World.
~~Although~~ I am very tired.

Now the sentences are complete because they contain a subject and a verb, and the ideas they express are complete in themselves.

Figure B-2.1 Identifying the Features of a Sentence

FEATURES	QUESTIONS TO ASK YOURSELF
Subject	*Who* or *what* is the sentence about?
Verb	What is the subject *doing, feeling,* or *being*? What is *happening* to the subject?
Complete thought	What *idea* is communicated? Is the idea *complete*? Does the sentence begin with a *subordinating conjunction* or a *relative pronoun: when, because, who*, etc.?

To correct a sentence fragment, determine whether you need to add a subject or a verb to complete the thought. Figure B-2.1 above lists features of a sentence and questions that can help identify them. Figure B-2.2 below shows you how to correct a fragment by adding the missing feature needed to make a complete sentence.

Exercise 14

For items 1–10 below, write F if the item is a fragment; write C if the item is a complete sentence.

_____ 1. Because many people do not like cold weather.

_____ 2. When my grandmother was growing up in Cuba.

_____ 3. No one knows how hard it was for me to get over losing my dog.

_____ 4. Too many cars for the few roads that we have in my community.

_____ 5. Holidays are my favorite times of the year.

Figure B-2.2 Making Fragments into Complete Sentences

FRAGMENT	WHAT IS MISSING?	COMPLETE SENTENCE
Tourists from all over the world.	A *verb* is missing. What do the tourists *do*?	Tourists from all over the world *come* to New Orleans.
Sing and dance in the streets.	A *subject* is missing. *Who* or *what* sing and dance?	*People* dressed in brightly colored costumes sing and dance in the streets.
When the King and Queen are crowned.	The *thought* is incomplete. What *explanation* is needed?	*Everyone celebrates* when the King and Queen are crowned.

_____ 6. For my birthday a trip to the Canadian Rockies.

_____ 7. *Love in the Time of Cholera* both a book and a film.

_____ 8. Who knew that we would go so long without rain?

_____ 9. Although athletic shoes come in many styles and colors.

_____ 10. Whenever they get a day off from work.

[Exercise 15] Test each of the word groups below for completeness. If a word group is a complete sentence, leave it alone. If you find any fragments, rewrite them to make them into complete sentences.

1. Because the car had 80,000 miles on it.

2. She needed to return the books to the library.

3. Such as hunting, fishing, and hiking.

4. That met in the auditorium last week.

5. So many obligations and responsibilities.

6. Working and attending classes at the same time.

7. What the dog needed most.

8. Not wanting to let them down.

9. Since he had always been a procrastinator.

10. If you do not study for the exam.

[Exercise 16] The following paragraph contains five sentence fragments. Underline them, decide what is missing, then rewrite the paragraph so that there are no fragments.

Luis and Silvana went mountain climbing in the Andes. Their trip took three weeks. They had to plan ahead and take enough food, water, and other supplies. Because there were no stores where they were going. They, another couple, and their two guides could not carry enough supplies for the six of them. A helicopter to drop off supplies at certain points along the way. Temperatures were often below zero. At night, they had to build a wall of snow to protect their tents from the wind. Once when Luis was walking across a frozen river. The ice cracked, and he fell into the freezing water. Silvana and the others helped him remove his wet clothes. Wrapped him in sleeping bags until his clothes could dry, and then they resumed their journey. At the top of the mountain, they laughed, cried, and hugged each other. Rested before the long trip back down.

B.3 Eliminating Fused Sentences and Comma Splices

When you edit your essays, you need to proofread them to find and correct any errors. Two errors to check for are the *fused sentence* and the *comma splice*. You should strive to eliminate these errors from *all* your writing. A *fused sentence* is one that contains two or more independent clauses without any mark of punctuation to separate them. Read the next sentence:

> Yvette spent the whole day registering for classes she did not even have time for lunch.

A *comma splice* error occurs when one sentence contains two or more independent clauses, and they are incorrectly separated by a comma. Read the sentence again.

> Yvette spent the whole day registering for classes, she did not even have time for lunch.

With or without the comma, the sentence expresses *two* complete thoughts:

1. Yvette spent the whole day registering for classes.

2. She did not even have time for lunch.

One way to correct a fused sentence or to eliminate a comma splice is to *state each complete thought in a separate sentence,* as in the previous example. However, if you think it would be more effective to express both these ideas about Yvette in one sentence, there is a correct way to connect them. The chart in Figure B-3.1 on page 413 explains five ways to correct fused sentences and comma splices.

☑ **CONCEPT CHECK**
For more information on conjunctions and how to use them, see Sections B4 and B5.

As a writer, you are free to choose the method of correction that you prefer. Do not get stuck on any one method, however. To add some variety to your writing, experiment with all the ways to correct your sentences. It *does* matter which conjunctions or relative pronouns you use to connect two complete thoughts or to connect a dependent clause to an independent clause. For one thing, determine how one thought relates to another; also, learn what each conjunction means so that you can choose the best one.

[Exercise 17]   The first sentence below is a fused sentence; the second one contains a comma splice. Rewrite each sentence five different ways so that you can try all five ways to correct the sentences. When you finish, you will have a total of ten sentences. Refer to the chart in Figure B-3.1 for help.

1. Mark stayed up all night cramming for a statistics test it didn't cover what he had studied.

2. Linda was well prepared for the test, she was sure she had made an A or a B.

Figure B-3.1 Five Ways to Correct Fused Sentences and Comma Splices

1. Use a period to separate complete thoughts within a fused sentence or a sentence containing a comma splice.

Fused:	Reynaldo got off the Metro at the wrong stop he had to walk several blocks to the museum.
Comma splice:	Reynaldo got off the Metro at the wrong stop, he had to walk several blocks to the museum.
Correct:	Reynaldo got off the Metro at the wrong stop. He had to walk several blocks to the museum.

2. Make a compound sentence by using a comma + a coordinating conjunction (*for, and, nor, but, or, yet, so*) to connect complete thoughts.

   Reynaldo got off the Metro at the wrong stop, **so** he had to walk several blocks to the museum.

3. Make a compound sentence by using a semicolon to connect complete thoughts that are closely related.

   Reynaldo got off the Metro at the wrong stop; he had to walk several blocks to the museum.

4. Make a compound sentence by using a semicolon + conjunctive adverb + comma to connect complete thoughts. (*However, therefore, furthermore, instead, in addition, also, moreover, as a result, consequently,* etc., are conjunctive adverbs.)

   Reynaldo got off the Metro at the wrong stop; **therefore,** he had to walk several blocks to the museum.

5. Make a complex sentence by using a subordinating conjunction (*because, since, although, after, when, before, until, as, that, if, unless*) or a relative pronoun (*who, which, that*) to create a dependent clause and connect it to the independent clause.

   First use a subordinating conjunction to create a dependent clause:

   Because Reynaldo got off the Metro at the wrong stop . . .

   Then connect the dependent clause to the independent clause:

   Because Reynaldo got off the Metro at the wrong stop, he had to walk several blocks to the museum.

   HINT: Always put a comma after the dependent clause when you connect it to an independent clause that follows it.

[**Exercise 18**]   Read the following paragraph and edit it for fused sentences and comma splices.

The electricity went off at my house several inconvenient things happened. My clock is electric, so the alarm did not go off luckily I wake up at about 5:30 every morning anyway. I had to take a cold shower, that was not the worst of it I could not use my blow dryer. "A good breakfast will make up for everything," I thought. I had forgotten that the stove and coffeemaker would not work without electricity, I had to go to class without my coffee. It looked like rain outside, but there was no way to know for sure I could not tune in The Weather Channel on TV. On the way to work, I realized that I take electricity and many other things I use every day for granted I expect them to always be there. Now our state officials are telling us we have to conserve water I have already started.

B.4 Sentence Combining: Coordination

As you revise your essays, you may find opportunities for sentence combining. Sometimes the ideas expressed in two separate sentences could be stated more effectively in a compound sentence that combines the ideas. One way to create a compound sentence is by *coordination.* The term *coordination* comes from a Latin word meaning "of equal rank." When you use coordination to combine independent clauses of equal importance, you join them with connecting words called *coordinating conjunctions.*

There are seven coordinating conjunctions: *for, and, nor, but, or, yet,* and *so.* Each of the coordinating conjunctions establishes a different relationship between the independent clauses. Your choice of which coordinating conjunction to use thus depends on the relationship you want to express. For example, *for* and *so* establish a cause-and-effect relationship. *For* introduces a reason; *so* introduces a result. Suppose you wrote the following two sentences:

1. Today would be a good day to go to the beach.

2. The weather is clear and sunny.

You can combine the sentences to establish a cause-and-effect relationship between the weather and a good day at the beach by joining them with either *for* or *so:*

reason

1. Today would be a good day to go to the beach, <u>for</u> the weather is clear and sunny.

result

2. The weather is clear and sunny, <u>so</u> today would be a good day to go to the beach.

CONCEPT CHECK
How many of the rules for using commas do you know? See section C.6 for comma rules.

In each sentence, the good weather is the *cause,* or reason; the *effect,* or result, of the good weather is that today is a good day to go to the beach.

Note that both sentences have a *comma* before the coordinating conjunction. When you use a coordinating conjunction to combine independent clauses, *put a comma before the coordinating conjunction.* This is rule 5 of the six rules for using commas explained in section C.6 on page 439.

Figure B-4.1 on page 415 shows how to use the seven coordinating conjunctions. Study the chart, paying special attention to the relationship each

Figure B-4.1 Coordinating Conjunctions and Sentence Relationships

CONJUNCTION	RELATIONSHIP	EXAMPLE SENTENCE
For	Cause and effect (reason)	Lupe was excited about the party, for she had not been to one in a long time. (The fact that Lupe had not been to a party in a while was the *cause* of her excitement.)
And	Addition	Carlos and Janet gave a party, and they invited all their friends. (Giving a party and inviting friends *add* up to two *equally* important things that Carlos and Janet did.)
Nor	No choice	Jackie said she didn't want to eat inside, nor did she want to eat outside. (Jackie made *no choice* between eating inside or outside.)
But	Exception, contrast	Kurt hoped that he would be back in town in time for the party, but he did not think he could make it. (The fact that Kurt did not think he could make it is an *exception* to his hope that he would.)
Or	Choice	Party guests could select items from the buffet and eat inside, or they could take their food outside. (Guests could make a *choice* to eat either inside or outside.)
Yet	Exception, contrast	Lucious said he would not be at the party, yet he showed up anyway. (Lucious came to the party *in contrast* to what he said.)
So	Cause and effect (result)	Jack arrived at the party fifteen minutes before it was scheduled to begin, so he was the first one there. (Being the first one at the party was the *result* of arriving fifteen minutes early.)

conjunction creates between the two independent clauses in each sentence. Then complete Exercises 19 and 20.

[Exercise 19] Combine each pair of sentences below into one sentence. First, decide how the sentences are related. Then connect them by using an appropriate coordinating conjunction. Refer to Figure B-4.1 if you need help remembering the conjunctions or the relationships they imply.

1. Robert B. Parker is a popular writer of detective novels. Most of his books are about Spenser, a private eye.

2. Spenser lives and works in Boston, Massachusetts. His work often takes him to other states.

3. Susan Silverman is Spenser's girlfriend. Hawk is Spencer's associate and a good friend.

4. Susan and Hawk must be regular characters in the stories. They would not appear in all the novels.

5. Susan is a psychiatrist. She does not always understand what motivates Spenser.

6. Spenser would not think of getting out of shape. Hawk would not think of getting out of shape.

7. Cooking is another of Spenser's accomplishments. He can put a meal together on short notice.

8. In *Pastime* Parker introduced Pearl, Spenser's dog. Following novels have included her.

9. Parker's mysteries are also travel guides. They inform readers about restaurants and other places of interest in Boston.

Exercise 20 Complete the sentences by adding your own independent clause after the comma and coordinating conjunction.

1. I have a pet boa constrictor, *and* . . .

2. I would love to sing at your wedding, *but* . . .

3. This cellular telephone does not work anymore, *so* . . .

4. Rick would either like to be a trapeze artist, *or* . . .

5. Myra wore a sequined cat-suit to the party, *yet* . . .

6. I cannot afford a new car right now, *for* . . .

7. The children did not want to go to the zoo, *nor* . . .

8. Please do not go bungee jumping today, *for* . . .

9. The job I really want would give me plenty of vacation time, *and* . . .

10. While rummaging in the attic, Mark found his old tuxedo, which was now too small, *so* . . .

Exercise 21 Most of the sentences in the following paragraph are short and choppy. Using coordinating conjunctions, combine some of them to create a more effective paragraph.

Years ago, I resisted learning to use a computer. I was convinced that typing was easier and faster. I did not think a computer could do anything my typewriter could not do. I was wrong. I discovered word processing. Then typographical errors were no problem. I could erase with the touch of a key. I was through with messy correcting fluids and crumbly erasers. If I wanted to take out a paragraph, I did not have to retype the entire page. I especially liked the spell-check feature. I missed some errors when proofreading. The computer found them for me. Word processing saved me hours of time. I soon gave up typing with no regrets.

B.5 Sentence Combining: Subordination

Subordination involves joining two clauses in such a way that one clause is clearly more important than the other. One clause remains independent, and the other is joined to it by a connecting word that shows the second clause is subordinate to, or dependent on, the main, independent clause. The resulting sentence is a *complex sentence*. The connecting word can be either a *subordinating conjunction* or a *relative pronoun,* and it always introduces the dependent clause.

The most common subordinating conjunctions are

although	if	though
as	in order that (to)	until
as if	once	when
as long as	provided that	where
as though	since	wherever
because	so that	whether
before	than	while
even though		

The meaning of the subordinating conjunction you choose establishes how the dependent and independent clauses are related. Figure B-5.1 on page 418 lists six commonly used subordinating conjunctions and illustrates how you can use them to relate ideas. Four additional conjunctions work well for establishing cause-and-effect relationships between the dependent and independent clauses. For example, *because* and *since* introduce a reason; *so that* and *in order that* introduce a result. Suppose you wrote the following two sentences:

1. I am going to wash my car.

2. It is dirty.

You can combine the sentences to establish a cause-and-effect relationship between the two ideas by subordinating one of them with *because* or *since.* The following examples show two ways you can do this. The dependent clause is underlined.

1. <u>Because it is dirty</u>, I am going to wash my car.

2. I am going to wash my car <u>since it is dirty</u>.

Figure B-5.1 Subordinating Conjunctions and Sentence Relationships

CONJUNCTION	RELATIONSHIP	EXAMPLE SENTENCE
After	Following	Carlos and Janet began cleaning up *after* the guests went home. (Cleaning up is an act that *followed* when the guests left.)
How	Process	Carlos and Janet did not know *how* they would get the spots out of the carpet. (The *process* they would use to get the spots out is what they didn't know.)
Even though	Although	Carlos started cleaning now *even though* he would rather wait until later. (Carlos will do the cleaning *although* he would rather wait.)
Unless	Except	*Unless* Janet agreed to help, Carlos would have to finish by himself. (Janet's agreeing to help would be an *exception* to Carlos's having to finish by himself.)
Whenever	Indefinite time	Janet said she would make breakfast *whenever* they got finished. (Janet will fix breakfast at some *indefinite time* in the future.)
While	During, at the same time	*While* Janet worked on the spots in the carpet, Carlos vacuumed the furniture. (Cleaning the spots took place *during* the vacuuming of the carpet.)

In both sentences, "dirty" is the *cause* of the *effect* of washing the car. Also, "I am going to wash my car" is the most important idea, and "because it is dirty" is subordinate to it. *The independent clause always states the most important idea. The dependent clause states the subordinate, or less important idea.* It does not matter whether the dependent clause begins the sentence or ends it; the idea expressed in the dependent clause is still *subordinate* to, or *less important* than, the idea expressed in the independent clause. Also, when the dependent clause is at the beginning of the sentence, a *comma* follows it. If the dependent clause comes at the end of the sentence, there is *no comma* before the subordinating conjunction.

The next example illustrates how to combine the four sentences below into one sentence by using a subordinating conjunction. The dependent clause is underlined.

1. The Weather Channel predicts a hurricane.

2. The hurricane is coming this way.

3. Residents should prepare for the storm.

4. Residents should buy candles, canned goods, flashlight batteries, and bottled water.

<u>Because the Weather Channel predicts that a hurricane is coming this way,</u> residents should prepare for the storm by buying candles, canned goods, flashlight batteries, and bottled water.

The new sentence is more effective than the four original sentences because it eliminates repetitive words and phrases.

When combining sentences, it is all right to change the wording or eliminate some words as long as the new sentence has the same meaning as the original group of sentences. Also, there are many possibilities for combining sentences. Although you and someone else might combine a group of sentences in entirely different ways, both of your new sentences might be equally effective.

[**Exercise 22**]   Combine each pair of sentences into one sentence by using subordination.

1. a. Mid-May through mid-November is hurricane season in Florida.

    b. Florida residents prepare for the season.

2. a. Florida residents keep track of the weather.

    b. Florida residents use a hurricane tracking map or watch the local weather forecast on television.

3. a. Hardware stores stock hurricane supplies.

    b. Hardware stores usually run out of supplies.

4. a. Hurricanes used to have women's names, such as Donna or Alice.

    b. Hurricanes now also have men's names, such as Hugo or Andrew.

5. a. Naming hurricanes only after women was considered sexist.

    b. Men's names were added to avoid sexism.

[**Exercise 23**]   Combine each group of sentences into one sentence by using subordination.

1. a. Nancy wants an unusual pet.

    b. Macaws are unusual.

    c. Macaws are a kind of parrot.

    d. Nancy is going to buy a macaw.

2. a. Electric eels live in South America.

   b. Electric eels carry a charge that is equal to about 160 volts.

   c. Electric eels can defend themselves against predators.

3. a. Dragonflies are harmless to humans.

   b. Dragonflies are useful.

   c. Dragonflies eat mosquitoes.

   d. Dragonflies have been used in research that has led to improvements in aircraft.

4. a. Roaches do not live only in filthy places.

   b. Hospitals have to exterminate roaches.

   c. Many clean, respectable restaurants have to exterminate roaches.

   d. Roaches are not choosy about where they live.

When a *relative pronoun* joins clauses in a relationship of subordination, the dependent clause is called a *relative clause*. The information contained in the relative clause is less important than that in the independent clause. Following is a list of the most commonly used relative pronouns and when to use them:

who	refers to people
that	usually refers to things but can refer to people
which	refers to things

If the relative clause comes at the end of the sentence, a comma precedes the relative pronoun only if the information contained in the clause can be omitted with no loss in meaning. If the information is essential, however, then no comma precedes the relative pronoun. When the relative clause interrupts the independent clause, and if the clause contains nonessential information, it is surrounded by commas. The following annotated examples illustrate these features of the relative clause within a relationship of subordination.

Betty Friedan, who has been called the mother of the women's movement, wrote *The Feminine Mystique*.

Iron John, which is a best-selling book by Robert Bly, is a male's response to feminism.

The first women who became members of the National Organization for Women were pioneers in women's rights.

The Feminine Mystique is the book that started the feminist movement.

Can you name the woman who was the first president of the National Organization for Women?

In the first two sentences, the relative clauses *interrupt* the independent clauses. The relative clauses in each of these sentences contain information that is not essential to the meaning of the sentence, so they are surrounded by commas. In the first sentence, the relative clause is nonessential because the independent clause names the woman who is the subject of the sentence. The relative clause in the second sentence is nonessential because the independent clause names the book that is the subject of the sentence.

In the third sentence, unlike sentences 1 and 2, the relative clause that modifies the independent clause does contain essential information that you need to identify the women who were pioneers. Commas do not surround this clause.

In the fourth and fifth sentences, the relative clauses *follow* the independent clauses. In the fourth sentence, there is no comma at the beginning of the relative clause because the information it contains is essential to the meaning of the independent clause. The relative clause specifies the book's importance. In the fifth sentence, the relative clause is essential because it provides information needed to identify the woman referred to in the independent clause. You do not need a comma before the relative clause in the fifth sentence.

[**Exercise 24**] Use relative pronouns to combine the following sentences. Add commas where necessary.

1. Mary McCarthy is an author.
   Mary McCarthy wrote *The Group.*

2. *The Group* is about a group of young women.
   The women go to the same college.

3. Some colleges used to be men's colleges.
   These colleges now admit women.

4. I remember the old chapel.
   The old chapel has been torn down.

5. Beverages are not permitted in the department store.
   Beverages are permitted in the lounge.

[**Exercise 25**] Most of the sentences in the following paragraph are short and choppy. Using subordinating conjunctions, combine some of the sentences to create a more effective paragraph. Also, add transitions where necessary to give your paragraph coherence.

Ireland is a great place to spend a vacation. Most people travel in southern Ireland. Southern Ireland has rocky coastlines, scattered villages, castles, and other interesting sights to see. The Cliffs of Mohr are a breathtaking sight. It is a long walk to the edge of the cliffs. It is a steep drop from the cliffs to the ocean. Waves thunder against the cliffs. Taking a country drive is like stepping back in time. A farmer will stop traffic to take his herd of sheep across the road. Thatch-roofed cottages dot the countryside. Northern Ireland is also an interesting place. Not many tourists go into northern Ireland. They have heard about the IRA activity there. They miss an opportunity to see another part of the country. White's Island is the site of pre-Christian ruins. This remote island is accessible only by boat. You can rent a small rowboat from a farmer. He lives across the lake from the island. There is nothing on the island but the ruins and grazing cattle. The silence and natural beauty add to the enchantment of the place. Some tourists believe that a trip into northern Ireland is worth the trouble and the risk.

B.6 Expanding Your Sentences: Phrases and Clauses

As you write and rewrite, sentences will become the focus of much of your revision: how to change, rearrange, combine, and correct them so that they express your ideas clearly and effectively. One way to get more detail into your sentences is to expand subjects and predicates by adding descriptive words, phrases, and clauses.

Phrases

Expanding subjects and predicates by adding words, phrases, and clauses gives you still more choices as a writer. A *phrase* is a group of words that is not a sentence because it lacks either one or both of the two basic parts: subject and predicate. To be a phrase, the group of words must function together as a single part of speech. Phrases can function as nouns, verbs, adjectives, or adverbs. If a phrase explains *who* or *what*, it acts as a *noun*. Phrases that explain *which* or *what kind* function as *adjectives*. A phrase that tells *when, where*, or *how* functions as an *adverb*.

Phrases add detail to your sentences. The following examples explain several types of phrases and illustrate how they function in sentences:

Prepositional phrases	They begin with prepositions: *for, to, around, through, over,* and so on. They describe relationships such as time, place, or direction.

After failing to stop, Maria's car skidded into a telephone pole.

Both phrases are functioning as *adverbs,* telling *when* and *where* the car skidded.

| Verbal phrases | They are forms of verbs that cannot stand alone as the main verb of a sentence. They act as nouns, adjectives, or adverbs. |

Maria decided <u>to call a wrecker.</u>

The phrase functions as a *noun* explaining *what* Maria decided.

<u>Tired and depressed</u>, Maria wondered how she would get to work the next day.

The phrase functions as an *adjective* describing Maria.

<u>Getting the car fixed</u> was the only thing on Maria's mind.

The phrase functions as a *noun* describing *what* Maria was thinking.

| An absolute phrase | It contains a noun or pronoun, an *-ing* or *-ed* verb form, and modifiers. It frequently modifies an entire sentence rather than a single word. |

<u>The car having been hauled away</u>, Maria waited for her sister to pick her up.

The phrase modifies the whole sentence, explaining why Maria had to wait.

The car was a mess, its windshield <u>smashed into pieces</u> and its front end <u>crushed to bits.</u>

These phrases function as adjectives, describing what happened to the windshield and front end.

| Appositive phrase | Placed next to a noun or pronoun to identify or rename it, the appositive phrase acts as a noun modifying another noun. |

Maria, <u>a college student</u>, did not know where she would get the money to pay for the car.

The phrase identifies Maria. It is a nonrestrictive phrase since it does not add essential information to the sentence. Nonrestrictive phrases are set off with commas.

Maria went home and read the book *Sex, Drink, & Fast Cars* by Stephen Bayley.

The phrase identifies the book's title. It is a restrictive phrase because it provides essential information; therefore, the phrase is *not* set off with commas.

Remember that a phrase is a group of words acting together as a single part of speech that cannot stand alone as a sentence because it lacks either a subject, a predicate, or both. Phrases are sentence expanders that add interest and detail to your sentences.

Exercise 26	Expand each of the following sentences by adding phrases.

1. The telephone rang. (Add a *verbal phrase* that tells how the phone rang.)

2. Toby sounded angry. (Add an *appositive phrase* that tells who Toby is.)

3. I gave Lisa the phone. (Add an *appositive phrase* that tells who Lisa is.)

4. She slammed it down. (Add a *verbal phrase* that describes how she slammed it down.)

5. I turned on the answering machine. (Add an *absolute phrase* that describes how the machine was turned on.)

6. Lisa turned it off. (Add a *prepositional phrase* that tells when she turned the machine off.)

Clauses

A *clause* is a group of words containing a subject and a predicate. There are two types: *independent* and *dependent* (or *subordinate*).

Independent clause	It can stand alone as a sentence because it expresses a complete thought.

Amigos is a new Mexican restaurant.

Dependent (subordinate) clause	It cannot stand alone as a sentence because the thought it expresses requires completion or connection to something more.

that opened in our neighborhood

The following sentence shows the relationship of an independent and a dependent clause:

 independent clause   **dependent clause**

My brother owns the restaurant that opened in our neighborhood.

The dependent clause explains which restaurant my brother owns.

Dependent clauses usually begin with a relative pronoun (such as *which, that, what, whatever, who, whose, whom, whoever,* or *whomever*) or a subordinating conjunction (such as *after, because, rather than,* or *when*). Section B.5 explains how to use these conjunctions and others like them to establish relationships within sentences. The following examples illustrate how to use dependent clauses to expand your sentences:

1. Maria wants a car. (unexpanded independent clause)

Maria wants a car that gets good gas mileage and has a high safety rating.
                  dependent clause

The dependent clause expands the sentence by telling you what kind of car Maria wants.

2. Maria wants a Volvo. (unexpanded independent clause)

dependent clause   **dependent clause**

Because safety is a high priority, Maria wants a Volvo that has a high safety rating.

The first dependent clause explains why Maria wants a Volvo. The second dependent clause describes the Volvo.

3. Maria will buy a Volvo. (unexpanded independent clause)

dependent clause

When she wins the lottery, Maria will buy a Volvo.

The dependent clause explains when Maria will buy a Volvo.

Notice how in these three examples, adding dependent clauses expands the original sentences by providing more information.

[Exercise 27] Expand the following sentences by adding clauses either at the beginning or the end as indicated in the previous examples.

1. A good friend is one *who* . . .

2. I would like to have a car *that* . . .

3. *Until* . . . I will have to put up with his behavior.

4. *When* . . . the kitchen flooded.

5. I believe I will get the job *because* . . .

[Exercise 28]

Working with a partner, read the following paragraph. Identify phrases and clauses the writer has used to expand the basic sentence parts of subject and predicate.

My cousin, Ned, is a great swimmer. The first summer he visited us in Florida, he saved a girl from drowning in the ocean. We had spent the morning at the beach. In the afternoon, Ned was sunbathing beside me when a young girl started splashing in the water. Then she started waving her arms over her head. She would disappear under the water, then come up to the surface. At first, we thought she was playing. Through his binoculars, Ned could see that she was in trouble. Ned raced to the water and dove into the waves. He swam hand over hand in long strokes until he reached her. She was almost drowned. After he got her on shore, he gave her mouth-to-mouth resuscitation, breathing air into her lungs. Fortunately, she revived. She said my cousin had saved her life. Ned said it was his swimming ability that had saved them both. He had taken a lifesaving course and knew how to keep her head above the water while slowly working his way back to shore. The girl's parents offered him money, but he would not take it. To that girl, Ned was more than a great swimmer. He was a hero.

B.7 Varying Your Sentences

You can improve your style by writing sentences that are more interesting and varied. To achieve sentence variety, try these four common methods:

1. Use a variety of sentence lengths.
2. Use a variety of sentence types.
3. Use a variety of sentence beginnings.
4. Use a variety of sentence relationships.

Use a Variety of Sentence Lengths

Sentences are either short, medium, or long. The best short sentences are simple and direct. Though too many may make your writing sound choppy and monotonous, a few carefully placed ones can give your writing balance and help you emphasize important ideas. Medium-length sentences occur most frequently, probably because it seems logical and more effective to combine related ideas from two or more simple sentences into one sentence. Long sentences are detail-filled and can help clarify complex ideas and relationships. However, too many of them may make your writing seem unnecessarily wordy. The six previous sentences in this paragraph illustrate all three sentence lengths. The first two sentences are short, the third and fourth sentences are long, and the fifth and sixth sentences are medium. Following are additional examples.

Short	Some students are afraid to ask questions in class.
Medium	They may lack confidence, or they may fear that other students will think they are trying to impress the instructor.
Long	Students' questions can help the instructor determine how much of the material they understand; moreover, one student may ask a question that many others had but were afraid to ask.

Should you have an equal mix of short, medium, and long sentences in your essays? Not necessarily. Short sentences are characteristic of Ernest Hemingway's bold, spare style. Another of America's greatest writers, William Faulkner, favored long sentences. They seemed to fit the complexity of his stories and his characters' lives. Sentence length is as much a part of the writing style of the nonfiction writer as it is of the fiction writer. The editorial pages of the newspaper contain the work of many fine writers: George Will, Ellen Goodman, Kathleen Parker, and Leonard Pitts to name a few. Though their writing differs in other ways, these writers use more medium-length sentences than short or long. Goodman uses short sentences for emphasis, often near the end of her pieces. Will's long sentences add depth to his writing and help him clarify complex issues.

Sentence length is a matter of choice, as are the other aspects of style. Your style will develop with time and practice. For now, try to use all three sentence lengths in your writing.

[**Exercise 29**] Examine one or more of your essays to determine whether your sentence length is varied. See how many examples you can find of short, medium, and long sentences; then decide what you need to do to vary your sentence length.

Use a Variety of Sentence Types

Sentences may be *loose, periodic,* or *balanced.* In a *loose* sentence, the subject and verb come first and are followed by information that helps to clarify them. Loose sentences are straightforward and easy to read because the subject and verb at the beginning let you know what the sentence is about. The *loose* sentence is also the most common type. The following example is a loose sentence: The subject and predicate are labeled and underlined:

> s   p
> The autumn leaves look like bright swipes of paint against a sky-blue canvas, a pleasant association for me.

The rest of the sentence clarifies what the leaves look like and that the association is a pleasant one.

In a *periodic* sentence, the subject, the verb, or the subject and verb come near the end of the sentence. Because the explanatory information comes first, readers have to wait to get to the key idea of the sentence. Writers use periodic sentences to build suspense, to add emphasis, or to create drama. In the following example of a periodic sentence, the subject and predicate of the independent clause are labeled and underlined.

> Since summer is their favorite time of year, the family vacations in August.
> s   p

By placing a dependent clause first—which, by definition, is an incomplete thought—the writer builds suspense for the clause that completes the thought. As you read the next example, notice the suspense that you feel while you are waiting to see what the sentence is about.

Spewing blue oily smoke from its exhaust, squealing its tires on the slick pavement, rumbling ominously in the bowels of its engine before it finally quit, the old <u>Chevrolet</u> <u>came</u> to a halt.

         s   p

The delayed subject and predicate in this periodic sentence create a more dramatic scene for the reader than if the subject and verb had come at the beginning.

[**Exercise 30**] Select a paragraph from an essay you have written, and either add a periodic sentence to it or revise one of your sentences to make it a periodic sentence.

A *balanced* sentence contains parallel words, phrases, or clauses in a series. Elements within sentences are *parallel* when they are used in similar ways or when they appear in the same grammatical form. In each pair of the following sentences, the first sentence contains an italicized element that is not parallel. The second sentence in each pair is a revised version in which all elements are parallel.

WORDS

a. The pasta was soggy, limp, and *it had been cooked too long.* (Not balanced: *Soggy* and *limp* are adjectives; *it had been cooked too long* is not parallel because it is a clause.)

b. The pasta was soggy, limp, and overcooked. (Balanced: Now all three modifiers are adjectives.)

PHRASES

a. Dr. Fractal is a caring teacher, *an expert in math,* and a reliable colleague. (Not balanced: *Caring teacher* and *reliable colleague* each consist of a noun modified by a preceding adjective; *an expert in math* is not parallel because it is a noun modified by a prepositional phrase.)

b. Dr. Fractal is a caring teacher, an expert mathematician, and a reliable colleague. (Balanced: Now all three phrases are parallel.)

CLAUSES

a. When Victor played the piano and sang, everyone *applauds* and asked for more. (Not balanced: *Played the piano and sang* is in the past tense; *applauds* is not parallel because it is in the present tense.)

b. When Victor played the piano and sang, everyone applauded and asked for more. (Balanced: Now both clauses are in the past tense.)

[**Exercise 31**] Select a paragraph from an essay you have written, and either add a balanced sentence to it or revise one of your sentences to make it balanced.

Use a Variety of Sentence Beginnings

Varying the way you begin your sentences is another way to improve your style. Basically, the way you begin a sentence depends upon how you want to introduce the subject and predicate. You have already learned that the *type* of sentence you use will create a difference in the way your sentences begin: In *loose* sentences, the subject and verb come first, whereas in *periodic* sentences, the subject and verb are delayed until near the end of the sentence. You can also begin your sentences with *adjectives, adverbs, modifying phrases, prepositional phrases, transitional words and phrases,* or *dependent clauses.* Following are examples of each type. The subjects and predicates are labeled and underlined.

Adjective

Tired and hot, the dog dug a hole in the wet dirt and lay down.   compound predicate

Crimson and gold, the fall leaves made a colorful backdrop for the white house.

Adverb

Carefully, the prowler eased open a basement window.

Quietly, the children crept out of bed to spy on the teenagers having a party downstairs.

Modifying phrases

Fearful of making any noise, Nancy called the police to report that she heard a prowler.

To reach a verdict of guilty, the jury would have to believe the prosecuting attorney's evidence.

Prepositional phrases

"Over the river and through the woods, to Grandmother's house we go."

Before taking off, the pilot completed his preflight checklist.

Transitional words and phrases	p For example, a vote for this candidate might split the ticket, resulting in a vote for the other party.

Consequently, Ed made a better grade on the test than he had thought he would.

Dependent clauses   Because there was a snack bar built right into the pool, the swimmers ate lunch in the water.

After the game was over, everyone went to a restaurant.

[Exercise 32]   Revise one of your essays for sentence variety by changing the beginnings of your sentences so that you have at least one of each type.

Use a Variety of Sentence Relationships

As you learned in sections B.4 and B.5, you can use *coordination* and *subordination* to combine sentences in a variety of relationships shown by the coordinating and subordinating conjunctions and the relative pronouns you choose. Be careful, however, not to overuse any one of the coordinating or subordinating conjunctions. It is easy to get hooked on a favorite conjunction, such as *and* or *but,* and use it several times in one paragraph. To vary your sentence structure, vary your use of conjunctions.

Sentence relationships are of two types: those that occur *within* sentences, and those that occur *between* sentences. Coordination and subordination help you combine independent clauses to express their relationship within a single sentence. *Transitional phrases* and adverbs such as *therefore, however,* and *nevertheless* can show relationships within or between sentences. By establishing clear sentence relationships, you are able to achieve coherence, as explained in Chapter 3. The following examples show how transitional phrases and certain adverbs establish relationships between sentences. The transitions and adverbs are underlined. Relationships are italicized.

Transitional phrases   Did you know that you have three types of memory? One type is your sensory memory. Another type is short-term memory. Your long-term memory is the third type. (The transitional phrases establish a *part-whole* relationship between the first sentence and the three sentences that follow; memory is broken down into three types.)

I wish I had a computer that was more convenient to use than my large desk model. For example, I would like to have one of the portable laptop models. (The transitional phrase establishes a relationship of *clarification* between the first sentence, which is a general statement, and the second sentence, which is an example.)

I did not study enough for the exam. As a result, I did not make a very good grade. (The transitional phrase sets up a *cause-and-effect* relationship between the two sentences.)

The computer has all but replaced the typewriter in today's offices. On the other hand, a typewriter may still be useful for small jobs. (The transitional phrase establishes a relationship of *contrast* between the two sentences.)

Adverbs

I really would love to go swimming with you at Rock Springs. However, I have a bad cold. (The adverb sets up a relationship of *contrast* between the two sentences.)

The painters did not do a very good job of painting my house. Moreover, they did not clean up the mess they made. (The adverb establishes a relationship of *addition;* the second sentence adds one more thing that the painters in the first sentence did not do well.)

You forgot my birthday, and you did not even call me until two weeks after you got back from your vacation. Therefore, I think our relationship is over. (The adverb establishes a *cause-and-effect* relationship between the sentences.)

You forgot my birthday, and you did not even call me until two weeks after you got back from your vacation. Nevertheless, I will give you one more chance to show you care. (The adverb sets up a relationship of *opposition* or *contrast* between the first and second sentences.)

[Exercise 33] Examine an essay in progress to see whether you have used coordination and subordination to add variety to your sentences. Determine whether you are overusing any one of the conjunctions. Revise a paragraph or a whole essay to improve your use of coordination and subordination and to eliminate overuse of a conjunction.

[**Exercise 34**] Examine an essay in progress. See whether you have used a variety of transitional phrases and adverbs to achieve coherence between sentences. Revise a paragraph or the whole essay to vary your use of transitional phrases and adverbs and to establish clearer relationships between sentences.

[**Exercise 35**] The following paragraph is composed exclusively of short simple sentences. In addition, the paragraph is not very well organized. Revise it to improve the organization and to add sentence variety, using all the methods explained in this section.

> Rick is a carpenter. Rick is forty-eight years old. Rick has been doing carpentry for more than twenty years. He is tired of building cabinets. He is tired of doing the finish work on houses. The work is hard. The work is time consuming. Rick no longer finds the work challenging. He wants to do something else. Rick likes to grow plants. He also likes to cook. He enjoys using a variety of herbs and spices. He cannot always find fresh herbs and spices. He has to use dried ones. Rick thinks there is a market for fresh herbs and spices. He would like to start an herb and spice business. He has the land. He knows how to build greenhouses. He has good business sense. The work would be challenging. He could get out of carpentry. He could start a new career.

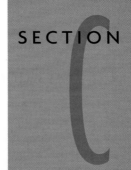
Punctuation Choices

Correct use of punctuation can help you communicate confidently and without confusion. Readers expect you to follow the rules and conventions of punctuation because errors can interfere with your message. What are your choices for effective punctuation? Section C reviews the marks and rules of punctuation.

C.1 End Punctuation Marks

Choose an appropriate punctuation mark to end a sentence.

The *period, question mark,* and *exclamation point* are marks of punctuation that you probably use correctly most of the time. Because these end marks are so familiar, it is easy to take them for granted. Following is a quick review of the three ways to end a sentence.

1. *Place a period at the end of a sentence that either makes a statement or issues a command:*

   Mark took his bicycle to the repair shop for an estimate.

   Fill out one of these forms.

2. *Place a question mark at the end of a sentence that asks a direct question, but place a period at the end of a statement that indirectly asks a question:*

   How soon can you fix my bicycle?

   Mark asked the mechanic how soon the bicycle would be ready.

   Mark wanted to know when the mechanic could fix the bicycle.

☑ **CONCEPT CHECK**
Exclamations can be forceful and effective if used very sparingly, but if you overuse them, they lose their punch. Use an exclamation point only when the intensity of feeling or surprise expressed in your writing justifies it.

3. *Place an exclamation point at the end of a statement to indicate surprise or intense feeling:*

   I must have my bicycle by next Friday!

   What an outrageous price!

   I cannot believe it will cost that much!

C.2 The Colon

Place a colon at the end of a statement if what follows is a list, quotation, explanation, or word needing special emphasis:

I will have to repair or replace the following: a wheel, the tire and tube, and the handlebars.

Mark thought of two proverbs that applied to his recent accident with the bicycle: "An ounce of prevention is worth a pound of cure" and "Better safe than sorry."

Here is what you can do if I do not finish repairing your bicycle in time: Use our loaner, but this time watch out for chuckholes.

At this point, Mark could think of only one thing to do: laugh.

C.3 The Dash

Place a dash before and after words that interrupt the flow of thought or before words that create a dramatic effect:

Mark was unhappy enough as it was, but the fact that his bicycle was brand-new—he had bought it only two weeks ago—added to his despair.

When the mechanic presented Mark with an estimate, he said that there was only one way to look at it—sitting down.

Dashes, like exclamation points, should be used sparingly and only when there is a good reason for doing so.

C.4 The Hyphen

1. *If two or more words that describe a noun function as a unit, connect them with a hyphen:*

Mark showed that he still had a sense of humor when he asked if the shop had a lay-away plan.

The mechanic laughed but told him the shop did have a time-payment plan.

Considering what the bill would do to his bank account, Mark wondered whether he would get into a charge-it-as-a-way-of-life routine.

2. *When you have to divide a word at the end of a line, use a hyphen. Break the word at the end of a syllable. If you do not know how to divide a certain word into syllables, consult your dictionary. Figure C-4.1 on page 436 lists rules for hyphenating words at the end of a line.*

[**Exercise 36**] Correctly place hyphens or dashes in the following sentences. The words in parentheses following each sentence tell you what to do.

1. The fight or flight response that is typical of animals who are confronted by an aggressor has also been observed in humans. (Use hyphens to connect words functioning as a unit.)

2. When an animal is backed into a corner so that he cannot retreat, he will do the only thing left to him fight back. (Use a dash for dramatic effect.)

3. Grizzly bears have a reputation for aggressiveness they actually prefer to avoid confrontation but they will often flee rather than fight if there is an escape route. (Use dashes to set off words that interrupt the flow of thought.)

Figure C-4.1 How to Hyphenate at the End of a Line

1. Do not hyphenate short words, one-syllable words, or words pronounced as one syllable.

2. Do not leave only one or two letters at the end of a line or carry over one or two letters to the next line.

3. Hyphenate only at the end of a syllable.

4. If a word already has a hyphen (self-confident, all-inclusive), divide it only after the hyphen.

4. Most people try to avoid physical conflict unless backed into a corner. (Use a dash for dramatic effect.)

5. Even the most mild mannered people, however, may react physically if they feel their lives or their children's lives are threatened. (Use a hyphen to connect words functioning as a unit.)

C.5 The Semicolon

1. *Place a semicolon between two independent clauses that are closely related:*

   Mark worried about the results of his bicycle repairs; would he be able to tell that his new bike had been in an accident?

2. *Place a semicolon before a conjunctive adverb when the semicolon joins two independent clauses. A comma follows the conjunctive adverb. See Figure C-5.1 on page 437 for a list of conjunctive adverbs and the relationships they signal.*

   On Friday, Mark's bike was ready; moreover, it looked as good as it did on the day he bought it.

3. *Use a semicolon to separate items in a series if the items already contain commas:*

   Listening to the shop radio, Mark heard three "oldies" that made him wish he had a car: "409," by the Beach Boys; "Oh Lord Won't You Buy Me a Mercedes Benz," by Janis Joplin; and "Little GTO," by Ronnie and the Daytonas.

Exercise 37 Examine your returned papers for errors in the use of the semicolon and other punctuation marks. Using what you have learned in this chapter, correct your errors.

Figure C-5.1 Conjunctive Adverbs and Sentence Relationships

RELATIONSHIP	CONJUNCTIVE ADVERBS
Addition	also, besides, furthermore, moreover
Contrast	however, instead, nevertheless, nonetheless, otherwise, still
Comparison	likewise, similarly
Result	accordingly, consequently, hence, then, therefore
Time	finally, meanwhile, next, subsequently, then
Emphasis	certainly, indeed

Exercise 38 In the following paragraph, all marks of punctuation except commas have been left out. Read the paragraph and supply the missing marks of punctuation.

Far from being merely a means of sweetening your breath, mouthwash in the United States has taken on a deeper meaning Mouthwashes have acquired certain images in consumers' minds no one knows this better than advertisers who use these images to sell their products According to some psychologists, a person's choice of mouthwash may be influenced by the image the mouthwash projects Product A projects a no-nonsense germ fighting image Product B, on the other hand, projects a sexual image clean breath is sexy breath Product B's latest ads show couples getting out of bed in the morning afraid to kiss each other until they've used their mouthwash Product A's purchasers may see themselves as sensible people who are more concerned about the germs that can cause bad breath than about being kissable however, Product B's users may see themselves as lovers whose mouthwash is just one more weapon in the arsenal of attraction Which mouthwash do you think more people buy

C.6 The Comma

In some cases, a comma is like a little pause in a conversation. The comma, or the pause, gives readers or listeners a chance to think about what is being said and the relation of one idea to another. Sometimes you can tell where a comma should go by reading your sentence aloud and listening for the natural pause that indicates a break in the flow of thought. In cases in which this practical suggestion does not work, a familiarity with the comma's six common uses may help.

1. *Commas separate items in a series.*

If you have three or more items in a series, separate them with commas.

Blake had bruises, lacerations, and contusions following his accident at work.

He had a cast on his arm, several bandages on his leg, and a brace on his neck.

In the first example, commas separate single words in a series. In the second example, commas separate phrases in a series.

2. *Commas separate two adjectives that modify the same word if the adjectives are coordinate and belong to the same class.*

The tired, overworked nurses worked on Blake for several hours.

but

One big black bruise covered most of Blake's face.

Adjectives are *coordinate* when they modify the same word and belong to the same class of ideas. In the first example, the adjectives *tired* and *overworked* are coordinate because they both modify *nurses* by telling how the nurses felt. Since both words describe feelings, they are of the same class, and they need a comma to separate them. In the second example, the adjectives *big* and *black* are not coordinate. Although they both modify *bruise,* they tell you two different things about the bruise. *Big* describes its size, and *black* describes its color. *Size* and *color* belong to different classes of ideas, so they do not need a comma to separate them.

If you have trouble deciding when to place a comma between two adjectives that modify the same word, try this classic method: Say the words with "and" between them, then say them in reverse. If they sound OK either way, put a comma between them. If they sound odd, leave the comma out. For example, "tired and overworked nurses" sounds OK; so does "overworked and tired nurses." However, "big and black bruise" sounds odd; so does "black and big bruise."

3. *A comma follows introductory words, phrases, and clauses.*

Fortunately, Blake's workman's compensation insurance covered the costs of his injuries.

On the other hand, he had already spent some money before he was able to file the claim.

Even after he had recovered from his injuries, Blake had occasional soreness.

In the first example, the comma follows an introductory word. In the second example, the comma follows an introductory phrase. In the third example, the comma follows an introductory dependent clause.

Commas also follow introductory transitions, as in the next four examples.

First, Blake was rushed to the hospital.

After that, emergency room personnel took care of him.

When they were finished, Blake was admitted to the hospital for a few days.

Finally, he was allowed to go home.

If you introduce a sentence with a transition, or any other introductory material, be sure to follow it with a comma.

4. *Commas come before and after interrupting words, phrases, and clauses that are not restrictive in meaning.*

Several coworkers, fortunately, were close by when Blake's accident happened.

Blake, hurt and frightened, lay in the ambulance wondering what would happen next.

The emergency room, which Blake had been to once before, was an efficiently run place.

In the first example, a word interrupts the sentence. In the second example, a phrase interrupts. In the third, a dependent clause interrupts. In each example, the interrupter is not restrictive (essential to the meaning of the sentence). It is set off with commas to show that it is simply added information that does not affect the meaning of the sentence as a whole. To test this out, either cross out or cover up the interrupter, and read what is left of the sentence. You will find that in each example the sentence makes sense without the interrupter. The insertion of interrupters provides you, the writer, with another option for constructing sentences. The use of interrupters can add interest to your sentences and can increase your sentence variety.

Restrictive phrases and clauses sometimes act as interrupters, but because they *are* essential to the meaning of a sentence, they are not set off by commas:

Blake remembered that the song *"Benny and the Jets"* was playing on the radio while he was in the emergency room.

The nurses *who were on duty* did their best to make Blake comfortable.

The phrase in the first example and the clause in the second example are both *restrictive* because they are essential to the meaning of the sentence. Therefore, they are not set off by commas. In the first example, the phrase *"Benny and the Jets"* identifies the song that was playing. In the second example, the clause "who were on duty" identifies which nurses took care of Blake.

5. *A comma comes before a coordinating conjunction joining two independent clauses.*

Blake fully recovered from his accident, *and* he returned to his job.

The company instituted new rules that they hoped would prevent accidents like Blake's in the future, *but* they would have to wait and see.

✔ CONCEPT CHECK
To review coordination,
see section B.4.

In each example, the coordinating conjunction joins two independent clauses. The comma before the coordinating conjunction signals that a new independent clause with its own subject and verb will follow the coordinating conjunction. There are seven coordinating conjunctions: *for, and, nor, or, but, yet,* and *so.* Each of these conjunctions has a different meaning and expresses a different relationship between two clauses.

6. *Commas set off certain ordinary material.*

Commas set off the names of people who are addressed directly:

This may hurt a little, Blake, when I remove the cast.

Can you move all of your fingers, Blake?

Commas separate parts of a date and divisions of numerical expressions:

Blake's accident happened on Friday, March 27, 2006.

Blake's insurance covered more than $5,000 in medical bills.

Commas separate the parts of an address:

The hospital is at 1500 Mercy Drive, Bloodworth, MA 02123.

Note that there is no comma between the state and the zip code.

Commas follow informal greetings and the closing in letters:

Dear Blake,

Sincerely,

In some formal letters, a colon (:) follows the greeting.

[Exercise 39] Place commas where needed in the following sentences:

1. Marta I want you to follow these steps exactly to use our new word processor.

2. First turn on the monitor.

3. When a list of icons appears click on your program's icon.

4. Wait for a blank screen a little flashing line in the upper left corner and some icons across the top and bottom of the screen.

5. Now you are ready to use the keyboard which works just like a typewriter to type whatever you want.

6. There are more things you will need to know but I cannot tell you all of them today.

7. I will be out of the office until Tuesday April 21.

8. A list of these instructions which I have typed out for you should help you remember the steps.

9. Also you can request a free manual from the downtown office at 1600 West Central Street Clarksville OK 32102.

10. I hope you have an interesting rewarding learning experience.

[Exercise 40] Read the following paragraph and insert commas where needed:

> When you have found the right place for your home office you are ready to select the furniture you will need. How much space you have will determine your choice of a desk or table. If your office is in a spare room you can choose almost any type of desk. You might want a desk that is big enough to hold a computer a printer and a fax machine. If you are converting a closet into an office you might want to install a pull-out shelf that can serve as a desktop. A sturdy comfortable chair is another piece of furniture you will want to consider. Make sure the chair has firm back support and that it is comfortable to sit in for long periods of time. As important as the desk and chair is the kind of lighting you have. If you are converting closet space hang a fluorescent light above your pull-out shelf. If you have a conventional desk you can position it under an existing light fixture or you can buy a lamp. Select one that does not take up too much space and that gives strong bright light. A bookcase and file cabinet are two other pieces of furniture you should have if space is unlimited. Use the bookcase for books supplies or other items. A file cabinet that you can lock is a good storage place for important papers and documents. If your office is in the closet simply install one or more shelves above your pull-out desktop for easy convenient storage. Cardboard file boxes are small stackable and affordable organizers for your closet workplace.

C.7 The Apostrophe

The *apostrophe* (') has two functions: to show possession and to indicate omitted letters or numbers.

1. *To show possession, add* 's *to the end of a singular noun even if the noun ends in* -s:

a student's book

Bob Jones's dog

Beethoven's Ninth Symphony

the car's transmission

the bat's wings

If a noun is plural, add only an apostrophe at the end.

several girls' dresses

hundreds of voters' wishes

two doctors' patients

If a noun is plural but does not end in -s, add 's.

women's friends

children's toys

men's watches

Do not use an apostrophe with possessive case pronouns.

The book is hers.

I forgot my pencil; may I borrow one of yours?

Whose backpack is this?

Every college has its rules.

2. *Use an apostrophe when making contractions. A contraction is a word or number that contains one or more missing letters or numerals. An apostrophe takes the place of what is omitted.*

they're (they are)

you'd (you would)

class of '97 (1997)

a '57 Chevy (1957)

To choose between a contraction and the expression it stands for, consider your audience and how informal you want to be. Generally speaking, contractions are inappropriate in academic or other formal writing. Figure C-7.1 on page 443 lists commonly used contractions.

C.8 Quotation Marks

Use double *quotation marks* (" ") to enclose direct quotations, and always use them in pairs. Use single quotation marks (' ') for a quotation within a quotation. Use quotation marks to enclose the titles of songs, short stories, articles, essays, and poems. (Underline or italicize the titles of longer works, such as books, movies, and television series.) Remember to punctuate quotations correctly. These rules are illustrated in the following list.

Figure C-7.1 Commonly Used Contractions

aren't = are not	I'm = I am	wasn't = was not
can't = cannot	isn't = is not	weren't = were not
didn't = did not	let's = let us	we'd = we would, we had
don't = do not	she'd = she would, she had	we're = we are
he'd = he would, he had	she's = she is	we've = we have
he's = he is	there's = there is	who's = who is
I'd = I would, I had	they'd = they would, they had	won't = will not
it's = it is	they're = they are	you're = you are

1. *Use quotation marks in pairs—at the beginning and end of the quotation.*

   "Hand in your papers," said the instructor.

   Chris said, "I'm not finished."

2. *For a quotation within a quotation, use single quotation marks.*

   "'A Person Worthy of Admiration' is the title of my essay," said the student.

✔ CONCEPT CHECK
Long passages of more than four typed lines should not be enclosed in quotation marks. Instead, indent each line of the quotation ten spaces from the left margin.

3. *Enclose titles of songs, short stories, articles, essays, and poems in quotation marks.*

   "Love Me Tender" (song made popular by Elvis Presley)

   "The Open Boat" (short story by Stephen Crane)

   "On Liberty" (essay by John Stuart Mill)

   "Stuck in an Elevator With a Dead Body? Here's What to Do" (newspaper article in *Wall Street Journal,* March 11, 1997)

   "Those Winter Sundays" (poem by Robert Hayden)

4. *Figure C-8.1, page 445, shows us how to punctuate quotations.*

[**Exercise 41**] In the following sentences, add apostrophes and quotation marks where they are needed.

   1. Have you read the poem Loveliest of Trees?

   2. Whos going with you to the dance?

3. Dont tell me you wouldnt like to have a chocolate shake.

4. This car gets poor gas mileage, said Boomer. I wish I could afford a new one.

5. Bill's article, Matadors Secure Another Win, appeared in the college newspaper.

6. Six boys coats need cleaning, and two girls shoes need polishing.

7. My dad has a 57 Thunderbird that he has restored.

8. Joan's favorite Beatles song is Love Me Do.

9. Ouch! the child cried.

10. The instructor always asks, May I have a volunteer?

[**Exercise 42**] Edit the following sentences by inserting the correct punctuation where needed. Choose from among the following punctuation marks and use each one only once: *dash, exclamation point, comma, hyphen, colon, apostrophe, semicolon, question mark.*

1. Lakes and ponds are the sites of year round activity.

2. Popular Lake Como is a fishermans paradise in the spring.

3. Wouldn't you like to win big money in a bass tournament

4. On some lakes, these are the sounds of fall ducks quacking, geese honking overhead, and the occasional sound of a rifle.

5. Skaters on a frozen pond in winter what a peaceful scene that is.

6. Everyone enjoys a summer picnic food tastes better outdoors.

7. My favorite water sports are swimming boating, and jet skiing.

8. Someone always says, I'll race you to the dock.

9. Watch out for that alligator

Figure C-8.1 Punctuate Quotations Correctly

PUNCTUATION MARK	CORRECT PLACEMENT	EXAMPLE SENTENCE
Period, comma	Inside quotation marks	"Thank goodness," said Russ. "My essay is finished."
Comma	After a phrase that introduces a quotation	The speaker asked, "Can you hear me in the back of the room?"
Comma	Before and after interrupting words	"If I can borrow some paper," said Than, "I'll pay you back tomorrow."
Colon, semicolon	Outside quotation marks	Tara said, "I'd like to go to the concert"; however, she did not have a ticket.
Exclamation point, question mark	Inside quotation marks unless they apply to the whole sentence	Juan said, "Hurry up!" Do you recall the song "I'll Be Seeing You"?

SECTION

Choices for Trouble Spots

This section deals with a few trouble spots that can cause difficulty for beginning writers. For example, agreement errors and misplaced and dangling modifiers distract and confuse readers. Articles can be especially troublesome for the person who speaks English as a second language. Many students say they need a review of the rules concerning the use of numbers in writing.

As you know, there are many ways to put words together to create sentences and paragraphs. Knowing how to overcome your trouble spots will help you make more successful choices.

D.1 Pronoun Case, Reference, and Agreement

Choosing a point of view and maintaining it throughout your essay depends upon a solid understanding of pronouns and how to use them. *Pronouns* are words used in place of nouns. They can help you avoid needless repetition, and they can also serve as a coherence device. The three essentials of pronoun usage are *case, reference,* and *agreement.* See section A.2 on pages 390–393 if you need a quick review of pronouns.

Pronoun Case

Pronoun case refers to a pronoun's function in a sentence. Since pronouns replace nouns, they can function in all the ways nouns function: as subjects, objects, or possessive modifiers.

Subjective case pronouns function as *subjects* and can replace noun subjects:

Edmundo could not find his backpack.

He could not find his backpack.

Objective case pronouns function as *objects* of verbs or prepositions and can replace noun objects:

Sue and Latrisha loaned Edmundo a pen and some paper.

Sue and Latrisha loaned him a pen and some paper.

They gave the pen and paper to Edmundo.

They gave the pen and paper to him.

Possessive case pronouns can appear anywhere in a sentence as modifiers; they show ownership and can replace possessive nouns:

Edmundo's backpack had been stolen.

His backpack had been stolen.

Edmundo used Sue's pen and Latrisha's paper.

Edmundo used their pen and paper.

Notice that personal pronouns also have different forms depending on whether they are singular or plural. Before doing Exercise 43, study Figure D-1.1, page 448, which lists all the forms of the personal pronouns.

Figure D-1.1 Cases of Personal Pronouns

	SUBJECTIVE	OBJECTIVE	POSSESSIVE
1st person singular	I	me	my, mine
1st person plural	we	us	our, ours
2nd person singular	you	you	your, yours
2nd person plural	you	you	your, yours
3rd person singular	he, she, it	him, her, it	his, hers, its
3rd person plural	they	them	their, theirs

Exercise 43

Replace the underlined nouns in each sentence with the appropriate subjective, objective, or possessive case of personal pronouns.

1. Elena bought a used camper; Elena had wanted a camper for a long time.

2. Elena bought the camper from someone who needed to get rid of it, so Elena got an unbelievably good deal.

3. Elena felt great behind the wheel of Elena's camper.

4. Elena took Elena's family for a ride, and the family congratulated Elena on finding such a good camper at such a low cost.

5. When the previous owner, Joe, called Elena a week later, the previous owner asked Elena how Elena liked the camper, and Elena answered, "Just fine."

Pronoun Reference

Always make clear which noun a pronoun refers to. If the *antecedent*—literally, the word that "goes before"—of your pronoun is unclear, your sentence will be confusing.

Unclear	**Clear**
Bob told Richard that his garbage disposal would not run. (Was it Bob's or Richard's garbage disposal? The reference is unclear.)	Bob said to Richard, "My garbage disposal will not run." (The pronoun *my* tells you that the garbage disposal belongs to Bob.)
Bob was sure that they had sold him a faulty garbage disposal. (Nothing in the sentence tells you who *they* are.)	Bob was sure that Ace Appliances had sold him a faulty garbage disposal. (Now it is clear who *they* are.)

Bob wanted to know what the store was going to do about <u>it</u>. (You cannot tell from the sentence what *it* means.)

Bob wanted to know what the store was going to do about the garbage disposal. (Now you can tell that *it* is the *garbage disposal*.)

[**Exercise 44**] Either rewrite the sentence or replace the underlined pronouns with words that make the reference clear.

1. Amy went with Nga to the department store to return <u>her</u> blouse.

2. Although it was Memorial Day, Amy thought that <u>they</u> would be open.

3. Amy was right, so she and Nga went inside to ask <u>them</u> to exchange the blouse for a smaller size.

4. The clerk said, "I'm sorry, but we're out of those. Do you want to exchange <u>it</u> for a different one or take a refund?"

5. <u>She</u> decided to take the money and go somewhere for lunch.

Whether to use *who, whom, whoever,* or *whomever* can be confusing. As explained below, these pronouns are both *relative pronouns* (useful for referring to a noun within a clause) and *interrogative pronouns* (useful for asking questions). They can be either singular or plural, as in the following sentences:

Janice is the only one <u>who</u> is talking.

Janice and Jeremiah are the only ones <u>who</u> are talking.

Finally, *who* and *whoever* also function as *subjective case pronouns,* but *whom* and *whoever* function as *objective case pronouns.* Several rules may help you to avoid confusion.

Use *who* or *whoever* as the subject of a sentence, clause, or question. To test whether you have used *who* or *whoever* correctly, you should be able to replace it with *he, she, they, I,* or *we* in the sentence or clause in which it appears.

<u>Who</u> is having the party? (<u>She</u> is having the party.)

<u>Who</u> should we say invited us? (We should say <u>she</u> invited us.)

<u>Whoever</u> brings the food should know how many are coming. (<u>He</u> brings the food.)

Please give an invitation to <u>whoever</u> might want to come. (<u>They</u> might want to come.)

Use *whom* or *whomever* as the object of a verb or the object of a preposition. To test whether you have used *whom* or *whomever* correctly, you should be able to replace it with *him, her, them, me,* or *us.* If you still are unsure, mentally rearrange the words in the sentence or clause so that the subject and verb are in the proper relationship; then substitute the appropriate pronoun for *whom* or *whomever,* as in the following sentences.

Whom did you invite to the party? (You did invite him to the party.)

To whom did you give the invitations? (You did give the invitations to them.)

She will invite whomever she likes. (She likes them.)

We will accept money from whomever we can get to contribute. (We can get them to contribute.)

[**Exercise 45**] Read each sentence. Then underline the appropriate pronoun in parentheses. Remember that *who* and *whoever* function as subjects, but *whom* and *whomever* function as objects.

1. The National Wildlife Federation is an organization that was founded to help people (who, whom) want to protect endangered species from abuse and extinction.

2. The organization awards research grants to (whoever, whomever) it chooses.

3. The photographer (who, whom) we invited to speak at our garden club meeting has been a frequent contributor to *National Wildlife* magazine.

4. For a small fee, anyone (who, whom) wants to support the organization's work can become a member of the National Wildlife Federation.

5. (Whoever, whomever) wants to help animals can serve in other ways as well.

6. Local groups, such as an animal shelter in your community, are always looking for people to (who, whom) they can turn for financial or other kinds of support.

7. Dick Morgan is the one in our community (who, whom) does the most to support wildlife causes.

8. (Who, whom) do you know in your community (who, whom) is a friend to animals?

Pronoun Agreement

A pronoun must *agree* in number and gender with its antecedent. Use a singular pronoun to refer to a singular antecedent; use a plural pronoun to refer to a plural antecedent. The gender of your pronouns (masculine: *he, his, him;* feminine: *she, hers, her;* or neuter: *it, its*) should also agree with that of

Figure D-1.2 Indefinite Pronouns

anybody	everybody	no one
anyone	everyone	one
each	neither	somebody
either	nobody	someone

their antecedents. For a quick review of pronoun types, see Figure A-2.1 on page 392.

> Because Parrish had studied for his test, he was prepared to do well.

> Because the students had studied for their test, they were prepared to do well.

In the first example, the singular masculine pronouns *his* and *he* refer to the singular masculine antecedent *Parrish.* In the second example, the plural pronouns *their* and *they* refer to the plural antecedent *students.*

Sometimes the antecedent of a personal pronoun is an indefinite pronoun, such as *everyone, someone, each,* or *one:*

> Has anyone left her coat behind?

Indefinite pronouns do not specify the things or individuals they refer to and therefore can cause some problems in agreement. In the example just given, both the verb *has left* and the personal pronoun *her* are singular. Indefinite pronouns are singular, and you should refer to them with singular personal pronouns. Avoid using the plural *their* to refer to an indefinite pronoun.

> Incorrect: Has anyone left their coat behind?

Another agreement problem with indefinite pronouns is that, because they are *indefinite,* their gender is unknown. Do not automatically use a masculine personal pronoun like *he, his,* or *him* unless you are specifically referring just to men. Either substitute *he or she, his or hers,* or *him or her* or, if these sound awkward, rewrite your sentence to avoid using them:

> Someone has left his or her answer sheet on the desk.

> Someone has left an answer sheet on the desk.

> I found an answer sheet on the desk.

Before doing the following exercise, review the list of indefinite pronouns in Figure D-1.2 at the top of this page.

[Exercise 46] Underline the pronoun in parentheses that agrees in number and gender with its antecedent.

1. Some students believe that algebra is (his, their) hardest course.

2. José, like many students, becomes anxious before (he, they) takes a test.

3. But if José goes into a test prepared, he will usually make a good grade on (them, it).

4. "Just between you and (I, me), I don't like algebra," said José.

5. "Then you and (I, me) agree on at least one thing," said his friend Rose.

6. Of Rose and José, it is (her, she) who makes better grades.

7. José and (her, she) often study together.

8. Unfortunately, a student who does not prepare sufficiently for a test will usually not do (his, his or her, their) best work.

9. Anyone who is willing to prepare for (his or her, their) tests has a good chance of succeeding.

10. Rewrite sentences 4 and 5 to eliminate the need for personal pronouns.

     If the antecedent consists of two singular pronouns joined by the correlative conjunctions *either . . . or, neither . . . nor,* or *not only . . . but also,* use a singular pronoun. If the antecedent consists of two plural nouns joined by these conjunctions, use a plural pronoun:

     Either Mary or Carrie will bring her notes to the meeting. (Mary, Carrie, and her are singular.)

     Neither the men nor the women want to give up their places in line. (Men, women, and their are plural.)

     Not only the group's president but also the other officers will give their reports.

     What if a correlative conjunction joins a singular noun and a plural noun, as in the third example just given? The rule for this type of sentence construction is that the pronoun should agree with the noun that is closer to it. However, following the rule can sometimes cause confusion, as in the next sentence:

     Either the students or the teacher will correct her answers.

     This sentence follows the rule of making the pronoun agree with the closest noun, but the meaning is confused. The students, not the teacher, are the ones whose answers should be corrected. To preserve this meaning and to follow the rule, simply reverse the order of the nouns:

     Either the teacher or the students will correct their answers.

To avoid confusion in your own writing when using correlative conjunctions, place the plural noun closer to the pronoun, as in the previous example.

[**Exercise 47**] Choose the pronoun in parentheses that agrees in number and gender with its antecedent.

1. Neither Larry nor Leroy wants to do (their, his) work.

2. Not only my aunt but also my cousins will bring (her, their) car.

3. We were upset because neither the dog nor the cats would eat (its, their) food.

4. My grandmother thinks that either an apple or some nuts would add (its, their) distinct flavor to the salad.

5. We asked neither this speaker nor that speaker to limit (their, his or her) time.

[**Exercise 48**] Read the following paragraph and correct any errors you find in pronoun case, reference, or agreement, either by changing the pronoun or by rewriting the sentence.

> Tinsey's job as a registered nurse is very demanding. She works in an intermediate care center where many of the patients are bedridden, so Tinsey has to bathe, change, and feed him or her. Others may be on tube feedings, and Tinsey must see that his or her pump is working properly, the lines are clear, and a new bottle of food is attached as soon as they are empty. Monitoring a patient's vital signs is also a part of Tinsey's job. She takes their temperature, pulse, and blood pressure several times during her shift. If a patient is on oxygen, Tinsey must make sure that the line remains attached to the oxygen supply and that they do not dislodge the tube. When a patient rings for their nurse, Tinsey must answer the call and attend to their needs. In addition to all her other tasks, Tinsey writes reports and attends staff meetings. At the end of her shift she has earned her rest.

D.2 Verb Tense Consistency and Agreement

Mistakes in verb tense consistency and agreement are among the most common types of errors college students make in writing. Before reading this section, see section A.3 on pages 393–396 for a quick review of verbs.

Tense Consistency

The verb in a dependent clause of a sentence should be *in the same tense* as the verb in the independent clause if the actions occurred at the same time. If the verb in the independent clause of a sentence is in the past tense, then the verb in the dependent clause should also express past time:

> Darryl wished (past) that he had bought (past perfect) the jacket when it was (past) on sale.

> Darryl missed (past) the sale because he was working (past progressive) late.

To help your readers avoid any confusion about what is happening and when the events you describe take place, maintain a consistent sequence of tenses throughout a paragraph or essay. In Example A, unnecessary tense shifts create confusion. In Example B, the paragraph is revised to achieve tense consistency. In both paragraphs, verbs are underlined.

EXAMPLE A

Choosing a restaurant was difficult. I want ethnic food such as Thai or Indian cuisine. However, my friend says he had a taste for something simple such as a hamburger or a salad. As a compromise, we chose a restaurant that offers something enjoyable for both of us.

EXAMPLE B

Choosing a restaurant was difficult. I wanted ethnic food such as Thai or Indian cuisine. However, my friend said he had a taste for something simple such as a hamburger or a salad. As a compromise, we chose a restaurant that offered something enjoyable for both of us.

In sentences having more than one verb, make sure that you maintain a consistent sequence of tenses as in the following examples:

> Darryl now thinks (present) that he is going (present progressive) to buy the jacket anyway.

> Darryl says (present) that he has never seen (present perfect) a jacket that he likes (present) as well.

> Darryl hopes (present) that the store will have (future tense) some jackets left.

> Darryl thought (past) that the store would have (past tense form of *will have*) some jackets left.

[Exercise 49] Circle the appropriate verb tense in the sentences that follow.

1. Linda (takes, took) Freshman Composition at 8:00 on Tuesdays and Thursdays this semester.

2. She (likes, liked) this class, but she (does not, do not) like to write.

3. At least that is how she (felt, has felt) when the semester began.

4. Now she (thinks, was thinking) that she (likes, liked) to write a little better than she used to.

5. In fact, she (is looking, was looking) forward to her next writing class.

6. Chuck, a friend of Linda's, (attends, attended) a creative writing class this semester.

7. He (wants, wanted) Linda to sit in on it sometime because he (knows, knew) she will like it.

8. Chuck (has talked, had talked) so much about this class that Linda has already decided to sign up for it.

9. She (worries, worried) that the class may be too hard for her.

10. "Don't worry," Chuck says. "The class (is, was) for beginners."

[Exercise 50] Fill in the blank in each sentence with the correct form of the verb *be, do,* or *have.* These verbs can be troublesome for some students.

1. The kind of car to buy _____ (be) a personal choice.

2. My dad _____ (have) always driven Chevrolets, but I prefer Fords.

3. I _____ (do) own a Corvette once, but I sold it to my brother-in-law.

4. Some people _____ (have) a need for a vehicle with lots of room.

5. Others _____ (have) big cars in the past but are now looking to downsize.

6. My friend says she _____ (do) care about gas mileage, even though the car she drives is not fuel efficient.

7. My last car _____ (be) not very reliable.

8. I hope my next car _____ (have) a good warranty.

9. Some say that the kind of car you choose _____ (have) a lot to do with your personality.

10. What kind of car _____ (do) you want to own?

Verb Agreement

The subject and verb of a sentence must agree in number. If the subject is singular (one person or thing), the verb form must be singular. If the subject is plural (two or more persons or things), the verb form must be plural. Note that the present tense of a verb in the third-person *singular* always ends in -*s* or -*es,* whereas the third-person plural form of the verb in the present tense has no -*s* or -*es.* This is just the opposite from nouns: Nouns normally form their *plural* by adding -*s* or -*es.*

> The rain falls. (*Rain* is singular; the verb adds -*s.*)
>
> Heavy rains fall. (*Rains* is plural; the verb drops the -*s.*)
>
> Careta plays the violin. (*Careta* is singular; the verb adds -*s.*)
>
> Careta teaches music. (*Careta* is singular; the verb adds -*es.*)

Where a correlative conjunction joins two nouns, not only must a pronoun agree with the closer antecedent, but the verb must also agree in number with the closer subject. Where one noun is plural and the other is singular, place the plural noun closer to the verb to avoid confusion. If the subjects are two different personal pronouns, then make the verb agree in person and in number with the subject closer to it. When meaning may be in doubt, write your sentences so that the plural subject is closer to the verb, and make the verb agree.

> Neither Ron nor Rita has brought a lunch today. (Singular subjects agree with singular verb.)
>
> Not only the students but also the teachers eat here. (Plural subjects agree with plural verb.)
>
> Neither Raymond nor his sisters have eaten yet. (A plural and a singular subject: Verb agrees with closer subject.)
>
> Either my brother or I fix dinner. (Third-person subject and first-person subject: Verb agrees with closer subject.)
>
> Not only fruit juices but also the fruit itself adds flavor to recipes. (A plural subject and a singular subject: Verb agrees with closer subject.)˙

[Exercise 51] At the end of each sentence are paired verbs. Pick the correct one to fill in the blank by first underlining the subject of the sentence or clause and then choosing the verb form that agrees with the subject.

1. Margaret and Steve _____ at the San Diego Zoo at 9:00 in the morning. (arrives, arrive)

2. They _____ to go their separate ways and meet back at the entrance for lunch. (decides, decide)

3. Margaret _____ on the skylift to get a view of the whole zoo. (rides, ride)

4. While she is riding, she _____ a strange animal. (spots, spot)

5. There are several others like it, and they _____ like pigs with long faces. (looks, look)

6. Their crooked little horns _____ up from the bottom of their mouths. (curls, curl)

7. The person who _____ the skylift says, "That's Charlie, the warthog." (operates, operate)

8. Steve _____ so much time looking at the timber wolves that he misses most of the other animals. (spends, spend)

9. After lunch, Margaret and Steve take each other to see the animals that each _____ best. (likes, like)

10. The wolves _____ no attention, but the warthog looks at Margaret and Steve and _____. (pays, pay) and (snorts, snort)

[**Exercise 52**] The following sentences contain subjects joined by correlative conjunctions. Read each sentence. Then underline the correct verb within parentheses.

1. Neither the employees nor their manager (like, likes) the store's new working hours.

2. Not only consumers but also employees (prefer, prefers) a store that is clean and up-to-date.

3. Either a department store or a specialty store (sell, sells) the items most consumers want.

4. Neither the mall's food court nor the various stand-alone restaurants surrounding the property (serve, serves) exactly what we want.

5. Not only my friends but also my family (like, likes) our area's newest movie theater.

[**Exercise 53**] Read the paragraph that follows and correct any tense or agreement errors that you find.

A few years ago, a really strange thing happens. A woman bought a wallet made out of eelskin and the next thing she knew, her Mastercard would not works. The clerk at the store where she tried to use the card said that something must have demagnetized it. The woman also had some gasoline credit cards that she kept in the back of her checkbook; these were working fine. While she was waiting to receive a replacement credit card, she heard on the news that other people is having the same problem. The rumor was that the wallets were made of the skin from electric eels and that they still contained traces of electricity, which had destroyed the credit cards. The company got so many complaints that they did some research. As it happened, the wallets were not even made of the skin of electric eels at all. They were made of hagfish skin. The mystery were solved by researchers who pointed out that some of the wallets had metal clips that could have demagnetized the cards. Not only that; they also said that if you lays a wallet down on a VCR, that action could demagnetize the card as well.

D.3 Misplaced and Dangling Modifiers

Modifiers are words, phrases, or clauses that describe or limit other words within sentences. As explained in Chapter 8, good descriptive writing contains numerous modifiers that specify *what* something looks, sounds, smells, tastes, and feels like and *how* it acts. The usual position for a modifier is next to the word it modifies. If modifiers are out of place, they can create confusion in your sentences, making it difficult for readers to understand what you mean. *Misplaced modifiers* and *dangling modifiers* are two common sentence errors you can learn to recognize and correct.

Misplaced Modifiers

A *misplaced modifier* is one that is not placed next to the word it describes. Figure D-3.1 on page 459 illustrates how to correct misplaced modifiers. Study the figure before you do Exercise 54.

[Exercise 54] Each sentence on page 459 has a misplaced modifier. Underline the misplaced word or word group in each sentence. Then rewrite the sentence so that the modifier is next to the word it modifies. Example:

Misplaced modifier: We <u>nearly</u> had eight inches of rain last week.
(The writer's intent is to explain how much rain.)

Correction: We had <u>nearly</u> eight inches of rain last week.
(Now the writer's intent is clear.)

1. For the person who needs to only lose a few pounds, exercise and a balanced diet will do the job.

2. Jack, however, wanted results fast because he did not want to go to the fraternity dance with his girlfriend wearing a tuxedo that was too small.

3. Jack tried the Super Skinny Diet advertised by a famous rock star who lost 30 pounds on television.

4. "All you have to do," the rock star said, "is drink a Super Skinny shake after being mixed up in a blender three times a day."

5. By the end of the first day, Jack was so hungry that he ate three hamburgers driving home in a pickup truck.

6. Jack's father, who was a nutritionist, told him to exercise and eat sensibly with his stationary bicycle.

7. Jack tried this plan and by the end of three weeks had nearly lost six pounds.

8. He returned the rest of the Super Skinny shake mix to the store where he had bought it for a refund.

9. The manager took the shake mix and gave Jack a refund after throwing it in the trash can.

10. Jack went to the dance with his girl wearing a tuxedo that fit just right.

Figure D-3.1 Misplaced Modifiers and How to Correct Them

MISPLACED MODIFIER

My brother keeps the trophy that he won for playing soccer <u>in the bookcase</u>. (My *brother* did not play soccer in the bookcase.)

We brought the car from a salesman <u>that has a five-year warranty</u>. (The *salesman* does not have a five-year warranty.)

We <u>almost</u> had fifty people come to our party. (The writer *does not* mean that fifty people were expected, but none of them came.)

CORRECTLY PLACED MODIFIER

The trophy <u>in the bookcase</u> is the one my brother won for playing soccer. (The *trophy* is in the bookcase.)

The salesman sold us a car <u>that has a five-year warranty</u>.) (The *car* has a five-year warranty.)

We had <u>almost</u> fifty people come to our party. (The writer *does* mean that about fifty people came to the party.)

Rule: *Place modifying words and word groups next to the words they modify.*

Dangling Modifiers

A modifier that begins a sentence but does not modify the subject of the sentence is a *dangling modifier*. Dangling modifiers confuse readers and, like misplaced modifiers, create errors in logic:

> Flying upside down, we watched the Blue Angels.

The sentence is illogical because the wording of it suggests that *we* are flying upside down, not the Blue Angels. You can correct the dangling modifier in two ways:

> Flying upside down, the Blue Angels performed for us. (The intended subject follows the modifier that begins the sentence.)

> We watched the Blue Angels, who were flying upside down. (The modifier becomes a dependent clause.)

Figure D-3.2 on page 461 provides additional examples of dangling modifiers and how to correct them.

[**Exercise 55**] Each of the following sentences has a dangling modifier. Underline the dangling modifier in each sentence, and then either rewrite the sentence so that the word or subject the modifier describes follows it, or make the modifier into a dependent clause.

1. Studying for the algebra exam, the chair was so uncomfortable that Kathy couldn't concentrate.

2. Finding another chair, now the temperature seemed too cool.

3. After adjusting the temperature, the light bulb in the desk lamp burned out.

4. Feeling hungry after all this work, a snack seemed like a good idea.

5. Trying once more to study, her concentration still wandered.

6. To do well on the test, studying was absolutely essential.

7. Ringing on the table beside her bed, Kathy got up from her desk to answer the phone.

8. Telling her friend she had to study, going out was a great temptation.

9. Sitting down once more, her roommate came in from class and started to play the stereo.

10. Deciding she needed a better study place, the library seemed inviting.

Figure D-3.2 Dangling Modifiers and How to Correct Them

DANGLING MODIFIER

Sitting in the bookcase, my brother won the trophy for playing soccer.
(My *brother* is not sitting in the bookcase.)

With a five-year warranty, the salesman sold me the used car.
(The *salesman* does not have a five-year warranty.)

To guarantee winning the lottery, tickets in every possible number combination are necessary.
(*Who* needs the tickets to guarantee winning?)

CORRECTED MODIFIER

The trophy sitting in the bookcase is the one my brother won for playing soccer.
(The *trophy* is sitting in the bookcase.)

The salesman sold me a car that has a five-year warranty.
(The *car* has a five-year warranty.)

To guarantee winning the lottery, you need tickets in every possible number combination.
(*You* need the tickets to guarantee winning.)

Rule 1: *Follow a modifier at the beginning of a sentence with the word or subject it modifies.*

or

Rule 2: *Make the modifier into a dependent clause. (You may need to change the verb also.)*

[**Exercise 56**] Find and correct the misplaced and dangling modifiers in the following paragraph.

Mr. Dohrmat decided to have a pool installed with his Christmas bonus. Hoping for a healthful summer of swimming laps every morning, a pool seemed like a great idea. Judy and Jimmy Dohrmat were distracted by the construction doing their homework. Finally the pool was filled, and all the neighborhood children came over for a look in their bathing suits. That afternoon Mrs. Dohrmat's relatives, the Freeloaders, called to say they were coming to spend their vacation in their camper with their three kids. For the next month, the Freeloaders' children, the neighborhood kids, and the two little Dohrmats monopolized the pool. Just when Mr. Dohrmat would start to relax on his air mattress, one of the children would capsize him by jumping in with the dog wearing an innertube around his waist. One morning Mr. Dohrmat told his wife he should have invested his Christmas bonus during breakfast. His wife said, "Never mind; the kids only are young once." Bobbing with children, Mr. Dohrmat eyed the pool wistfully. "I suppose you are right," he said.

Figure D-4.1 Guidelines for Using Numbers

Dates	February 9, 1945
	1918–1992
Addresses	33 Poplar Avenue
	6509 Grapevine Road
	Mt. Dora, FL 32756
Times	3:02 P.M.; three o'clock
Mathematical expressions	3.1416; 2½; one-third; 50 percent
Chapters and pages	Volume 4, page 21; Chapter 8, page 102
Scores and statistics	3–1 odds; a score of 14–0
Identification numbers	radio station 105.9; (telephone numbers, social security numbers, zip codes)
Measurements	36 inches; 120 pounds; 16 liters; 4 tablespoons; 3" x 5"
Act, scene, line	Act II, scene 3, lines 10–17
Temperatures	212°F; 100°C
Money	10 cents; $3.2 million; $12.00

D.4 Numbers

Numbers can be expressed in words or figures. The choice depends on how many numbers appear in your paper and what they signify. If you use only a few numbers, and if they can be expressed in one or two words, spell them: *fifty* percent, a population of *six thousand*, *twenty-five* copies. Remember to hyphenate numbers from twenty-one through ninety-nine. However, if numbers occur frequently in your paper, spell out those from one to nine, but use figures for 10 or higher. When writing papers for the humanities, do not begin a sentence with a number. Either spell the number or revise your sentence so that the number does not come first. Figure D-4.1 above lists guidelines for using numbers.

Word Choice

As a writer, you have many choices to make, but your word choice is your most important one. What words will you choose? What combinations of words will result in the best sentences you can write? What words and the ideas they represent will appeal to your readers? Three strategies can help you make these decisions: knowing a word's stated and implied meanings, being able to choose among words that look or sound alike, and learning a few spelling tips so that spelling does not become a stumbling block.

E.1 Denotation and Connotation

To make effective word choices, understand the difference between a word's *denotation* and its *connotation*. The dictionary definition is a word's *denotation*. The emotional associations that a word evokes are its *connotations*. For example, *thin, slender, slim, skinny,* and *emaciated* all have the same denotation: weight that falls below the average. However, each of these words has different connotations. *Skinny* connotes unattractiveness; *emaciated* connotes malnourishment; and *thin, slim,* and *slender* usually connote degrees of attractiveness. However, people may disagree about a word's connotation. Some people might say that fashion models are skinny, whereas others would call them slender. Your choice of one of these words to describe a fashion model would depend upon whether you think that a typical model's size and body type are attractive.

Connotations also can change over time. For example, *awesome,* an adjective that denotes mixed feelings of wonder, reverence, and dread, used to be reserved for use in a spiritual context. The word still has this connotation in the following two sentences:

> As Greta listened to the <u>awesome</u> strains of Beethoven's *Ninth Symphony,* her eyes filled with tears.

> Some people say that while standing before El Greco's <u>awesome</u> painting *The Crucifixion,* they can feel the presence of God.

Beginning in the nineteen-seventies, *awesome* developed a new usage as a slang term and therefore new connotations, as in the following two sentences:

> Mikey whipped out the plastic minicar from the cereal box and said, "Wow, this is <u>awesome!</u>"

> Jennifer said to Angela, "Wear your red leather miniskirt to the party; it looks <u>awesome</u> on you."

Used as slang, *awesome* still carries connotations of wonder, but the wonder is more generalized to cover anything that might be called "great" or "terrific."

Understanding the difference between denotation and connotation can help you select the words that will most effectively communicate your ideas.

☑ **CONCEPT CHECK**
When writing a definition essay, consider both the denotation and connotation of the word or term you define. For more on definition, see Chapter 13.

[Exercise 57] Each of the word groups in the following exercise contains three words that have approximately the same *denotation* but different *connotations.* For each word group, do the following:

1. Write a single *denotative* definition for the word group.

2. Write the *connotative* meanings of each of the three words.

3. Rate each of the three words as positive, neutral, or negative in its connotation.

> Example: preowned, used, worn-out
>
> Denotation: The terms all mean "not new."
>
> Connotation: <u>Worn-out</u> suggests "unusable" and is the negative term. <u>Used</u> means "not new," though there may be some use left. <u>Used</u> is the neutral term, and <u>preowned</u> is the positive term. It suggests that an item had a prior owner but is neither used up nor worn out.

WORD GROUPS

a. obese, large, plump

b. persistent, stubborn, unyielding

c. synthetic, fake, artificial

d. act, stunt, trick

e. stroll, swagger, walk

f. to boss, to control, to manage

g. disrobe, strip, undress

h. cheap, bargain-priced, inexpensive

i. show, expose, display

[**Exercise 58**] Because of their connotations, the six underlined words in the following paragraph do not match the tone of the rest of the paragraph. First determine why each of the six words is inappropriate; then replace each one with a word that has an appropriate connotation.

> Three friends meet once a week to play poker. Although they play for only pennies, the game can get very intense, with heated arguments on all sides. Before they know it, one is accusing another of cheating. To solve these problems so they can all relax and have an enjoyable game, they have come up with some new rules. First of all, they have to wear ski masks so that the expressions on their <u>mugs</u> will not reveal the cards they are <u>hugging</u>. Second, they have to keep their <u>mitts</u> above the table at all times. In addition, they play at a glass-topped table to prevent anyone from sneaking a hand underneath to <u>pluck</u> a hidden card. Also, they always play with a new pack of cards so that no one can mark the cards ahead of time or <u>cram</u> extras into the deck. The friends find their game amusing and think they are wonderfully creative to have come up with a way to play it and avoid getting <u>peeved</u>.

E.2 Making Sense of Confusing Words

Words can be confusing when they look alike or sound alike. It is easy to write one word when you really mean another one that happens to look or sound like it. Though many of the most commonly confused words are simple ones whose meanings you know when you stop to think about them, it is easy to confuse them when you are writing. Call it a slip of the pen or the computer key. Two things can help you make sense of confusing words. First, review their meanings. Second, proofread your essays for any of the following words you may have confused.

accept, except

Accept is a verb meaning "to receive with pleasure." *Except* is most commonly used as a preposition meaning "excluding."

> I accept (receive with pleasure) your apology.

> Everyone except (excluding) Roxanne is invited.

advice, advise

Advice is a noun meaning "opinion concerning what to do." *Advise* is a verb meaning "to give advice or an opinion."

> My counselor gave me some good advice (opinion) about what course to take.

> My counselor advised me (gave an opinion) to take a study skills course.

affect, effect

Affect used as a verb means "to influence." *Effect* used as a verb means "to bring about." *Effect* used as a noun means "a result."

affect and *effect* used as verbs:

> Your jokes affect (influence) me in a negative way.

> The new fertilizer will effect (bring about) new growth.

effect used as a noun:

> We do not know what effect (result) this new drug will have.

brake, break

Brake used as a verb means "to stop." *Break* used as a verb means "to crack, smash, or shatter."

> I brake (stop) for animals.

> To break (shatter) a mirror is to invite bad luck.

choose, chose

Choose is the present-tense form of the verb *to choose,* meaning "to select." *Chose* is the past-tense form of the same verb.

> Every four years voters choose (select) a new president of the United States.

> After an election, pollsters try to determine why voters chose (selected) their candidates.

coarse, course

Coarse is an adjective meaning "rough" or "vulgar." *Course* is a noun meaning "subject" or "direction."

> Burlap is a coarse (rough) material.

> Some people do not like to hear coarse (vulgar) jokes.

> Algebra is a required course (subject) at most colleges.

> The explorers followed the river's course (direction).

everyday, every day

Everyday is an adjective meaning "ordinary." *Every day* is an adverbial phrase meaning "each day."

> A tornado is not an everyday (ordinary) weather condition.

> The mail arrives every day (each day) at 10:30 A.M.

its, it's

Its is a possessive pronoun meaning "belonging to." *It's* is a contraction of "it is."

> The dog buried its (belonging to, his) bone in the yard.

> Because it's (it is) raining, you will need your umbrella.

loose, lose

Loose is an adjective meaning "not tight." *Lose* is a present-tense form of the verb *to lose,* meaning "to misplace."

> Loose (not tight) clothing is comfortable on hot days.

> Every time I lay down my keys, I lose (misplace) them.

passed, past

Passed is the past-tense form of the verb *to pass,* meaning "to move on or ahead." *Past* used as an adjective means "over and done." *Past* used as a noun means "a former time."

We <u>passed</u> (moved ahead of) the cars on the right.

There is no use crying over <u>past</u> (over and done) mistakes.

Some people enjoy thinking about the <u>past</u> (a former time).

peace, piece

Peace is a noun meaning "harmony." *Piece* is a noun meaning "part."

We would like all nations to live in <u>peace</u> (harmony).

I would like another <u>piece</u> (part) of pie.

quiet, quite, quit

Quiet used as an adjective means "silent"; used as a verb, it means "to silence." *Quite* is an adverb meaning "completely." *Quit* is a verb meaning "to stop" or "to leave."

After the storm, it was <u>quiet</u> (silent).

Is there no way to quiet (to silence) that noisy dog?

I am not <u>quite</u> (completely) finished with this essay.

Do not <u>quit</u> (leave) your job unless you find a better one.

their, there, they're

Their is a possessive pronoun meaning "belonging to them." *There* is an adverb meaning "in that place." *They're* is a contraction of "they are."

These are <u>their</u> (belonging to them) books.

Put your jacket over <u>there</u> (in that place).

<u>They're</u> (they are) noisy today.

to, too, two

To is commonly used as a preposition meaning "in a direction toward." *Too* is an adverb meaning "also" or "more than enough." *Two* is a noun meaning "the sum of one plus one."

Send the check <u>to</u> (toward) me.

I like chocolate ice cream <u>too</u> (also).

You have paid <u>too</u> much (more than enough) for this VCR.

There will be <u>two</u> (one plus one) for dinner.

wear, where, were, we're

Wear is a verb meaning "to have on." *Where* is an adverb meaning "at what place." *Were* is a past-tense form of the verb *to be*. *We're* is a contraction of "we are."

I wish you would <u>wear</u> (have on) your new suit to the wedding.

<u>Where</u> (at what place) did you put my new suit?

I did not know you <u>were</u> (to be) going to the reception.

<u>We're</u> (we are) a cute couple.

who's, whose

Who's is a contraction meaning "who is." *Whose* is a possessive pronoun meaning "belonging to whom."

<u>Who's</u> (who is) ready for a swim?

<u>Whose</u> (belonging to whom) swimming trunks are these?

your, you're

Your is a possessive pronoun meaning "belonging to you." *You're* is a contraction of "you are."

This must be <u>your</u> (belonging to you) sister.

I hope <u>you're</u> (you are) not intending to eat these doughnuts.

[**Exercise 59**] In each sentence, fill in the blank with the correct word.

1. This _____ (passed, past) week, I was invited to a friend's birthday party.

2. I decided to _____ (accept, except) the invitation.

3. Because I could not decide on a gift to take, I finally _____ (choose, chose) a gift certificate instead.

4. The invitation said not to dress up, so I wore my _____ (everyday, every day) clothes.

5. When I took a wrong turn, my friend said, "Do you know where _____ (were, we're) going?"

6. My friend said he had been _____ (there, their) before.

7. I took his _____ (advice, advise) and changed _____ (coarse, course).

8. The party was _____ (quiet, quite) a lot of fun.

9. "I can't wait to have a _____ (peace, piece) of that cake," my friend said.

10. When the food is good, _____ (its, it's) easy to eat _____ (to, too) much.

[Exercise 60] Edit the following paragraph by finding and correcting any confusing words.

> Having a rat die in you're office is an experience you will not forget. In the first place, you do not always know where the rat is. It may be in the attic caught in a trap you put up their the last time one died, or it may be decaying inside a wall were it crawled to try to escape. Secondly, the smell is so strong its hard to concentrate on anything else. It really disrupts the piece of the office. Passed experience may have shown you that if this rat has died, another probably will to, so you had better call a construction company and try to find out how there getting in the building. If someone can find the holes and seal them up, then you're problems will be over. If not, then you will just have to except the situation as it is and realize that once the air is clear, you may have to go through all this again.

E.3 Spelling Tips

Careless errors, especially in spelling, can interrupt the flow of even the most well-organized and logically supported essay because they call attention to themselves. When you proofread your essays to find and correct surface errors, don't forget spelling. Following are some common spelling rules and tips for improving your spelling.

1. *You may have learned this rule long ago:* i *before* e *except after* c *or when pronounced* ay, *as in* neighbor *and* weigh.

   believe, grieve   (use i before e)

   receive, perceive   (except after c)

   Some exceptions: either, foreign, forfeit, height, leisure, neither, seize, weird

2. *When adding an ending to a word that ends in* e: *keep the* e *before a consonant; drop it before a vowel. (Vowels are* a, e, i, o, u, *and sometimes* y; *all the other letters are consonants.)*

   hope + ful = hopeful   (keep e before a consonant)

   cope + ing = coping   (drop e before a vowel)

   Some exceptions: argue + ment = argument
   judge + ment = judgment or judgement
   true + ly = truly
   damage + able = damageable
   advantage + ous = advantageous

3. *When adding an ending to a word that ends in* y: *If the* y *is preceded by a vowel, keep the* y; *if the* y *is preceded by a consonant, change the* y *to* i.

buy + ing = buying   (vowel u precedes y)

copy + ed = copied   (consonant p precedes y)

4. *Generally, when adding an ending to a one-syllable word that ends in a consonant: Double the final consonant if it is preceded by a single vowel; leave it alone if it is preceded by two vowels.*

ship + ed = shipped   (p preceded by single vowel i)

seat + ed = seated   (t preceded by two vowels ea)

5. *Generally, when adding an ending to a multisyllable word that ends in a consonant: Double the final consonant if it is preceded by a single vowel; leave it alone if it is preceded by two vowels or by a consonant + vowel.*

commit + ing = committing   (t preceded by single vowel i)

despair + ing = despairing   (r preceded by two vowels ai)

benefit + ed = benefited   (t preceded by consonant + vowel fi)

Some exceptions: quitting, cancellation, excellent, questionnaire

6. *To form plurals of nouns, add* -s *to most nouns; add* -es *to most nouns ending in* o, ch, sh, ss, x, *or* zz.

plan + s = plans

star + s = stars

hero + es = heroes

lunch + es = lunches

toothbrush + es = toothbrushes

sphinx + es = sphinxes

mix + es = mixes

Some exceptions: words that end in two vowels, such as *radios* and *zoos*

[**Exercise 61**] Examine several of your returned essays for spelling errors that have been marked. Make a list of your errors and try to determine which of the six rules you need to review.

Tips for Improving Your Spelling

1. Keep lists of words that you misspell and that you frequently look up in the dictionary. Try to learn the spelling of these words by figuring out which rule applies.

2. Use a memory aid. For example, choose a word you commonly misspell and memorize some spelling points about it—for example:

   accommodate contains two *c*'s, two *m*'s, two *o*'s, and *a date.*

   There is a rat in separate.

3. Try the following method for learning the spelling of difficult words: Pronounce the word; spell it aloud one letter at a time; write the word without looking at it; check your spelling; repeat the steps until you can spell the word from memory.

4. Use the dictionary; keep it handy when you write.

5. Review basic spelling rules; seek extra help from your college library or learning lab, which may have programmed materials you can check out for improving spelling.

6. If you use a word processor, use the spelling check feature. However, a spell checker is no substitute for your desk dictionary because your computer's dictionary may not contain *all* the words you misspell. Moreover, a spell checker will not catch misspellings that are actually another word. For example, if you write *peace* when you mean *piece,* your spell checker will not make the distinction.

ESL Concerns and Choices

English is a rich language that has roots in and connections to many other languages. Standard English—the version used in *The Confident Writer*—is expected in academic and business settings. English is the language of international trade and communication and is spoken around the world, as Figure F-1.1 on the following page shows. Being able to write correct English sentences and paragraphs is a career asset for both nonnative and native speakers.

Standard English has many exceptions and irregularities. Therefore, if English is not your native language, and you are sometimes confused, then you are not alone! This section answers some of the nonnative speaker's frequently asked questions. Perhaps one of your questions or concerns is among the following:

- What is the proper word order in English?
- How do I use negatives like *no* and *not?*
- How do I use *there* and *it* to begin a sentence?
- What are *articles,* and how do I use them?
- How do I use *idioms* such as *afraid of* or *sign up?*

Figure F-1.1 Circle of World English

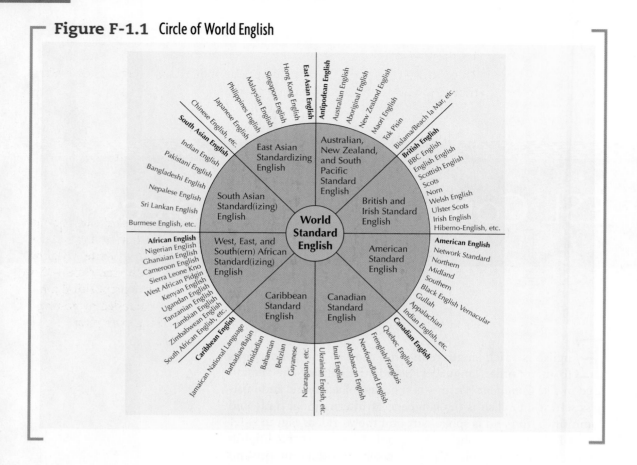

F.1 Basic Sentence Patterns

What is the proper word order in English?

Every language has a standard *word order,* or rules for the placement of words in a sentence. The English language has several sentence patterns that describe word order. Mastering these patterns will enable you to improve your sentence structure. First, let's review the parts of a sentence: The *subject* (**S**) is who or what the sentence is about. The *verb* (**V**) describes an action that the subject takes or receives or the subject's state of being. The verb's object (**O**) is of two types: The direct object (**DO**) receives an action. The indirect object (**IO**) is the person, place, or thing for or to whom the action is performed. The indirect object comes between the verb and the direct object. These relationships are expressed in three basic sentence patterns. There are other sentence patterns, of course, but these three are a good beginning.

      S   V

1. My sister baked.

This is the most basic pattern: A subject is followed by a verb. The combination of the two expresses a complete thought.

      S   V   DO

2. My sister baked a cake.

In this pattern, the direct object, *cake,* receives the action of the verb.

      S   V   IO   DO

3. My sister baked me a cake.

In this pattern, the indirect object, *me,* explains for whom the cake was baked. The indirect object comes before the direct object. Notice that in this pattern, *for* is understood and is not stated. It would be incorrect to write *My sister baked for me a cake.* If *for* were written in this version of the sentence—"My sister baked a cake for me"—*me* would be the object of the preposition *for.*

    In fact, each of the three sentence patterns can be expanded by adding a modifier such as a prepositional phrase as in the following examples:

      S V **prep. phrase**

The dog ran [up the stairs.]

      S   V   DO   **prep. phrase**

My sister baked a cake [before breakfast].

      S   V   IO   DO **prep. phrase**

My mother bought me a coat [at the store].

    If you doubt whether a sentence you have written follows the correct word order, first try to identify the parts by asking yourself these questions: *Who or what is the subject? What is the action? Who or what receives the action?* When you are sure that you have identified the parts accurately, you can rearrange the parts in the correct order, as in the following example:

Incorrect: My sister a cake baked.
Correct: My sister baked a cake.

[Exercise 62] Following are several pairs of sentences. Beside each sentence, write C if the word order is correct; write I if the word order is incorrect.

_____ 1. Jonah a toy airplane has built.

_____ 2. Jonah has built a toy airplane.

_____ 3. Eric sent an email to me.

_____ 4. Eric to me an email sent.

_____ 5. To Atlanta for Thanksgiving went I.

_____ 6. I went to Atlanta for Thanksgiving.

_____ 7. Will you make a cake for me?

_____ 8. For me a cake will you make?

_____ 9. For sale, provides the department store many items.

_____ 10. The department store provides many items for sale.

[**Exercise 63**] In each of the following sentences, the word order is incorrect. Rewrite each sentence to correct the word order.

1. For his brother a baseball cap Joe bought.

2. Watching play the Red Sox enjoys Amy.

3. The World Series this year won the Red Sox.

4. Been to a baseball game have you ever?

5. On TV watching sports enjoy many people.

F.2 Understanding Negatives

How do I use negatives like no *and* not?

The words *no* and *not* are two different parts of speech that are used in different ways. *No* is an adjective that modifies a noun. *Not* is an adverb that when used with a verb, adjective, or another adverb changes that word's meaning to a *negative* meaning. Some examples will illustrate how to use *no* and *not*.

1. We make *no* excuses.

2. We wash *no* cars here.

In the first sentence, *no* modifies the noun *excuses;* in the second sentence, *no* modifies the noun *cars.* Now read the next group of sentences.

3. He has *not* cleaned the garage.

4. She has *not* talked to anyone.

In sentences 3 and 4, *not* is used with a verb. In each case, the sentence explains actions that have *not* taken place.

5. This tire is *not* flat.

6. The color of the chair is *not* pretty.

In sentence 5, *not* is used with an adjective that describes the tire. In sentence 6, *not* is used with an adjective that describes the chair's color.

Figure F-2.1 Helping Verbs (also called Auxiliary Verbs)

to be	is, was, were, am, are, been, being
to do	do, does, did
to have	have, has, had
other helpers	can, could, may, might, should, will, shall

7. He is *not* very tired.

8. She is *not* too happy.

In sentence 7, *not* is used with an adverb that explains how tired he is—not *very* tired. In sentence 8, *not* is used with an adverb that explains to what extent he is happy—not *too* happy.

By now, you may have noticed two interesting things about negative expressions. First of all, *no* and *not* can be used to change positive statements into negative statements, as in the following examples. The sentences in each pair are opposites in meaning:

9. Tran has money. (positive) Tran has *no* money. (negative)

10. Yolanda will go to the party. (positive) Yolanda will *not* go to the party. (negative)

Second, when *not* is used with a helping verb in a negative sentence such as "I have *not* read the book," the helping verb comes before *not*. Also, the helping verb is required. It is incorrect to write "I not read the book" or "I no read the book." Here are four more examples. See Figure F-2.1 for a list of helping verbs.

11. They *will not* answer the phone

12. I *am not* going to call again.

13. She *does* not care.

14. He *is not* angry.

[**Exercise 64**] Edit the following sentences to correct any misuse of negatives. Bracket the incorrect parts, and write your corrections above them, as in the following example:

is not

Example: He [no is] angry.

1. Maria will no walk the dog.

2. The dog not eaten his food today.

3. Maybe he not like this kind of dog food.

4. Although dogs make good pets, some people not like dogs.

5. Large dogs no are the best choice for apartment living.

6. Do no put candy on the table where the dog can get it.

7. Why do you no want to walk the dog, Maria?

8. "I not like to go out in the rain," said Maria.

[**Exercise 65**] Rewrite the positive statements below as negative ones.

1. We want to see the new musical.

2. We are taking everyone in our family.

3. My sister enjoys singing and dancing.

4. She goes to the theater very often.

5. The tickets are too expensive for some people.

6. I am excited about the show.

F.3 Using *There Is, There Are,* and *It*

How do I use there is, there are, *and* it *to begin a sentence?*

The words *there* and *it* can be troublesome for writers, but they serve several important purposes in English. The word *there* is used to indicate that something exists or happens. Use *there* for beginning a sentence in the present tense (*there is* or *there are*) or for beginning a sentence in the past tense (*there was* or *there were*). The word *it* is used for weather, distance, time, surroundings, and in common expressions such as *it is important* and *it is obvious*. These expressions place emphasis on the details that come after them. You can also use *it* as an indefinite subject (filler) in some expressions. The following examples illustrate when to begin sentences with *there* and *it*.

1. To show that something exists/existed or happens/happened:
   • There is a park where my children love to play. (the park exists)
   • There are swings and slides in the park. (swings and slides exist)
   • There was a war in Kosovo in the nineties. (the war happened)
   • There were bombings of neighborhoods in the war. (bombings happened)

2. To ask a question:
- Are there any drinks in the refrigerator?
- Is there a fly in your soup?
- Was there an empty seat on the bus?
- Were there some people waiting outside?

 Although you can begin a statement with *there is,* you must reverse the word order when you write a question.

3. To indicate weather, time, distance, or surroundings:
- It is raining outside. (weather)
- It is morning in California. (time)
- It is several miles to the next town. (distance)
- It is quiet in my neighborhood. (surroundings)

4. To place emphasis on what comes next:
- It is necessary for you to bring your book to class.
- It is required that you take Algebra 1.
- It is essential that you arrive at the airport two hours before your flight.
- It is important to floss your teeth regularly.

 In some sentences, *it* may serve as filler. In sentences like the ones that follow, *it* cannot be left out.

1. As you may know, it is almost midterm. (correct)

2. As you may know, is almost midterm. (incorrect)

3. I thought it was time to go home. (correct)

4. I thought was time to go home. (incorrect)

5. You know, it is a good idea to hand in assignments on time. (correct)

6. You know, is a good idea to hand in assignments on time. (incorrect)

[**Exercise 66**] Read the following sentences. If *there* or *it* is used correctly, write C in the blank. If *there* or *it* is used incorrectly, write I in the blank. Edit all incorrect sentences so that they are correct.

_____ 1. It was a fair in my town last week.

_____ 2. There were rides, concessions, and farm displays at the fair.

_____ 3. Like most fairs, was crowded with children.

_____ 4. Was fun to participate in the pie-eating contest.

_____ 5. Unfortunately, was soon time to go home.

_____ 6. There is anything more exciting than a fair?

[**Exercise 67**]

Working with a partner, read each other's essays to find sentences that begin with *there* or *it*. Underline the sentences. Then determine whether *there* or *it* has been used correctly in each sentence. If not, rewrite the sentence so that it is correct. Write your new sentences on a separate sheet of paper, either to hand in or discuss in class, as your instructor recommends.

F.4 How to Use Articles

What are articles, *and how do I use them?*

Let's begin our discussion of articles with a review of nouns. As explained in section A.1, nouns can be grouped into several categories, two of which are *proper nouns* (Grand Canyon, New Year's Eve, Golden Gate Bridge) and *common nouns* (home, responsibility, desk, curtain). Proper nouns name specific people, places, and things, and they always begin with a capital letter. Common nouns name general classes of people, places, and things, and they are not capitalized. Common nouns can be divided into two more categories: countable nouns and uncountable nouns.

A *countable noun* has two features: You can place a number before it, and you can form its plural by adding *-s* or *-es* (one night, five books, several days, many horses). An *uncountable noun* cannot be numbered (happiness, hunger, dark, information). Uncountable nouns have additional features as well:

1. Uncountable nouns do not have plurals.

   Correct: I have not finished my homework for math and English.
   Incorrect: I have not finished my homeworks for math and English.

   Correct: Put all of your clean clothing away.
   Incorrect: Put all of your clean clothings away.

2. When the subject of a sentence is an uncountable noun, the verb is always singular.

   Correct: Their research is accurate.
   Incorrect: Their research are accurate.

   Correct: My furniture is very old.
   Incorrect: My furniture are very old.

3. Although an uncountable noun is always singular, you can quantify it with words and phrases, as in the following examples:

   Correct: I looked up several kinds of information.
   Incorrect: I looked up several informations.

   Correct: Let me give you a piece of advice.
   Incorrect: Let me give you some advices.

One more thing you need to know about nouns is that some nouns can be either countable or uncountable, depending on the context in which they are used. Take a look at the next three pairs of sentences:

I bought several yards of cloth. (a quantity of cloth cut from a single bolt)
Bring one clean cloth from the stack on the shelf. (one cloth among several)

I love chocolate (any kind of chocolate)
Would you like a chocolate? (one piece from a bag or box)

You can never have enough time. (*time* used as an abstract concept)
"It was the best of times; it was the worst of times." (*times* as eras or periods of history)

Keep in mind the categories and features of nouns as we consider a few rules for the use of the articles *a, an,* and *the.* Figure F-4.1 on page 482 summarizes the basic rules for using articles and lists some examples. Keep in mind that there are exceptions to these rules, many of which you will learn from experience as you read and use the English language.

[**Exercise 68**] Read each sentence. Then circle the correct article in parentheses. If no article is required, circle *none.*

1. Do you have (a, an, the, none) good memory?

2. Did you know that you can improve (a, an, the, none) memory?

3. (A, An, The, none) human memory operates through three stages: encoding, storage, and retrieval.

4. During the first stage, your brain takes in (a, an, the, none) impressions from your senses.

5. By focusing your attention, you can choose (a, an, the, none) information that you want to remember.

6. Why is it easier to remember (a, an, the, none) zip code than a hotel confirmation number?

7. Zip codes have only five digits, whereas (a, an, the, none) maximum number you can hold in memory is about seven or nine.

8. Your brain is like (a, an, the, none) computer that takes in, sorts, and stores information that you can later retrieve.

9. But like (a, an, the, none) computers, our brains can only do what we tell them to do.

10. For (a, an, the, none) process of memory to work efficiently, you must first decide to remember.

Figure F-4.1   How to Use Articles (*a, an,* and *the*)

ARTICLE	RULES	EXAMPLES
a	Use *a* before a singular noun that begins with a consonant.	a box, a toy, a room
	Use *a* before singular nouns that are countable.	one box = a box, one toy = a toy, one room = a room
	Use *a* before a singular countable noun when its identity is either unclear or unknown.	Bring me a box from the closet. (Any box in the closet will do.)
an	Use *an* before a singular countable noun that begins with a vowel.	an acrobat, an employee, an item, an oboe, an undertaker (exceptions: a ukulele, a uniform)
	Use *an* before a singular countable noun beginning with a vowel when its identity is either unclear or unknown.	An employee took an item from the supply closet. (Any employee might have taken any item.)
the	Use *the* before a plural noun, whether it begins with a consonant or a vowel.	the apples, the violins, the toys, the eggs
	Use *the* before a plural noun when the identity is known.	I want one of the apples in the refrigerator. (The apples wanted are specified.)
	Use *the* before an uncountable noun when its identity is known.	Give me the information that you found on the Internet. (The source of the information is known.)
no article, some	Use either no article or *some* before an uncountable noun when its identity is unknown, when it refers to a general category of things or people, or when it refers to an unspecified amount.	Do you want some help? The kind or type of help is unknown.)
		The police have information on the robbery that took place last night. (*Information* is a general category.)
		There is some dirt on my chair. (How much dirt is unclear.)

[Exercise 69] Select a short passage from one of your textbooks. Underline every article in the passage. Determine whether the noun that follows is a countable or uncountable noun, singular or plural, and which one of the rules in Figure F-4.1 applies.

[Exercise 70] Read the following paragraph. Then choose *the, a,* or *an* to fill in each blank.

Nepal is 1 _____ kingdom in India. It has 2 _____ population of 20,827,000. 3 _____ capital of Nepal is Kathmandu. Nepali is 4 _____ official language, but Maithir and Bhojpuri are also spoken. Nepal is 5 _____ only official Hindu state in the world. Hindus make up 90 percent of 6 _____ population in 7 _____ country that is also 5 percent Buddhist, 3 percent Muslim, and 2 percent Christian. Nepal has hot, humid summers and mild winters. It is bounded by 8 _____ Himalayas, whose peaks are permanently covered with snow. 9 _____ monsoon season lasts from June to September. Nepal has 10 _____ annual rainfall of 56 inches. Agriculture is 11 _____ mainstay of the economy, but tourism is 12 _____ rapidly developing industry.

F.5 Prepositions and Idioms

How do I use idioms such as afraid of *or* sign up?

As explained in Section A, prepositions are one of the six parts of speech, and they consist of many common words such as *in, out, over, under, around,* and *about.* A prepositional phrase consists of a preposition plus its object. *Over the fence* and *behind the house* are two examples. Prepositions have three characteristics:

1. They show relationships of time, space, direction, and condition.

2. A preposition usually comes before its object, but it can follow the object.

3. Compound prepositions consist of more than one word: *as well as* and *because of* are two examples.

For a list of common prepositions, see Figure A-5.1 on page 484.

Prepositions combine with other parts of speech in various ways to form idioms. An *idiom* is a common expression whose meaning cannot be understood by defining the individual words of which it consists. Idioms have to be memorized. One way to learn them is by making your own lists of idioms as you encounter them in your reading. However, the best way to learn idioms is by using them in your speaking and writing. Figure F-5.1 on page 485 lists idioms that begin with the prepositions *at, in,* or *on.*

Figure F-5.1 Idioms That Begin with *At, In,* or *On*

AT	IN	ON
at school	in bed	on time (punctual)
at home	in love	on foot (walking)
at work	in Florida	on vacation
at lunch	in English	on Thanksgiving
at 9 o'clock	in December	on Saturday
at the bank	in the oven	on the porch
at a concert	in the afternoon	on the bookshelf

Did you notice that many of the idioms in Figure F-5.1 are made by combining a preposition with a noun (at home) and that in some of the idioms the noun is preceded by an article (on *the* porch)? Prepositions also combine with other parts of speech to make idioms, as in the following examples. See also Figure F-5.2, which lists more idioms and examples.

1. **Adjective + preposition:**
   - I am *grateful for* the book you gave me.
   - I am *proud of* my son's accomplishments.

2. **Verb + preposition:**
   - We have nothing to *complain about.*
   - The instructor *insists on* participation from everyone.

3. **Other verb + preposition combinations:** The meaning of the idiom is different from the meaning of the verb used alone.
   - This printer will *run out* of ink soon. (*Run out* means "become used up.")
   - Are you *making fun of* me? (*Make fun of* means "to ridicule.")
   - *Get over* it! (*Get over* means "to recover from.")

4. **Same verb + different preposition = different meanings:** Many idioms consist of the same verb combined with a different preposition, such as *call on* or *call off.* The meanings of the resulting idioms differ, depending on the preposition, as in the following examples.
   - call on (choose): Can I *call on* you to help with the decorations?
   - call off (cancel): Unfortunately, I have to *call off* tomorrow's meeting.
   - fill in (fill up space): *Fill in* the blank with your answer.
   - fill up (make full): Take the car to the gas station and *fill up* the tank.

- fill out (complete): Please *fill out* the application form.
- break down (malfunction): No one likes to have a car *break down* on the highway.
- break up (come apart): Jennifer wants to *break up* with her boyfriend.
- look into (examine): Detective Roberts will *look into* the fire's causes.
- look down on (despise): Do not *look down on* others who are different from you.
- look up to (admire): Everyone needs someone to *look up to* or respect.
- look forward to (anticipate): We are *looking forward to* the party next week.

Figure F-5.2   More Idioms and How to Use Them

TYPE	EXAMPLES	HOW TO USE
Adj. + Prep.	afraid of	Vince is *afraid of* spiders.
	ashamed of	Do not be *ashamed of* making mistakes.
	aware of	Are you *aware of* the impression you make?
	confused by	People are *confused by* many things.
	content with	It is good to be *content with* what you have.
	fond of	We are *fond of* our new puppy.
	full of	The box is *full of* cookies.
	interested in	Are you *interested in* earning some money?
	sorry for	I am *sorry for* the trouble I have caused.
	tired of	We are all *tired of* hearing bad news.
Verb + Prep.	complain about	Ben always *complains about* something.
	concentrate on	Try to *concentrate on* the test.
	depend on	Children *depend on* their parents for support.
	find out	*Find out* who left the garage door open.
	hand in	Always *hand in* your assignments on time.
	keep on	This clock *keeps on* ticking.
	lock up	*Lock up* the house before you leave.
	pick out	*Pick out* a dress to wear to the party.
	explain to	Let me *explain to* you why I am late.
	apply for	You can *apply for* a job online.
Other Idioms	drop in (visit)	Please *drop in* tomorrow afternoon.
	put off (postpone)	Do not *put off* studying for your test.
	sign up (register)	*Sign up* for your courses early.
	go over (review)	Let's *go over* your homework now.
	take after (resemble)	Diane *takes after* her mother.
	break down (malfunction)	My car *broke down* on the highway.
	put up with (endure)	I will not *put up with* complaints.
	stand up for (defend)	It is time to *stand up for* your country.
	take care of (care for)	Do not worry; I will *take care of* you.
	get along with (cooperate)	Can we all *get along with* each other?

[Exercise 71] As previously mentioned, one way to learn idioms is to make your own list of those that you find in your reading. To make a chart for listing your idioms, fold a sheet of notebook paper in half. On one side of the fold, list the idioms that you find. On the other side of the fold, explain what each idiom means. See the example in Figure F-5.3 below. Share your list in a class discussion. Review the idioms frequently so that you learn them.

[Exercise 72] Working with a partner, scan each other's essays for use of prepositions and idioms. Underline each prepositional phrase that you find. Then determine whether it is used correctly or incorrectly. Make your corrections on a separate sheet of paper. Ask your instructor for help if you have trouble.

Figure F-5.3 Chart for Listing and Explaining Idioms

Idioms and Prepositions

1. on time	1. punctual
2.	2.
3.	3.
4.	4.
5.	5.
6.	6.
7.	7.
8.	8.
9.	9.
10.	10.

Credits

CHAPTER 1

STEPHEN CHAPMAN By permission of Steve Chapman and Creators Syndicate, Inc.

CHAPTER 2

ROBERT M. PIRSIG Excerpt from pp. 170-2 from *Zen and the Art of Motorcycle Maintenance* by Robert Pirsig. Copyright © 1974 by Robert M. Pirsig. Reprinted by permission of HarperCollins Publishers.

CHAPTER 3

LEIGH ANNE JASHEWAY-BRYANT By Leigh Anne Jasheway-Bryant, © 2002 Meredith Corporation. First published in *Family Circle* Magazine. Reprinted with permission.

CHAPTER 4

STEPHEN KING "Ever Et Raw Meat" by Stephen King. Originally appeared in *The New York Times Book Review*, December 6, 1987. Reprinted With Permission. © Stephen King. All rights reserved.

CHAPTER 5

GREGG EASTERBROOK Gregg Easterbrook, "Stress is the Dirty Secret of Success," *The Orlando Sentinel*, February 26, 2004. Reprinted by permission of Inkwell Management.

CHAPTER 6

WILLIAM ZINSSER "Clutter" from *On Writing Well*, Seventh Edition, by William Zinsser. Copyright © 1976, 1980, 1985, 1988, 1990, 1994, 1998, 2006 by William K. Zinsser. Reprinted by permission of the author.

CHAPTER 7

GILLIAN SILVERMAN From *Newsweek*, July 15, 2002, © 2002 Newsweek, Inc. All rights reserved. Used by permission and protected by the Copyright Laws of the United States. The printing, copying, redistribution, or retransmission of the Material without permission is prohibited.

CASSANDRA BJORK Reprinted by permission of the author.

CHAPTER 8

LANGSTON HUGHES "Salvation" from *The Big Sea* by Langston Hughes. Copyright © 1940 by Langston Hughes. Copyright renewed 1968 by Arna Bontemps and George Houston Bass. Reprinted by permission

of Hill and Wang, a division of Farrar, Straus and Giroux, LLC.

STEVE HACKNEY Reprinted by permission of the author.

CHAPTER 9

DAVID H. LEVY David H. Levy, "When the Big Clouds Gather," *Parade Magazine*, May 18, 2003, p. 4. Reprinted with permission from *Parade*, copyright © 2003, and Scott Meredith Literary Agency.

SARAH COLEMAN-BRANTLEY Reprinted by permission of the author.

CHAPTER 10

SARA D. GILBERT Sara D. Gilbert, "The Different Ways of Being Smart" is reprinted with permission of the author.

HEATHER ARTLEY Reprinted by permission of the author.

CHAPTER 11

ROBB WALSH "The Inkblot Test" copyright © 2003 by Robb Walsh from *Are You Really Going to Eat That?* Reprinted by permission of Counterpoint.

ALEXANDRA STOWE Reprinted by permission of the author.

CHAPTER 12

SHARON BEGLEY AND ANDREW MURR From *Newsweek*, July 2/July 9, 2007, © 2007 Newsweek, Inc. All rights reserved. Used by permission and protected by the Copyright Laws of the United States. The printing, copying, redistribution, or retransmission of the Material without express written permission is prohibited.

ANDREA WOODHAMS Andrena Woodhams, "Anti-Conservative Bias," from New Voices, a Forum for Readers Under 30, *The Orlando Sentinel*, April 24, 2004. Reprinted by permission of the author.

CHAPTER 13

ALICE HOFFMAN "The Perfect Family" by Alice Hoffman. From *The New York Times*, November 1, 1992. Copyright © 1992 by The New York Times Co. Reprinted by permission. All rights reserved.

ARIC MITCHELL Reprinted by permission of the author.

CHAPTER 14

JOE QUEENAN Joe Queenan, "The World is Watching, and No One Cares," *Los Angeles Times*, July 16, 2007, OpEd. Reprinted by permission of the author.

Index